Hispanics in the Labor Force

Issues and Policies

ENVIRONMENT, DEVELOPMENT, AND PUBLIC POLICY

A series of volumes under the general editorship of
Lawrence Susskind, *Massachusetts Institute of Technology, Cambridge, Massachusetts*

PUBLIC POLICY AND SOCIAL SERVICES
Series Editor: Gary Marx, *Massachusetts Institute of Technology, Cambridge, Massachusetts*

AMERICANS ABROAD: A Comparative Study of Emigrants from the United States
Arnold Dashefsky, Jan DeAmicis, Bernard Lazerwitz, and Ephraim Tabory

THE DIFFUSION OF MEDICAL INNOVATIONS: An Applied Network Analysis
Mary L. Fennell and Richard B. Warnecke

DIVIDED OPPORTUNITIES: Minorities, Poverty, and Social Policy
Edited by Gary D. Sandefur and Marta Tienda

FATAL REMEDIES: The Ironies of Social Intervention
Sam D. Sieber

HISPANICS IN THE LABOR FORCE: Issues and Policies
Edited by Edwin Melendez, Clara Rodriguez, and Janis Barry Figueroa

INNOVATION UP CLOSE: How School Improvement Works
A. Michael Huberman and Matthew B. Miles

OSHA AND THE POLITICS OF HEALTH REGULATION
David P. McCaffrey

RACIAL AND CULTURAL MINORITIES: An Analysis of Prejudice and Discrimination (Fifth Edition)
George E. Simpson and J. Milton Yinger

Other subseries:

ENVIRONMENTAL POLICY AND PLANNING
Series Editor: Lawrence Susskind, *Massachusetts Institute of Technology, Cambridge, Massachusetts*

CITIES AND DEVELOPMENT
Series Editor: Lloyd Rodwin, *Massachusetts Institute of Technology, Cambridge, Massachusetts*

Hispanics in the Labor Force

Issues and Policies

Edited by
EDWIN MELENDEZ

Massachusetts Institute of Technology
Cambridge, Massachusetts

CLARA RODRIGUEZ
and
JANIS BARRY FIGUEROA

Fordham University at Lincoln Center
New York, New York

Plenum Press • New York and London

Library of Congress Cataloging in Publication Data

Hispanics in the labor force: issues and policies / edited by Edwin Melendez, Clara Rodriguez, and Janis Barry Figueroa.
    p.   cm. — (Environment, development, and public policy. Public policy and social services)
    Includes bibliographical references and index.
    ISBN 0-306-43799-6
    1. Hispanic Americans — Employment. I. Melendez, Edwin. II. Rodriguez, Clara. III. Barry Figueroa, Janis. IV. Series.
HD8081.H7H575 1991   91-20344
331.6′368073 — dc20   CIP

ISBN 0-306-43799-6

© 1991 Plenum Press, New York
A Division of Plenum Publishing Corporation
233 Spring Street, New York, N.Y. 10013

Printed in the United States of America

We dedicate this book to

Tamarinda Jean, Edgardo Jose,
Oscar Javier, Clara Gelvina,
and Jose Angel

Contributors

JANIS BARRY FIGUEROA, Division of the Social Sciences, Fordham University at Lincoln Center, New York, New York 10023

MARTIN CARNOY, School of Education, Stanford University, Stanford, California 94305

HOWARD CHERNICK, Department of Economics, Hunter College and the Graduate School of the City University of New York, New York, New York 10021

HUGH DALEY, Data Center, Stanford University, Stanford, California 94305

RAUL HINOJOSA-OJEDA, Institute for International Studies, University of California, Berkeley, California 94720

EDWIN MELENDEZ, Department of Urban Studies and Planning, Massachusetts Institute of Technology, Cambridge, Massachusetts 02139

VILMA ORTIZ, Department of Sociology, University of California, Los Angeles, California 90024

CORDELIA REIMERS, Department of Economics, Hunter College and the Graduate School of the City University of New York, New York, New York 10021

FRANCISCO L. RIVERA-BATIZ, Institute of Urban and Minority Education, and Department of Economics and Education, Teachers College, Columbia University, New York, New York 10027

CLARA E. RODRIGUEZ, Division of the Social Sciences, Fordham University at Lincoln Center, New York, New York 10023

TERRY J. ROSENBERG, Community Service Society, 105 East 22nd Street, New York, New York 10010

CARLOS E. SANTIAGO, Department of Economics, State University of New York at Albany, Albany, New York 12222

WALTER STAFFORD, Urban Research Center, Robert F. Wagner Graduate School of Public Service, New York University, New York, New York 10003

ADELA DE LA TORRE, Health Care Administration Program, California State University Long Beach, Long Beach, California 90840

ANDRES TORRES, Center for Puerto Rican Studies, Hunter College of the City
    University of New York, New York, New York 10021
RODOLFO D. TORRES, Graduate Center for Public Policy and Administration,
    California State University Long Beach, Long Beach, California 90840

Foreword

The bright side of the 1980s, or the "Hispanic decade," as it was dubbed early on, may ironically turn out to be the detail and sophistication with which the economic and social reversals affecting most Latinos in this period have been tracked, with a fresh cohort of Latino scholars playing an increasingly prominent role in this endeavor. As this volume conveys, these analyses are steadily probing more deeply into the fine grain of the processes bearing on the social conditions of U.S. Latinos and particularly into the diversity of the experiences of the several Latino-origin nationalities until recently generally treated in the aggregate as "Hispanics."

Though still fragmented and tentative in perspective, as are the disciplines on which they draw and the research apparatus on which they rest, the quest among these new voices for a unifying perspective also comes across in this collection of essays. There is manifestly more under way here than a simple demand for inclusion of neglected instances on the margin of supposedly well understood larger or "mainstream" dynamics. The 1990s open with a more confident assertion of the centrality of the Latino presence and Latino actors in the overarching transformations reshaping U.S. society, and especially in the playing out of these restructurings in the regions and cities of Latino concentration. In that sense, each of these inquiries adds to a newly accumulating "critical capital"—questionings of reigning concepts and approaches, insights drawn from empirical observations at odds with received social science and policy wisdom, and a new sense of connectedness and motivation springing from newly available modalities of research collaboration.

Significantly, in my view, there are no strident claims advanced here imputing decisive or overriding centrality to ethnic or cultural factors in determining behaviors or social outcomes, but rather a call for more careful attention to larger structural or, as in the case of employment and earnings, "demand-side" considerations. Nevertheless, in subtler ways, these essays highlight the necessary social legitimation of research-grounded knowledge and policy solutions and the place of ethnicity in the social construction of whatever larger consensus is to see the United States through the coming decade.

FRANK BONILLA

Inter-University Program for Latino Research
Hunter College of the City University of New York
New York, New York

Preface

This volume is the outgrowth of a series of eight seminars that were held at the Massachusetts Institute of Technology, the Centro de Estudios Puertorriqueños (Center for Puerto Rican Studies) at Hunter College, and the Center for Immigrant and Population Studies at the College of Staten Island. In addition to some of the contributors to this volume, participants in these seminars included Alice Colon-Warren, Palmira Rios, Luis Falcon-Rodriguez, Marisa Alicea, Robert Aponte, Miren Gaston-Uriarte, Rick McGahey, William Radison, Roberto Fernandez, Luis Prado, Tom Bailey, Roger Waldinger, Thierry Noyelle, Carolle Charles, Nina Glick, Linda Basch, Joyce Toney, Patricia Pessar, Mary Corcoran, Darlene Kalke, and Roy Bryce-Laporte.

The impetus for the seminars was a growing concern on the part of the editors about the deteriorating economic situation of Puerto Ricans and other Latinos in the last two decades. These seminars sought to bring together researchers from numerous disciplines to consider various dimensions of the labor-market problems affecting Puerto Ricans and other Latinos in the Northeast. We focused on three areas we considered critical to such an analysis. These were: trends in the characteristics and composition of Puerto Rican and Latino labor markets, the effects of industrial restructuring, and policies affecting the labor-market participation of Puerto Ricans and other Latinos in the Northeast.

The focus of the seminars was on new ideas and new research. We invited senior and junior researchers; works presented were, to the greatest extent possible, comparative in approach and focused largely on Latinos in the Northeast. Specific areas addressed were: the underclass, Hispanic women, income, migration, policy and program options in education and employment, industrial restructuring, and the economic role of new immigrants. The discussion in these seminars subsequently led us to consider the regional issues we had addressed within a broader, more national Latino framework—thus the birth of this volume.

This volume seeks to examine many of the above issues within a larger context and from a variety of perspectives. It begins with an introduction that reviews current issues and approaches to the study of the Latino labor force. An overview of the economic situation of Latinos in the United States then provides the context within which to examine the effects of literacy and race on earnings. The relationship between labor-market segmentation and industrial change is examined regionally and comparatively. Hispanic employment and segmentation within the public sector are also examined. The feminization of poverty, women, family, and work also receive special attention. A critical assessment of labor-force policy and its effects on Latinos is provided. The volume concludes with an epilogue that examines the future implications of the problems and policy concerns that are raised. It is our hope that this volume will facilitate discussions leading to the development of more concrete solutions to enhance the employment situation of Latinos in the United States.

We would like to thank the following for their support of the original seminar series: the Inter-University Program for Latino Research, the Ford Foundation, the American Sociological Association Small Grants Program, the Rockefeller Foundation, and the Massachusetts Institute of Technology, Department of Urban Studies and Planning, for providing much needed resources and space. We would also like to gratefully acknowledge the support of the Centro de Estudios Puertorriqueños at Hunter College, City University of New York, and the Center for Immigrant and Population Studies at the College of Staten Island, who cosponsored and organized some of the seminars. Special thanks also go to the seminar participants and to Betty Radwanski, whose assistance was invaluable in making the original seminar series a success and the current volume a reality. We would also like to acknowledge the very important commentary and editorial suggestions made by the editors at Plenum and by Gary Marx, the Series Editor. In the process of compiling the chapters for this book, we have also received valuable ideas, support, and participation from Frank Bonilla, Rudy de la Garza, Bill Diaz, Bennett Harrison, Tunney Lee, Robert Reischauer, Errol Ricketts, Palmira Rios, Raquel Ovrin Rivera, and Harriett Romo. We thank them now for their immeasurable contributions. Finally, special thanks go to the presenters and contributors to the volume, not just for their written contributions, but also for their indispensable comments on the other papers presented.

Contents

Vilma Ortiz

III. Government Employment

Cordelia Reimers and Howard Chernick

V. Policy

Rodolfo D. Torres and Adela de la Torre

Edwin Melendez, Clara E. Rodriguez, and Janis Barry Figueroa

1

Hispanics in the Labor Force

An Introduction to Issues and Approaches

EDWIN MELENDEZ, CLARA E. RODRIGUEZ, AND JANIS BARRY FIGUEROA

Twenty years ago, a researcher studying Hispanics in the United States would have found a somewhat limited list of titles. How dramatically different the situation is today. The study of Hispanic history and social development in the United States has progressed to the point where, in the early 1990s, there is now an entire literature dedicated to Hispanic studies, which certainly reflects the greater importance and visibility given to Hispanics as an ethnic group. Hispanic studies encompasses a diversity of research issues and theoretical approaches that compete in order to understand and interpret the Hispanic reality.

Initially, research questions and methodologies that were deployed to understand the complexity of the Hispanic experience in the United States were, to a large degree, an extension of existing disciplinary paradigms. These questions often revolved around the origins and causes of Hispanic migration and, to a lesser extent, their process of incorporation or assimilation into the economy and the society at large.

EDWIN MELENDEZ • Department of Urban Studies and Planning, Massachusetts Institute of Technology, Cambridge, Massachusetts 02139.   CLARA E. RODRIGUEZ and JANIS BARRY FIGUEROA • Division of the Social Sciences, Fordham University at Lincoln Center, New York, New York 10023.

Hispanics in the Labor Force, edited by Edwin Melendez *et al.* Plenum Press, New York, 1991.

1

In Hispanic studies, the dominant theme has been the immigrant experience. The "immigrant" paradigm, which is utilized in many social sciences, has a relatively well-defined set of assumptions, and these were easily extended to the analysis of Hispanics. Like previous European immigrants, Hispanics were and still are attracted to the United States by expectations of a higher standard of living or, in some cases, by the need to escape political persecution.

Since the vast majority of Hispanics are induced to emigrate because of economic factors, these immigrants are usually the younger, more motivated and able individuals among the population in their native country. At first, when they are compared to native workers, the Hispanic immigrants have lower educational levels and bring lower skill levels to labor markets in the United States. These human capital characteristics act to limit immigrants to low-wage occupations and industries during their early years in the host country. But, as immigrants adapt their skills to the new working environment and as young workers invest in education, it is assumed that wages, employment tenure, and occupational mobility will converge to native–worker levels (Chiswick, 1979). The full incorporation and eventual assimilation of immigrants into the mainstream of society can occur despite the existence of ethnic institutions and customs that tend to reproduce group solidarity and social differentiation (Gordon, 1964).

Although the immigrant paradigm takes a somewhat different form across disciplines, the central themes and assumptions presented above seem to be inherent in most arguments. Labor market analysis, for example, has devoted substantial attention to what factors determine differences in labor market outcomes among workers. Given the assumptions of the immigrant model, differences in labor market outcomes between Hispanics and other groups should be explained by differences in human capital variables, particularly differences in schooling, on-the-job training, and labor market experience.

In this context, immigrant background variables, such as fluency in the English language and length of residence in the host country should have a strong influence on long-term income gains. Individual economic prosperity should result from occupational mobility, employment tenure, and adaptation of skills to the United States labor market. For immigrant children or second generations, the influence of ethnic institutions should weaken and tend to induce a social and economic convergence that would make labor market outcomes for these workers similar to those of non-Hispanic workers. During the initial phase of Hispanic research, much effort was devoted to testing various hypotheses that can be derived from this immigrant model (Bryan, 1971; Casal & Hernandez, 1975). Yet the now vast literature on Hispanics tends to portray a more complex picture of their experience rather than the one derived from research based on past immigration flows to the United States (Bean & Tienda, 1987; Borjas & Tienda, 1985; Massey, 1981; Portes & Bach, 1985).

The Hispanic migratory experience has obvious similarities to those of northwestern, southern, and eastern Europeans, who migrated to the United

States during the late nineteenth and early twentieth centuries. Certainly, the admission of the early European immigrants and the later Hispanic arrivals was welcomed by employers, who tended to place these workers in the lowest-skilled and worst-paid jobs within the American labor market. Historically, employers in the United States have successfully used new immigrant groups to exert pressure upon the living standard of native American workers and to divide working-class unity (Cheng & Bonacich, 1984). In fact, popular concern about recent immigrants and their use of government transfer programs has once again caused many Americans to support restrictive immigration policies that are, in spirit, not unlike the nativist and racist policies that were proposed in order to restrict the flow of immigrants during the early twentieth century (Parmet, 1981).

However, recent analyses indicate that differences between the earlier European immigrants and the post-World War II Hispanic entrants, in terms of their migratory and assimilation experiences, are of major importance for understanding the situation of Hispanics today. The socioeconomic decline of Hispanics during the 1980s poses a critical problem in research for social scientists, community organizations, and policymakers. Consequently, the shift in research emphasis from the "immigrant" to the "Hispanic" experience is, therefore, an attempt to understand why Hispanics have not been integrated more successfully into American labor markets and society.

HISPANIC DIVERSITY AND IMMIGRANTS' ASSIMILATION

The incorporation of different Hispanic groups into American society has been very different from the experience of earlier European immigrants. Mexicans, who form the largest immigrant Hispanic group in the United States, were first incorporated into the United States through the military conquest and annexation of the southwest territories (California, Arizona, New Mexico, Colorado, and Texas) in the 1840s. However, it was the economic expansion in the United States at the turn of the century coupled with social instability in Mexico that induced the first significant wave of Mexican immigrants across the border and provided the cheap laborers needed for agricultural production (Barrera, 1979). This migratory flow was interrupted during the economic decline of the 1930s but continued after World War II. The composition of Mexican immigration, however, was significantly changed by the post-World War II period. New legal restrictions caused many Mexican workers to enter the United States illegally, and their concentration in agricultural production diminished as increased mechanization in this sector caused the demand for agricultural labor to decline (Estrada *et al.*, 1981).

The situation of Puerto Ricans migrating to the United States was circumstantially similar to that of the Mexicans, in that surplus labor conditions in an agricultural economy had pushed people to migrate. A major difference between migrating Puerto Ricans and Mexicans lies in the fact that Puerto Ricans were granted United States citizenship in 1917 and therefore did not face any immigration restrictions. Although Puerto Rican migration to the United States in the pre-World War II period had created many communities that were located on the East Coast and in the northcentral United States, the larger number of Puerto Ricans had migrated between 1945 and 1960 (Centro de Estudios Puertorriquenos, 1979). Migrating largely to urban centers in the Northeast, Puerto Ricans became concentrated in unskilled blue-collar manufacturing jobs, but by the 1970s, the economic restructuring of the Northeast economy had displaced significant numbers of Puerto Rican workers (Cooney, 1979; Cooney & Warren, 1979).

In contrast to the Mexicans and the Puerto Ricans, two other large Hispanic groups, the Cubans and the Central Americans, have a somewhat different history and origin. The genesis of their recent migratory flows has a strong political-refugee component related to the Cuban Revolution in 1959 and to the political instability in Central America of the 1970s and the 1980s (Moore & Pachon, 1985). The relative wealth of the first wave of Cuban immigrants, in combination with the assistance they received from United States government sources, allowed them to form an ethnic enclave in Miami (Wilson & Portes, 1980). Today Cubans tend to have socioeconomic characteristics that are more similar to those of non-Hispanic white Americans than to those of other Hispanic groups.

Central Americans (largely Salvadorans, Guatemalans, and Nicaraguans) are the most recent immigrants, and they have settled largely in California, Washington, D.C., and New York State. The success of their integration into American society is still unclear because of the recency of their arrival. However, Cubans and Central Americans do share with the other Hispanic groups a unique historical connection because of the tradition in the United States of geopolitical expansionism throughout much of Latin America and the Caribbean during the nineteenth and twentieth centuries.

Consequently, the origins and initial incorporation of Hispanic groups into the United States reflect the impact of United States territorial expansion (e.g., in Mexico and in Puerto Rico), it's sphere of political influence (e.g., in Central America), and American economic interdependencies (e.g., in Central America, Puerto Rico, and Mexico). These were not factors that motivated European migration to this country, and their influence on the rates of economic and social progress for the various Hispanic groups should not be underestimated.

Disparities in economic progress between European immigrant groups and Hispanic immigrants also suggest that a substantially different set of employment circumstances has confronted the vast majority of Hispanics. European immigrant labor was instrumental to the economic expansion of the late 1800s and the early 1900s. Kolko (1976) estimated that, in 1909,

> 58 percent of the workers in the twenty principal mining and manufacturing industries were foreign born; and coming overwhelmingly from farm and unskilled rural origins. [They composed] 45 percent of all unskilled labor and 38 percent of the semiskilled in the United States. (p. 74)

European immigrants played a key economic role in this period of industrial expansion in the United States.

In contrast to the European immigrants, the employment opportunities made available to Mexicans and Puerto Ricans were overwhelmingly low-skilled jobs, located in agriculture or in the declining sectors of manufacture. By 1970, the increasing economic and social marginality of many Hispanics residing in the United States was compounded by the "new immigration," composed largely of Central Americans, Cubans, and undocumented Mexicans. Legal changes in American immigration law, civil war in Central America, the global economic crisis of the early 1970s, and structural shifts in the world economy affected large pools of unskilled workers in the Third World and helped to dramatically change the volume and composition of the immigrant flows. When compared to the immigrants who entered the country before 1965, these new immigrants have shown significantly increased rates of poverty (Jensen, 1988).

Yet, for all the differences between the new and the old immigrants, Hispanics share another commonality of experience that distinguishes them from the early Europeans. This distinction lies in the racial heterogeneity of the Hispanic peoples (Rodriguez, 1989). The Latin American lineage results from the integration of both the Spaniard and other Europeans with the Indian and the African peoples. Historically, the practice of racial intermarriage has been maintained throughout the Caribbean and in Latin America, resulting in populations that have a wide variety of racial types. Additionally, the Spanish heritage provides a common language and cultural unity among Hispanic groups that tends to reinforce ethnicity. In contrast, European immigrants were and are necessarily more fragmented by differences in both language and cultural heritage.

This brief outline of migratory histories, labor market experiences, and cultural and racial difference offers a preliminary explanation for the divergence in assimilation patterns evidenced between the earlier European immigrants and those of later Hispanic arrivals. The European experience has proceeded in a manner that is more in keeping with the key elements advanced by the traditional "immigrant model." If past groups of European immigrants and African-Americans are seen as benchmark examples of successful and unsuccessful cultural assimilation and socioeconomic progress, respectively, then Hispanics are more likely to be sensitive to—and affected by—the limitations that are placed on people of color within American society.

IMMIGRATION AND LABOR MARKET OUTCOMES

As previously mentioned, one of the more important predictions of the immigrant model is that differences in labor market outcomes between Hispanic and non-Hispanic workers can be explained by human capital and immigrant background variables. Thus, labor market outcomes will tend to converge as migrants adapt their skills to new requirements and gain country-specific experience. But given the tremendous diversity within the Hispanic population, it is not surprising that wage, unemployment, and labor force participation rates show great variation among the different groups. These differences in labor market outcomes, however, can only be partially attributed to differences in human capital and immigrant background. Other factors, such as race, gender, household composition, and local labor market conditions, have a critical influence in determining labor market outcomes for Hispanics.

Empirical studies of Hispanic-Anglo wage differentials have revealed that differences in individual characteristics explain most of the discrepancy for some Hispanic groups (Mexican men and women, and Puerto Rican and Cuban women) but not for others (Puerto Rican and Central American men). Thus, some Hispanic groups are subjected to wage discrimination to a larger extent than others (Reimers, 1983). A similar pattern is found when considering labor force participation rates. Hispanic groups show significant diversity by gender, nativity, residential location, marital status, and even age (Borjas, 1983).

Perhaps the dilemma posed by these studies to the immigrant model is best illustrated by life-cycle earnings among different Hispanic groups. According to Borjas (1982), it takes about fifteen years for Mexican and about twenty-five years for Puerto Rican men to have significant gains in earnings when compared to other recent immigrants. It appears that conventional approaches fall short of explaining why some Hispanic groups are subjected to discrimination and others are not, and why there appear to be factors, other than those of nativity and time of arrival, that act to determine Hispanic labor force participation and earnings trends.

The recent empirical evidence on Hispanics represents a challenge to simplistic extensions of the immigrant model. Perhaps more important, recent empirical studies represent a shift in emphasis away from the immigrant experience to the Hispanic experience. This shift in emphasis, both in research questions and theoretical approaches, represents a second phase in the ongoing effort to understand the incorporation of Hispanics into American society in general and into its labor markets in particular. The focus has shifted to structural barriers found in the schools, the political arena, the private-sector and public-sector labor markets, and other institutions—all of which may have acted to aggravate the economic and social well-being of the Hispanic population. In this context, immigration plays an important role in understanding the Hispanic reality, but a comprehensive analysis of labor market institutions and of American civil and political society is required as well.

SOCIOECONOMIC PROFILE OF HISPANICS IN THE 1980S

In this volume, we focus on the process of Hispanic incorporation into national and key regional labor markets. If we take the median income ratio of

Hispanic families to all non-Hispanic families as an index of relative economic well-being, the economic situation of Hispanic families has deteriorated during the last decade, despite the economic expansion of the late 1980s. Hispanic median family income as a proportion of all non-Hispanic family income declined from 85.1% in 1979 to 64.2% in 1988, a dramatic 20.9% decline (U. S. Department of Commerce, 1989). Although there is no simple explanation for this trend, several factors seem to be contributing to the decline in the relative position of Hispanic families; the stories are unique for Mexicans and for Puerto Ricans.

Among the most important factors contributing to relative economic decline are demographic changes affecting household composition, age distribution, and population growth, and labor market-related factors, such as the decline in Mexican relative earnings and the loss of operative jobs among Puerto Ricans. These factors contribute to the disproportionate increase in poverty among Hispanics and Hispanic families. As shown in Table 1, the poverty rate for non-Hispanic families increased from 8.8% in 1980 to 9.7% in 1988, a small increase of less than 1%. However, the poverty rate for Hispanic families increased 4.5 percentage points, to 25.8% by 1988.

The proportion of all non-Hispanic female heads in poverty relative to all non-Hispanic families declined from 43.7% in 1980 to 32.3% in 1988, a substantial improvement of 11.4 percentage points. But, in sharp contrast, the percentage of all Hispanic female-heads in poverty rose to 51.8% in 1988, up from 44.0% in 1980. Poor, female-headed families among Mexicans experienced a 12.9 percentage point increase during this period, and Puerto Rican female heads 9.2 percentage points. Puerto Rican female-headed families continued to have the highest poverty rate with 65.3% of all households living below poverty. The increase in poverty among Hispanic female heads is all the more significant when one considers the increase in the number of households of this type, from 19.4% in 1980 to 23.4% in 1988. Still, factors other than household composition patterns may be just as important in determining the Hispanic socioeconomic profile.

Hispanics are growing at a much faster rate than other populations in the United States; they are concentrated in a few states in the Southwest and the Northeast, are much younger, and have larger families. These trends, which were discerned over the period from 1960 to 1980, have continued throughout the 1980s. Table 2 shows the distribution of the Hispanic population by state and the percentage of change in the population between 1980 and 1988. Population growth among Hispanics was five times larger than the average for the United States. The rates of population growth were highest in the states with the largest concentration of Hispanics, particularly in the Southwest where rates of growth were above the 33% average for all Hispanics in Florida, Arizona, California, and Texas. Three northcentral and northeastern states followed with rates of growth higher than 25% (New York, New Jersey, and Illinois).

8   EDWIN MELENDEZ *et al.*

Table 1. Family Characteristics

	All persons	Total[a]	Mexican	Puerto Rican	Cuban	All non-Hispanics[b]
			Hispanic origin			
1980						
Total	226,546	14,604	8,674	2,005	806	211,942
Type of family						
Married couples (%)	82.8	75.4	78.6	60.1	82.1	83.1
Female householder (%)	13.9	14.4	15.9	34.8	14.2	13.5
Below poverty level						
Families (%)	9.6	21.3	20.6	34.9	11.7	8.8
Female householder (as % of families in poverty)	43.8	44.0	34.2	66.7	33.0	43.7
1988						
Total	241,155	19,431	12,110	2,471	1,035	221,724
Type of family						
Married couples	79.5	69.8	74.4	51.6	78.1	80.3
Female householder (%)	16.3	23.4	18.5	44.0	16.1	15.8
Below poverty level						
Families (%)	10.8	25.8	25.5	37.9	13.8	9.7
Female householder (as % of families in poverty)	34.3	51.8	47.1	65.3	NA	32.3

[a]Includes other Hispanics not listed on table.
[b]Includes whites, blacks, American Indians, Eskimos, Aleutians, Asians, Pacific Islanders, and other races not elsewhere classified.
SOURCE: U. S. Department of Commerce, 1983 and 1988.

Although the larger proportion of this growth can be attributed to immigration, Hispanics have a younger population—as indicated in Table 3 by the percentage of the population under 5 years of age and median age—and a larger number of persons per family. These demographic and social trends (changes in household structure, regional population growth, and a higher proportion of preschool children) combine to reduce the number of wage earners per family, causing more family members to depend on fewer income earners.

Table 2. Distribution of Hispanic Population
for Selected States

	1980	1988	Percentage of change
Total	14,609	19,431	33.0
California	31.1	33.9	45.0
Texas	20.4	21.3	38.4
New York	11.4	10.9	27.9
Florida	5.9	7.6	71.7
Illinois	4.4	4.1	25.9
Arizona	3.0	3.3	46.9
New Jersey	3.4	3.3	31.3
New Mexico	3.3	2.8	13.8
Colorado	2.3	1.9	8.2
Other states	14.9	10.9	−3.2
United States	226,546	241,155	6.4

SOURCE: U. S. Department of Commerce, 1983 and 1988.

Earnings

Perhaps more important for understanding the relative economic decline of Hispanic families during the 1980s are the trends revealed in median yearly earnings for 1987. Table 4 shows that from the period 1979 to 1987, Hispanic women saw their share of non-Hispanic women's earnings decrease from 90.2% to 79.6%. Hispanic men had an even greater decline in their share of non-Hispanic men's earnings, with a decline from 90.7% in 1979 to only 61.1% by 1987.

Table 3. Age Characteristics of the Population
and Number of Persons per Family, 1988

	All persons	Hispanic origin				All non-Hispanics
		Total	Mexican	Puerto Rican	Cuban	
Under 5 years (%)	7.6	10.7	11.8	10.6	4.7	7.3
65 years+ (%)	12.0	4.7	4.0	4.0	12.8	12.4
Median age	32.2	25.5	23.4	24.9	38.7	32.9
Persons per family	3.17	3.79	4.06	3.39	3.16	3.13

SOURCE: U. S. Department of Commerce, 1983 and 1988.

A disaggregation of the figures by Hispanic groups suggests that a great deal of variation in wage and employment conditions existed among Puerto Ricans, Cubans, and Mexicans between the years 1979 and 1987. The median income among all Cuban, Puerto Rican, and Mexican earners is compared to the median income for all non-Hispanic earners in Table 4. There are no adjustments made for variations in number of hours and weeks that were worked during the year or for human capital characteristics. The amount of the earnings differences that can be attributed to these factors is a subject for future empirical investigation. However, at this time, we can make some conjectures about the trends that are apparent from these data.

In Table 4, all groups, except Puerto Rican women, saw a decrease in their share of median non-Hispanic earnings during the period between 1979 and 1987. Mexican men and women appear to have experienced the worst decline, with the men going from an 88.5% share of non-Hispanic men earnings in 1979, to a mere 57.5% share in 1987. Mexican women saw their share decline from 86.8% in 1979 to 73.6% in 1987. Cuban men also saw a large decline in their share from 1.02% of non-Hispanic male earnings in 1979, to only 81.1% by 1987. Cuban women seem to have just about maintained their share during this period.

The smallest decline in earnings share that was evidenced among the men, and the only female group to improve their share, was found among the Puerto Ricans. The earnings gain for Puerto Rican women may be associated with changes in their occupational distribution during the period (see Table 8). However, labor force participation figures (see Table 6) for Puerto Rican women are the lowest among all women and did not increase significantly over the 1980 to 1988 period. Therefore, it can be assumed that among this group the older cohorts are leaving the labor force as rapidly as the younger and better educated cohorts are entering. Thus, the apparent earnings gain could represent the greater occupational mobility of the younger replacement cohorts and a positive selectivity of both old and young women in the labor force.

Education

Although Hispanics had significant educational gains in the 1980s, these gains were not sufficient to close the educational gap between them and the non-Hispanics. In Table 5, the data show that the median years of school completed for non-Hispanics, who were 25 years and older, increased from 12.4 to 12.9 years between 1980 and 1988. In contrast, the median years of school completed for Hispanics increased from 10.8 to 12.0 years. Among the Hispanic origin groups, Puerto Ricans experienced the largest educational gains, improving their median years of school completed from 10.5 years in 1980 to 12.4 years in 1988, a 1.9 percentage point gain.

Table 4. Median Earnings and Family Income in 1979 and 1987
(15 Years and Older with Earnings)

| | All persons | Hispanic origin | | | | All non-Hispanics |
		Total	Mexican	Puerto Rican	Cuban	
			1979			
Males (N)	12,192	9,078	8,858	8,519	10,249	10,005
Percentage of non-Hispanic male earnings	—	90.7	88.5	85.1	102.4	100.0
Females (N)	5,263	4,733	4,556	4,473	5,307	5,244
Percentage of non-Hispanic female earnings	—	90.2	86.8	85.2	1.01	100.0
Median family income	19,914	14,714	14,765	10,734	18,245	17,280
Percentage of non-Hispanic median family income	—	85.1	85.4	62.1	105.6	100.00
			1987			
Males (N)	19,878	12,527	11,791	15,672	16,634	20,496
Percentage of non-Hispanic male earnings	—	61.1	57.5	76.4	81.1	100.0
Females (N)	10,618	8,554	7,912	11,327	11,364	10,745
Percentage of non-Hispanic female earnings	—	79.6	73.6	105.4	105.8	100.0
Median family income	30,835	20,306	19,968	15,185	27,294	31,610
Percentage of non-Hispanic median family income	—	64.2	63.1	48.0	86.3	100.0

SOURCE: U. S. Department of Commerce, 1983 and 1988.

In Table 5, a disaggregation of the educational gains by educational levels shows that the percentage of non-Hispanic high school graduates increased by 14.5% between 1980 and 1988, whereas the percentage of Hispanic graduates increased by 8.3%. The proportion of non-Hispanic college graduates increased by 3.4%, whereas Hispanics had a smaller gain of 2.4%. Mexicans, who were the Hispanic group with the lowest proportion of college graduates, had a modest

Table 5. Educational Characteristics of the Population in 1980 and 1988
(25 Years and Older)

| | All persons | Hispanic origin | | | | All non-Hispanics |
		Total	Mexican	Puerto Rican	Cuban	
			1980			
Median years completed	12.5	10.8	9.6	10.5	12.2	12.4
High school grad-uate (%)	66.5	44.0	37.6	49.1	55.3	63.4
College graduate (%)	16.2	7.6	4.9	5.6	16.2	17.6
			1988			
Median years completed	12.7	12.0	10.7	12.0	12.4	12.9
High school grad-uate (%)	76.2	51.0	44.6	50.7	60.5	77.9
College graduate (%)	20.3	10.0	7.1	9.6	17.2	21.0

SOURCE: U. S. Department of Commerce, 1983 and 1988.

gain of 2.2% and Puerto Ricans gained by 4.0 percentage points. The proportion of Cubans with a college degree (17.2%) remains closer to the 21% average for non-Hispanics, and Mexicans (7.1%) and Puerto Ricans (9.6%) continue to be disproportionately underrepresented among the college graduate group. Overall, because a large proportion of Hispanics drop out of high school and the difficulties in being able to afford a college education have become more acute for many Hispanic families, the future economic significance of these educational gains for the aggregate population remains unclear.

Employment and Unemployment

In 1988, the employment situation for Hispanics remained very similar to that in 1980. There was little significant change in participation rates for any of the Hispanic groups. Table 6 does show that in 1988, labor force participation rates for Hispanic men (78.9%) continued to be slightly above the average for non-Hispanic men (73.89%). On the other hand, Hispanic women had a participation rate (52.1%) that was below that for non-Hispanic women (56.2%) in 1988. A significant exception to the trend of higher participation rates among Hispanic men, is that of Puerto Rican men with only 68.6% participating in the labor force in 1988. Puerto Rican women also continued to have the lowest rate of participation among all women, with only 40.9% in the labor force in 1988.

Unemployment rates are more reflective of business cycle fluctuations, industrial restructuring, and general demand shifts. Unemployment rates for both Hispanic men (9.5%) and women (7.0%) were well above the rates for non-Hispanics, but there were differences among Hispanic groups. By 1988, Mexican men had the highest unemployment rate (11%) among all Hispanic men (see Table 6). Cuban men, on the other hand, had an unemployment rate (4.1%)

Table 6. Labor Force Status, 1980 and 1988

| | All persons | Hispanic origin | | | | All non-Hispanics |
		Total	Mexican	Puerto Rican	Cuban	
1980						
Female						
16 years and over	89,482	4,887	2,702	675	353	84,595
Civilian labor force	44,523	2,400	1,320	269	195	42,124
Participation rate (%)	49.7	49.1	48.8	39.8	55.2	49.7
Employed	41,635	2,169	1,189	235	181	39,466
Unemployed (%)	6.4	9.6	9.9	12.7	7.2	6.3
Male						
16 years and over	81,732	4,726	2,781	608	311	77,007
Civilian labor force	59,927	3,593	2,174	411	240	56,333
Participation rate (%)	73.3	76.0	78.1	67.5	77.1	73.1
Employed	56,005	3,288	1,985	365	228	52,716
Unemployed (%)	6.5	8.4	8.6	11.1	5.0	6.4
1988						
Female						
16 years and over	96,516	6,656	3,790	918	437	89,860
Civilian labor force	53,987	3,466	1,985	376	234	50,521
Participation rate (%)	55.9	52.1	52.4	40.9	53.6	56.2
Employed	51,018	3,223	1,832	337	230	47,793
Unemployed (%)	5.5	7.0	7.7	10.5	1.7	5.4
Male						
16 years and over	88,522	6,608	4,112	728	431	81,944
Civilian labor force	66,738	5,216	3,308	499	333	60,522
Participation rate (%)	74.2	78.9	80.4	68.6	77.2	73.9
Employed	66,467	4,720	2,944	453	319	56,830
Unemployed (%)	6.4	9.5	11.0	9.2	4.1	6.1

SOURCE: U. S. Department of Commerce, 1983 and 1988.

which was lower than that for non-Hispanics (6.1%). Thus, among the men, Puerto Ricans had the lowest rates of participation and Mexicans the highest unemployment rate.

In the case of Hispanic women, the unemployment rate fell from the 1980 figure of 9.6% to 7.0% in 1988. This reflects the differential demand shifts affecting working women during this period. Puerto Rican women had a 1988 unemployment rate (10.5%) that was higher than that for all other women; whereas Cuban women had an unemployment rate (1.7%) that was much lower than the 5.4% rate for non-Hispanic women. Thus, among women, Puerto Ricans had the lowest rates of participation and the highest rates of unemployment.

Occupations

By 1988, the occupational distribution of Hispanics continued to reflect the changing occupational structure in which lower-level, blue-collar occupations (e.g., farmers, laborers, and operatives) had diminished in importance and in availability. Therefore, the degree to which changes in occupational distribution represent an improvement in Hispanic employment conditions remains an open question until more detailed information—possibly the results of the current (1990) United States Census of Population and Housing—is available.

Hispanics continued to be underrepresented in upper white-collar (e.g., managerial and professional) categories and in lower white-collar (technical, sales, and clerical) occupations. They are overrepresented in lower blue-collar occupations (e.g., operatives, farmers, and laborers), which means they are concentrated in occupations that are and have been in decline throughout the 1980s. Table 7 shows how these trends looked in 1988, by indicating underrepresentation in the occupational category with a value below 1 and overrepresentation with a value above 1.

In Table 8, the change in the group share of employment over the period from 1980 to 1988 is provided. Hispanics had different patterns of occupational mobility in the 1980s, except for the employment gains realized by all groups in the service occupations. Hispanic men lost a 6.0% share in operative, fabricator, and laborer occupations, but gained a 13.0% and 48.0% share in service and farming occupations, respectively. However, there was no significant change in their shares of managerial, professional, technical, sales, and clerical occupations. Hispanic women were able to make modest gains in upper white-collar occupational categories and lower white-collar jobs (technical, sales, and clerical).

An examination of the data by Hispanic-origin group shows some interesting variations. Mexican men had marginal gains in managerial, professional, craft, and service occupations, and lost significant employment shares in the lower blue-collar jobs. However, they continued to obtain significant em-

Table 7. Occupational Share of Hispanics, 1988[a]

Occupation	All Hispanic	Mexican	Puerto Rican	Cuban
Male				
Managerial and professional	0.50	0.39	0.58	0.91
Technical, sales, and clerical	0.77	0.62	0.83	1.40
Services	1.57	1.42	2.02	1.14
Farming, forestry, and fishing	2.00	2.81	0.44	0.39
Precision, products, craft, and repair	1.05	1.13	0.90	0.77
Operators, fabricators, and laborers	1.34	1.46	1.44	1.01
Female				
Managerial and professional	0.62	0.50	0.81	1.08
Technical, sales, and clerical	0.91	0.93	0.99	0.93
Services	1.23	1.24	0.86	0.73
Farming, forestry, and fishing	1.67	2.33	0.00	0.00
Precision products, craft, and repair	1.52	1.57	1.57	1.39
Operators, fabricators, and laborers	1.89	2.05	1.80	1.67

[a]Computed as the group share in a given occupation divided by the group share of total employment; a value below 1 indicates underrepresentation, and above 1 overrepresentation.
SOURCE: Author's estimates based on data taken from U. S. Department of Commerce, 1983 and 1988.

Table 8. Change in Occupational Share, 1980–1988[a]

Occupation	All Hispanic	Mexican	Puerto Rican	Cuban
Male				
Managerial and professional	−0.01	0.01	0.09	−0.04
Technical, sales, and clerical	−0.01	−0.02	−0.15	0.18
Services	0.13	0.09	0.14	−0.20
Farming, forestry, and fishing	0.48	0.66	−0.08	0.06
Precision products, craft, and repair	0.06	0.08	0.12	−0.13
Operators, fabricators, and laborers	−0.06	−0.74	−0.05	0.06
Female				
Managerial and professional	0.04	0.00	0.19	0.35
Technical, sales, and clerical	0.06	0.10	0.07	−0.01
Services	0.07	−0.04	0.02	0.04
Farming, forestry, and fishing	0.22	−0.68	0.00	−0.33
Precision products, craft, and repair	−0.15	−0.15	0.06	−0.48
Operators, fabricators, and laborers	0.01	0.17	−0.38	−0.41

[a]Computed as the group share in a given occupation divided by the group share of total employment.
SOURCE: Author's estimates based on data taken from U. S. Department of Commerce, 1983 and 1988.

ployment shares in low-paid farming occupations, and this may be a causal factor in their earnings decline over the period. Thus, Mexican men did not exhibit any clear occupational gains during this period. Mexican women had gained employment shares in lower white-collar jobs and lower blue-collar jobs, but they lost shares in all other occupational categories.

Cuban men and women are in a better occupational position than other Hispanic groups and have a more similar occupational distribution than that of the non-Hispanic population. Cuban women increased their employment share significantly in managerial and professional occupations, while reducing their shares in both the upper and lower blue-collar jobs. Yet Table 7 shows that Cuban women as well as all other Hispanic women are still overrepresented in blue-collar jobs. Cuban men lost shares in upper-level white-collar occupations, services, and crafts (which may explain some of their earnings decline), but made gains in lower-level white-collar jobs especially. Overall, both Cuban men and women experienced a continued improvement in their occupational distribution.

Puerto Rican women experienced an improvement in their occupational distribution by moving out of lower-level blue-collar jobs and into managerial and professional occupations. As mentioned before, this movement by the younger, more educated Puerto Rican women probably accounts for the increase in relative earnings over the 1979 to 1987 period. Overall, Puerto Rican women continued to be concentrated in the poorly paid, lower blue-collar jobs. However, Puerto Rican men showed clear signs of occupational loss. Despite a 9% gain in employment shares of managerial and professional occupations and a 13% gain in services, they lost a 14% share in lower-level white-collar jobs. Thus, Puerto Rican males are overrepresented in both lower-level blue-collar and in white-collar jobs (see Table 7).

In conclusion, the above analysis suggests that the labor market situation of Hispanic workers has contributed significantly to the decline in their relative socioeconomic position during the 1980s. In many ways, the shift in research emphasis from the immigrant to the Hispanic experience represents an attempt to understand why Hispanics have not been successfully integrated into the social and economic mainstream of the labor market. In the next section, we discuss the type of research questions that have gained recent prominence, and the way in which the contributors to this volume have begun to construct their answers.

ORGANIZATION OF THE VOLUME

The primary focus of this book is on Hispanics in the labor force, even though several other topics are also evident in the volume. Several contributors have generated regional-specific studies that focus on particular Hispanic groups and not others. In those chapters, for example, that target the northeastern United

States for investigative purposes (Barry Figueroa [Chapter 9], Melendez [Chapter 5], Rodriguez [Chapter 4], Stafford [Chapter 8], Ortiz [Chapter 6], and Rosenberg [Chapter 10]), the authors are necessarily concerned with Puerto Ricans, who are the largest Hispanic group residing in this region. The growing evidence of the uniquely disadvantaged position of Puerto Ricans within labor markets in the United States has motivated several authors whose research findings are contained in this volume. Similarly, the chapters on income inequality among Hispanics (Hinojosa-Ojeda, Carnoy, and Daley [Chapter 2] and Torres and de la Torre [Chapter 13]), Hispanic employment in the public sector (Reimers and Chernick [Chapter 7] and Stafford [Chapter 8]), and the effects of literacy on Hispanic employment (Rivera-Batiz [Chapter 3]) continue to explore the extent to which Hispanics, as a group, can be distinguished economically and socially.

Many labor economists propose that, despite the economic expansion of the late 1980s, real wages have stagnated or fallen and the distribution of income has become more unequal. Harrison and Bluestone (1988) have referred to this reversal in the postwar gains in real income as "the great U-Turn." Raul Hinojosa-Ojeda, Martin Carnoy, and Hugh Daley argue that minority groups, and especially Hispanics, have experienced an even greater loss in real and relative earnings. In their findings, the "polarization of jobs" appears to be an explanation for a significant proportion of the decline in relative incomes. However, discrimination and educational differences still remain significant problems.

Earlier, we remarked that labor market analysts have devoted a lot of attention to the question of what factors determine wage differences between workers. The effect of education is examined more closely by Francisco Rivera-Batiz. Using 1985 data, he investigates the effect of measured literacy levels on Hispanic men and women and finds that literacy is a major predictor of wage differentials, although there is a distinction made in the type of literacy skill that is of importance to men relative to women. His chapter takes the important step of separating the issues of the quantity and quality of the education that is received.

An especially provocative investigation of stratification among Puerto Ricans by race is provided in Clara Rodriguez's chapter. Her analysis of a number of socioeconomic variables (including poverty status, occupational and industrial location) shows that Puerto Ricans who identify themselves as "white" fare better than those who identify themselves as black or "other-Spanish." Also, her further analysis of earnings determinants reveals that identifying as "other-Spanish" significantly and negatively affects male hourly wage rates, whereas racial self-identification is not a significant predictor of wages for women.

The work of Edwin Melendez, who investigated the significance of labor market segmentation on the hourly wages of Hispanics in New York City, is especially notable for its inclusion of both demand and supply-side factors in the estimated earnings function. Melendez finds that holding other factors constant, the labor market structure explains a substantial proportion of the wage gap between non-Hispanic whites and Hispanics in New York City. He finds that Hispanics are overly represented in secondary labor markets, relative to their qualifications, and that discriminatory employment practices play a significant part in lowering their earnings.

Vilma Ortiz examines how industrial change has affected the employment of Hispanics. She tests the relative explanatory power of three competing hypotheses. These theories are known in the literature as the skills-mismatch, the service sector expansion, and the job queues hypotheses. Using 1970 and 1980 census data for New York and Los Angeles, two regions affected by both rapid industrial change and large Hispanic immigration, she finds support for the skills-mismatch hypothesis. However, this is a better explanation of the experiences of blacks and Puerto Ricans than that of Mexicans.

Government has often been viewed as the "employer of last resort" for minorities who are seeking economic advancement. Jobs in the public sector (at the federal, state, and local levels) have functioned in this way for blacks, but it is not clear that this has been the case for Hispanics. Cordelia Reimers and Howard Chernick's multivariate logit analysis of 1980 census data leads them to conclude that Hispanics are not necessarily gaining less access than whites to government jobs, but they do seem to have less access than blacks. The findings show that women are especially more likely to be employed in the public sector, and that citizenship, English language fluency, and veterans status may all be variables that contribute to the likelihood of securing employment. The research explores not only the impact of human capital variables on the probability of securing a government job, but the role of political and financial influences on government managers' decisions to hire Hispanics, blacks and other minorities.

Walter Stafford's chapter also looks at the racial, ethnic, and gender mix found in government employment, but within the context of New York City municipal government. He finds considerable segmentation of race/ethnic and gender groups within the public sector. During the period from 1975 through 1986, blacks and Hispanics gained jobs only in those areas where they already had a foothold; entry into other city agencies remained closed. Although the proportion of whites in city government has been declining, he finds that whites are still overly represented, especially in higher-paying positions. Moreover, he attributes the increased number of women holding official and manager occupations to the "broad-banding of titles"; this procedure often involves a change of title with appreciable increase in salary. Overall, he finds Hispanics have made the smallest public-sector gains.

The role of family structure in explaining changes in median family incomes and poverty rates is today a standard feature of the inequality literature. With regard to Puerto Ricans, it is often suggested that it is the rapid growth of Puerto Rican female-headed households that has contributed to the deteriorating economic position of Puerto Ricans.

The previous section on the socioeconomic status of Hispanics between the years 1980 and 1988 demonstrated that Puerto Rican women have the lowest rates of labor force participation and the highest rates of poverty. Although other women's labor force participation rates have increased, that of Puerto Rican women has remained constant in spite of the demographic trends that would seem to indicate that Puerto Rican women should be increasing their labor force participation—for example, because of their greater educational attainments, their lower fertility rates, the increase in the percentage of Puerto Rican women who are now born in the United States, and increases in the number who are heading households.

Two chapters in this volume, by Janis Barry Figueroa and Terry Rosenberg, examine these perplexing trends more closely. Rosenberg examines the labor force participation rates, educational levels, family structure, and child-care responsibilities of Puerto Rican women at various stages of their life cycle. Particular emphasis is given to analyzing differences between Puerto Rican married women aged 30 to 39 and their non-Hispanic black and white counterparts. Her work expands our understanding of Puerto Rican women by exposing how the timing of education, employment, and childbearing in a woman's life affects her labor force status.

In her chapter, Barry Figueroa investigates the distinctions between Puerto Rican female householders and their spouse-present counterparts. Single mothers have a significantly lower labor force participation rate. But once they are working, these women are more likely to work full time when compared to married mothers. The hours worked estimates suggest distinct labor supply behavior for each group, with female heads of household being unaffected by many of the factors (such as presence of small children) that act to deter the number of hours worked by married mothers. The research indicates that variations in household composition factors between the two groups of women merit continued investigation for insight into the forces motivating their labor supply.

It has been argued that the lack of progress of Puerto Ricans is due to their "circulating migration pattern" (*Wall Street Journal*, 1/23/86, p. 1; *New York Times*, 8/28/87, p. A31; 6/5/87, p. B1; *Los Angeles Times*, 3/16/86, Section IV). Puerto Ricans lacked or did not develop a labor force commitment because they kept traveling back and forth between Puerto Rico and the United States in a circular migration pattern. In addition to the influential news media, variations of this thesis can be found in the research literature.

Because Puerto Rico is an unincorporated territory of the United States, the migration of Puerto Ricans to the United States is bound to be influenced by the economic and the policy changes that occur here as well as in Puerto Rico. Just as the economic changes in Puerto Rico propelled surplus workers to the states in search of jobs, so too do changes in the wage policy of the United States spur migrations.

Carlos Santiago's chapter examines the effect of minimum wage policies in Puerto Rico on the migration of Puerto Ricans to the United States during the 1970s. Citing the intentions of policymakers to forestall migration from Puerto Rico by increasing wages, he shows why the policy proved ineffectual in practice. The mistaken notion that policies based on economic conditions in the United States could be successfully implemented under different economic circumstances in Puerto Rico indicates that policymakers need to reformulate their models of the existing economic interdependencies between Puerto Rico and the United States.

Andres Torres and Clara Rodriguez present a discussion of the relationship between research and policy, using Puerto Rican poverty as a case study to discuss alternative views on the causes of poverty and how these approaches may influence policy prescriptions. Policy effectiveness is many times hampered because the uniqueness of Hispanic disadvantage is subsumed under conventional approaches to poverty. They conclude with a discussion of policy recommendations that have specific reference to the situation of Hispanics.

Rodolfo Torres and Adela de la Torre conclude the volume with a critical review of the literature on earnings, employment, and occupational inequalities between Hispanics and non-Hispanics. They suggest that conventional human capital treatments of earnings differences logically lead to a limited set of policy recommendations which ultimately view the problem as being one of individual initiative. In contrast, a class/structuralist model—which recognizes that production in capitalist economies is shaped by competition and conflict between capitalists, as well as between workers and capitalists—provides an analytical framework in which the relative position of Hispanics within the labor market can be identified and understood more readily. The chapter concludes with a discussion of industrial policy initiatives and the role of full employment and affirmative action policies in improving opportunities for Hispanics.

REFERENCES

Barrera, M. (1979). *Race and class in the Southwest: A theory of Racial Inequality*. Notre Dame, IN: University of Notre Dame Press.

Bean, F. D., & M. Tienda. (1988). *The Hispanic population in the United States*. New York: Russell Sage.

Borjas, G. J. (1982). The earnings of male Hispanic immigrants in the United States. *Industrial and Labor Relations Review, 35,* 343–353.

Borjas, G. (1983). The labor supply of male Hispanic immigrants in the United States. *International Migration Review, 17,* 653–671.

Borjas, G., & M. Tienda. (1985). *Hispanics in the U. S. Economy*. Orlando, FL: Academic Press.

Bryan, S. (1971). Mexican immigrants in the labor market. In W. Moquin & C. Van Doren (Eds.), *A documentary history of the Mexican Americans*. New York: Bantam Books.

Casal, L., & A. Hernandez. (1975). Cubans in the U. S.: A survey of the literature. *Cuban Studies, 5*, 25–51.

Centro de Estudios Puertorriquenos, History Task Force. (1979). *Labor migration under capitalism: The Puerto Rican experience*. New York: Monthly Review Press.

Cheng, L., & E. Bonacich. (1984). *Labor immigration under capitalism: Asian workers in the United States before World War II*. Berkeley: University of California Press.

Chiswick, B. R. (1979). The economic progress of immigrants: Some apparently universal patterns. In W. Fellner (Ed.), *Contemporary economic problems*. Washington, DC: American Enterprise Institute.

Cooney, R. S. (1979). Declining female participation among Puerto Rican New Yorkers: A comparison with native white non-Spanish New Yorkers. *Ethnicity, 6*, 281–297.

Cooney, R. S., & A. C. Warren. (1979). Intercity variations in Puerto Rican female participation. *Journal of Human Resources, 14*, 222–235.

Estrada, L. F., C. Garcia, R. F. Macias, & L. Maldonado. (1981). Chicanos in the United States: A history of exploitation and resistance. *Daedalus, 110*, 103–131.

Gordon, M. (1964). *Assimilation in American life: The role of race, religion and national origins*. New York: Oxford University Press.

Harrison, B., & B. Bluestone. (1988). *The great U-turn*. New York: Basic Books.

Jensen, L. (1988). Poverty and immigration in the United States: 1960–1980. In G. D. Sandefur & M. Tienda (Eds.), *Divided opportunities: Minorities, poverty, and social policy*, New York: Plenum Press.

Kolko, G. (1976). *Main currents in modern American history*. New York: Pantheon Books.

Massey, D. (1981). Dimensions of the new immigration to the United States and the prospects for assimilation. *Annual Review of Sociology, 7*, 57–85.

Moore, J., & H. Pachon. (1985). *Hispanics in the United States*. Englewood Cliffs, NJ: Prentice-Hall.

Nazar, S. L. (1986, January 23). Forever outsiders, Puerto Rican children who move too much suffer severely. *Wall Street Journal*, p. 2.

Parmet, R. (1981). *Labor and immigration in industrial America*. Boston: Twayne Publishers.

Portes, A., & R. Bach. (1985). *Latin journey: Cuban and Mexican immigrants in the United States*. Berkeley: University of California Press.

Reimers, C. W. (1983). Labor market discrimination against Hispanic and black men. *Review of Economics and Statistics, 65*(4), 570–579.

Rodriguez, C. (1989c). *Puerto Ricans: Born in the U.S.A.* Boulder, CO: Westview Press.

Rodriguez, N. P. (1987). Undocumented Central Americans in Houston: Diverse populations. *International Migration Review, 21*(1), 4–26.

Thurow, L. (1986, March 16). Latinos enter mainstream quickly. *Los Angeles Times*, Section IV.

Tienda, M., & W. A. Diaz. (1987, August 28). Puerto Ricans' special problems. *New York Times*, p. 31.

U. S. Department of Commerce, Bureau of the Census. (1983). *General social and economic characteristics* (Summary Report, Vol. I, Chapter C., pp. 166, 168). Washington, DC: U. S. Government Printing Office.

U. S. Department of Commerce. (1988). *The Hispanic population in the United States: March 1988*. Washington, DC: U. S. Government Printing Office.

Wilson, K., & A. Portes. (1980). Immigrants enclaves: An analysis of the labor market experiences of Cubans in Miami. *American Journal of Sociology, 86*, 295–319.

I

Earnings

2

An Even Greater "U-Turn"

Latinos and the New Inequality

RAUL HINOJOSA-OJEDA, MARTIN CARNOY, AND HUGH DALEY

A CHANGING U. S. POLITICAL ECONOMY

Since the mid-1970s the United States has been experiencing a profound shift in both the nature and political management of the post-World War II pattern of economic development and income distribution. This "Great U-Turn," so labeled by Bluestone and Harrison (1988), has been characterized by the dramatic reversal after 1973 of the postwar rise in real wages and relative stability or decline in inequality. Since that time, real wages have stagnated or fallen and the distribution of income and wealth has become more unequal.

A publication of Latinos in a Changing U. S. Economy, a project of the Inter-University Program for Latino Research. Work on this chapter was sponsored by the Ford Foundation. The responsibility for the research is entirely the authors and should not be attributed to the Foundation. Originally prepared for presentation at the Inter-University Program for Latino Research National Conference *Latino Research Perspectives in the 1990s* in Pomona, California, May 25–27, 1990.

RAUL HINOJOSA-OJEDA • Institute for International Studies, University of California, Berkeley, California 94720.   MARTIN CARNOY • School of Education, Stanford University, Stanford, California 94305.   HUGH DALEY • Data Center, Stanford University, Stanford, California 94305.

Hispanics in the Labor Force, edited by Edwin Melendez *et al.* Plenum Press, New York, 1991.

What is not as well known, however, is that all minority groups, and especially Latinos, have experienced an *even greater* reversal in real and relative income levels. After making significant strides in real income growth relative to whites from the 1940s through the 1960s, the recent past has produced

1. A widening of the gap between minority male and white male mean income, as minority real incomes fell more rapidly than white male decline in real income
2. A widening between minority female and white female incomes despite a narrowing of the overall gender income gap
3. A more rapid widening of the income gap among Latinos and among African-Americans than that among whites.

These trends are particularly disturbing given the rapidly expanding share of Latinos in the work force—a trend that is expected to continue into the next century. Note that in this chapter we concentrate on Census and Current Population Survey (CPS) data for the relative incomes of only those workers with jobs, thus introducing a conservative bias in estimating the actual level of ethno-racial inequality.[1]

In this chapter, we describe first the dimensions of this reversal in real and relative wage levels and then attempt to determine the key causal dynamics behind the sharp turnaround toward greater income inequality among Latino, African, and European white Americans. With the use of regression and simulation methodologies, we have sought to examine the relative explanatory power of the four major factors traditionally put forward in the literature for explaining inequality: (1) differences in human capital endowments (including education, age, and immigrant status); (2) the persistence of wage discrimination against different ethno-racial groups; (3) the pattern of industrial-occupation structural change; and (4) continued immigration.

Our research findings show that from the 1940s through the 1960s, declining inequality was due primarily to

1. The shift in the structure of Latino employment from agriculture to industry and services
2. Significant increases in the proportion of Latinos with high school education
3. Intermittent yet sharp declines in discrimination in the 1940s and especially in the 1960s, when it was the dominant factor in increasing Latino relative incomes.

---

[1]Although the analysis presented here is for the sum total of the labor force, in a longer manuscript we have differentiated between full- and part-time workers (see Carnoy, Daley, & Hinojosa, 1990).

The research also indicates that the principal dynamics responsible for increased wage inequality since the mid-1970s are:

1. A widening gap between higher- and lower-income earners and a declining share of middle-income earners within most ethnic/gender subgroups of the population
2. A widening gap between the white concentration in upper-income groups and a disproportionate minority concentration in lower-income groups
3. A widening gap between immigrant and nonimmigrant incomes
4. Widening gaps in high and low educational achievement
5. Renewed increased ethno-racial wage discrimination.

We conclude the chapter with some thoughts on what the experience of Latinos tells us about the dynamics of late twentieth-century political economy in the United States, concentrating on what trends and processes are commonly impacting all groups and what are the key areas for innovation in public policy.

DIMENSIONS OF THE REVERSAL

The "Great U-Turn" is best characterized by a reversal of the 60% rise in real weekly earnings from 1947 to 1973, to a 15% decline in real earnings from 1973 to 1987. This reversal was accompanied by a slowdown in productivity growth from 2.4% annually in the previous period to 0.8% after 1973. In addition, during the two most recent recessions (1974–1975 and 1980–1982) real wages fell sharply, 7% in 1974–1975 and 8% in 1980–1982, while the subsequent periods of economic recovery resulted in minimal increases in net earnings.

Throughout this reversal in relative incomes, the composition of the labor force has also changed dramatically. Fifty years ago, the employed labor force was predominantly white male (65%), and about 70% male. Now it is only about 45% white male and 56% male (see Table 1). Nonwhites were 9% of employed males in 1960 but almost 20% in the late 1980s. Among employed females, the percentage of nonwhites also increased, from 13 to 20%. The fastest growing groups—Latinos and Asian-Americans—together increased their share of employment from 3% to almost 10% in this period, with most of the increase occurring in the last 20 years.

The rise and fall in real wages of those in the labor force who have jobs, however, has been very different for each ethnic and gender subgroup. Although while male real wages rose 26.9% in the 1960s, they stagnated in the 1970s and fell −6.6% from 1980–1986. Real wages of Latino males, on the other hand,

Table 1. Percentage of Ethno-Racial and Gender Composition of the Labor Force

Group	1940	1950	1960	1970	1976	1980	1983	1988
White males	64.6	62.8	60.8	54.8	54.0	49.1	49.2	46.1
White females	24.4	26.6	26.6	31.0	32.3	34.1	35.4	36.0
Latino males	0.7	0.7	1.8	2.5	2.8	3.3	3.4	4.5
Latino females	0.1	0.2	0.7	1.2	1.5	2.2	2.1	2.9
Black males	6.3	5.9	5.9	5.3	5.1	4.8	5.0	5.2
Black females	3.6	3.4	3.5	4.2	4.3	4.7	4.9	5.2
Asian males	0.2	0.3	0.4	0.6	—	0.9	—	—
Asian females	0.0	0.0	0.2	0.4	—	0.8	—	—

SOURCES: 1/1000 Public Use Census Sample, 1960, 1970, 1980; Current Population Survey, 1976, 1980, 1983, 1986, 1988. In CPS years, those workers who are not white, Latino, or black are excluded from the sample; therefore, the percentage shown represent the percentage of the sample including only those three groups. If the 2–3% of "other" workers were included, the percentage of whites, Latinos, and blacks would be slightly lower.

peaked at the end of the 1960s and then fell −4.2% in the 1970s and −11.3% in the 1980s. Native Mexican males experienced the deepest total declines with −6.7% in the 1970s and −9.5% in the 1980s. Native Puerto Rican males fell −2.2% in the 1970s and −12.2% in the 1980s.

By contrast, female real income has improved steadily over the last 30 years, despite intermittent setbacks. White female real income increased substantially in the 1960s (+21%), slowed in the 1970s (+2.4), and rebounded in the 1980s (+4.8). Real income of Latino females also rose dramatically in the 1960s (+49.5%) but then increased very slowly in the 1970s (+.2%) and in the 1980s (+1.6%). Cuban females in the 1970s and 1980s and Puerto Rican females in the 1980s have recently outstripped even white female income growth while Mexican females continue to lag even further behind.

Growing Overall Income Inequality

Since the mid 1970s, increasing inequality has become endemic in society in the United States. Differences in real income change across ethnic groups has resulted in increasing income inequality *between* race and ethnic groups. During this period, the United States also experienced increases in income inequality *within* virtually all ethnic/gender subgroups. Rising inequality between whites and minorities and inequality within minority groups is becoming an increasingly important determinant of the dramatic overall growth in inequality in the work force as a whole.

Given the uneven declining trends in real wages, it is not surprising to find a widening gap in relative income *between* whites and minorities (see Table 2).

Even though in the late 1960s Latino male income had reached its peak of 71% of white male income, this ratio has continued to fall to 64% in 1987. Black to white male income ratios continued to rise through the late 1970s to 66% and then dipped to 64% by 1987. Latino female income relative to white female income also peaked in the late 1960s at 87% and has widened to 83% by 1987. Although the black-to-white female income ratio did close dramatically until it reached parity in 1979, it has since 1987 widened to 90%.

We measured inequality *within* groups by calculating the variance of log income for the work force as a whole and for its component subgroups. Here we deal with observations on *individuals* from Census and CPS data for all *employed and self-employed workers,* but with "extreme" observations removed.[2] The variance of incomes in these sets of individuals is less than in the entire labor force or of all income earners and the changes over time may also be different.[3]

After decades of falling or relatively stable overall wage–income inequality, a substantial surge in inequality within the work force occurred after 1975. Among all workers, wage inequality measured by the variance of log income, went up from .887 in 1975 to 1.070 in 1985. Our results (see Table 3) suggest that income distribution became more unequal among employed individuals in the labor force in the United States, particularly after 1975. The most interesting facet of this greater inequality is that much of it occurred in a period of declining real mean income and that it occurred in almost every group, male and female.[4] Income inequality among employed male workers also became more similar to female worker income distribution, as male inequality grew more rapidly to catch up with the traditionally higher female levels.[5]

Inequality within Ethnic/Gender Subgroups

During the period that we witnessed the surge in overall inequality and inequality among subgroups, we also witnessed increasing inequality within all major subgroups in the population. Among white males, the variance of log

[2]Such extreme observations were defined in terms of unusually low or high hourly and weekly incomes (see Smith & Welch, 1986).

[3]Income distribution measures, such as the variance of log income or the Gini coefficient, are extremely sensitive to the definition of the set of income earners included in the distribution. The set of all income earners yields the most unequal distribution; the variance of incomes of everyone in the labor force, employed and unemployed, is also high. The distribution of family incomes can vary significantly from the distribution of individual incomes.

[4]The data also suggest some variation where the time worked is analyzed. In the 1960s, when real incomes were increasing, income inequality was rising among full-time workers as rapidly or more rapidly than among all workers. In the 1970s, particularly after 1975, income inequality among all workers (part-timers included) increased more rapidly than among full-time workers (see Carnoy *et al.*, 1990).

[5]Income distribution of full-time male workers, however, remained much more unequal than that of full-time female workers.

Table 2. Employed and Self-Employed Mean Incomes, by Ethno-Racial Origin
and Gender, as a Proportion of White Male Mean Incomes

Subgroup	1940	1950	1960	1970	1976	1980	1988
White males	1.00	1.00	1.00	1.00	1.00	1.00	1.00
Black males	0.43	0.51	0.52	0.61	0.65	0.66	0.64
Latino males	0.49	0.56	0.64	0.71	0.69	0.67	0.64
MOL males	0.46	0.55	0.65	0.68	0.65	0.63	0.60
PROL males	0.81	0.56	0.60	0.68	0.68	0.66	0.61
COL males	—	—	0.76	0.74	0.83	0.78	0.73
White females	0.58	0.57	0.48	0.46	0.47	0.47	0.54
Black females	0.24	0.31	0.30	0.38	0.44	0.47	0.49
Latino females	0.32	0.44	0.35	0.41	0.39	0.41	0.45
MOL females	0.30	0.42	0.33	0.38	0.37	0.38	0.40
PROL females	0.59	0.49	0.40	0.52	0.40	0.41	0.46
COL females	—	—	0.36	0.42	0.45	0.45	0.52

SOURCES: 1/1000 Public Use Census Sample, 1960, 1970, 1980; Current Population Survey, 1976, 1980, 1983, 1986, 1988. Sample of all employed and self-employed workers with income; "extreme" observations removed. MOL = Mexican-origin Latinos; PROL = Puerto Rican-origin Latinos; COL = Cuban-origin Latinos.

income rose from .748 in 1975 to .986 in 1982. Among Latino males, it rose from .653 in 1975 to .928 in 1982. Income inequality rose much more rapidly among employed black workers, males and females, than among whites or Latinos.[6]

Among women we also found increasing inequality between race/ethnic subgroups as well as within them. Among white females, the variance of log has increased from .784 in 1975 to .980 in 1985. Among Latinas, it rose from .754 in 1975 to .936 in 1985.

Table 3 also shows differences and changes over time in log income vari-

[6]These results differ from those based on family incomes, and for good reason. Levy (1988) estimated that the Gini coefficient of the distribution of family income declined in the 1960s, from 0.361 to 0.349, then rose to 0.365 in 1979 and 0.385 in 1984 (see his Table 2.1). In part, the difference with our figures can be explained by the use of Ginis, which tend to emphasize changes at the high-income end of the distribution, whereas variance of log income puts a lower weight on high-income end changes. But another part of the explanation comes from combining male and female incomes into a family income. In the 1960s, the distribution of female income was more unequal than male, but female inequality declined during the decade as male increased. If low-income females tend to marry low-income males, then declining inequality would offset rising male inequality in the family income computations. Similarly, Levy's results for the 1980s, showing more rapid increases in family income inequality than we showed for individual incomes, is partially caused by the more rapidly increasing inequality among female incomes accentuating male income inequality.

Table 3. Income Distribution of Employed and Self-Employed Workers, by Race, Ethnic Group, and Gender (Variance of Log Income)

Group	1960	1970	1976	1980	1983	1986	1988
All workers	.882	.923	.887	1.004	1.068	1.070	1.039
All Latinos	.780	.826	.763	.889	.935	.912	.893
White males	.696	.756	.748	.868	.986	.937	.946
Black males	.686	.694	.676	.883	1.167	1.104	1.028
Latino males	.659	.679	.653	.817	.928	.848	.845
MOL males	.704	.682	.703	.794	.937	.824	.843
PROL males	.525	.551	.539	.755	.905	.906	.804
COL males	.700	.654	.574	.958	.870	1.028	.867
White females	.847	.818	.784	.889	.926	.980	.943
Black females	.853	.809	.819	.876	.953	1.101	1.013
Latino females	.812	.860	.754	.843	.852	.936	.895
MOL females	.942	.891	.825	.873	.878	.979	.894
PROL females	.326	.780	.609	.807	.829	.846	.825
COL females	.978	.816	.511	.626	.604	.682	.965

SOURCES: 1/1000 Public Use Census Sample, 1960, 1970, 1980; Current Population Survey, 1976, 1983, 1986, 1988.

ance among Latino subgroups. The variance was more equal among groups in 1969 than in the mid-1980s. But income inequality increased most rapidly for Cuban males and least rapidly for Cuban females. Exactly the opposite occurred for Mexican males and females when compared with other ethnic groups of the same gender. Variance did generally decrease for both male and female subgroups (with the notable exception of Puerto Rican females) in 1959–1969 and generally increased substantially in 1969–1985, especially in 1975–1985. Mexican males, who had the most unequal income distribution in 1975 and more unequal than Puerto Rican males in 1969, had the most equal distribution among males in 1985. Mexican females, with the most equal income distribution in 1969, were most unequal in 1985.

EXPLAINING INCREASING INEQUALITY

What can explain this sharp turnaround in the minority male economic position even relative to *declining* white male real income? Also what explains the relative decline of minority female incomes relative to (rising) white female incomes?

Previous studies (e.g., Barrera, 1979; Bergman, 1986; Hartmann, 1981; Myrdal, 1944; Reich, 1981) have focused on the larger issue of explaining wage discrimination against minorities of color and of women in the labor market.

Although they discussed changes in relative wages, the importance of their analyses lies more in their explanation of discrimination (the persistence of wage differences) and what is its impact on the American labor market. The essence of their argument is that the nature, or structure, of America's economy and society keeps minorities and women in low-income jobs and pays them less for similar work. In different degrees, the analysis contends that discrimination serves the system (even though it may be contradictory to the system's avowed ideology); so it is maintained.

There are those who argue that the discrimination factor is less important than the amount of human capital brought to the labor market by minority groups. This argument suggests that increased education is the key to increasing relative wages for minorities (e.g., Freeman, 1976; Hanushek, 1981; McCarthy & Burciaga Valdez, 1985; Smith & Welch, 1986, 1989). McCarthy and Burciaga Valdez argue that a key variable explaining lower relative income of Latinos (primarily Mexican-origin) is their lower rate of attending and completing college; and that college completion, unlike many other variables, does not increase appreciably as Latinos move two and three generations away from initial immigration. These researchers also show that in addition to improvements in education, shifts out of agriculture and from the South to the North were significant in raising black male relative incomes in the period before 1960, and that the Civil Rights Movement had a significant impact on black male relative incomes after 1960.

Yet a third argument claims that structural changes in the economy are fundamental to understanding changes in the relative wages of minorities and women who were discriminated against. Historical shifts from an agricultural to a manufacturing-based economy and, more recently, from traditional manufacturing to restructured manufacturing and services because of increased world economic competition have, in this instance, had an important effect on the relative economic position of various groups in the economy. In particular, these changes, combined with the reaction of American business to them and the discrimination that is endemic in society, have produced greater inequality (Bluestone & Harrison, 1982; Levy, 1988; Thurow, 1987; Wilson, 1987).

Continued immigration also has been presented as an argument for increasing the inequality gap. These immigration-focused arguments are really based on the theories previously examined: immigrants are either more discriminated against, possess less education and language skills, and lack entrepreneurial drive, or they are seen to function in very segmented labor markets, competing with any native workers who are also localized in those segments.

Drawing on these previous studies, we have developed a set of independent variables and a simulation methodology that analyzes the relative incomes of minorities from 1959 to 1987. Our results suggest that two major changes in the

American labor market since 1973 go far in explaining the decline in Latino and black incomes in the late 1970s and the 1980s: namely, the various "gaps" and "price discrimination."

Five crucial *gaps* in minority group labor market attributes have increased in the 1970s and 1980s. First, there is the increasing gap in the number of minority members who have completed a college education. Black and Latino males and females are involved primarily in levels of education (high school and in-completed college) that have become less valuable in the 1980s than in the 1960s and early 1970s. This gap is critical for Latino males and females but less so for black females. Second, for both black males and females and for Latino males, there is the increasing gap in employment in higher-paying occupations, which is tied in part to the education gap, but also to segmentation. Third, there is, for Latino males, the increasing gap in employment in higher-paying industries. Fourth, there is the increasing gap in time worked by minorities in the high unemployment environment of the late 1970s and 1980s. Fifth, there is the increasing gap between immigrant and nonimmigrant incomes, within the Latino community but more so with respect to white workers.

The tendency to *price discriminate* against minorities in the labor market has increased in the 1980s. The wages paid to minority males and females for work in the same industries and for the same human capital went down relative to the wages paid to whites. The tendency is more marked for younger minorities and for those in certain education groups (i.e., those who have completed high school). As such, minorities are becoming less valued in the labor market, no matter what their education and experience, or where they work.

After estimating the importance of each of these gaps, we compiled a rank ordering of the relative importance of these factors on increasing inequality.

Human Capital Gaps

The data indicate that while there is a convergence in the percentages of white and minority workers with middle-level education, there is growing divergence at the lower- and upper-educational levels. Improvements have been made in closing the gap in middle-educational levels (i.e., high school completion and some college). Yet Latinos are dropping further behind in the very rewarding college completion and postgraduate levels. Although whites and even blacks have made important strides in reducing the number of workers who did not complete high school, Latinos are still making very little progress in this regard.

The average years of schooling in the employed labor force has increased substantially in the past twenty years for every group (see Table 4), but education differences among these groups remain substantial, especially in terms of the percentage of those employed workers who have completed college or graduate

Table 4. High School Completion, College Education, and College Completion, by Race, Ethnic, and Gender Group, 1960–1988 (as Percentage of All Workers in Group)

	1960	1970	1976	1980	1983	1986	1988
White males							
High school completed	27	33	38	36	39	38	39
Some college[a]	11	14	17	19	18	20	19
College completed	11	15	20	22	25	26	27
Latino males							
High school completed	13	23	27	27	31	31	30
Some college[a]	6	10	11	14	14	14	14
College completed	4	8	8	9	8	9	11
MOL males							
High school completed	13	23		26			29
Some college[a]	5	9		12			12
College completed	2	3		2			5
PROL males							
High school completed	11	24		26			35
Some college[a]	5	4		16			16
College completed	2	2		3			8
COL males							
High school completed	11	22		25			31
Some college[a]	22	15		21			19
College completed	4	4		8			12
White females							
High school completed	37	43	46	44	46	45	44
Some college[a]	12	16	16	20	21	22	23
College completed	10	11	15	17	20	21	22
Latino females							
High school completed	22	30	38	33	39	38	38
Some college[a]	7	11	12	19	16	18	19
College completed	2	6	5	8	10	10	12
MOL females							
High school completed	24	33		32			38
Some college[a]	7	11		15			16
College completed	2	5		4			6
PROL females							
High school completed	26	30		39			42
Some college[a]	2	8		18			21
College completed	0	2		4			9
COL females							
High school completed	33	25		35			32
Some college[a]	0	11		19			24
College completed	0	3		8			14
Graduate school	0	6		8			6

[a]"Some college" represents less than four years of college completed. "College completed" also includes postgraduate work.

SOURCE: 1/1000 Public Use Census Sample, 1960, 1970, 1980; Current Population Survey, 1976, 1983, 1986, 1988.

study. In 1960, 51% of white males and 77% of Latino and black males who were employed had not completed high school. The average education of employed females was higher, but even so, more than 40% of employed white women and about 70% of Latino and black women had less than four years of high school completed.

By 1988 (only one generation later), a drastic change had occurred: only 15% of employed white males, 44% of Latino males, and 26% of black males had not completed high school. For females, the percentages were 11%, 32%, and 20%. At the other end of the spectrum, the 11% of white males who had completed college or graduate study in 1960 had risen to 27% in 1988. For Latino males, the figure had risen from 4 to 11%, and for black males, from 3 to 12%. Although the proportion of white females with completed college or graduate study increased less rapidly than for white males, the opposite was the case for minority females. Yet, particularly among males, the percentage of whites who came to the labor market with completed college or graduate studies was much higher than the percentage of Latinos and blacks with those levels, and the percentage of whites who entered the labor force with high school completed or less was much lower.

Data on Latino subgroups are also shown in Table 4. Until 1980, the education of employed Mexican and Puerto Rican males was equally low, and that of Cuban males was much higher, with the percentage of those who had completed college or graduate study about the same as for white males. Apparently, in 1980 and since then, with the influx of Cuban immigrants of much lower socioeconomic (SES) origins, education of the average male Cuban has dropped, and, as we show, below, so has relative mean Cuban income. Education of the Puerto Rican male, on the other hand, rose more rapidly than for Mexicans, especially in terms of college completion or graduate study. This difference is especially striking between Mexican and Puerto Rican females, both of whom have considerably higher average education than their male counterparts. The difference between Mexican females and males, however, is primarily in the percentage that completes high school, whereas for Puerto Rican females it is in the percentage that completes high school and goes to college.

The growing differences in relative educational structures between race/ethnic groups, particularly at the upper- and lower-educational levels, has an even greater impact on income inequality because of the shifting rates of returns to education for each group. Real wages for a given level of education, or for returns to education, are generally falling for the lower- and middle-educational levels and increasing only at the upper levels. Real incomes of college educated Latinos are rising as fast as comparable white incomes but real wages of the middle- and lower-educational levels for Latinos are falling faster. Under these circumstances, gradual improvements in average education are no longer a guarantee of increasing income.

Industrial-Occupational Employment Gaps

American industries have also changed dramatically during the period studied. In 1960, about 30% of males were employed in traditional manufacturing, but by 1987,this percentage had dropped to 20% (see Table 5). About 20% of women also worked in the same industry in 1960; by 1987, only about 12% did. Most of the males in traditional manufacturing shifted into the service sector (a high fraction into office and professional work), and a very small percentage advanced into high tech manufacturing. These shifts were broadly similar across male race/ethnic groups, except for two notable exceptions: in the 1960s, a significant shift from agriculture occurred for Latino and black males—a shift that was completed earlier for white males. Similarly, the shift out of traditional manufacturing was slower for Latino and particularly black males than for white males, so that the sharp drop in the percentage of black workers in manufacturing did not occur until the 1980s, whereas for white workers, it had already occurred in the 1960s and 1970s.[7]

Sectoral shifts in female employment vary much more across race/ethnic groups. Also, females are much more highly concentrated in a few industrial sectors, but these sectors vary across groups. Like white males, about 10% of employed white females shifted from traditional manufacturing to service industries between 1980 and 1987. This shift was mostly to office and professional work (high services), and a small percentage into high tech manufacturing. By 1986, 46% of white females were working in high services. The shift for Latino females was similar but greater, with a higher share working in manufacturing in 1960, and a larger shift from manufacturing to services (with some also shifting into retail trade). For black females, however, the shift was not from manufacturing into services but within the service sector, from low services (housework) into high services (office and professional work), and some shift into retail trade.

By the 1980s, Mexican, Puerto Rican, and Cuban males worked in similar industries, except that more Mexican males were still employed in agriculture and construction and less in office and low services than were either Puerto Rican or Cuban males (Table 6). This was not always the case. Until recently, because of their concentration in the northeastern states, Puerto Rican males were more apt to work in traditional manufacturing jobs. Thus, they were potentially hit much harder by the decline of manufacturing than were other groups. As we

---

[7]For *full-time* minority male workers, the shift out of manufacturing has also been much slower. The percentage of Latino males in traditional manufacturing evolved from 28% in 1970 and 27.3% in 1980 to 24.5% in 1987. For black males, the traditional manufacturing percentage rose from 27.6% in 1970 to 28.7% in 1980 and then fell to 13.7% in 1987.

Table 5. Characteristics of Employed and Self-Employed Labor Force,
by Race, Ethnic, and Gender Group

Variable	White males	Latino males	Black males	White females	Latino females	Black females
Industrial sector				1960		
Agriculture	7.5	14.8	10.7	0.8	3.9	2.1
Traditional manufacturing	29.6	28.3	26.3	22.1	32.1	11.2
Low services	4.7	7.5	7.3	8.7	15.5	43.5
High services	17.2	11.1	15.7	37.4	21.1	24.5
Retail trade	13.1	12.1	10.2	18.7	13.4	9.7
Hightech management	0.5	0.4	0.2	0.4	0.5	0.1
Defense management	1.5	1.6	0.5	0.5	0.5	0.2
Industrial sector				1970		
Agriculture	4.4	7.1	4.8	0.6	2.1	0.9
Traditional manufacturing	25.3	27.0	26.9	17.4	28.3	12.4
Low services	5.0	7.7	6.1	7.5	11.9	22.3
High services	21.0	15.9	18.9	40.1	32.4	40.1
Retail trade	13.4	13.6	9.3	18.7	12.6	8.6
Hightech management	1.4	1.2	0.5	1.4	1.4	1.0
Defense management	1.9	1.0	1.3	0.7	0.4	0.5
Industrial sector				1980		
Agriculture	3.8	7.3	2.9	1.0	2.9	0.5
Traditional manufacturing	23.4	25.2	27.8	14.9	22.4	16.7
Low services	5.7	8.2	7.3	7.7	11.9	14.6
High services	22.8	16.9	22.3	45.2	34.4	48.1
Retail trade	13.5	14.4	10.6	20.0	17.3	10.4
Hightech management	2.2	2.0	1.3	1.9	3.0	1.6
Defense management	1.3	1.2	1.1	0.6	0.5	0.5
Industrial sector				1986		
Agriculture	3.3	6.8	2.5	0.9	1.7	0.2
Traditional manufacturing	20.3	22.1	21.3	11.7	18.1	12.5
Low services	7.0	10.0	10.7	10.4	14.7	16.6
High services	23.7	16.0	23.1	45.8	36.4	44.8
Retail trade	13.8	16.7	13.8	19.8	18.5	14.8
Hightech management	2.3	1.3	1.4	1.8	2.0	1.7
Defense management	1.5	1.4	1.0	0.7	0.9	0.6

SOURCE: 1/1000 Public Use Census Sample, 1960, 1970, and 1980. Income data refer to previous year. Current Population Survey, 1986. Income data refer to 1985.

Table 6. Sector of Employment, All Worker Latino Sample
(in Percent)

Ethnic origin/gender/sector	Year				
	1960	1970	1980	1986	1988
MOL males					
Agriculture	18.9	10.6	10.4	9.7	11.2
Traditional manufacturing	22.9	23.3	24.7	22.2	21.8
Low services	6.8	7.3	7.3	8.1	9.6
High services[a]	11.3	14.3	14.0	13.3	14.4
Retail trade	11.2	11.5	14.6	16.3	14.9
Construction	10.7	10.2	11.4	14.2	13.5
PROL males					
Agriculture	4.4	0.7	0.9	1.6	1.4
Traditional manufacturing	47.8	38.2	32.6	25.9	22.7
Low services	6.9	7.2	6.5	14.2	9.4
High services[a]	6.9	16.7	21.2	22.4	25.1
Retail trade	16.7	15.7	13.8	17.3	14.8
Construction	1.5	3.4	4.3	3.9	7.8
COL males					
Agriculture	0.0	2.5	0.9	0.8	2.2
Traditional manufacturing	44.4	26.2	21.8	20.3	15.6
Low services	18.5	10.0	11.4	13.3	12.5
High services[a]	3.7	16.9	25.8	20.0	21.4
Retail trade	11.1	21.9	15.3	13.0	16.5
Construction	3.7	6.3	9.6	12.3	8.2
MOL females					
Agriculture	6.2	2.9	5.0	2.6	2.5
Traditional manufacturing	16.9	21.4	21.9	17.6	16.1
Low services	19.4	14.1	11.6	14.0	16.2
High services[a]	27.7	34.1	32.5	34.4	35.7
Retail trade	15.7	15.1	18.8	20.8	18.6
PROL females					
Agriculture	0.0	0.8	0.4	0.4	0.0
Traditional manufacturing	69.2	43.2	27.1	19.6	14.6
Low services	5.5	4.5	10.2	12.7	14.8
High services[a]	8.8	28.8	40.3	45.3	49.1
Retail trade	7.7	9.8	12.7	15.3	12.2
COL females					
Agriculture	—	2.2	0.0	0.5	1.0
Traditional manufacturing	—	36.0	29.7	22.2	16.1
Low services	—	10.1	11.5	10.4	13.8
High services[a]	—	34.8	32.7	39.4	35.5
Retail trade	—	7.9	10.3	13.7	13.3

[a]Includes public administration.

show below, this was apparently the case after 1979, because the shift in the 1970s for Puerto Rican males was out of manufacturing and into office services, where salary levels were not significantly different from those in traditional manufacturing. After 1979, however, the job shift was from manufacturing to low-paying low services and construction, with a slowdown in the move to high services. COL males also left traditional manufacturing jobs and went into lower-paying low services, retail trade, and construction. After the shift out of agriculture in the 1960s, Mexican employment distribution was amazingly stable. What is notable is that the distribution for the other groups had become more like that for the Mexicans.

The same pattern can be observed for Mexican females. Their sectoral employment distribution has not been quite as stable as that of Mexican males, with some job shifts for females in the 1980s from traditional manufacturing to low and high services. But the job shift out of traditional manufacturing even in the 1980s has been less marked for Mexican females than for either Puerto Rican or Cuban females. All three groups shifted from manufacturing jobs to low services, but Puerto Rican females also had the largest shift to office services and other sectors (transportation and communication), whereas jobs for Cuban females shifted to retail trade and other sectors. By 1988, the employment percentage of the three female groups in traditional manufacturing and low services was similar.

A Polarization in Jobs

The reversal in income inequality has been accompanied by a renewed polarization in the job structure of the United States. The kinds of jobs whites, Latinos, and blacks work in has changed significantly in the 1980s when compared with the 1960s, but even after twenty years of increased incorporation into "better jobs," blacks and Latinos are still disproportionately employed in low-income jobs. What is even more important, the changes occurring in the employment structure for minorities and whites in the 1980s suggest a significant slowdown in the incorporation process of the previous two decades.

To measure these differences, we constructed a matrix of high- to low-income one-digit industries and high- to low-income one-digit occupations (see Figure 1). The industries and occupations were ranked in each data year according to the relative mean incomes of those who worked in that industry or occupation. Although in time a few rankings changed, a consistency of high- and low-paying industries and occupations was maintained when incomes were estimated separately for males and females. Note, however, that mean real incomes rose in the 1960s and fell in the 1970s and 1980s. So the terms *high-paying* and *middle-paying* are relative to a declining mean. More important, relative incomes for

Figure 1

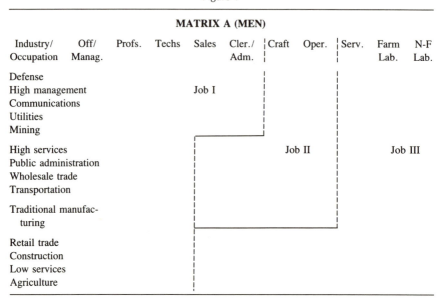

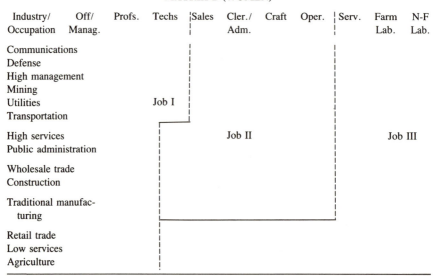

high-paying jobs rose relative to middle- and low-paying jobs in the 1970s and 1980s.

Once the high-to-low income ranking shown in the Matrices A (for males) and B (for females) was constructed, we divided jobs into three categories based on 1988 data: high-, middle-, and low-paying, which were defined as Job I, Job II, and Job III. We then estimated the percentage of each ethnic/gender group in each job definition in 1960, 1970, 1980, 1986, and 1988. The results of this analysis are shown in Table 7. The data suggest a general trend in relative job

Table 7. Employment Shares by Industry/Occupation, and Ethnic-Gender Group, All Workers

Job level/group	1960	1970	1980	1986	1988
Total employed					
Job I (high)	24.6	25.5	28.2	30.9	32.4
Job II (middle)	40.2	39.6	38.2	34.5	34.2
Job III (low)	35.1	35.0	33.6	34.5	33.4
White males					
Job I	28.4	29.4	32.3	35.6	37.2
Job II	41.2	38.9	36.5	32.3	32.1
Job III	30.4	31.8	31.3	32.1	30.7
Black males					
Job I	7.9	9.1	13.8	15.4	16.3
Job II	30.8	40.3	42.6	37.2	37.0
Job III	61.4	50.7	43.5	47.3	46.7
Latino males					
Job I	10.5	13.9	16.2	15.5	16.9
Job II	37.8	40.2	37.8	34.8	33.7
Job III	51.6	45.8	46.0	49.6	49.4
White females					
Job I	19.2	20.2	24.6	28.6	30.5
Job II	47.5	46.0	43.7	40.2	39.4
Job III	33.2	33.8	31.7	31.2	30.4
Black females					
Job I	9.1	13.5	17.8	18.5	18.8
Job II	19.0	33.3	42.2	39.8	41.1
Job III	71.8	53.1	40.0	41.8	40.2
Latino females					
Job I	5.2	11.5	13.6	15.6	17.3
Job II	50.0	52.3	46.1	44.8	42.5
Job III	44.9	36.2	40.3	39.7	40.3

SOURCE: U. S. Department of Commerce, Bureau of the Census, 1/1000 Public Use Sample, 1960, 1970, 1980; Current Population Survey, 1986, 1988.

growth toward higher-paying jobs and a decline in middle-income jobs, with an accentuation of this trend in the 1980s. This polarization, however, was experienced differently by each ethnic/gender subgroup. Among white males, there has been a steady shift which accelerated in the 1980s from middle- to higher-income jobs, whereas the percentage of white males in lower-paying jobs has stayed the same.

Among Latino males, although there was an expansion of middle- and higher-paying jobs in the 1960s, this trend has been reversed in the 1980s with an expansion in lower-paying jobs, a decline in middle-paying jobs, and slow growth in the upper-paying jobs. In the 1960s, Mexican males had the largest expansion in middle-income jobs as they moved out of agriculture into traditional manufacturing. Puerto Ricans have shifted out of middle-income jobs since 1960. The polarizing trend toward upper- and lower-income jobs of the 1980s was most pronounced among Puerto Rican males, whereas Mexican males experienced a declining middle- and upper-share with an expanding lower share. Cuban males, on the other hand, displayed a shift from lower- and middle- to upper-income jobs.

Among white females, a rapid and steady shift occurred from both lower- and middle-paying jobs to higher-paying jobs. Latino women experienced a similar job shift in the 1960s but then began experiencing a declining middle and a polarizing growth in the upper and lower shares. Again, Puerto Rican females exhibited the most pronounced upper and lower polarizing trends whereas Mexican females' middle-income job loss was absorbed by upper-income jobs. Although having the highest share of upper-level jobs among Latinos, Cuban females have recently expanded their lower-level share as well.

Immigration and Demographic Change

Immigration played different roles in relative income determination for all three Latino subgroups in ways that are not typically expected. Mexican-origin Latinos displayed the highest percentages of native born that peaked in 1970 and then fell in 1980 with the influx of new immigrants (Table 8). The native born do not earn significantly more than immigrants, although the gap between foreign and native-born Mexicans widened in the 1970s (Table 9). No corresponding data are available from the CPSs, so we do not know how the most recent immigrants compare to native-born Mexicans in the 1980s. The results have suggested to some that a large part of the decline of relative incomes for Mexicans in the 1970s was due to the increased percentage of foreign-born Mexicans and the decline in their incomes, as the new immigration brought in younger and lesser-educated workers than either the existing foreign-born or native-born work force (see the increases in percentages of foreign-born by level of education and age in Table 10). But the data also show that even the relative median incomes of

Table 8. Proportion of Native-Born Latinos by Ethnic Origin

Ethnic origin/gender	Year				
	1940	1950	1960	1970	1980
All males	0.52	0.55	0.72	0.69	0.60
MOL males	0.55	0.63	0.72	0.74	0.64
PROL males	0.00	0.05	0.11	0.24	0.31
COL males	—	—	—	0.18	0.10
All females	0.59	0.58	0.76	0.68	0.66
MOL females	0.66	0.79	0.82	0.80	0.73
PROL females	0.00	0.05	0.07	0.26	0.40
COL females	—	—	—	0.11	0.09

SOURCE: U. S. Census 1/1000 Public Use Sample, 1940, 1950, 1960, 1970, 1980.

native-born Mexicans fell in the 1970s. It is also true, as the figures in Table 10 suggest, that for most schooling and age levels, the foreign-born workers earn less than native-born, and the income gap did increase somewhat between the two groups in the 1970s after decreasing in the 1960s, once schooling and age are controlled for. These results mean that among Mexicans the effect on income of foreign birth apparently increased in the 1970s. After controlling for age and education, income differences of the native and foreign born can be attributed to the fact that the native born working more often during the year than the foreign born. We tested this proposition more systematically below.

Table 9. Median Incomes of Native- and Foreign-Born
Mexican-Origin Latinos Relative to White Male Incomes

Group/gender	Year				
	1939	1949	1959	1969	1979
Native-born male MOLs/WM	0.42	0.62	0.67	0.72	0.69
Foreign-born male MOLs/WM	0.57	0.48	0.57	0.70	0.61
All male MOLs/WM	0.48	0.56	0.64	0.72	0.66

SOURCE: U. S. Census 1/1000 Public Use Sample, 1940, 1950, 1960, 1970.

Table 10. Incomes of Employed Mexican and Puerto Rican-Origin Foreign-Born Males Relative to All Employed Mexican and Puerto Rican-Origin Males

Level of education	MOL males			PROL males		
	1959	1969	1979	1959	1969	1979
Age 16–24 years old						
< High school	0.87	1.02	1.04	1.01	1.08	1.27
	(17)	(22)	(46)	(88)	(61)	(37)
Completed high school	0.49	1.34	0.93	1.10	1.02	1.61
	(10)	(13)	(15)	(83)	(67)	(15)
Age 25–34 years old						
< High school	0.74	0.95	0.98	0.94	0.92	1.00
	(21)	(34)	(60)	(85)	(88)	(82)
Completed high school	0.85	0.88	0.91	1.00	0.86	1.12
	(7)	(14)	(24)	(100)	(70)	(67)
Age 35–44 years old						
< High school	0.77	0.96	0.89	0.99	0.92	0.97
	(29)	(31)	(57)	(95)	(83)	(96)
Completed high school	1.20	0.83	0.90	0.83	0.85	0.93
	(17)	(9)	(9)	(60)	(70)	(80)

*a*Percentage of foreign born in each cell in parentheses below income ratio.
SOURCE: 1/1000 Public Use Census Sample, 1960, 1970, 1980.

In contrast, for Puerto Rican males, birth on the island implies more of an earnings cost relative to native birth. This gap has been falling, however, since more Puerto Ricans in the United States in the 1980s are also native born. For all Latino females, the impact of being foreign born is not as important as for males. This variety of results further substantiates the claim that immigration status *per se* is not a reliable indicator of economic performance but rather depends heavily on the specifics of the international, regional, and labor market experience of each Latino subgroup population in which immigrants are situated.

The employed labor force became younger (and less experienced) in the 1960s and 1970s and is now (in the 1990s) becoming older (and more experienced) again. This pattern has two important elements: (1) those employed from whatever race, ethnic, or gender group were younger in the 1960s and 1970s; (2) the average age of the total number of those who were employed dropped somewhat because the Latino labor force, which is younger than other groups, grew more rapidly than the others. By 1980, 20% of the employed males and 25% of the employed females were under 25. One other important point: the percentage of under-25 Latino males increased less rapidly than the percentages among white or black males who were employed in the 1960s; but in the 1970s, it rose more rapidly. As we shall see below, the surging growth of under-25, native-born, Mexican-origin males has played a more significant part in the fall of Mexican-origin males than has Mexican immigration.

THE RELATIVE IMPORTANCE OF ALTERNATIVE EXPLANATIONS

To assess the relative strength of each of these factors in explaining increased inequality, we used a technique for simulating relative incomes that was based on coefficients obtained from estimated regression equations. In this section, we used the estimated coefficients to estimate a simulated log income—the log income that would be earned by individuals in a particular group assuming that each individual in that group received a value equal to the estimated regression coefficients for his or her (or some other group's) human capital attributes, where they worked (industry and region), their civil status, the time they worked, and so forth.

In such a simulation, individual attributes within a group can vary, but the "prices" (or regression coefficients), which they receive for those attributes, are fixed. We fixed those "prices" as the set of regression coefficients estimated for a particular group (Latino males, black males, etc.) or for white males or white females, depending on the comparison. Using such simulations, we can then estimate the effect that changing the prices has on estimated log income for the group. Similarly, we can keep prices the same but change the attributes of individuals in the group: we can assume that they have the attributes of another reference group—in this case white males, or, for minority females, the attributes of white females.

All this manipulation allows us to assess the effect on differences in income that these different groups in the labor force receive when compared to white males (or females) for different sets of variables—industrial structure (which industry they worked in), their human capital, the time worked during the year, and the region they worked in, and also their marital status. We can also implicitly assess the effect that differences in attributes have on differences in income by using white income coefficients in simulating the log income of the other groups. With this technique we can determine how much of the inequality in relative income between whites and minorities is due to differences in each group's characteristics (education, age, industry worked in, time worked, region, and civil status) and how much is due to differences in what is paid for the same characteristics across groups (thus measuring discrimination).[8]

---

[8]To explain differences in relative incomes, we adapted a method of simulation analysis that uses estimated regression equations to simulate the incomes of minority groups, assuming that they had the attributes of the white male population in a particular year. Similarly, we simulated white incomes, assuming that the white population had the attributes of the minority population that same year.

Tables 11 and 12 present the results of the white and Latino simulations with column (1) showing inequality ratios of simulated incomes, column (2) showing the effect of wage discrimination, and column (3) showing the effect of differences in characteristics. The results in Table 11 indicate that income inequality between Latino and white males is due more to differences in characteristics between groups than to wage discrimination given the same characteristics. For Latino males, the discrimination effect decreased in the 1960s, has gradually increased in the 1970s, and was relatively constant during the 1980s. On the other hand, for Latino females compared to white males (Table 11), the discrimi-

---

With this method, the regression equation provides an estimated relationship between, say, experience and education as independent variables and log income as the dependent variable. With the estimated coefficients for Latino males, we estimated a "new" mean log income by running this estimated equation on the white male sample data. For each set of independent variables, we know how much giving Latinos the same attributes as white males in that same year (but retaining the Latino payoff to those attributes) would increase Latino mean log income. This simulation yielded the price effect on, say, Latino male income—the effect that lower Latino payoffs have on income, even were Latino labor market attributes the same as white males. Economists would refer to this as the "price discrimination" effect (i.e., the lower payoffs to discriminated-against groups for the same human capital and other variables offered in the labor market).

Similarly, we ran white male estimated regression coefficients on, say, the Latino male sample in each year to estimate the mean log income for whites, assuming that they had the attributes of Latinos but white payoffs for those attributes. This simulation measured the impact on relative incomes of lower-income groups from having lower-valued labor market attributes, such as a lower-valued distribution of education and experience in that group's labor force, working in lower-paid industries or lower-income regions, being less or more likely to be married, or working less time per year.

We called this the "attributes" effect, although some others could argue that it, too, has discriminatory elements, such as certain groups having less access to school; other groups being crowded into low-paying industries and occupations; and other groups working less time than they would find desirable because of the lack of full-time work and high unemployment rates.

We therefore estimated three simulated mean log incomes: (1) the simulated mean for each minority group based on its regression coefficients applied to its own sample data in each year; (2) the simulated mean based on its regression coefficients applied to the white male sample in each year; and (3) the simulated mean based on the white male regression coefficients applied to the sample data for each minority group in each year. The three simulated means were then divided by the simulated means for white males in each year. These simulations and their comparisons to simulated white male log income are represented by these equations:

R_k = Estimated mean $(\log Y)_k$ − Estimated mean $(\log Y)_{AM}$

$\quad = b_{jk} \cdot x_{ijk} - b_{jAM} \cdot x_{ijAM}$

$P_k = P_k * Q_{AM} / P_{AM} * Q_{AM} = b_{jk} * x_{ijAM} - b_{jAM} * x_{ijAM};$

$C_k = P_{AM} * Q_k / P_{AM} * Q_{AM} = b_{jAM} * x_{ijk} - b_{jAM} * x_{ijAM};$

where R_k = the ratio of the simulation estimate of the log income of group k (e.g., Latino males) and the simulation estimate the log income of white males; P_k = the price effect for group k; C_k = the attributes effect for group k; b_{jk} = the estimated regression coefficient for the jth variable in the estimated regression equation for group k; and x_{ijk} = the value of variable j for individual i in group k.

Table 11. Mean Log Incomes of Latino Males and Females Relative to White Males, Based on Simulations from Various Regression Estimates for All Workers' Equations, by Type of Estimate and Year, 1940–1988

Year and regression estimate	(1)[a] Income ratios	(2)[a]	(3)[b] Discrimination	(4)[b]	(5)[c] Characteristics	(6)[c]
	LM/LM relative to WM/WM	LF/LF relative to WM/WM	WMd/LMc relative to WM/WM	WMd/LFc relative to WM/WM	WMc/LMd relative to WM/WM	WMc/LFd relative to WM/WM
1960 Census (1959)						
Industry	0.66	0.34	0.70	0.39	0.98	0.98
Human K	0.66	0.34	0.90	0.38	0.85	0.84
All factors	0.66	0.34	0.94	0.63	0.79	0.61
1970 Census (1969)						
Industry	0.74	0.39	0.76	0.42	0.97	1.00
Human K	0.74	0.39	0.84	0.44	0.94	0.87
All factors	0.74	0.39	0.94	0.61	0.89	0.68
1974 CPS (1973)						
Industry	0.70	0.39	0.70	0.41	0.96	1.01
Human K	0.70	0.39	0.81	0.45	0.89	0.89
All factors	0.70	0.39	0.86	0.57	0.85	0.69
1980 Census (1979)						
Industry	0.69	0.42	0.72	0.44	0.96	0.96
Human K	0.69	0.42	0.87	0.49	0.85	0.84
All factors	0.69	0.42	0.89	0.64	0.82	0.66
1983 CPS (1982)						
Industry	0.68	0.46	0.72	0.50	0.93	0.98
Human K	0.68	0.46	0.87	0.57	0.80	0.80
All factors	0.68	0.46	0.90	0.66	0.78	0.68
1988 CPS (1987)						
Industry	0.65	0.45	0.70	0.50	0.92	0.96
Human K	0.65	0.45	0.84	0.57	0.80	0.82
All factors	0.65	0.45	0.88	0.70	0.78	0.66

[a]Simulated mean log income from regression estimated equation for Latinos run on Latino data relative to simulated mean log income from regression estimated equation for white males run on white male data.

[b]Simulated mean log income from regression estimated equation for Latinos run on white male data relative to simulated mean log income from regression estimated equation for white males run on white male data.

[c]Simulated mean log income from regression estimated equation for white males run on Latino data relative to simulated mean log income from regression estimated equation for white males run on white male data.

SOURCE: Regression estimates which served as the basis of these simulations were made from the 1/1000 Public Use Sample, U. S. Census, 1960, 1970, and 1980, and the Current Population Survey data, 1974, 1983, and 1988.

Table 12. Mean Log Incomes Based on Simulations from Various Regression Estimates for All Workers' Equations, by Type of Estimate and Year, 1939–1987

Year and regression estimate	(1) MNB/MNB[a] relative to WM/WM	(2) MI/MI[b] relative to WM/WM	(3) WMd/MNBc relative to WM/WM	(4) WMd/MIc relative to WM/WM	(5) WMc/MNBd relative to WM/WM	(6) WMc/MId relative to WM/WM
	Income ratios		Discrimination		Characteristics	
1960 Census (1959)						
Industry	0.69	0.58	0.73	0.68	0.93	0.82
Human K	0.69	0.58	0.95	0.74	0.88	0.87
All factors	0.69	0.58	0.97	0.73	0.82	0.66
1970 Census (1969)						
Industry	0.73	0.68	0.76	0.75	0.97	0.93
Human K	0.73	0.68	0.90	0.79	0.91	0.89
All factors	0.73	0.68	0.97	0.86	0.84	0.80
1980 Census (1979)						
Industry	0.69	0.61	0.71	0.64	0.96	0.90
Human K	0.69	0.61	0.91	0.82	0.78	0.78
All factors	0.69	0.61	0.94	0.86	0.78	0.78

[a]Mexican origin U. S. native born = MNB.
[b]Immigrant males = MI.
SOURCE: 1/1000 Public Use Sample, U. S. Census, 1960, 1970, and 1980, and the Current Population Survey data, 1974, 1983, and 1988.

nation effect was more important than differences in characteristics in the 1960s and 1970s. In the 1980s, the discrimination effect diminished whereas the impact of differences in characteristics began to increase. Discrimination relative to white females, however, has increased for Latinas in the 1980s.

In analyzing the impact of differences in characteristics between white and Latino males, human capital differences were more important than differences in what industries were worked in. Yet, although differences in industrial characteristics became less important in the 1960s, they have grown in importance in the 1970s and 1980s much faster than have differences in human capital. The sectoral composition of employment for minorities relative to white males is consistently the largest for Latino males among minority males and females. Furthermore, for all minority groups, the industry attributes effect decreased in the 1940s, 1950s, and 1960s, and increased in the 1980s for minority males, especially in this all worker sample of Latino males. For that group, the attributes effect increased from 4% to 8% in 1979–1987. We have previously suggested that this was probably due to a shift of Latino males from traditional manufacturing into lower-paying construction, retail trade, and service jobs rather than into higher-paying service jobs (as in the case of white males). Differences in time worked and regional concentration, while less important than industry, also diminished in the 1960s and then also grew in the 1970s and 1980s.

For Latino females compared to white males (Table 11), human capital differences were also more important than differences in industrial employment. Although when examined at the same education level discrimination fell significantly in the 1960s, differences in educational attainment nonetheless grew in the 1970s and 1980s. Differences in industrial work narrowed in the 1960s, grew in the 1970s, and then remained stable in the 1980s. Discrimination within industries increased more for Latino females than for males. The impact of differences in time worked and regional concentration also declined in the 1960s and then increased in the 1980s. Differences in time worked were more important in explaining lags in incomes of Latino females than for Latino males but grew worse after the 1982 recovery.

The Immigration Issue

Table 12 also shows the results of the simulation exercise applied to immigrant and native-born Mexican males compared to white males. The results suggest that the large difference in median income between native- and foreign-born Mexicans in 1960 declined substantially by 1970 for two main reasons: (1) wage discrimination suffered by the foreign-born fell 10 percentage points to 17%, whereas wage discrimination against the native-born rose 3 percentage points to a still low 6%; and (2) the attributes gap fell substantially, mainly because of a sharp drop in foreign-born workers in agriculture (from 33% to 18% of the foreign-born labor force) and a sharp increase in the number of weeks worked per year by foreign-born workers.

The results showed that while overall discrimination has been increasing for native-born and falling for immigrant workers, immigrants were still much more discriminated against than native-born Mexican males. In the 1970s, discrimination increased for both native-born and immigrant workers, given a similar pattern of industrial employment as white males. The rate of discrimination declined, however, when given a similar pattern of educational attainment.

In the 1970s, the income difference increased slightly between natives and foreign-born even though both medians were falling relative to white incomes. The main reasons for the drop in the relative medians were different for each group, though both reasons came from an increasing attributes gap. For native-born MOLs, the attributes gap increased because the native-born Mexican-origin labor force grew younger very quickly in the 1970s, even more quickly than the white male labor force. For the foreign-born Mexicans, the attributes gap grew also, but mainly because their average education grew more slowly than that of White males or native-born Mexican-origin males. In addition, foreign-born Mexicans worked increasingly in lower-paying industries in the 1970s, and got paid increasingly less than white males in those industries, even though for the same education and age, they got paid somewhat more than white males in 1979 than in 1969.

These results suggest that the falling incomes of the native-born Mexican-origin Latinos (MOLs) did not result from increased competition with new immigrants, but rather from the increased youthfulness of the native-born MOL labor force relative to white males. This is an effect that is independent of immigration and of the changing structure of jobs in the labor market and also suggests that the declines in the 1980s for MOL relative incomes as a whole were the result of forces that affected all workers of lower education rather than those groups, such as MOLs, where large numbers of working people came into the labor market from abroad.

PUBLIC POLICY IMPLICATIONS AND FUTURE RESEARCH

The results of our research have a number of implications for the debate on what is the appropriate public-policy response to the growing inequality of whites and minorities. Our results also point to new directions where research needs to be advanced in order to understand the dimensions and dynamics of this new inequality.

First, our research indicates that the major areas that have historically been the focus of public policy—particularly discrimination and poor education—remain significant problems. Important changes have occurred however, in the nature of these problems that require renewed attention and policy innovation.

Since the important progress in the 1960s, inequality because of discrimination in the labor market has not declined over the last 20 years. Discrimination has actually increased for Latino women compared to white women, for Mexican native-born males compared to white males and for Mexican immigrants given similar patterns of industrial employment compared to white men. This persistence and/or renewal of discrimination coincides with the end of major initiatives and some reversals in the area of affirmative action. Research by the General Accounting Office on the 1986 Immigration Reform and Control Act has already found discrimination to increase against Latinos. The slowdown in public employment has also contributed to the closing off of some arenas where discrimination was less of a problem than in the private sector labor market. Research on the evolution of discrimination in the private sector should be advanced, a task that has been made more difficult since important data sources, like the Equal Employment Opportunity Commission, have been curtailed in the 1980s.

Although progress has been made in the Latino completion of middle-educational levels, there is increasing urgency to focus attention on the dynamics that lead to the persistence among Latinos of the highest national rates of high school dropouts, which is particularly urgent because of the falling real wages for high school dropouts. This trend is caused, in part, by the swelling of the number of people competing for lower paying jobs as employers continue to up-grade the educational requirements for all jobs. Continued immigration of less educated workers places additional supply pressures on the lowest wage sector of the labor market.

Immediate attention must also be directed at increasing the rate of Latino college completion and enrollment in graduate schools. With cutbacks to aid in higher education, Latino enrollment fell back significantly relative to whites. In part this is responsible for the shortage, and rising relative costs, of high-skilled workers in the United States. Finally, continuing progress must also be made in Latino attainment at middle-educational levels; yet attention must also be placed on why this level of education is becoming less rewarding. More research needs to be conducted on the causes and implications of growing polarization in returns to education, including changes in the interface between educational policy, changing skill requirements, and the structural evolution of the economy. Simply concentrating on a gradual improvement in average education is no longer a guarantee of increasing relative incomes.

Second, our research has pointed to a disturbing dynamic that is driving the new inequality: overall polarization in employment and wage growth in the American job market. The nature of this dynamic, however, is much more complicated, and the public-policy issues much less specific than the traditional explanations and policy approaches to inequality. What is clear is (1) that this is the most rapidly growing source of the increase in inequality; (2) that any policy agenda that is serious about Latino economic advancement and inequality in general must begin to address these issues; and (3) that these trends are impacting all minority groups of the population and are thus creating the need and constituency for concerted action.

Further research conducted as part of this project suggests that the sources of this polarized structural change are of both a domestic and international nature.[9] Domestically, this polarization is linked to the collapse of the "Fordist" social pact that was characterized by balanced mass production manufacturing growth tied to improving real wages and income distribution, all regulated under a government commitment to education, employment generation, and civil rights

---

[9]See Carnoy, Daley, and Hinojosa-Ojeda (1990).

enforcement. International factors accelerated polarization through import competition and a collapse of manufacturing export markets in the United States, particularly because of the Latin America debt crisis that is also exacerbating migratory pressures toward the low wage sectors of the American labor market.

There is a need to understand clearly how changes in the international economy and the role of the United States are impacting on labor market polarization in order to analyze adequately Latino inequality in the broader debates concerning macroeconomic and incomes policies, as well as industrial, regional, international trade, investment, and migration policies. Thus, this study should be seen as a first contribution, along with other parallel regional and binational studies of Latinos in a changing economy project, toward laying the foundation for broader research and a policy agenda in the United States.

REFERENCES

Barrera, M. (1979). *Race and class in the southwest.* South Bend: University of Notre Dame Press.

Bluestone, B., & B. Harrison. (1982). *The deindustrialization of America.* New York: Basic Books.

Becker, G. (1964). *Human capital.* New York: National Bureau of Economic Research.

Bergman, B. (1986). *The economic emergence of women.* New York: Basic Books.

Bureau of the Census, Current Population Reports. *Money Income and Poverty Status in the United States: 1987.* Washington, D.C.: U. S. Dept. of Commerce, 1988.

Carnoy, M., H. Daley, & R. Hinojosa-Ojeda. (1990). *Latinos in a Changing Economy: Comparative Perspectives on the U. S. Labor Market Since 1939.* New York: Inter-University Program on Latino Research Monograph.

Freeman, R. (1976). *Black elite.* New York: McGraw-Hill.

Hanushek, E. (1981). *Sources of black-white earnings differentials.* Stanford: Stanford University, Institute of Educational Finance and Governance.

Harrison, B., & B. Bluestone. (1988). *The great U-turn:* Corporate restructuring and the polarizing of America. New York: Basic Books.

Hartman, H. (1981). *Women, work and wages.* Washington, DC: National Academy Press.

Levy, F. (1988). *Dollars and dreams.* New York: W. W. Norton.

McCarthy, K., & R. Burciaga Valdez. (1985). *Current and future effects of Mexican immigration in California.* Santa Monica: Rand Corporation.

Myrdal, G. (1944). *An American dilemma.* New York: Random House.

Reich, M. (1981). *Racial inequality,* Princeton University Press

Smith, J., & F. Welch, Eds. (1986). *Closing the gap: Forty years of economic progress for blacks.* Santa Monica: Rand Corporation.

Smith, J., & F. Welch. (1989, June). Black economic progress after Myrdal. *Journal of Economic Literature, 27,* 519–564.

Thurow, L. (1987, May). A surge in inequality. *Scientific American, 256*(5), pp. 30–37.

U. S. Department of Labor. (1989). *The effects of immigration on the U. S. economy and labor market.* Immigration and Policy Research Report 1. Washington DC: U. S. Government Printing Office.

Wilson, W. J. (1987). *The truly disadvantaged.* Chicago: University of Chicago Press.

3

The Effects of Literacy on the Earnings of Hispanics in the United States

FRANCISCO L. RIVERA-BATIZ

In March 1989, close to 20 million persons (or about 8%) of the population of the United States was of Spanish origin. In recent years, the economic condition of Hispanics has received much attention, and studies examining the determinants of earnings among this group have proliferated (see, for instance, Bean & Tienda, 1987; Borjas & Tienda, 1985; and DeFreitas, 1990). One aspect that has not received much attention in this literature is the role that literacy skills play in constraining the economic opportunities of Hispanics.

Broadly speaking, *literacy* refers to the set of skills required to use printed and written information to function effectively in society and to pursue one's goals and aspirations. One can thus expect literacy to be a key factor influencing individual performance on the job and, therefore, employment and earnings (see Sum, Harrington, & Goedicke, 1986, 1987; Venezky, Kaestle, & Sum, 1987). In this chapter, I intend to specify statistically the relative importance of literacy skills as a determinant of Hispanic earnings.

FRANCISCO L. RIVERA-BATIZ • Institute of Urban and Minority Education, and Department of Economics and Education, Teachers College, Columbia University, New York, New York 10027.

Hispanics in the Labor Force, edited by Edwin Melendez *et al.* Plenum Press, New York, 1991.

RESEARCH ON LITERACY AND ITS ECONOMIC EFFECTS

Research on the labor market effects of literacy has been hampered by the lack of data on the literacy skills of individuals who are in the labor market. Since 1860, the U. S. Census of Population has collected data on literacy based on questions that require the respondent to rank how well he or she reads or writes. This type of information is based on subjective, self-reported assessments that are difficult to use for comparison purposes and are subject to personal inaccuracies and misperceptions. Furthermore, in concentrating on reading and writing, other aspects of literacy are ignored. For instance, processing printed or written material in the everyday activities of a modern society often requires quantitative skills of varying degrees. Such is the case when the cost of a dinner at a restaurant has to be computed, or when the total amount of a set of deposits at a bank has to be written on a checking deposit slip. Arithmetic computations of varying degrees of complexity are almost surely to appear in the performance of jobs in any technologically complex economy.

The desire to produce more detailed measures of literacy led to the surveys that have been conducted by the National Assessment of Educational Progress (NAEP). Although NAEP surveys have focused on the literacy skills of students, in 1985 a survey was carried out which included mostly individuals in the labor market. The 1985 Young Adult Literacy Survey interviewed a nationally representative household sample of young adults, aged 20 to 25, who were living in the contiguous 48 states of the United States. Individuals in these households were asked a set of demographic and socioeconomic background questions and then were asked to perform tasks related to literacy. In particular, they were administered written tests to measure proficiency in reading and in quantitative skills. The latter involved applying numerical operations of varying degrees of difficulty to information contained in printed materials, such as a restaurant menu, a checkbook, or an advertisement. On the basis of the tasks in each literacy test, proficiency scales were developed, and individuals were assigned scores based on them (for more details, see Kirsch & Jungeblut, 1987).

In this chapter, I will use these reading and quantitative literacy measures in a multivariate analysis to explain the wages of Hispanics in the United States. I expect literacy to be a particularly important factor affecting economic success among Hispanics. First, the ability to use printed material is very much mediated by English language proficiency. Because a large fraction of Hispanics are immigrants (approximately 40%), their knowledge of English is often quite limited. English reading and writing proficiency can thus be expected to be a major factor affecting Hispanic economic performance in labor markets in the United States. Indeed, although some research has found a lack of impact of English proficiency on Hispanic earnings (Borjas, 1984; Reimers, 1983, 1985), studies that have used the most comprehensive measures of English language proficiency suggest that deficiencies in English skills severely curtail earnings (Grenier, 1984; Kossoudji, 1988; McManus, Gould, & Welch, 1983; Rivera-Batiz, 1988; Tainer, 1988). I shall use the NAEP reading proficiency test (a short, standardized test of English reading comprehension) to measure English proficiency in this chapter.

English language proficiency is not the only literacy-related skill that may enable fuller adjustment of Hispanics in the American economy. There are job possibilities that do not require extensive use of English for their performance; such is the case of some highly unskilled jobs in the garment industry, agriculture, and in ethnic enclaves, among others. These employment opportunities, however, are unlikely to provide a great degree of upward mobility.

Achieving job mobility requires successful entry into mainstream labor markets. With inadequate English proficiency, other skills must be possessed that compensate for the language deficiency. Quantitative skills, for example, are a growing requirement of jobs that offer opportunities for advancement. Proficiency in such skills can provide a competitive advantage to prospective job applicants and offset any English language deficiency the worker may have. Currently, many firms supply on-the-job training programs that teach quantitative skills to new employees because of an inability to find workers proficient in them. The problem is a severe one among young workers in urban labor markets and is illustrated by the following case. In 1986, a group of New York City banks pledged to fill 250 entry-level positions with high school graduates from South Brooklyn schools. But by June 1987, only about a hundred graduates had been hired; most of those interviewed had failed the entry-level test, the equivalent of an eighth-grade math exam (as reported by Cuomo Commission, 1988, p. 122). The suggestion here is that the acquisition of quantitative skills may substitute for inadequate English language proficiency, allowing entry into mainstream job ladders. In my sample, I used the NAEP test of quantitative literacy as a measure of proficiency in quantitative skills, adding it as an explanatory variable in my analysis of Hispanic earnings.

I shall introduce the questions to be examined in this chapter by briefly surveying the economic progress of Hispanics in the United States and the links between education and labor market outcomes. Then I will proceed to specify the empirical model used in explaining how literacy skills affect wages and to report my results and conclusions.

THE ECONOMIC CONDITION OF HISPANICS IN THE UNITED STATES

Although there are many parameters involved in measuring the economic condition of a population, the level and distribution of income rank high in the list. In both counts, the economic status of the overall Hispanic population in the

United States, and of Puerto Ricans in particular, has been substantially below that of non-Hispanic whites. Furthermore, this situation has deteriorated since the 1970s. For instance, Puerto Rican family income in 1970 was 58% of that of non-Hispanic whites, 51% in 1980, and 47% in 1987. For the overall Hispanic population, family income in 1970 was 72% of non-Hispanic family income; by comparison, in 1980 this proportion was 70% and in 1987 it was 63%. The major exception to this trend lies in the Cuban population, whose family income in 1980 was 82% of the non-Hispanic white income, while in 1987, it was equal to 84%. (All data reported in this section are from U. S. Department of Commerce, 1971, 1983, 1989a,b).

That the family income of Hispanics—especially Puerto Ricans—has deteriorated over the last 20 years relative to that of non-Hispanic whites is now widely recognized. What is less often realized, however, is that the level of real income among overall Hispanics has not risen since 1970 and, for Puerto Ricans, real family income has actually declined (as has been noted by Rodriguez, 1989, p. 36, and Tienda, 1989). Expressed in 1985 dollars, Hispanic real family income in 1988 was less than $200 higher than in 1972; among Puerto Ricans, real family income declined from $17,676 in 1972 to $15,940 in 1988. By comparison, among non-Hispanic whites there was an upward trend in real family income from $30,476 in 1972 to $33,915 in 1988.

Although the figures supplied so far depict a lack of economic progress among Hispanic families, they fail to provide the full picture for persons of Hispanic origin in the United States. The reason is that average family size diverges across ethnic/racial groups, giving rise to further differentials in *per capita* income. On the average, Hispanic families are larger than non-Hispanic families. The average size of a Hispanic family is 3.79 family members as compared to 3.11 among non-Hispanic whites. As a result, *per capita* income differences between non-Hispanic whites and Hispanics tend to be larger than family income differences. Dividing family income by the number of family members yields *per capita* income. As of March 1987, the *per capita* income in an average Hispanic family was $5,358 compared to $10,377 among a non-Hispanic white family. That is, Hispanic *per capita* income was close to 50% of that among non-Hispanic whites; for Puerto Rican families the percentage was even smaller, equal to only 43%.

Per capita family income levels are used to provide a picture of the average level of economic welfare of a population. This does not necessarily show, however, how most families in that population may have fared. To consider such an issue requires a look at the distribution of family income. It is possible, for instance, to observe two populations with identical average income but with widely different number of people living in poverty. Let us therefore consider poverty levels among the Hispanic population. In 1987, the poverty level in the United States was defined to be equal to $11,611 for an urban family of four (consisting of two parents and two children). If, hypothetically, one were to assume that income is equally distributed among all families in the United States, then the family income figures quoted above would imply that the poverty level among Hispanics is zero: even among Puerto Ricans, the average family income in 1988 was $15,185, which exceeds the poverty level. In reality, things are very different. A picture of the extent of income inequality results from looking at the actual data on the number of families living under the poverty threshold. Among Hispanics, the percentage of families living on poverty equaled 23.6 in 1987, compared to 8.1% among non-Hispanic whites. For Puerto Ricans, the proportion of families on poverty was equal to 38.0%.

Previous research indicates that substantial income inequality is associated with the presence of female-headed households (Garfinkel & McLanahan, 1986; Wilson & Neckerman, 1987). The presence of children, combined with a relatively low average income earned by the female head, results in low *per capita* income among these households. Indeed, as much as 60% and 70% of households in poverty are female-headed households. For Hispanics, the proportion of female-headed families is about twice that among non-Hispanic whites. For Puerto Ricans, 42.3% of the families are headed by women, the highest proportion among any other ethnic/racial group in the United States.

FACTORS DETERMINING SOCIOECONOMIC STATUS

What explains the relatively low levels of income received by Hispanic families? Labor market earnings compose the largest share of family income. These earnings, in turn, are equal to the wages of each employed family member multiplied by the number of employed family members. Consider the latter. The proportion of employed in a family is linked to two variables: the proportion of persons in the labor force and the proportion of the latter who are actually employed. In March 1988, the overall Hispanic labor force participation rate was equal to 65.5%, which was approximately equal to the 65.8% participation rate among non-Hispanic whites. On the other hand, the 53.2% participation rate among Puerto Ricans was substantially below the rate for other Hispanics and for non-Hispanics. Looking at unemployment rates, the Hispanic unemployment rate in March 1988 was equal to 8.5%, significantly higher than the 5.3% unemployment rate among non-Hispanic whites. Among Puerto Ricans, the unemployment rate was 9.2%. Overall, then, part of the lower family income among Hispanics can be attached to their greater likelihood of nonemployment.

The second key component of family income involves the earnings received by employed family members. In general, Hispanics tend to receive lower hourly wages than non-Hispanic whites. As an example, the ethnic/racial hourly wage differentials computed by Reimers (1985) for her sample of men from the 1976

Survey of Income and Education indicate that the average wage rate for non-Hispanic whites was equal to $5.97, but among non-Hispanic blacks it was $4.65 and among Hispanics $4.31. Within the Hispanic population, Cubans received wages closer to those of non-Hispanic whites whereas Puerto Ricans and Mexicans received wages closer to those of non-Hispanic blacks.

These patterns of wage differences among ethnic/racial groups (as well as the labor force patterns noted above) are due partly to demographics. Usually, older workers tend to receive higher wages because of their greater on-the-job experience. Non-Hispanic whites are older than Hispanic workers. Overall, the median age among non-Hispanic whites is equal to 32.7 years, while for Hispanics the median age is equal to 25 years. Among Hispanics, however, Cubans tend to be older, with a median age of 38 years. The implied differences in experience levels partly explain wage differentials.

A second factor behind the ethnic/racial wage differentials noted above is differences in levels of schooling. Some skepticism exists about what is the real influence of education on the relative economic position of ethnic/racial minorities in the United States (Hirschman, 1988, p. 73). Such skepticism is generated partly by the figures depicted in Table 1, where I show years of schooling completed by various racial/ethnic groups from 1970 to 1987. The data show that median years of schooling among blacks, whites and Hispanics have been

Table 1. Median Years of School Completed,
by Race/Ethnicity

Subjects	Non-Hispanic white[a]	Non-Hispanic black[a]	Hispanic (overall)[a]
		1970	
Overall	12.1	9.8	9.1
Men	12.1	9.4	9.3
Women	12.1	10.1	8.9
		1980	
Overall	12.5	12.0	10.8
Men	12.5	12.0	11.1
Women	12.6	12.0	10.6
		1987	
Overall	12.7	12.4	12.0
Men	12.8	12.4	12.1
Women	12.6	12.4	12.0

[a]Persons 25 years of age or older.
SOURCES: U. S. Department of Commerce, 1971, 1983, 1989a,b.

converging. Yet, as was discussed earlier, the relative economic position of the three groups has not narrowed over these years.

There are two problems in using median years of schooling completed to measure educational attainment. First, data on median years can be misleading as a measure of average educational progress when the underlying educational attainment is not normally distributed and is, instead, skewed. Second, for Hispanics, educational attainment can diverge substantially by ancestry. In Table 2, figures show the proportion of persons 25 years of age and older who have completed high school by race/ethnicity. For all groups, high school completion rates have increased. However, wide gaps in high school completion rates between Hispanics and non-Hispanics remained in 1987: among non-Hispanic whites (25–34 years old) the rate was 87.2%, whereas for Hispanics of the same age group it was 60.3%. The 33.2 percentage point gap in high school completion rates between these two groups in 1987 was in effect higher than the 22.4 percentage point difference between them in 1970. Among the overall Hispanic population, then, there has been no convergence in educational attainment toward the non-Hispanic white level. Within the Hispanic population, some convergence has occurred for Puerto Ricans and Cubans; but among the Mexican population, the high school completion rate in 1987 was below the 1970 rate for non-Hispanic whites.

There is another reason for suspecting the use of median years of schooling as a measure of educational attainment: there are obvious differences in the quality of schooling. As a result, persons with the same years of education may exhibit widely different educational skills. Although there is a voluminous literature on the determinants of wages, very little existing work examine how the

Table 2. Percentage of High School Completion Rates, by Race/Ethnicity

Year	Non-Hispanic white[a]	Non-Hispanic black[a]	Hispanic (overall)[a]	Mexican[a]	Puerto Rican[a]	Cuban[a]
1970	54.5	31.4	32.1	24.2	23.4	43.9
1980	68.8	51.2	44.0	37.6	40.1	55.3
1987	75.6	63.4	50.9	44.8	53.8	61.6
1987[b]	87.2	81.7	60.3	54.0	68.4	83.1
Differential in high school attainment rates						
1970	—	23.1	22.4	30.3	31.1	10.6
1980	—	17.6	24.8	31.2	28.7	13.5
1987	—	12.2	24.7	30.8	21.8	14.0
1987[b]	—	5.5	26.9	33.2	18.8	4.1

[a]Persons 25 years of age and older.
[b]Including only persons 25–34 years old.
SOURCE: U. S. Department of Commerce 1971, 1983, 1989a,b.

quality of schooling affects earnings. My purpose in this chapter is to use literacy as a direct measure of the skills acquired by persons in school and to examine how it influences the wages of Hispanics. The next section specifies the specific empirical framework used for these purposes.

LITERACY AND EARNINGS: THE EMPIRICAL FRAMEWORK

The economic participation of men and women in labor markets has been found to differ sufficiently so that separate analyses were done for each group. Human capital studies examining the determinants of earnings postulate that the natural logarithm of the wage rate of a person i of sex j is given by

$$\ln W_{ij} = \beta' X_{ij} + U_{ij} \qquad (1)$$

where W_{ij} is the wage rate received by the individual, β is a vector of coefficients to be estimated, X_{ij} is a vector of human capital and demographic characteristics affecting wages, and U_{ij} is a stochastic disturbance term. This model is to be estimated using the NAEP data set described in detail below. The critical step at this point is to specify the variables included in X_{ij}; that is, the determinants of wages.

Human capital theory suggests that the skills of individuals determine their productivity and, therefore, labor market earnings (see Willis, 1986). The type of skills an individual is endowed with include academic, school-related skills in addition to out-of-school skills acquired through on-the-job training or vocational training programs.

In terms of academic skills, empirical studies in this field have universally used years of schooling as a proxy, looking at how this variable influences earnings (the early studies here include Mincer, 1974; Welch, 1973). As noted earlier, however, years of schooling do not accurately measure the academic skills that a person has been able to learn. Not only does the quality of teaching differ across schools, but the ability of students to absorb knowledge is influenced by many psychological and socioeconomic factors. As a result, if you take any class of graduating high school seniors, you will find a wide dispersion of academic proficiency, suggesting that years of schooling should be supplemented with other, perhaps more direct, measures of the academic skills that persons acquire in school.

Previous studies have incorporated quality of schooling (measured, for instance, by school expenditures per child) or pure academic achievement (measured by grade point average or Scholastic Aptitude Test [SAT] scores) as variables added to years of schooling in explaining earnings (see Bishop, 1989; Card & Krueger, 1990; Orazem, 1987; Smith & Welch, 1989; Wachtel, 1976; Welch,

1973; Wise, 1975). In this chapter, literacy—measured through scores on tests explicitly designed to assess literacy skills—is used as a direct yardstick of the academic knowledge absorbed by individuals in reading and quantitative skills (see also Rivera-Batiz, 1990, 1991). Since education supplies skills other than reading and quantitative literacy, the latter are introduced as additional variables influencing wages, with years of schooling also included in the equation.

English reading proficiency was measured by scores on a test administered to individuals in the NAEP sample. Based on their responses to the test questions, individuals were assigned scores based on a scale of 0 to 500, with higher scores indicating improved levels of English reading proficiency. As standardized by NAEP, a score of 150 indicates very rudimentary reading skills, a score of 200 indicates basic reading skills, 250 shows intermediate reading proficiency, 300 reflects adept reading skills, and 350 advanced reading proficiency. It is to be emphasized that the NAEP tests are explicitly developed to measure basic English reading comprehension—not general scholastic achievement or intelligence—and are administered to students in the United States as part of periodic assessments of their reading skills.

In addition to reading proficiency, a measure of proficiency was added in quantitative skills as a factor influencing wages. The quantitative skills test administered to persons in the NAEP sample was designed to measure proficiency in basic computation skills (e.g., addition, subtraction, multiplication, and division) arising in printed material encountered in everyday personal and occupational activities. The scale is similar to the one described for the reading test, ranging from 0 to 500. In order to evaluate levels of proficiency using this scale, the following reference values are given by NAEP. Individuals who scored around 233 points were generally able to carry out simple arithmetic operations, such as adding up two deposits that had already been entered on a bank deposit slip. Scores between 275 and 300 reflected an ability not only to add or subtract but also to transfer information accurately onto a form (keep a running balance in a checkbook). Individuals achieving a score of 325 were able to make more complicated computations, such as calculating the cost of a specified meal from a menu. Finally, a score of 375 was given to persons who could combine several types of computations, such as transforming cents per ounce into dollars per pound and comparing different items on the basis of their price.

There are non-academic skills that can affect productivity and, thus, wages. Not all knowledge comes from academic schooling. On-the-job training and/or vocational training programs can substitute for a lack of academic schooling. To account for these, total weeks of participation in vocational training programs and years of on-the-job experience—measured by age minus years of education minus six—were included as explanatory variables in the analysis. (Most studies incorporating on-the-job experience as a variable in earnings equations take into account decreasing returns to experience by adding a quadratic term; given the young population under consideration in this chapter, this effect is unlikely to be significant and it is not introduced in the empirical analysis.)

Location of residence is another important variable influencing wages. On account of major structural shifts of industrial production in the United States over the last two decades, there are areas of low-income growth and regions of high-income growth coexisting with each other. For the workers who reside in depressed areas, employment opportunities and earnings may decline relative to those in growing regions (see Kasarda, 1989). Such seems to be the case in the northcentral states where industrial restructuring has been connected to unemployment rates that are about twice those in other areas. In the industrial centers of this region (e.g., Chicago, Cleveland, and Detroit) the unemployment rate is two or three times that of major cities in other regions (e.g., Houston, Dallas, and Atlanta).

Marital status and the presence of children have been found in previous studies to influence labor market participation and wages. This is so particularly for females, for whom marriage and the presence of children have been traditionally associated with reduced labor market activity and with a downgrading of employment opportunities (see Reimers, 1985).

Among Hispanics, a large proportion of the population is composed of immigrants. Since the education and experience of foreign-born workers are not necessarily comparable with the education and experience of American-born workers, a dummy variable was introduced that distinguishes American-born workers from immigrants (equal to 1 if the person is native-born). It is expected that this dummy variable will have a positive coefficient in the wage equations because education and experience received by American-born workers can be expected to be more appropriate for participation in domestic labor markets than their foreign-based equivalents.

Wage differentials among occupations persist over time because of nonpecuniary aspects of employment, temporary occupational labor demand disequilibria, and sluggish adjustments to relative supplies of labor by occupation. To take into account wage differences that are due to occupation, a dummy variable was incorporated that separates white-collar occupations from others (equal to 1 if the person is white collar and 0 otherwise). It is anticipated that the coefficient on this variable in the wage equations is positive.

SCHOOLING, EMPLOYMENT, AND SELECTIVITY BIAS

The previous section specified an array of variables that influence wages. Algebraically, these variables form part of the vector x_{ij} in Equation 1. On this basis, the wage equation to be estimated should be given by

$$\ln W_{ij} = \beta_0 + \beta_1 EDUCAT2_{ij} + \beta_2 EDUCAT3_{ij} + \beta_3 READ_{ij} + \beta_4 COMP_{ij}$$
$$+ \beta_5 WCOLLAR_{ij} + \beta_6 TEXPER_{ij} + \beta_7 OCCUT_{ij} + \beta_8 AMERICAN_{ij}$$
$$+ \beta_9 REGION3_{ij} + \beta_{10} MARRIED_{ij} + \beta_{11} KIDS_{ij} + U_{ij} \qquad (2)$$

where W_{ij} will be measured by the hourly wage rate, so that the left-hand side is the logarithm of the hourly wage rate, $EDUCAT2$ is a dummy variable that equals 1 if the person has 12–15 years of schooling; that is, if the person has graduated from high school and/or has some college education, and 0 otherwise; $EDUCAT3$ equals 1 if the person has graduated from college and/or has some additional (graduate-level or professional) education, and is 0 otherwise. The variables $READ$ and $COMP$ are the scores on the reading proficiency and quantitative skills tests taken by persons in the sample. The dummy variable $WCOLLAR$ is equal to 1 if the person is in a white-collar occupation and 0 otherwise. $TEXPER$ is a proxy for years of experience and is computed as age minus maximum years of schooling minus six; $OCCUT$ shows the weeks of vocational (out-of-job) training the individual has had. The dummy variable $AMERICAN$ is equal to 1 if the person was born in the continental United States and 0 otherwise (individuals born in the Island of Puerto Rico are catalogued as immigrants); $REGION3$ is a dummy variable for residence in the northcentral United States; $MARRIED$ is equal to 1 if the person is married and 0 otherwise; $KIDS$ is equal to 1 if the individual has children living in the household and 0 otherwise. Finally, U_{ij} is an error term assumed to be randomly distributed among the population. Note, however, that the sample for which wages are observed is not randomly selected from the population; it represents individuals that have a preference for participation in the labor market vis-à-vis other activities, such as schooling. As a result, taking expected values in Equation 1:

$$E(\ln W_{ij} \mid X_{ij}, W_{ij} > 0) = \beta' X_{ij} + E(U_{ij} \mid W_{ij} > 0) \qquad (3)$$

where X_{ij} is the vector of human capital characteristics of the individual in the wage sample (which includes $EDUCAT2, EDUCAT3$, etc.), and where the expectation is taken conditional on individuals having a positive wage, meaning that the last term in the right-hand side may differ from zero, making the least squares estimates of Equation 2 subject to specification error and biased.

To adjust for the sample selection bias involved in the exclusion of persons for whom there is no wage and cannot therefore be in the wage regression sample, the two-stage procedure postulated by Heckman (1979) was followed. Mainly, a binary probit analysis was performed where the dependent variable is 1 if the person is an employee in the wage sample and 0 if the person is in school. (There is a third category that includes the unemployed and those out of the labor force; but since only a relatively small proportion of the Hispanic sample was in this category, and previous studies have suggested that the selectivity bias involved in excluding the unemployed and out-of-labor-force persons from samples of young workers may be negligible [see Hoffman & Link, 1984], no adjustment was made for this selectivity in this chapter.) The independent variables in the probit equation are the following.

First, the variables *READ* and *COMP* were included as proxies for the academic proficiency of a person. It is expected that the stronger a person's academic achievement, the more likely he or she is to continue education and thus be a student in the sample. Also used was the variable *IADULT,* which is equal to 1 if the person is a Hispanic immigrant who moved to the United States less than 5 years before the survey interview, and 0 otherwise. The reason this variable is included is because, among Hispanics in the present sample, the proportion of recent immigrants that are students is high, particularly among females. The probability of being in the wage sample is therefore negatively correlated with being a recent foreign immigrant (*IADULT* = 1).

In addition, marital status and having children are represented by the dummy variables *MARRIED* and *KIDS* (defined before). Both can be expected to raise the probability that the individual will be employed vis-à-vis being in school. Indeed, previous research has suggested that, among women, high school and college dropout rates are strongly correlated with teenage pregnancy and early marriage (see Garfinkel & McLanahan, 1986, p. 23).

The dummy variable *FWHITEC* is equal to 1 if the person's father has a white-collar occupation and 0 otherwise; *MWHITEC* is equal to 1 if the mother is white-collar. The choice of these variables reflects the fact that a person's socioeconomic background, particularly parental occupation background, intimately affects whether college and postcollege schooling is sought or not (see Borus, 1984; Fligstein & Fernandez, 1985; and Willis & Rosen, 1979).

The probit equations whose variables have just been described are estimated using *Maximum Likelihood* and the results used to find the inverse Mills ratios that are then introduced into the original regression for Equation 3—in place of $E(U_{ij} \mid W_{ij} > 0)$—to adjust for the selection bias in this equation (see Heckman, 1979). The variable *MILLS* represents the inverse Mills ratio in the tables in this chapter. The wage equation can then be estimated using ordinary least squares, providing consistent estimates.

FIRST STAGE ESTIMATION: DETERMINANTS OF THE PROBABILITY OF EMPLOYMENT

A total of 3,618 individuals were interviewed by NAEP. The sample of Hispanics (with ethnicity catalogued on the basis of self-assessed ethnicity) used here consists of 301, of which 155 were men and 146 women. Of the 155 males,

114 (or 73.5%) were employed and 41 were still in school. Of the 146 females, 95 (or 65%) were in the labor market and 51 were students. It should be stressed that the great majority of the Hispanic sample (65% of the men and 52% of the women) consists of persons of Mexican origin. The results below are thus more applicable to this group and may not be representative for Puerto Ricans, Cubans, or other Hispanics. Unfortunately, the analysis could not be carried out separately by national origin because of the small sample sizes.

The sample means and results of the first stage of the estimation procedure for Hispanic males and females are presented in Tables 3 and 4, respectively. As

Table 3. Sample Means: Probit Analysis for the Probability
of Being in the Wage Sample

Variable	Mean for $DSTUD = 0$	Mean for $DSTUD = 1$	Mean for all
	Independent variable means for men[a]		
READ (Test-based reading proficiency)	275.5	245.0	253.1
COMP (Test-based quantitative literacy)	287.3	250.3	260.1
FWHITEC (Proportion of sample with white-collar father)	0.29	0.21	0.23
MWHITEC (Proportion of sample with white-collar mother)	0.34	0.09	0.16
IADULT (Proportion of sample immigrating to the United States as an adult)	0.15	0.13	0.14
MARRIED (Proportion of sample that is married)	0.07	0.23	0.19
KIDS (Proportion of sample with children)	0.07	0.19	0.16
Number of observations	41	114	155
	Independent variable means for women[a]		
READ (Test-based reading proficiency)	271.9	243.8	253.6
COMP (Test-based quantitative literacy)	276.7	263.3	267.9
FWHITEC (Proportion of sample with white-collar father)	0.35	0.18	0.24
MWHITEC (Proportion of sample with white-collar mother)	0.37	0.22	0.27
IADULT (Proportion of sample immigrating to the United States as an adult)	0.21	0.11	0.15
MARRIED (Proportion of sample that is married)	0.23	0.45	0.38
KIDS (Proportion of sample with children)	0.29	0.40	0.36
Number of observations	51	95	146

[a]Dependent variable: Binary categorical variable DSTUD, where DSTUD equals 1 if the person is an employee in the wage sample and 0 if the person is in school.
SOURCE: National Assessment of Educational Progress, 1988.

a basis for comparison, Equation 1 in Table 4 displays the probit results for males excluding the *COMP* and *READ* variables; Equation 2 then shows the results when the literacy variables have been added. At the bottom of each equation is shown the value of the likelihood ratio test statistic for the null hypothesis that all the coefficients of the model with the exception of the constant term are equal to 0. Asymptotically, this statistic has a chi-squared distribution with degrees of freedom equal to the number of independent variables. For instance, the value of 17.3 reported in Equation 1 for males is above 16.7, the critical value of the chi-squared distribution for the 99.5% confidence level (with 5 degrees of freedom). Therefore, the hypothesis that the coefficients of the probit equation depicted in

Table 4. Binary Probit Analysis for the Probability of Being in the Wage Sample

Variable	Equation 1		Equation 2	
	Maximum likelihood estimate	*T*-statistic	Maximum likelihood estimate	*T*-statistic
	Estimated coefficients for men			
INTERCEPT	0.7684	4.97	2.2880	3.64
READ	—	—	−0.0008	−0.35
COMP	—	—	−0.0049	−2.11
FWHITEC	−0.1377	−0.50	−0.0926	−0.33
MWHITEC	−0.9253	−3.15	−0.7494	−2.42
IADULT	−0.2772	−0.83	−0.5711	−1.51
MARRIED	0.6199	1.25	0.7867	1.56
KIDS	0.1293	0.25	−0.1011	−0.18
(−2.0) times				
Log-likelihood ratio:	17.3		24.7	
Number of observations:	155		155	
	Estimated coefficients for women			
INTERCEPT	0.5201	2.84	2.1560	2.72
READ	—	—	−0.0049	−2.51
COMP	—	—	−0.0012	−0.46
FWHITEC	−0.5338	−1.96	−0.3826	−1.34
MWHITEC	−0.2821	−1.09	−0.1904	−0.72
IADULT	−0.4689	−1.55	−1.1485	−2.79
MARRIED	0.7671	2.64	0.7882	2.66
KIDS	−0.2972	−1.02	−0.2629	−0.88
(−2.0) times				
Log-likelihood ratio:	16.8		25.6	
Number of observations:	146		146	

SOURCE: National Assessment of Educational Progress, 1988.

Equation 1 are equal to 0 can be rejected with a great degree of confidence. Similar conclusions can be obtained for the other equations reported in Table 4.

The coefficients in Table 4 provide estimates of the impact of the variables defined above—*IADULT, FWHITEC*, etc.—on the probability of being an employee (in the wage sample) vis-à-vis being a student. The signs of the estimated coefficients are mostly as expected, at least in the cases where they are statistically significant. In particular, note that, for Hispanic males, (1) being a recent immigrant increases the probability of his being a student; (2) being married reduces the likelihood of his being in school; (3) higher scores on the test-based measure of English reading proficiency makes the individual more likely to be in the student sample, although the coefficient is not statistically significant; (4) higher scores on the test-based measure of quantitative skills makes the person more likely to be a student; and (5) if the mother's, but not the father's occupation is white-collar, the person is much more likely to be in school.

There are some significant differences in the estimated coefficients of the probit equations for women when compared to those for men. Interestingly, the role of the father's occupation in raising the probability of being in school appears to be stronger among females: if the father is a white-collar worker, females are more likely to be in school. A similar role was played by the mother's occupation in the male sample. In addition, among women, the impact of reading proficiency is to sharply increase the probability of being a student, a connection that is of no importance among males. On the other hand, for men, proficiency in quantitative skills appears to be strongly associated with a greater probability of being in school, but among females this variable has no significance. Finally, marriage has a stronger negative effect on the probability of being in school for women.

THE EFFECTS OF LITERACY ON EARNINGS: RESULTS OF THE WAGE EQUATION

The second stage of the estimation procedure applies ordinary least squares to the wage equations, where the MILLS variable computed from the first stage has been added as an explanatory variable. The results to be reported below are, therefore, adjusted for sample selection bias.

The means for the variables in the wage equation are depicted in Table 5. The sample wage was much higher for males than for females. For males, the average sample hourly wage was equal to $6.879, whereas for females it was equal to $5.537. Interestingly, females in the sample had average scores on the quantitative skills test that were significantly higher than for males (263 points versus 250 for males). For most of the other variables, however, sample means do not differ substantially by gender. The exceptions are the marriage rate, which

Table 5. Sample Means for Wage Equations

	Men		Women	
	Mean	Standard deviation	Mean	Standard deviation
Hourly wage	6.879	3.118	5.537	2.161
READ (test-based reading proficiency, 0–500)	245	74	243	85
COMP (test-based quantitative literacy, 0–500)	250	58	263	52
EDUCAT1 (proportion with 0–11 years of schooling completed)	0.377	—	0.221	—
EDUCAT2 (12–15 years of schooling completed)	0.474	—	0.653	—
EDUCAT3 (16+ years of schooling completed)	0.149	—	0.126	—
WCOLLAR (proportion of sample with white-collar occupation)	0.316	—	0.611	—
TEXPER (years of job experience)	5.561	2.358	5.600	2.566
OCCUT (weeks of vocational training)	10.21	20.27	16.03	24.71
AMERICAN (proportion of sample born in the continental U. S.)	0.561	—	0.568	—
REGION3 (proportion of sample residing in northcentral U. S.)	0.070	—	0.053	—
MARRIED (proportion of sample that is married)	0.228	—	0.453	—
KIDS (proportion of sample with children)	0.193	—	0.400	—
MILLS (to adjust for sample selection bias)	0.400	0.186	0.488	0.265
Number of observations:	114		95	

SOURCE: National Assessment of Educational Progress, 1988.

is almost twice as high among females when compared to males, and the presence of children, which again is twice as large for females; in this sample of employed persons, approximately 45% of Hispanic females were married and 40% had children who were living in the same household.

The wage equation estimates are presented in Table 6. I first report the results for men, which are presented at the top of the table. For comparison purposes, Equation 1 depicts the male equation results when the literacy variables READ and COMP have been excluded from the analysis. Equation 2 then shows the results for the full wage equation, with the literacy variables added. Note that the coefficients on the MILLS variable are not statistically significant, indicating that the problem of sample selection bias may not be a severe one for this group. Observe also that the adjusted R^2 for the male wage equations rises substantially when the literacy variables are added, from 0.13 to 0.16, indicating the relevance of literacy in explaining the variance of wages among male Hispanics in this sample. The estimated coefficients suggest, however, that it is quantitative skills—as represented by the *COMP* variable—which has a significant effect on male wages. The coefficient of the reading proficiency variable, *READ,* is negligible in absolute value and statistically insignificant.

In addition to the importance of quantitative skills in raising the earnings of Hispanic males, the results presented in Table 6 indicate that years of schooling have a strong effect on wages independently of literacy skills. This is a result that has been found in previous research incorporating scholastic achievement into earnings equations. Bishop (1989) concluded that this result "suggests that schooling develops or signals other economically productive talents such as discipline, perseverance, and occupationally specific skills" (p. 181).

On-the-job experience also has a sharp positive impact on wages among this group but weeks of participation in vocational training programs do not seem to help much in raising wages among Hispanic males. Some previous studies have found similar results. Glazer (1986), for instance, has noted that many vocational training programs fail on account of relatively short time spans, high dropout rates, and inability to adjust to the variety of needs of the different participants. Finally, marriage is associated with lower wages but having children raises them, and location in the northcentral United States has a strong negative impact on earnings, holding other things equal.

The bottom part of Table 6 reports the results for females, with Equation 1 showing the wage equation excluding the READ and COMP variables and Equation 2 the estimated coefficients with the literacy skills included. Note that the MILLS variable is, as in the male equations, statistically insignificant, indicating again that selection bias may not be an influential problem in the sample.

The adjusted R^2 rises significantly when the literacy variables are included, from 0.25 to 0.28. On this, the results for males and females coincide. There are, however, considerable differences in the estimated coefficients of the wage equations for the two groups. First, the reading proficiency and quantitative skills variables have opposite effects on wages. Although for men quantitative skills seem to matter greatly in affecting wages, among women it is reading proficiency that seems to matter the most, with quantitative skills having a negligible effect and lacking statistical significance. One possible explanation is that this difference is due to the overrepresentation of women in clerical, sales, and professional occupations (61% of females in the sample were employed in white-collar occupations, as opposed to only 31.6% for males), occupations that require ample English language interaction for their performance and more limited profi-

Table 6. Estimated Coefficients: Wage Equations

	Equation 1			Equation 2		
Variable	Parameter estimate	T-statistic	Prob > |T|	Parameter estimate	T-statistic	Prob > |T|
		Men				
INTERCEPT	1.4461	7.14	0.0001	1.0135	4.05	0.0001
READ	—	—	—	0.00005	0.08	0.936
COMP	—	—	—	0.0021	2.11	0.037
EDUCAT2	0.2395	2.48	0.015	0.2027	2.03	0.045
EDUCAT3	0.5837	3.83	0.0002	0.5037	3.22	0.002
WCOLLAR	0.0851	1.02	0.312	0.0768	0.92	0.361
TEXPER	0.0429	1.95	0.054	0.0471	2.14	0.034
OCCUT	0.0025	1.38	0.169	0.0019	1.03	0.303
AMERICAN	−0.0098	−0.13	0.895	−0.0599	−0.75	0.453
REGION3	−0.2859	−1.99	0.049	−0.2902	−2.04	0.044
MARRIED	−0.2378	−1.52	0.130	−0.3574	−2.18	0.032
KIDS	0.2570	1.67	0.098	0.3524	2.23	0.028
MILLS	−0.1662	−0.69	0.490	−0.3104	−1.21	0.230
Number of observations:	114			114		
Adjusted R-SQ.:	0.13			0.16		
Dependent variable mean:	1.841					
		Women				
INTERCEPT	1.3692	6.57	0.0001	1.0859	4.73	0.0001
READ	—	—	—	0.0011	2.09	0.040
COMP	—	—	—	0.0006	0.79	0.439
EDUCAT2	0.2187	2.29	0.025	0.1500	1.54	0.128
EDUCAT3	0.3989	2.67	0.009	0.3091	2.00	0.048
WCOLLAR	0.1342	1.84	0.070	0.0895	1.22	0.226
TEXPER	0.0037	0.22	0.829	0.0079	0.46	0.647
OCCUT	0.0011	0.83	0.408	0.0012	0.87	0.387
AMERICAN	0.1381	2.03	0.045	0.0604	0.81	0.419
REGION3	0.1420	0.99	0.322	0.0583	0.41	0.685
MARRIED	−0.0292	−0.27	0.784	−0.0591	−0.56	0.575
KIDS	−0.1266	−1.35	0.179	−0.1430	−1.55	0.126
MILLS	−0.1054	−0.57	0.570	−0.1503	−0.84	0.406
Number of observations:	95			95		
Adjusted R-SQ.:	0.25			0.28		
Dependent variable mean:	1.650					

SOURCE: National Assessment of Educational Progress, 1988.

ciency in quantitative skills. If this is so, inadequate English language proficiency should be expected to severely curtail female employment opportunities and, thus, wages. Among males, on the other hand, the shortcomings of English language deficiency may be circumvented by employment in jobs that require quantitative skills, thus making this the critical variable influencing job opportunities and earnings.

Another major difference with the results for men is that on-the-job experience has a negligible positive effect on female wages, whereas the exact opposite holds for men. This is traditionally explained as resulting from the statistically higher rate of labor market withdrawal among women, which induces employers to supply them with less on-the-job training (or pass the costs of the specific training to the female employee in the form of lower wages). This reduces the slope of age–earnings profiles. Note, however, from Table 5 that, for the 1985 sample of young adults, female labor market experience exceeded that of men. For this group, then, the traditionally lower-experience levels of women do not hold. Of course, this does not preclude employers from making relatively low-salary and low-advancement offers based on high probabilities of future labor market withdrawal. But insofar as those decisions are not based on the behavior of the current cohort—and instead on national data which includes older cohorts—they constitute in effect statistical discrimination (see Bergmann, 1986; Blau, 1984). An alternative explanation is that on-the-job training is more important in the blue-collar jobs where men concentrate than in the white-collar jobs where women are clustered. In this view, occupational segregation explains the lower returns to experience among women (see England, 1982).

CONCLUSIONS

This chapter has made use of test-based measures of reading proficiency and quantitative literacy to estimate the role played by literacy skills in explaining the earnings of young adult Hispanics in the United States. The statistical analysis unequivocally suggests that literacy skills are a major variable explaining wage differentials among Hispanics. There is, however, a major difference in the type of literacy skill that is of relevance in the determination of wages for men and women. Among Hispanic females, English reading proficiency is the critical skill that is rewarded through higher wages. Quantitative skills do not appear to be as significant. For Hispanic males, on the other hand, quantitative literacy has a strong positive impact on wages and English proficiency a more modest effect.

An explanation for the difference in the type of literacy skill that is of importance in the determination of wages by gender may lie in the overrepresentation of females in the sample among white-collar occupations. A total of 61%

of Hispanic females and only 31.6% of Hispanic males were employed in white-collar occupations. Since it can be expected that the clerical, sales, and professional occupations in which women in the sample were more likely to be employed require the heavy use of the English language for their performance—and relatively minimal use of quantitative skills—it may not be surprising that reading proficiency is a variable of more significance in the female wage equation. At the same time, the concentration of men in blue-collar jobs, for which quantitative skills may serve to compensate for lack of English language proficiency, may be the explanation behind the significance of quantitative literacy in explaining the wages of Hispanic males.

Thus, policies encouraging the acquisition of broad literacy skills among Hispanic workers can have a large payoff in terms of higher wages. Let me observe that literacy skills appear to vary quite widely among Hispanic persons with similar years of schooling, suggesting that differences in the quality of schooling may be generating an unequal distribution of literacy skills among the Hispanic population. Targeting literacy directly, through English as a second language or bilingual education programs, must be the approach to follow if the earnings of Hispanics from low socioeconomic background are to be influenced. It must also be emphasized that quantitative literacy appears to be highly significant in substituting for inadequate English language proficiency among males. Literacy programs intended to help Hispanic workers in general may be more likely to succeed if they combine the development of quantitative skills with English language proficiency improvement.

I conclude by noting that, as in previous studies, the results presented here show how, even though measured human capital characteristics explain a significant portion of wage variation, a large fraction remains unexplained. Unmeasured productivity variables and the stochastic nature of labor market outcomes account for some of this unexplained wage variation. Labor market discrimination is also another influence. Indeed, our finding on the relative ineffectiveness of job experience in affecting the wages of women as compared to men suggests that statistical discrimination and/or occupational segregation may be operating in constraining female labor market outcomes. To explore this issue in more detail, as well as questions relating to ethnic/racial discrimination must be the task of future research.

ACKNOWLEDGMENTS

I have benefited from the valuable comments of Janis Barry Figueroa and the participants of seminars at the Employment Policy Conference held at the Massachusetts Institute of Technology in April, 1988, the American Economic Association Meetings in New York in December, 1988, and the American Educational Research Association Meetings in Boston in April, 1990. The first version of this paper was written while I was a postdoctoral Fellow at the Center for the National Assessment of Educational Progress at Princeton, New Jersey. I also gratefully acknowledge the financial assistance of grants provided by Educational Testing Service and the Rutgers University Research Council.

REFERENCES

Bean, F., & M. Tienda. (1987). *The Hispanic population in the United States.* New York: Russell Sage.

Bergmann, B. (1986). *The economic emergence of women.* New York: Basic Books.

Bishop, J. H. (1989). Is the test score decline responsible for the productivity growth decline? *American Economic Review, 79,* 178–197.

Blau, F. (1984). Discrimination against women. In W. Darity, Ed., *Labor economics: Modern views.* Boston: Kluwer-Nijhoff.

Borjas, G. (1984). The economic status of male Hispanic migrants and natives in the United States. In R. Ehrenberg, Ed., *Research in labor economics.* Greenwich: JAI Press, pp. 65–122.

Borjas, G., & M. Tienda, Eds. (1985). *Hispanics in the U. S. economy.* Orlando, FL: Academic Press.

Borus, M. (1984). *Youth and the labor market: Analyses of the national longitudinal survey.* Kalamazoo, Michigan: Upjohn Institute for Employment Research.

Card, D., & A. Krueger. (1990). *Does school quality matter? Returns to education and the characteristics of public schools in the United States.* Department of Economics, Princeton University, New Jersey.

Cuomo Commission on Trade and Competitiveness. (1988). *The Cuomo commission report.* New York: Simon & Schuster.

DeFreitas, G. (1990). *Migration, unemployment and inequality: Hispanics in the U. S. labor force.* Oxford: Oxford University Press.

England, P. (1982). The failure of human capital theory to explain occupational sex segregation. *Journal of Human Resources, 17,* 358–370.

Fligstein, N., & R. Fernandez. (1985). Educational transitions of whites and Mexican-Americans. In G. Borjas & M. Tienda, Eds., *Hispanics in the U. S. economy.* Orlando, FL: Academic Press, pp. 161–192.

Garfinkel, I., & S. Mclanahan. (1986). *Single mothers and their children: A new American dilemma.* Washington, DC: Urban Institute Press.

Grenier, G. (1984). The effects of language characteristics on the wages of Hispanic-American males. *Journal of Human Resources, 19,* 35–52.

Heckman, J. J. (1979). Sample selection bias as a specification error. *Econometrica, 47,* 153–162.

Hirschman, C. (1988). Minorities in the labor market: Cyclical patterns and secular trends in joblessness. In G. D. Sandefur & M. Tienda, Eds., *Divided opportunities: Minorities, poverty, and social policy.* New York: Plenum Press.

Hoffman, S., & C. Link. (1984). Selectivity bias in male wage equations. *Review of Economics and Statistics, 66,* 320–324.

Kasarda, J. (1989). Urban industrial transition and the underclass. *Annals of the American Academy of Political and Social Science, 501,* 26–47.

Kirsch, I., & A. Jungeblut. (1987). *Literacy: Profiles of America's young adults.* Princeton: Center for the Assessment of Educational Progress, Educational Testing Service, Report No. 16-PL-01.

Kossoudji, S. A. (1988). English language ability and the labor market opportunities of Hispanic and East Asian immigrant men. *Journal of Labor Economics, 6,* 205–228.

McManus, W., W. Gould, & F. Welch. (1983). Earnings of Hispanic men: The role of English language proficiency. *Journal of Labor Economics, 1,* 101–130.

Meyer, R. H., & D. A. Wise. (1984). The transition from school to work: The experiences of blacks and whites. In R. Ehrenberg, Ed., *Research in labor economics.* Greenwich: JAI Press, pp. 123–176.

Mincer, J. (1974). *Schooling, experience and earnings.* New York: National Bureau of Economic Research.

Murname, R. J. (1988). Education and productivity of the Work Force: Looking Ahead. In M. N. Bailey, M. Blair, R. W. Crandall, F. Levy, & R. J. Murnane, Eds., *American living standards: Threats and challenges.* Washington, DC: Brookings Institution, pp. 215–245.

National Assessment of Educational Progress. (1988). *Young adult literacy survey public use data tape.* Princeton: Center for the National Assessment of Educational Progress.

Orazem, P. F. (1987). Black-white differences in schooling investment and human capital production in segregated schools. *American Economic Review, 77,* 714–723.

Ortiz, V. (1987). *Literacy among Hispanic young adults.* Princeton: Educational Testing Service.

Reimers, C. (1983). Labor market discrimination against Hispanic and black men. *Review of Economics and Statistics, 65,* 570–579.

Reimers, C. (1985). A comparative analysis of the wages of Hispanics, blacks and non-Hispanic whites. In G. Borjas & M. Tienda, Eds., *Hispanics in the U. S. Economy.* Orlando, FL: Academic Press, pp. 27–76.

Rivera-Batiz, F. (1988). *English Language proficiency and the economic progress of immigrants. Research report.* Washington, DC: Division of Immigration Policy and Research, Bureau of International Labor Affairs, U. S. Department of Labor.

Rivera-Batiz, F. (1990). Literacy skills and the wages of young black and white males in the U. S. *Economics Letters, 32,* 377–382.

Rivera-Batiz, F. (1991). Quantitative literacy and the likelihood of employment among young adults in the United States. *Journal of Human Resources,* forthcoming.

Rodriguez, C. (1989). *Puerto Ricans: Born in the U.S.A.:* Boston: Unwin Hyman.

Smith, J., & F. Welch. (1989). Black economic progress after Myrdal. *Journal of Economic Literature, 27,* 519–564.

Sum, A., P. Harrington, & W. Goedicke. (1987). One fifth of the nation's teenagers: Employment problems of poor youth in America, 1981–1985. *Youth and Society, 18,* 195–237.

Sum, A., P. Harrington, & W. Goedicke. (1986). *Basic skills, high school diplomas and the labor force: Employment, unemployment, and earnings experiences of young adults in the U. S.* Research Report. New York: Ford Foundation.

Tainer, E. (1988). English language proficiency and the determination of earnings among foreign-born men. *Journal of Human Resources, 23,* 108–122.

Tienda, M. (1989). Puerto Ricans and the underclass debate. *Annals of the American Academy of Political and Social Science, 501,* 105–119.

U. S. Department of Commerce, Bureau of the Census. (1989a). *Current population reports: The Hispanic population in the United States: March 1988.* Series P-20, No. 438 (July). Washington, DC: U. S. Government Printing Office.

U. S. Department of Commerce, Bureau of the Census. (1989b). *Current population reports: Money income and poverty status in the United States: 1988,* Series P-60, No. 166 (October), Washington, DC: U. S. Government Printing Office.

U. S. Department of Commerce, Bureau of the Census. (1983). *1980 census of population: Characteristics of the population: General Social and Economic characteristics, Part I.* Washington, DC: U. S. Government Printing Office.

U. S. Department of Commerce, Bureau of the Census. (1971). *Current population reports: Selected characteristics of persons and families of Mexican, Puerto Rican and other Spanish origin.* Series P-20, No. 224 (November). Washington, DC: U. S. Government Printing Office.

Venezky, R. L., C. F. Kaestle, & A. M. Sum. (1987). *The subtle danger: Reflections on the literacy abilities of America's young adults*. Princeton: Center for the Assessment of Educational Progress, Educational Testing Service, Report No. 16-CAEP-01 (January).

Wachtel, P. (1976). The effects on earnings of school and college investment expenditures. *Review of Economics and Statistics, 58,* (August), 326–331.

Welch, F. (1973). Black-white differences in returns to schooling. *American Economic Review,* 63 (December), 893–907.

Willis, R. J. (1986). Wage determinants: A survey and reinterpretation of human capital earnings functions. In O. Ashenfelter & R. Layard, Eds., *Handbook of labor economics*. Amsterdam: North Holland Publishing, pp. 525–602.

Willis, R. J., & S. Rosen. (1979). Education and self-selection. *Journal of Political Economy, 87,* Part 2 (October), S7–S36.

Wilson, W. J., & K. Neckerman. (1985). Poverty and Family Structure: The widening gap between evidence and public policy issues. In W. J. Wilson, Ed., *The truly disadvantaged*. Chicago: University of Chicago Press.

Wilson, W. J., R. Aponte, J. Kirschenman, & L. Wacquant. (1988). The ghetto underclass and the changing structure of urban poverty. In F. Harris & R. W. Wilkins, Eds., *Quiet riots: Race and poverty in the United States*. New York: Pantheon Books, pp. 123–151.

Wise, D. A. (1975). Academic achievement and job performance. *American Economic Review,* 65 (June), 350–366.

4

The Effect of Race on Puerto Rican Wages

CLARA E. RODRIGUEZ

The manner in which Hispanic individuals chose to identify themselves by race in the 1980 census was quite different from the manner in which non-Hispanics chose to classify themselves. Although 40% of all Latinos classified themselves as neither white nor black, but as *other,* fewer than 2% of non-Hispanics in any state used this classification. This classification accounted for 7.5 million of all Latinos in the United States. For Puerto Ricans who were living in New York, the group that was the focus of this research, 48% responded that they were other and wrote in an additional Spanish descriptor (i.e., they were Boricua, Puerto Rican, etc.). Another 44% said they were white and 3.9% said they were black.[1] Thus, it would appear from these results that Latino racial identity, as revealed in the 1980 census, is a complex and intriguing phenomenon.[2]

---

[1] Another 4% said they were other but did not write in a Spanish descriptor, and 1% said they were Asian or Native American Indian (Rodriguez, 1989).

[2] Some researchers have argued that these responses to the race item on the census were the result of a misunderstanding of the question. Tienda and Ortiz (1986), for example, suggested that the format of the race item may have led to some misinterpretation. Although the item did not specifically mention race, it did precede the Hispanic identifier and included as possible answers to the race question various Asian groups, which may have induced some Latinos to respond culturally. However, the work of Martin, DeMaio, and Campanelli (1988) and Chevan (1990) has suggested otherwise. Moreover, a misunderstanding of such magnitude typically implies another understand-

---

CLARA E. RODRIGUEZ • Division of the Social Sciences, Fordham University at Lincoln Center, New York, New York 10023.

Hispanics in the Labor Force, edited by Edwin Melendez *et al.* Plenum Press, New York, 1991.

THE RESEARCH QUESTION

Viewed within the context of the labor-market discrimination literature, the divergent racial self-identification pattern of Latinos raises an interesting question. Is the racial identification of Latinos as white, black, and other associated with differential labor-market outcomes? This is the question that is addressed in this research. Employed Puerto Rican men and women in New York City were examined to determine whether racial identification had an effect on hourly wages—once other human capital, industry, and occupational variables were controlled.

On a broader, more theoretical level, this research assumes that by examining a racially heterogeneous ethnic group within a regional labor market,—that is, holding constant ethnicity and regional factors, and holding constant the usual human capital characteristics that have been found to be important determinants of wage rates—greater insight will be gained into the relative effect of race and gender on labor-market outcomes.

The data used were the responses of Puerto Ricans who were living in New York City to the race item on the 1980 census. These data are, in the main, self-reported data, since over 95% of the census questionnaires were self-administered. The census does not provide objective measures by which any of the collected information can be verified. Therefore, how much self-reported race equates with phenotypic race is not known. Earlier research indicates there is, for some Puerto Ricans, a difference between self-reported race and objective race, that is, how the person is seen by others (Rodriguez, 1974; Tumin & Feldman, 1961). What is being measured in my research is the impact of self-reported race.

The question of why Puerto Rican or Latino self-identification as white, black or other would be expected to influence labor market outcomes is an important one. To the degree that self-identification reflects phenotype, the relationship is relatively straightforward. Those who identify as white or black and who are seen by potential employers as white or black, would be expected to enjoy or suffer the same discrimination or preference as American whites and blacks. Those who are seen as intermediate in color would be expected to have intermediate outcomes, with darker individuals receiving the greatest discrimination. The research by Telles and Murguia (1990) has supported this expectation. Using a phenotype scale, they found that

> Dark and Native American Indian looking individuals of Mexican descent suffer significantly greater earnings disadvantages than their lighter and more European looking counterparts [and that this was] primarily because of labor market discrimination. (p. 16)

---

ing of the question. In addition, my current survey research indicates that even when the question about race is very clearly stated and restated, the responses are similar to those in the census. The question still elicits a similar "Other-Spanish" response among a great number of those who are interviewed.

However, such identification may also influence socioeconomic outcomes even when phenotype and self-identification are not consonant. For example, individuals who identify as white would be expected to feel more entitled to apply for jobs where American whites are dominant (i.e., they may try harder because they would expect more equitable treatment, or they may look for more desirable jobs). In addition, those who identify as white may be viewed by employers as more culturally assimilated and may be more favored in predominantly white job sectors—regardless of the extent to which they are phenotypically white. A similar phenomenon may be at work with regard to those who identify as black.

PUERTO RICANS AND RACE

Although the effect of race on Puerto Rican socioeconomic outcomes has seldom been the subject of systematic, scientific inquiry, the issue has been consistently mentioned in the literature. The early descriptive literature, for example, noted the significance of race especially when Puerto Ricans migrated to the United States. A common theme in this literature was the more benign quality of race relations in Puerto Rico as compared with the United States (Chenault, 1970; Giles, Llado, McKirnan, & Taylor, 1979; Glazer & Moynihan, 1970; Mintz, 1960; Petrullo, 1947; Steward et al., 1956). Tumin and Feldman (1961) further corroborated this theme when they studied in depth the question of whether men in Puerto Rico were "heirs to different social fates because of their colors" (p. 227). Their survey showed that skin color in Puerto Rico was *not* a significant differentiating variable with regard to educational attainment, employment type, or other features of Puerto Rican life.[3]

Upon the migration of Puerto Ricans to the United States, the picture in the literature is quite different because it presents Puerto Ricans as experiencing many difficulties because of their race. For example, Chenault (1970), writing on the early pre-World War II Puerto Rican community, found frequent instances of difficulty on account of color. While Steward et al. (1956, p. 127) found that dark skin was a handicap in New York when compared to Puerto Rico, he added that the realization of this attitude could shock the dark-skinned immigrant. The negative economic consequences for dark Puerto Ricans in New York were also noted by C. Wright Mills (Mills, Senior, & Goldsen, 1950, pp. 72–74), who found that in the late 1950s "colored" or intermediate men, earned less than white men and experienced less mobility.[4] Senior (1965) also found (somewhat

[3]They did note, however, its salience at the "fringes and interstices of personal relations, where public policy is not an issue and where public controls are not available" (p. 233).
[4]Mills (1950) also found white men to experience greater upward and downward mobility than the intermediate group, who tended to stay in semi-skilled and unskilled jobs in New York and in Puerto Rico (pp. 72–74).

later) that in New York the colored Puerto Ricans had a problem getting jobs. However, Katzman (1968), using 1950 census data found that "Negro" Puerto Ricans were more underemployed and underpaid than white Puerto Ricans, but had few differences with regard to white-collar employment.[5] Difficulties in the area of housing because of race or color were also noted by Chenault (1970, pp. 92, 127), Gosnell (1945, p. 313), and Senior (1961:28).

There are also references in the literature to negative social and psychological changes experienced by immigrants to the United States as a result of race (Gosnell, 1945, pp. 310–311; Mills *et al.*, 1950, p. 7; Padilla, 1958, p. 75). Such changes can be seen to have indirect effects on labor-market functioning. For example, Berle (1958) found that black Puerto Ricans seemed to be predominant among Puerto Ricans who were drug addicts and Malzberg (1967) noted that black Puerto Ricans were admitted to New York State psychiatric hospitals more frequently than non-black Puerto Ricans. Teichner and Berry (1981, p. 281) and Longres (1974, p. 67) spoke more generally to the psychological significance of race among Puerto Ricans in the United States and the need to address it in the treatment of Puerto Rican clients. Race was also cited as a salient factor to be considered in determining jobs, housing, and relations with other groups in the memoirs and literary works of the Puerto Rican migration (Colon, 1961; Iglesias, 1980; Rivera, 1983; Thomas, 1967).

Along with the noted effect of race on jobs, housing, and social and mental health, there were also expectations voiced by many authors concerning the assimilation of white and black Puerto Ricans. It was predicted that those Puerto Ricans who could pass for white would assimilate into the white communities in the United States; those who could not, would assimilate into the black community; and that a small group of standard bearers, who did not assimilate into either community, would be left to represent the Puerto Rican community (Chenault, 1970; Fitzpatrick, 1971; Handlin, 1959; Mills *et al.*, 1950). Yet this does not appear to have occurred. As noted, a very small proportion of Puerto Ricans identified themselves as black, whereas the largest group said they were other and wrote in a Spanish descriptor. (There were no significant differences by gender; Rodriguez, 1990.) Thus, it appears that Puerto Ricans have not divided themselves into black and white as social scientists had predicted earlier.

More recent research, utilizing these census data, found this other-Spanish (OS) group to differ significantly from the white Puerto Rican group. Denton and Massey (1989) found differences with regard to housing segregation. Rodriguez (1990) found that the other-Spanish group was consistently disadvantaged relative to the white group on a number of socioeconomic variables.[6] In other words, identification as white was associated with higher socioeconomic status, whereas

[5]Katzman (1968) also found black Puerto Ricans to be "more successful in obtaining white collar jobs" than black Anglos (p. 373).
[6]The black group was similar to the white group with regard to some variables, while, in other respects, it was more similar to the other-Spanish group.

identification as other-Spanish was associated with lower socioeconomic attainments. The postulate that the OS group was less assimilated and, therefore, less remunerated than the white group was also investigated; however, the results did *not* confirm this hypothesis.[7]

The Rodriguez (1990) study was based on all adults, both in the labor force and outside of the labor force, the current research focuses only on those who are employed. It looks specifically at the effect of self-identified race on wages received in the labor market and asks the question of whether those who identify as other-Spanish (i.e., as neither white nor black), have lower hourly wages than those who identify as white or black.

DATA AND METHODOLOGY

The 1980 5% Public Use Microdata Sample (Tape File A) for the five New York City boroughs was used. These data were selected because they are the largest and most reliable sources of information for Puerto Ricans within one regional labor market. The decision to focus on one labor market was made in order to achieve greater insight into the role of race, holding ethnicity constant. In addition, the author wished to control for regional variations by looking at one region. New York City provided a large number of cases and has been the site of much of the previous research on Puerto Ricans.[8]

In the 1980 census, all individuals were asked, "Is this person of Spanish/Hispanic origin or descent?" Those in New York City who responded to this question by indicating that they were "Puerto Rican" constituted the sample for this research. This sample was examined in terms of how they responded to the race item in the 1980 census. The race item in the census asked "Is this person . . ." and provided check-off responses for 17 different categories, including white, black, and an *other* category that had space for a write-in response. Thus, in the text that follows, "white" refers to Puerto Ricans who classified themselves as white, "black" to those who classified themselves as black, and "other-Spanish" to those who checked off the other category and wrote in, Puerto Rican, Boricua, or some other Spanish descriptor. To avoid confusion with Euro-

---

[7]The OS group was younger and less educated, but it did *not* have more children, nor was a higher proportion born in Puerto Rico as compared with the white group. The OS group also did not speak Spanish at home to any greater degree than did the white group and it did not clearly report less English proficiency than the white group. Interestingly, although the OS group was not significantly different from the white group, both groups appeared to be significantly different from the black group. The analysis suggested that the black group may be more assimilated (as measured by these indicators) than the white or OS groups.

[8]Other research has shown that the proportion of Hispanics who identify as white, black or Other varies by state and is correlated with the proportion of blacks and Hispanics in a state (Rodriguez, 1989).

American whites, African-American blacks, and other Spanish in New York City, these Puerto Rican subgroups will be referred to as the *W*, the *B*, and the *OS* groups.

Puerto Ricans responding that they were Asian or American Indian were omitted, as were those who checked off *other* but did not write in a Spanish descriptor. This was done because of their smaller size and because a substantive interest was to evaluate the white, black, and larger other-Spanish categories.[9]

Regression analysis was used to determine whether self-identification was a significant predictor of wage rates when all other variables were held constant. For the empirical estimation, the sample was restricted to civilian men and women, aged 18 and over, who were wage and salary workers in the labor force in 1979 and who had positive annual hours and positive age and salary income.

The dependent variable, which was the wage rate, was transformed into logarithmic form because of the skewed distribution of earnings. The coefficients can be interpreted roughly as percentage changes in the dependent variable in response to unit changes in the independent variables, or returns to investments in the case of such variables as education. The wage-earnings function was estimated using ordinary least squares regression. Since the data have not been corrected for self-selection, the issue of selection bias must be acknowledged.

The basic equation used was

$$1nY_{ij} = X_{ij}\,B_j + e_{ij}$$

where $1nY$ is the natural logarithm of the wage rate earned in the labor market by individual i in group j, where j consists of six groups: Puerto Rican men and women who identify as white, black, or other-Spanish. X_{ij} is a vector of human capital and demographic variables; B_j is a vector of coefficients that are common to members of each group but that may vary across groups; and e_{ij} is a stochastic error term with the distribution $N\,(0,\ o^2{}_e)$.

The variables used in this OLS equation are defined in Table 1 and the means are given in Table 2. The dependent variable was the natural logarithm of hourly wages. Hourly wages were computed using total wage and salary earnings in 1979, divided by the product of total weeks worked and usual hours worked in those weeks.[10] Log N was used because the earnings function has been shown to

---

[9]In preliminary runs using the five groups, the analysis did not reveal any consistent or marked differences between the "other-unspecified" group and the white, black, or Spanish write-in groups.

[10]Because of the debate in the literature (Blinder, 1976; Rosenzweig, 1976) concerning the use of the natural logarithm of annual earnings or wage rates as dependent variables, two equations were estimated, one using the natural logarithm of annual earnings as the dependent variable and another using the natural logarithm of the hourly wage rate. Results did not differ significantly in either equation.

Table 1. Definitions of Variables

Variable	Definition
LNHRLYWG	Natural logarithm of hourly wage rate, calculated as annual earnings/weeks worked × usual hours worked per week in 1979.
Ascribed characteristics	
BRACE	1 if identify as black; 0 otherwise.
SRACE	1 if identify as other-Spanish write in; 0 otherwise.
BIRTHPL	1 if born in the United States; 0 otherwise.
DISABIL1	1 if had a work disability; 0 if not.
Social characteristics	
COGRP	1 if lived in the Bronx, Brooklyn, or Manhattan; 0 otherwise.
LANG1	1 if another language (Spanish) spoken at home; 0 if only English spoken at home.
CHU6	1 if children under 6 at home; 0 otherwise.
CH17	1 if children between 6 and 17 at home; 0 otherwise.
Achieved characteristics	
GRADE	Continuous variable = highest grade attended.
WRKEXP	Potential work experience; Age − grade − 6.
WRKEXPSQ	Square of WRKEXP.
ENGL	1 if indicate they speak English well or very well; 0 if indicate they do not speak it well or at all.
Job-related characteristics	
UWC	1 = employed in upper white-collar occupation, i.e., professionals, technical, and managerial personnel; 0 otherwise.
LWC	1 = employed in lower white-collar occupation, i.e., clerical and sales; 0 otherwise.
UBC	1 = employed as upper blue-collar or crafts workers; 0 otherwise.
SERV	1 = employed as service worker, including private household workers, farm workers, and a residual category of those without stated occupations.
CONSTR	1 = employed in construction industry; 0 otherwise.
NDMFG	1 = employed in nondurable manufacturing; 0 otherwise.
DMFG	1 = employed in durable manufacturing; 0 otherwise.
FARMG	1 = employed in farming or mining; 0 otherwise.
FINBUS	1 = employed in finance, real estate, insurance, or business services; 0 otherwise.
TRANSP	1 = employed in transportation, communications, or utilities; 0 otherwise.
PROF	1 = employed in professional services; 0 otherwise.
PUB	1 = employed in public sector; 0 otherwise.
PERSL	1 = employed in personal services; 0 otherwise.

CLARA E. RODRIGUEZ

Table 2. Means of Variables

	Males	Females
BRACE	0.43	.040
SRACE	.449	.452
GRADE	12.543	13.289
BIRTHPLACE	.268	.337
LANG1	.932	.933
ENGLISH	.842	.858
COGRP	.850	.840
CHU6	.133	.102
CH17	.274	.294
DISABIL1	.039	.031
WRKEXP	18.127	16.613
WRKEXPSQ	510.075	471.311
FARMG	.001	.001
CONSTR	.031	.004
NDMFG	.132	.212
DMFG	.124	.086
TRANSP	.111	.038
FINBUS	.176	.160
PRSL	.142	.289
PROF	.042	.033
PUB	.044	.047
LOGHRWG	1.654	1.539
UWC	.130	.146
LWC	.215	.455
UBC	.143	.036
SERV	.236	.129
N	6016	3922

be nonlinear. The independent variables included in the x vector incorporate different types of human capital variables. However, these traditional human capital variables were organized into four components: Personal, Social, Achieved, and Job-Related characteristics. These items reflect a locus of control gradient (see Table 1). Thus, the variables embodied in the unit of labor being supplied ranged from those over which workers have very little control (e.g., race and birthplace), to those that require a certain degree of self-exertion (e.g, education), to those that are outcome variables or job-related characteristics (e.g., seasonal construction work). The intent of this organization was to determine if there was any clustering of significant variables within these categories. Such a finding would provide insight into the policy debates over whether individuals' behaviors and attitudes toward work should be the object of program policy or whether more external impediments should be altered.

The model attempted to isolate the effect of race, holding constant the usual human capital characteristics that have been found to be important determinants of earnings and wage rates for men and women. The *Personal* group of variables included race, which consisted of two dummy variables: BRACE in which those identifying as black equal 1 and all others equal 0; and SRACE in which those identifying as other and writing in a Spanish descriptor equal 1. The white group is the omitted category. Based on earlier research results (Rodriguez, 1990), it was expected that SRACE would be negatively correlated with hourly wage, and that BRACE would *not* have a significant relationship with wage rate.

Since birthplace was included, it was expected that foreign birth would yield a negative association with wage rate. As other social scientists have argued, foreign birth can be a disadvantage because it represents cultural and social differences in preparedness for the labor market in the United States, as well as differences in the transferability of specific employment skills (Bean & Tienda, 1988, pp. 395–396). If foreign birth is manifested via accented speech or cultural styles, it may also trigger discriminatory treatment on the part of employers. It was anticipated that the coefficient for this variable would be positive. A disability variable was also included in the model; it was expected that the coefficient for this variable would be negative.

The *Social* set of variables included human capital characteristics that are, to a greater degree, influenced by others. These included residence, language spoken at home, and the presence of children at home. Because of the increasing attention paid to inner city or ghetto residence as a barrier to securing better job opportunities and higher earnings (Kasarda, 1985; Kasarda & Friedrichs, 1985; Wilson, 1987), a measure of inner city residence was included in the model. A residence variable labeled *COGRP* was created, and it was coded 1 for those living in the inner city boroughs of New York City (i.e., the Bronx, Brooklyn, or Manhattan) and 0 for those living in the outer boroughs of Queens and Staten Island. It was anticipated that this variable would be negatively associated with wage rate.

Although recent research has found that the presence of children affects the reservation wage and not the market wage of women (Heckman, 1974), this variable was included to maintain comparability with earlier studies of women's wages. In keeping with traditional expectations, the presence of children under 6 years of age was expected to have a stronger negative effect than the presence of older children at home on women's wage rates. To capture these various effects, two dummy variables were included in the model: one for children under 6, and the other for children between 6 and 17 living at home. The last variable in this set, *speaking Spanish at home,* is discussed below, along with English proficiency.

The third set of variables, *Achieved characteristics,* included education and work experience and it was expected they would both be positive. *GRADE,* a continuous variable, was used to measure the highest grade attended. To approximate experience, the conventional proxy of work experience was used (i.e., age minus grade minus six). In order to capture the nonlinear relationship between potential work experience and earnings, this variable was also squared.

There has been debate about the relative influence on earnings of a foreign language spoken at home (Grenier, 1984; Tienda, 1983a; Tienda & Niedert, 1984). A dummy variable was created to capture the effect of speaking Spanish at home, and it was anticipated that this variable would have a negative coefficient. Also included was a measure of English proficiency that measured self-reported proficiency in English and was expected to be predictive of higher earnings.

The fourth set of variables were *Job-related*. Industry and occupation were included because they are known to affect wages and because of the separate earnings equations for men and women and the acknowledged occupational segregation between genders. To measure the effect of occupations on wage rate, a series of dummy variables were created. Lower blue-collar occupations were the baseline category; it was expected that all other occupations would be positive predictors of the wage rate. Following the Telles and Murguia (1990) model, the industrial employment sector was coded into nine dummy variables, with wholesale and retail trade being the omitted category. Previous research on the Puerto Rican labor force has revealed that employment concentration in declining manufacturing industries has had a depressing effect on the economic status of Puerto Rican women in particular (Rios, 1985; Rodriguez, 1989; Santana-Cooney, 1979; Santana-Cooney & Colon-Warren, 1984). In effect, displacement has caused many women to leave the labor force or take lower-paid jobs, which would tend to affect the community as a whole. But for those women who were still employed in manufacturing, we would expect the coefficient to be positive, because, relative to wholesale and retail trade, manufacturing wages have remained higher. There is a greater possibility that wages in the manufacturing sector are affected by union wages, while the wholesale and retail trade industries tend to be nonunionized.

The model was estimated with and without the occupation and industry variables in order to ascertain whether controlling for job-related variables affected the relationship of other variables, especially race, to hourly wages.

FINDINGS

Most importantly, Table 3 shows that, all other things being equal, identifying as other-Spanish is significant and negatively correlated with the log of male hourly wage rates. That is to say, a Puerto Rican male who classifies himself as other and writes in a Spanish descriptor earns 8% less than another Puerto Rican male who indicated he was white on the 1980 census form. Puerto Rican women,

Table 3. Male Wage Equation[a]

	1	2
Ascribed		
BRACE	−.047	−.042
	(.052)	(.051)
SRACE	−.079**	−.081**
	(.022)	(.021)
BIRTHPL	.061*	.048
	(.028)	(.028)
DISABIL	−.17**	−.182**
	(.053)	(.053)
Social		
COGRP	−.109**	−.099**
	(.029)	(.029)
CHU6	.025	.02
	(.032)	(.032)
CH17	.043	.04
	(.024)	(.024)
LANG1	−.075	−.07*
	(.043)	(.042)
Achieved		
GRADE	.05**	.037**
	(.004)	(.004)
WRKEXP	.029**	.027**
	(.003)	(.003)
WRKEXPSQ	−.0004**	−.0003**
	(.00005)	(.00005)
ENGLISH	.063*	.044
	(.031)	(.031)
Job-related		
UWC		.175**
		(.04)
LWC		.115**
		(.032)
UBC		.177**
		(.034)
CONSTRUC		.113
		(.034)
FARMG		.39
		(.28)
FINBUS		.096**
		(.034)
DMFG		.092*
		(.039)

(*continued*)

Table 3   (*Continued*)

	1	2
NDMFG		.15**
		(.038)
PERSL		.217**
		(.038)
PROF		.097
		(.056)
PUB		.235**
		(.055)
SERV		.046
		(.034)
TRANSP		.406**
		(.039)
CONSTANT	.82**	.79**
	(.083)	(.086)
N	6015	6015
Adjusted R^2	.059	.082
Standard error	.798	.788

[a]Dependent variable: LNHRLYWG.
[b]Standard errors in parentheses.
$*p < .05; **p < .01.$

on the other hand, who indicated they were other-Spanish had coefficients that were similarly negative, but that were not statistically significant. As anticipated, identifying as black did not have a statistically significant impact on the hourly wages of men or women.

Variable groupings also show some interesting gender differences. Although most of the *Achieved* characteristics were significant for both men and women, more of the *Ascribed* variables were significant for men. Similarly, *Job-related* variables were important for both genders, but more so for males. The results of specific variables are discussed below by variable grouping.

A key finding is that the introduction of occupation and industry variables (see Equation 2 in Tables 3 and 4) did not significantly alter the effect of the race variables on hourly wages. In fact, the inclusion of job-related variables altered the significant relationship of only three variables to hourly wages, namely, English proficiency, birthplace, and whether Spanish was spoken at home. The inclusion of Job-related variables also increased the amount of variance explained. The adjusted R^2 rose for both males and females.

Personal variables, birthplace, and disability had dissimilar results. Disability showed the expected negative coefficient for both genders, but it was a significant predictor of income only for males, reducing male wages by an average of 17%. With regard to birthplace, there was another striking gender difference. Contrary to the expectation that the coefficients would be positive for both genders, they were negative for women and positive for men. Only for men were they significant and this significance was diluted when the occupation and industry variables were introduced. Nonetheless, all other things being equal, being born in the United States was associated with a 5% increase in men's hourly wage rate.

Social characteristics also showed diverging results. As hypothesized, residence was a significant and negative predictor of the hourly wage rate for both men and women. The estimated wage loss from living in inner-city boroughs varied from an average of 8% for women to 10% for men. The hypothesis concerning the effect of speaking Spanish at home was also confirmed. But even though the signs of the coefficients were negative in all instances, only in Equation 2 was the effect statistically reliable for men. The presence of children of any age was not significantly associated with male or female wage rates.

Many of the hypotheses concerning *Achieved* characteristics were confirmed. As expected, and as the literature has consistently found, education and potential work experience were significant for both men and women (Bean & Tienda, 1988; Borjas & Tienda, 1985; Reimers, 1983, 1984a,b; Telles & Murguia, 1990; Tienda, 1983a,b; Torres, 1988). As Tables 3 and 4 indicate, women have slightly lower returns to grade attainment than men (3% vs. 4%), but when occupation and industry variables are not included in the equation, the returns to education are the same. Similarly, English proficiency was a significant predictor of men and women's wage rate but only when job-related variables were omitted. English proficiency rendered greater pay-offs to Puerto Rican women—a 13% gain as compared with a 6% gain for males. Apparently, the introduction of job-related variables attenuated the effect of education and English proficiency on the wage rate.

As anticipated, men and women in white-collar occupations netted significantly higher wage rates than those in lower blue-collar occupations. However, only men (and not women) in upper blue-collar occupations had significantly higher wage rates than the lower blue-collar occupations. The industrial sector where Puerto Ricans worked was also an important determinant of the hourly wage. However, the hypothesis that employment in manufacturing would be a positive predictor of wages was supported for men but not for women. Another area where a gender difference was evident was in the personal services area. Here the coefficients were positive and significant but only for men.

However, there were certain sectors that afforded both male and female workers higher wage rates relative to those in the wholesale and retail industries. These were the financial and business services sector, where the wage gain was 15% for women and 10% for men; the transportation, communications, and utilities sector, where the respective figures were 37% and 41%; and the public

Table 4. Female Wage Equation[a]

	1	2
Ascribed		
BRACE	.091	.05
	(.062)	(.061)
SRACE	−.035	−.036
	(.025)	(.024)
BIRTHPL	.029	−.014
	(.030)	(.030)
DISABIL	−.024	−.029
	(.068)	(.067)
Social		
COGRP	−.079*	−.068*
	(.032)	(.032)
CHU6	.051	.034
	(.041)	(.040)
CH17	−.047	−.041
	(.027)	(.027)
LANG1	−.038	−.021
	(.049)	(.048)
Achieved		
GRADE	.053**	.028**
	(.005)	(.005)
WRKEXP	.013**	.014**
	(.003)	(.003)
WRKEXPSQ	−.0001*	−.0001**
	(.00005)	(.00005)
ENGLISH	.131**	.066
	(.038)	(.038)
Job-related		
UWC		.431**
		(.057)
LWC		.217**
		(.046)
UBC		.077
		(.066)
CONSTRUC		.08
		(.178)
FARMG		.035
		(.323)
FINBUS		.147**
		(.043)
DMFG		−.03
		(.057)

(*continued*)

Table 4   (*Continued*)

	1	2
NDMFG		−.025
		(.049)
PERSL		.071
		(.041)
PROF		−.035
		(.074)
PUB		.152*
		(.063)
SERV		.099
		(.055)
TRANSP		.373**
		(.067)
CONSTANT	.675**	.823**
	(.096)	(.107)
N	3922	3922
Adjusted R^2	.058	.099
Standard error	.734	.718

[a]Dependent variable: LNHRLYWG.
[b]Standard errors in parentheses.
*$p < .05$; **$p < .01$.

sector, where the figures were 15% and 24%, respectively. Lastly, and surprisingly, employment in the professional sector was not significant for either sex; indeed, the coefficient was negative for women.

In summary, relative to employment in wholesale and retail trade, Puerto Rican men and women had higher wage rates if they were employed in the financial and business sectors, in transportation, communication, and utilities, and in the public sector. While employment in manufacturing and in personal services netted significantly greater returns for men, women did not benefit from employment in these sectors.

RACE RESULTS

What is perhaps most surprising about the results are the gender differences that emerged. With regard to the main question pursued, identification as OS was a significant and negative predictor for men, but not for women. Even after controlling for those elements that might be interacting with race—that is, language, disability, work experience, inner-city residence, the presence of children, and the industrial and occupational location of those involved—identifying as OS had a negative effect on the hourly wages that men received, but this was not the case for women.

To some degree, these results parallel findings for men and women in general, which have found that within the female labor market there is less variance with regard to income than within the male labor market (Carlson & Schwartz, 1988; Reimers, 1985). An example of the smaller variance that exists within the female labor market is the diminished earnings gap between black and white American women. But these results do not necessarily indicate that racial identification is *less* important for Puerto Rican women. It may be an important variable affecting other labor market phenomena, such as the decision of Puerto Rican women to enter the labor market, their rate of unemployment, and the jobs that they get.

Interestingly, and as anticipated, identifying as black was *not* a significant predictor of the wage rate of men or women. Superficially, this finding might appear to be consistent with Reimers (1984b) research, since she also did not find race to be significant when utilizing a dichotomous (i.e., white or nonwhite) variable for Puerto Rican males. But it would be incorrect to compare dichotomous data on race with the threefold classification used here.

Nonetheless, the results on race are curious. The descriptive data on men and women within race groups shed little light on the gender difference that was found. On the whole, human capital differences between OS men and women are not major; only job-related variables show important differences. For example, there are higher proportions of OS women in nondurable manufacturing and personal services as compared with OS men, and lower proportions of OS women in finance, business, transportation, and retail industries. Also more OS women are to be found in lower white-collar jobs and fewer in upper blue-collar and service-sector jobs.[11]

The fact that these OS gender differences in occupational and industry distribution exist, in spite of the lack of major human capital differences, is surprising. This raises questions about the exact mechanisms by which gender, racial identity, and labor-market outcomes become linked. The mechanisms may work in a number of ways, for example, by affecting the labor-market behavior of individuals, or the way potential employers relate to individuals and channel them into one job or another. The issue of causation is also important here. In sum, these results on race require further in-depth investigation into the determinants of racial identity. Also needed is an investigation why identifying as OS is an important determinant for male and not for female wage rates.[12]

---

[11]Figures are available from the author.

[12]See Rodriguez (1989) for a discussion of the perceptions that people bring to racial self-classification.

OTHER FINDINGS

The gender differences in returns to skilled blue-collar employment raise questions concerning the role that discrimination may play in determining the occupations of men and women in this area, and, consequently, the hourly wages they earn. Men benefit from employment in skilled blue-collar work, but women do not. The data indicate that there are five times as many men in these occupations as women. It may be that women in these jobs have been there for relatively shorter periods and therefore hold lower-paying jobs within these occupations, get to work less overtime, experience more and longer spells of unemployment while waiting for assignment to jobs, and receive less on-the-job training. The role of unions *vis à vis* women as compared with men may also be a factor explaining these results.

Sectoral employment results also showed significant areas of gender differentiation. Here men in manufacturing had a significantly higher income, but women did not. Yet both men and women had higher wage rates if they were employed in the financial and business sectors, in transportation, communication, and utilities, and in the public sector than if they were employed in wholesale and retail trade. This latter finding would seem to be consistent with the sectoral growth theory that argues that those employed in high-wage and growing sectors of the economy have higher wages relative to those in wholesale and retail trade, even when human capital is held constant. The gender difference in returns to work in manufacturing suggests that women may be concentrated in the declining garment-manufacturing sector (where wages may not have kept pace with other sectors), while men may be employed more often in firms that have *not* experienced sectoral decline and that have had greater wage increases.[13] Table 2 does show a higher proportion of women in nondurable manufacturing as compared with men.

What is surprising is that employment in the professional sector was not significant for either sex. It may be that the wage variance in this category is quite large and many jobs within this category are not particularly well-paying. Thus, a Puerto Rican professional can be a modestly paid teacher or social worker, or a highly paid real estate or securities lawyer. Just being a professional does not have a predictable effect on income.

Although it was expected that the birthplace coefficients would be positive for both genders, they were statistically significant only for men and only when job-related variables were *not* included. These findings on birthplace are not too surprising if one reviews the empirical research on Puerto Ricans—as contrasted

---

[13]Waldinger (1985) found that hourly and relative earnings declined in the apparel industry in New York during the 1970s.

with other Hispanics and immigrants—more closely. Borjas (1983), for example, found that there was little difference between the employment propensities of island-born and mainland-born Puerto Rican males. Similarly, Tienda (1983b) did not find statistically significant differences between island- and mainland-born Puerto Ricans with regard to annual earnings. In another study, Puerto Rican men born in the United States enjoyed a higher payoff from schooling than their counterparts on the island, but length of time since migration did not apparently improve the earnings of Puerto Ricans (Tienda, 1983a, p. 66). These studies suggest that there are not strong nativity differentials among Puerto Ricans, and that this may be related to the pattern of circulating migration that has been discussed by some authors (Bonilla & Campos, 1981; Nelson & Tienda, 1985, p. 58; Rodriguez, 1988; Tienda, 1985). As Tienda (1983a, p. 66) has noted, it may be that in a strict sense Puerto Ricans are not immigrants.[14]

The fact that *residence* depresses the wage rates of both men and women, in a statistically significant way, is consistent with current discussions of residential concentrations of persistent poverty. It also raises the question researched by Tienda and Neidert (1984) of whether (in contrast to other groups) "Puerto Ricans are penalized for living and working in ethnic enclaves" (p. 533). It appears that if Puerto Ricans reside in areas where there is a higher density of Puerto Ricans (i.e., the Bronx, Brooklyn, or Manhattan), they are penalized.

Although speaking Spanish at home had the anticipated negative coefficient, it was significant only for men and only when job-related variables were included. Thus, it may be that for Puerto Rican men in New York speaking Spanish at home may be negatively associated with certain jobs and industries. Despite these findings, research on a national sample of Puerto Rican and other Hispanic men has found that the "retention of Spanish does not hinder the socioeconomic achievement of Hispanic groups provided a reasonable level of proficiency in English is acquired" (Tienda & Neidert, 1984, p. 533). Thus, there may be at work in this sample a regional labor-market effect particular to New York, wherein even with equivalent occupational and sociodemographic characteristics, those men who speak Spanish at home are not earning as much as those who do not.[15] The results of this investigation, however, require additional research to substantiate.

On the other hand, English proficiency was a significant predictor of both men and women's wage rate; but when we control for occupations and industry, it was no longer significant. The differences here may lie, again, in the nature of jobs held: certain types of jobs require very good English proficiency, whereas

[14]It is of interest in this regard that in Equation 1, where the job-related variables are omitted, birthplace is a significant and positive predictor for men.

[15]See Nelson and Tienda (1985) for an analysis of the relationship of this variable to other sociodemographic characteristics.

others may not require as much. Thus, English helps within certain job categories.

In general, the research literature in this area is inconclusive. As Melendez (1988) pointed out, some have argued that with greater time in the United States and greater English proficiency, wages would increase, but others have found that this path was not the same for all groups and that it takes longer for Puerto Ricans to have significantly higher earnings. Tienda (1983a) also found that the influence of English proficiency on earnings varies depending on the Hispanic group. Yet, as Melendez (1988) pointed out other researchers attribute most of Hispanic wage differentials to this factor. Reimers (1983, 1984b) consistently found that lack of English was a significant factor affecting earnings; Grenier (1984) used it to explain one-third of the differences; and Garcia (1984) concluded that it has little if any effect. Tienda and Neidert (1984) suggested a middle position when they stated that "adequate command of English is necessary to function effectively in the United States labor market, but such command does not, of course, ensure access to high status positions" (p. 534).

SUMMARY

The most interesting empirical findings are that, even when controlling for human capital, industry, and occupation variables,

1. Puerto Rican men who racially identify as other-Spanish earn a significantly lower hourly wage than those who indicate they are white. For Puerto Rican women, racial identification is not significant.
2. Interesting gender differences were also found with regard to the significance of both ascribed characteristics (i.e., birthplace, race, and disability) and job-related variables (e.g., employment in upper blue-collar occupations, manufacturing, and personal services) in wage–rate determination.
3. Furthermore, for men, employment in upper blue-collar occupations and in manufacturing and personal services was associated with significantly higher wages than employment in lower blue-collar occupations and in retail and wholesale trade areas. Women, however, did not benefit from employment in these areas. Disability also was significant for men but not women.
4. Variables that were positive and significant for both men and women included: education, work experience, employment in white-collar occupations, and in the financial, business, transportation, and public sectors, and residence in inner-city boroughs (this latter variable was associated with lower hourly wages). English proficiency was also significant

for both men and women but only when industry and occupation variables were excluded.

CONCLUSION

In looking at the impact of race within a racially heterogeneous ethnic group, this research has introduced a novel dimension to the wage discrimination literature. It has also raised many questions about the meaning of race, gender, and the mechanisms by which racial identities and labor-market outcomes become linked. In so doing, it has relevance to the long-standing theoretical debate over which system of inequality (i.e., race, gender, ethnicity, national origin, or class) is most important in determining life chances. The results underscore that there is a pressing need to better understand the functioning of all these systems of inequality, as well as their interactions, within the labor market.

REFERENCES

Arce, C. H., E. Murguia, & W. P. Frisbie. (1987). Phenotype and life chances among Chicanos. *Hispanic Journal of Behavioral Sciences, 9*(1), 19–32.

Bean, F., & M. Tienda. (1988). *Hispanic population in the U. S.* New York: Russell Sage Foundation.

Berle, B. (1958). *80 Puerto Rican Families in New York City.* New York: Columbia University Press.

Blinder, A. S. (1976). On dogmatism in human capital theory. *Journal of Human Resources, 11*(1), 8–21.

Borjas, G. (1983). The labor supply of male Hispanic immigrants in the United States. *International Migration Review, 17,* 4.

Borjas, G., & M. Tienda. (1985). *Hispanics in the U. S. Economy.* New York: Academic Press.

Bonilla, F., & R. Campos. (1981). A wealth of poor: Puerto Ricans in the new economic order. *Daedulus, 110,*(2), 133–176.

Carlson, L. A., & C. Swartz. (1988). The earnings of women and ethnic minorities. *Industrial and Labor Relations Review, 41*(4), 530–552.

Chenault, L. (1970). *The Puerto Rican migrant in New York City.* New York: Columbia University Press.

Chevan, A. (1990). "Hispanic racial identity: Beyond social class." Paper presented at the American Sociological Association meetings, Washington, DC.

Colon, J. (1961). *A Puerto Rican in New York and other sketches.* New York: International Publishers.

Denton, N. A., & D. S. Massey. (1989). Racial identity among Caribbean Hispanics: The effect of double minority status on residential segregation. *American Sociological Review, 54,* 790–808.

Fitzpatrick, J. S. J. (1971). *Puerto Rican Americans.* Englewood Cliffs, NJ: Prentice-Hall.

Garcia, P. (1984). Dual language characteristics and earnings: Male Mexican workers in the U. S. *Social Science Research, 13*(3), 221–235.

Giles, H., N. Llado, D. J. McKirnan, & D. M. Taylor. (1979). Social identity in Puerto Rico. *International Journal of Psychology, 14*(3), 185–201.

Glazer, N., & D. P. Moynihan. (1970). *Beyond the melting pot* (2nd ed.). Cambridge: MIT Press.

Gosnell-Aran, P. (1945). The Puerto Ricans in New York City. Unpublished doctoral dissteration, New York University.

Grenier, G. (1984). Shifts to English as usual by Americans of Spanish mother tongue. *Social Science Quarterly, 65,* 537–550.

Handlin, O. (1959). *The newcomers: Negroes and Puerto Ricans in a changing metropolis.* Cambridge, MA: Harvard University Press.

Heckman, J. (1974). Shadow prices, market wages, and labor supply. *Econometrica, 42*(4), 679–694.

Iglesias, C. A. (1980). *Memorias de Bernardo Vega: Una contribución a la historia de la comunidad Puertorriqueña en Nueva York.* Rio Piedras, P.R.: Ediciones Huracán.

Kasarda, J. D. (1985). Urban change and minority opportunities. In The Brookings Institution, *The new urban reality.* Washington, DC: Author.

Kasarda, J. D., & J. Friedrichs. (1985). Comparative demographic-employment mismatches in U. S. and West German cities. *Research in the Sociology of Work, 3,* 1–30.

Katzman, M. (1968). Discrimination, subculture and the economic performance of Negroes, Puerto Ricans and Mexican-Americans. *American Journal of Economics and Society, 27*(4), 371–375.

Longres, J. F. (1974). Racism and its effects on Puerto Rican continentals. *Social Casework,* February, 1974, 67–99.

Martin, E., T. J. DeMaio, & P. C. Campanelli. (1988). *Context effects for census measures of race and Hispanic origin.* Paper presented at the Annual Meeting of the American Statistical Association, New Orleans, La.

Malzberg, B. (1967). Internal migration and mental disease among the white population of New York State, 1960–61. *International Journal of Social Psychiatry, 14*(3), 184–191.

Melendez, E. (1988). *Labor market structure and wage inequality in New York City: A comparative analysis of Hispanics and non-Hispanic Blacks and Whites.* Final Report to the Inter-University Program, Committee on Public Policy Research on Contemporary Latino Research, Grant number: 26-7502-1928.

Mills, C. W., C. Senior, & R. Goldsen. (1950). *The Puerto Rican journey: New York's newest migrants.* New York: Harper.

Mintz, S. W. (1960). *Worker in the cane: A Puerto Rican life history.* New Haven, CT: Yale University Press.

Nelson, C., & M. Tienda. (1985). The structuring of Hispanic ethnicity: Historical and contemporary perspectives. *Ethnic and Racial Studies, 8*(1), 49–74.

Padilla, E. (1958). *Up from Puerto Rico.* New York: Columbia University Press.

Petrullo, V. (1947). *Puerto Rican paradox.* Philadelphia: University of Pennsylvania Press.

Reimers, C. (1983). Labor market discrimination among Hispanic and Black men. *Review of Economics and Statistics, 65*(4), 570–579.

Reimers, C. (1984a). Sources of the family income differentials among Hispanics, Blacks and White Non-Hispanics," *American Journal of Sociology, 89*(4), 889–903.

Reimers, C. (1984b). The wage structure of Hispanic men: Implications for policy. *Social Science Quarterly, 65*(2), 401–416.

Reimers, C. (1985). Cultural differences in labor force participation among married women. *American Economics Association Papers and Proceedings, 75*(2), 251–255.

Rios, P. (1985) Puerto Rican women in the United States labor market. *Line of March, 18*(Fall), 1985.

Rivera, E. (1983). *Family installments: Memories of growing up Hispanic.* New York: Penguin.

Rodriguez, C. E. (1974). Puerto Ricans: Between Black and White. *Journal of New York Affairs, 1*(4), 92–101.

Rodriguez, C. E. (1988). Puerto Ricans and the circular migration thesis. *Journal of Hispanic Policy, 3,* 5–9.

Rodriguez, C. E. (1989c). *Puerto Ricans: Born in the USA*. Boulder, CO: Westview Press.

Rodriguez, C. E. (1990). Racial classification among Puerto Rican men and women in New York. *Hispanic Journal of Behavioral Sciences, 12*(4).

Rosenzweig, M. R. (1976). Nonlinear earnings functions, age, and experience: A nondogmatic reply and some additional evidence. *Journal of Human Resources, 11*(1), 23–27.

Santana-Cooney, R. (1979). Intercity variations in Puerto Rican female participation. *Journal of Human Resources, 14*(2), 222–235.

Santana-Cooney, R. & A. Colon-Warren (1984). Work and family: The recent struggle of Puerto Rican families. In C. Rodriguez, V. Sanchez-Korrol, & O. Alers, Eds., *The Puerto Rican struggle: Essays on survival in the U. S.* Maplewood, NJ: Waterfront Press.

Senior, C. (1965). *Strangers, then neighbors: From pilgrims to Puerto Ricans*. Chicago: Quadrangle Books.

Steward, J. H., Manners, R. A., Wolff, E. R., Padilla Seda, E., Mintz, S. W., & Scheele, R. L. (1956). *The people of Puerto Rico: A study in social anthropology*. Chicago–Urbana: University of Illinois Press.

Telles, E. E., & E. Murguia. (1990). Phenotypic discrimination and income differences among Mexican Americans. *Social Science Quarterly, 71*(4).

Teichner, V. J., & G. W. Berry. (1981). The Puerto Rican patient: Some historical and psychological aspects. *Journal of the American Academy of Psychoanalysis, 9*(2), 277–289.

Thomas, P. (1967). *Down these mean streets*. New York: Alfred A. Knopf.

Tienda, M. (1983a). Market characteristics and Hispanic earnings: A comparison of natives and immigrants. *Social Problems, 31*(1), 59–72.

Tienda, M. (1983b). Nationality and income attainment among native and immigrant Hispanic men in the United States. *Sociological Quarterly, 24*, 253–272.

Tienda, M. (1985). The Puerto Rican workers: Current labor market status and future prospects. In National Puerto Rican Coalition, Inc., *Puerto Ricans in the mid '80s: An American challenge*. Washington, DC: Author.

Tienda, M., & J. Glass. (1985). Household structure and labor force participation of Black, Hispanic, and White mothers. *Demography, 22*(3), 381–394.

Tienda, M., & L. J. Niedert. (1984). Language, education and the socioeconomic achievement of Hispanic origin men. *Social Science Quarterly, 65*, 519–536.

Tienda, M., & V. Ortiz. (1986). "Hispanicity" and the 1980 Census. *Social Science Quarterly, 67*(1), 3–20.

Torres, A. (1988). *Human capital, labor segmentation and inter-minority relative status: Blacks and Puerto Rican labor in New York City, 1960–1980*. Unpublished doctoral dissertation, New School for Social Research.

Tumin, M., & A. Feldman. (1961). *Social class and social change in Puerto Rico* (2nd ed.). Princeton: Princeton University Press.

Waldinger, R. (1985). Immigration and industrial change in the New York City apparel industry. In G. Borjas & M. Tienda, Eds., *Hispanics in the U. S. economy*. New York: Academic Press.

Wilson, W. J. (1987). *The truly disadvantaged: The inner city, the underclass and public policy*. Chicago: University of Chicago Press.

II

Segmentation and Industrial Change

5

Labor Market Structure and Wage Differences in New York City

A Comparative Analysis of Hispanics and Non-Hispanic Blacks and Whites

EDWIN MELENDEZ

The question of the differences between the average wages received by Hispanic workers and average wages received by their white counterparts has received extensive attention during the last decade.[1] Previous studies have found that differences in human capital, immigrants' ability to adapt to new labor markets, and discrimination are important factors in explaining low wages for Hispanics. In contrast to findings regarding black men's earnings, differences in measurable characteristics, particularly in education, explain the largest proportion of wage differences for Hispanics. On this account, a lower proportion of the wage gap is attributable to discrimination. Such findings, however, are based on the assumption of a competitive labor market in which there are no barriers to worker mobility and in which market forces therefore tend to eliminate wage or employment differences as Hispanic workers adapt to their new working environ-

---

[1]Hispanics and non-Hispanic blacks and whites are mutually exclusive categories. A Hispanic is a person of Mexican, Puerto Rican, Cuban, or other Spanish-speaking ancestry. The categories of black and white exclude persons of Hispanic descent.

EDWIN MELENDEZ • Department of Urban Studies and Planning, Massachusetts Institute of Technology, Cambridge, Massachusetts 02139.

Hispanics in the Labor Force, edited by Edwin Melendez *et al.* Plenum Press, New York, 1991.

ment. To the extent that labor markets are noncompetitive and workers' attributes contribute to the support of industrial dualism and segmentation, however, there could be a premium attached to labor-market location, that is, to the sector or segment of the labor market in which a particular worker is employed. Despite the growing research measuring the effects of human capital and immigrant background, very few studies have measured the relative effect of labor-market location on earnings for Hispanics.

In this chapter, I will compare the effects of labor market structures on the hourly wages of Hispanic and non-Hispanic blacks and whites in New York City. The sample, drawn from the 1980 Census Public Use Microdata Sample (PUMS) (A), is subdivided by race (black, white), sex (men, women), and Hispanic origin (Mexican, Puerto Rican, Cuban, other Hispanic). I have defined labor market structures along two dimensions, as core or periphery industrial sectors and as primary or secondary occupational segments.

Estimating separate regressions for each group, I have found that labor market structures are important determinants of earnings and explain a substantial proportion of wage differences for blacks and Hispanics. Decomposing the wage gap into explanatory percentages corresponding to human capital, immigrant and socioeconomic background, government employment, and labor market structure, I found that primary segment location explains between 16 to 19% of Hispanic men's and between 36 to 58% of Hispanic women's observed wage differences; that core industrial location explains from 7 to 14% of observed differences for Hispanic men, and between 4 and 7% for Hispanic women; that discrimination accounts for one-third to one-half of Hispanic men's wage differences and for one-fifth to one-half that of Hispanic women; that education is the single most important factor explaining many Hispanic groups' wage differences; and, that immigrant background explains from 8 to 20% of Hispanic men's wage differences and 5 to 15% for Hispanic women.

These findings suggest that policies targeting the supply side of the market are likely to be ineffective in the absence of a strong enforcement of anti-discrimination laws and regulations. Thus, there is a need to pursue both supply- and demand-side policies as complementing strategies to increase black, Hispanic, and white women's earnings.

DETERMINANTS OF HISPANICS' EARNINGS

Most research on the earnings of Hispanics has focused on the effects of human capital, immigrant background, and discrimination. The most important finding is that, in contrast to similar studies concerning blacks and female earnings, most of the variations in earnings among Hispanic groups are attributable to group differences in measurable characteristics, such as education, experience, language skills, and hours worked (Cotton, 1985; Grenier, 1984; Hirschman & Wong, 1984; Stolzenberg, 1975). However, the effects of measurable characteristics vary significantly among Hispanic groups. Returns to education and experience, for instance, not only are generally lower for Hispanics than those for non-Hispanic whites but also vary for Hispanics of different national origins (Carlson & Swartz, 1988; Gwartney & Long, 1978; Kalacheck & Raines, 1976; Long, 1977; Reimers, 1984, 1985). Because of these variations in the effects of measurable characteristics, discrimination is also an important factor affecting Hispanic workers, particularly Mexicans and Puerto Ricans (Carliner, 1976; Poston, Alvirez, & Tienda, 1976; Reimers, 1983; Verdugo & Verdugo, 1984).

Empirical studies estimating the effects of immigrant background on earnings are less conclusive. After controlling for human capital and other attributes, research shows that such factors as being foreign born, English proficiency, country of origin, and the number of years a worker has lived in the United States are important in stratifying earnings. The effects of these variables on earnings, however, vary widely depending on the sample, the data, and the method utilized in the study. For instance, studies comparing the earnings of immigrants and of natives have found that the immigrants have lower earnings than do the native workers. However, for the typical immigrant, earnings will rise relatively fast during the first few years, become equal to those of the native-born workers after 10 years, and exceed native-born workers' earnings in 15 years (Chiswick, 1978). Furthermore, length of time in the country affects Hispanic immigrant groups differently. For example, although it takes 15 years for Mexicans to experience a significant increase in wages, it takes Puerto Ricans 25 years (Borjas, 1982). In regard to country of origin, studies have shown that, between 1970 and 1980, Mexican and Puerto Ricans had consistently lower earnings than did Cuban, Central and South Americans, and other Hispanics (Bean & Tienda, 1987).

The relative effect of English-language proficiency on wage differences is also the subject of controversy. Even though some studies have attributed up to one-third or more of Hispanics' wage differences to English-language proficiency (Grenier, 1984; McManus, 1985; McManus, Gould, & Welch, 1983), other studies have suggested that it has only a small effect (Reimers, 1983, 1984, 1985), or else they have found that English-language fluency affects earnings not directly but through its interaction with other variables (Garcia, 1984). Likewise, recent research suggests that English-reading proficiency is a more critical skill for increasing the wages of young Hispanic women than for young Hispanic men. Proficiency in English has a negligible effect on young Hispanic men's wages, whereas quantitative literacy has a significant impact (Rivera-Batiz, Chapter 3, this volume).

In short, previous research has found that the effects of measurable characteristics explain a large proportion of Hispanic wage differences, but these studies are less conclusive about the relative importance of human capital and immigrant background. In particular, it is not clear why the effects of human capital and immigrant background variables vary substantially among Hispanic groups of different national origin (Tienda, 1983a,b). Despite the above-cited variations in findings and explanations, most research on Hispanics has emphasized the immigrant experience as the underlying cause of their lower earnings.

It is clear from the previous discussion that differences in human capital and the immigrant background of Hispanics are important determinants of lower earnings when compared to high-income reference groups, whether they are Anglos or non-Anglo natives. However, it is equally important to investigate the specific labor market processes that mediate the effects of these conventional variables on wages. In particular, language, nationality, color, and other immigrant characteristics may serve as screening devices for employers. Hispanics could be preferred in certain jobs but be excluded from others, as when ethnic traits are used to restrict access by Hispanics to high-wage industries and occupations.

LABOR MARKET STRUCTURES

Previous assessments of the significance of labor market structures on the low earnings of Hispanics have been based on dual labor market or segmentation theories. Dual labor market theorists propose that the economic system is characterized by the existence of two distinct industrial sectors. In the core sector, firms have oligopoly power in their product markets, employ large numbers of workers, have vast financial resources, and are favored by government regulations and contracting, and their workers are more likely to be in unions. Core industries have well-defined internal labor markets and job ladders that regulate promotions and rely on ethnic and community networks for recruitment of workers. Firms in the periphery are smaller, have less influence over product markets, lack access to financial resources, and are usually dependent on subcontracting or retailing for larger firms. In the core sector, concentration and centralization of capital allows technological development and long-range planning, while firms in the periphery are more affected by fluctuations in economic conditions and rely more on contingent labor. These industrial characteristics lead to two different sets of labor market outcomes. In core industries, earnings are higher, returns to education and experience are higher, workers have more mobility, employment is more stable, and so forth, whereas in peripheral industries, labor market outcomes tend to be the opposite (Averitt, 1968; Osterman, 1975).

The evidence concerning the explanatory power of a dual labor market approach regarding the earnings of Hispanics is mixed. Tienda and Neidert

(1980) found that labor market location was an important determinant of Hispanics' earnings. However, they could not provide unequivocal support for their contention that labor market location was more important than nativity in stratifying the earnings of Hispanics. Natives had larger returns to education than immigrants in all Hispanic groups. Returns to education in the core sector were larger than in the periphery, as predicted by the duality hypotheses, but only among foreign-born Mexicans, Puerto Ricans, and other Hispanics. Contrary to dual labor market predictions, all native Hispanic groups and other foreign-born groups included in the study had equal or higher returns in the periphery than in the core sector. In a separate study not comparable in method, Hirschman and Wong (1984) found that core industrial location was not a significant factor affecting earnings for Asians, blacks, and Hispanics.

In a more recent study of Hispanic migration and labor market location, DeFreitas (1988:212) asserted that although "Hispanic migrant workers are disproportionately concentrated in low-wage jobs," the core–periphery scheme is not directly applicable to Hispanic immigrants. In the trade and services sectors, a significant number of industries with a large number of immigrant workers are excluded from the typical peripheral category.[2] Despite the classification limitations, Hispanic migrants' earnings in the periphery are substantially lower than the native Anglo average. Hispanic immigrants who are employed in low-skill jobs in the periphery, both men and women, received wages 50% lower than did Anglos.

Segmentation theorists offer a second variation of the noncompetitive labor market model. For them, labor markets are organized along occupational segments, although industrial characteristics are important to differentiate workers in the lower strata of occupations. Jobs in the primary labor market are divided between subordinated and independent segments. Jobs in the primary independent segment are characterized by the existence of educational credentials, or state regulation (licensing) of the occupation. Such jobs have a well-defined hierarchical structure, offer a clear path for advancement, and are better paid. Jobs in the primary subordinated sector are characterized by the presence of unions and technical or machine-paced systems of control. In contrast, jobs in the secondary segment require little formal training and education, tend to be low paying with no job security, and are characterized by high turnover. In this segment, simple control or direct supervision of workers characterizes the organization of the workplace. Race and gender are key mechanisms dividing the working class and reducing their bargaining power; thus, discrimination against women and racial and ethnic minorities is reinforced by labor market dynamics

---

[2]DeFreitas's criticism is particularly valid for earlier methods that focused on manufacturing and production workers. Sectoral classification of workers is less of a problem with more recent core–periphery classification schemes in which nonproduction sectors are explicitly accounted for.

(Edwards, 1979; Gordon, Edwards, & Reich, 1982; Reich, Gordon, & Edwards, 1973).

Torres (1988) used a segmentation model to assess the relative earnings of white, black, and Puerto Rican workers in New York City from 1960 to 1980. Intertemporal variations in earnings for blacks and Puerto Ricans generally corresponded to changes in the segmentation structure. Nevertheless, labor market segmentation was less important in explaining relative earnings through time than were race and human capital variables. In summary, the existing literature on the effects of industrial sector or occupational segments on earnings for Hispanics is limited and inconclusive. In particular, the relative effects of labor market structure on wage differences for Hispanics remains an open question.

I will now assess the relative importance of labor market structure in explaining differences between wages for Hispanics and those of white workers. For example, Hispanics may be more likely to be hired by smaller firms in peripheral industries and to occupy jobs in secondary segments. I hypothesize that, to the extent that Hispanics are preferred in low-wage jobs and their ethnic traits prevent them from entering in primary industrial sectors or occupational segments, labor market location should be a significant determinant of earnings for Hispanics and explain an important proportion of their wage differences. Since there is a vast literature on the differences in earnings and of the significance of discrimination for women and blacks, I will use these sectors of the population as comparison groups.

METHOD AND DATA

For my research, I used microdata from the 1980 Census (5% sample) for New York City. The sample included salary workers, 16 to 65 years old, with positive earnings.[3] Tables 1 and 2 show the distribution of racial and ethnic groups by industrial sector and occupational segment, respectively. Although white men are evenly distributed between core and periphery industries, blacks, Hispanics, and white women are underrepresented in core industries. The distribution within core industries is equally important: blacks, particularly black women, are excluded from the private sector and concentrated in government employment. Hispanics are also underrepresented in the private sector, and only

[3]All Hispanics are included in the sample but only a subsample of non-Hispanic blacks and whites, corresponding to 1% of the population, has been included. The census data not only offer a large number of Hispanic cases, but also most of the variables commonly used to estimate an earnings function. However, the data have some important shortcomings; among them the need to estimate hourly wages and postschooling experience and the absence of union membership information. In addition, I have not included a direct measure of how many years immigrants remained in the country because these data are not available for Puerto Ricans—the largest Hispanic group in New York City—and there is no meaningful way to estimate a figure.

Table 1. Percentage of Distribution of Racial and Ethnic Groups
by Industrial Sector (New York City, 1980)

Location	White	Black	Mexican	Puerto Rican	Cuban	Other-Hispanic
			Men			
Periphery	50.8	55.6	67.1	61.4	62.2	63.9
Core	49.2	44.4	32.9	38.6	37.8	36.1
Private	32.0	18.7	21.3	20.9	27.7	27.8
Government	17.2	25.7	11.6	17.7	10.1	8.3
Federal	3.9	6.4	5.2	4.9	2.4	2.3
State	2.4	3.9	2.0	2.1	1.6	1.4
Local	10.9	15.4	4.4	10.7	6.1	4.6
			Women			
Periphery	59.7	65.9	70.0	65.6	65.7	73.1
Core	40.3	34.1	30.0	34.4	34.3	27.9
Private	25.6	2.8	14.7	13.0	21.6	18.7
Government	14.7	31.3	15.3	21.4	12.7	9.2
Federal	2.4	4.7	1.5	4.6	1.9	1.6
State	2.3	5.2	3.8	3.1	1.8	1.9
Local	10.0	21.4	10.0	13.7	9.0	5.7

SOURCE: 1980 Census, 5% Public Use Microdata Sample.

Table 2. Percentage of Distribution of Racial and Ethnic Groups
by Occupational Segment (New York City, 1980)

Location	White	Black	Mexican	Puerto Rican	Cuban	Other-Hispanic
			Men			
Primary independent	51.4	30.0	34.2	29.1	39.4	32.3
Control	21.8	10.9	14.9	10.7	19.6	11.0
Professional/technical	16.7	7.3	5.2	5.6	9.8	6.6
Craft	12.9	11.8	14.1	12.8	10.0	14.7
Primary subordinated	25.9	28.7	17.7	23.9	26.8	22.1
Secondary	22.7	41.3	48.1	47.0	33.8	45.6
			Women			
Primary independent	33.2	20.1	16.2	18.1	20.8	14.0
Control	14.8	10.1	6.2	7.5	8.9	7.0
Professional/technical	16.4	8.5	8.5	8.9	10.3	5.2
Craft	2.0	1.5	1.5	1.7	1.6	1.8
Primary subordinated	51.7	52.8	43.1	47.5	44.3	36.9
Secondary	15.1	27.1	40.7	34.9	34.9	49.1

SOURCE: 1980 Census, 5% Public Use Microdata Sample.

Puerto Ricans have government employment in proportion equal or greater than that of whites. Overall, two-thirds of Hispanics are concentrated in periphery industries.

The vast majority of blacks, Hispanics, and white women are concentrated in the lower tier of occupations. The proportion of Hispanic men in secondary subsegments ranges between 33.8% for Cubans and 48.1% for Mexicans. Ethnic women are also concentrated in these occupations with blacks having the lowest concentration (27.1%) and other Hispanics the highest (49.1%). In contrast to minorities and white women, white men are concentrated in the upper tier of the primary segment, particularly in the control, and in the professional and technical subsegments.

The concentration of Hispanics in peripheral and secondary jobs is problematic because workers in these labor markets earn substantially less than workers with similar characteristics in the upper strata of industries and occupations (Table 3). Average hourly wages in New York City are stratified by labor market location, but race, ethnicity, and sex are important as well. In general, white workers have higher hourly wages than blacks and Hispanics irrespective of labor

Table 3. Hourly Wages by Industrial Sector and Occupational Segments
(New York City, 1979)

	White	Black	Mexican	Puerto Rican	Cuban	Other-Hispanic
Men						
Average	8.83	6.60	6.20	6.17	7.47	5.96
Industrial sector						
Core	9.53	7.36	7.68	7.36	8.37	7.08
Periphery	8.17	6.03	5.52	5.49	6.96	5.36
Occupational segment						
Primary independent	10.84	8.08	7.01	7.36	9.16	8.29
Primary subordinated	8.01	6.60	6.13	6.91	7.36	5.83
Secondary	6.86	6.30	5.70	5.60	6.59	5.15
Women						
Average	6.90	6.27	4.71	5.57	6.20	4.90
Industrial sector						
Core	7.09	6.37	5.58	6.99	6.83	5.62
Periphery	6.77	5.93	4.36	4.91	5.89	4.64
Occupational segment						
Primary independent	8.70	9.11	6.19	7.36	—	6.79
Primary subordinated	6.54	6.48	5.40	5.72	5.52	5.48
Secondary	4.75	4.93	3.92	5.16	4.47	4.28

SOURCE: 1980 Census, 5% Public Use Microdata Sample.

market location. This pattern persists throughout labor markets, with the exception of Cuban men and women in core industries and primary independent segments, who have about the same hourly wages as white workers in the periphery or in secondary segments. A second pattern is that women in a similar labor market location and who are of similar ethnicity or race earn less than men. Considering the above qualifications, workers in core industrial sectors earn higher wages than those in the periphery, and workers in primary occupational segments earn higher wages than those in secondary jobs. By way of illustration, white men in core industries earn 17% more than white men in the periphery. However, white men in the periphery earn 11% more than do black men in core industries.

It is important to consider that there is a great variation of hourly wages among Hispanics. Cubans in particular have a higher average wage than Mexicans, Puerto Ricans, and other Hispanics. Mexicans, Puerto Ricans, and other Hispanics are clustered at the bottom of the wage distribution, where wage differences among workers are smaller and less significant. For instance, the average wage difference between Mexican, Puerto Rican, and other-Hispanic men is less than 5%; for women, less than 20%. In comparison, white men earned 43% more than did Puerto Rican men on average, and white women earned 24% more than did Puerto Rican women.

Observed variations in hourly wages could be misleading, since a significant proportion of these differences could be affected by a person's education, experience and age, English-language proficiency, and other factors. The most common method to estimate the relative importance of these variables is to estimate a wage equation for each group and then decompose the difference into proportions attributable to each variable. Following previous research on earnings for Hispanics, I estimated regression equations for each racial, Hispanic, and gender group.[4] The wage equation for group j can be specified as

$$ln\ W_j = B_j X_j + e_j$$

where $ln\ W_j$ = the natural logarithm of hourly wages, B_j = the vector of regression coefficients, X_j = the vector of measured characteristics, and e_j = the residual.

Hourly wages are computed in logarithmic form so that the estimated coefficients can be interpreted as measuring the proportionate effect of changes in measured characteristics on wages. The estimated equations are used to decompose the black and Hispanic wage gap into two components: (1) differences

[4]I decided to follow this method in order to make findings comparable to those in previous studies on earnings of Hispanics. Alternatively, labor market structure studies estimate regressions by dividing the sample by the industrial sector or the occupational segment. See Cain (1976) for a critique of this method.

attributable to measurable characteristics and (2) unexplained differences. Let ln $W_j = B_j X_j$ represent the estimated regression equation evaluated at the mean values of the variables. Then the average wage difference between a high-income group (h) and a low-income group (l) can be decomposed as:

$$ln\ W_h - ln\ W_l = B(X_h - X_l) + X_l(B_h - B_l)$$

The first term $B_h(X_h - X_l)$ specifies the proportion of earning differences between h and l groups given by differences in levels of characteristics. The second term $X_l(B_h - B_l)$ is a measure of racial, ethnic, or gender discrimination insofar as it reflects different market valuations of workers' characteristics.[5] Thus, $B_h(X_h - X_l)$ / ($ln\ W_h - ln\ W_l$) represents the percentage of the wage differential explained by differences in characteristics, and $X_l(B_h - B_l)$ / ($ln\ W_h - ln\ W_l$) the percentage attributable to discrimination.

Table 4 presents the definitions of the variables included in the model. The natural logarithm of hourly wages is the dependent variable; independent variables correspond to human capital, socioeconomic and immigrant background, government employment, and labor market structure regressors—industrial sector or occupational segments. I estimated two alternative models measuring the effects of labor market structure on earnings. The first model includes a categorical variable THBsect indicating employment in the core industrial sector as defined by Tolbert, Horan, and Beck (1980). The second model includes categorical variables for each primary subsegment (control, professional and technical, craft, and subordinate) as defined by Gordon (1986) and Reich (1984).

DECOMPOSITION OF WAGE DIFFERENCES

Tables 5 and 6 summarize the data for the decomposition of the wage gap into explained and unexplained effects.[6] For analytical convenience, the explained effect is divided into partial sums corresponding to human capital, socioeconomic and immigrant background, government employment, and labor market structure and is expressed as a percentage of the wage difference. The relative effect of labor market structure on hourly wages is measured by the inclusion of variables indicating government employment, location in core in-

---

[5]This is provided that all factors affecting earnings are included in the equation and that the estimated majority wage function will prevail in the absence of discrimination. See Reimers (1983) for a discussion of these issues.

[6]The regression equations from which these results were derived are available from me upon request, as is a more detailed analysis of the results, including the equations and regressors' significance by group.

Table 4. Definition of Variables

Lnwageh	Natural logarithm of hourly wages, hourly wage rate = (annual earnings in 1979) / (weeks worked in 1979) × (average hours worked per week in 1979).
Educa	Highest grade of school.
Exp	Potential experience = age − educa − 5.
Expsq	Square of Exp.
Married	1 if married and not separated; 0 if widowed, divorced, separated or single.
Children	1 if family with own children; 0 otherwise (women only).
Veteran	1 if veteran of active-duty military service; 0 otherwise (men only).
Notable	1 if work disability; 0 otherwise.
Nativity	1 if foreign-born, including Puerto Rico; 0 otherwise.
Fluency	1 if ability to speak English is "not well" or "not at all"; 0 otherwise.
Natflu	Nativity × Fluency.
Natexp	Nativity × Experience.
Fedgov	1 if federal government worker; 0 otherwise.
Stagov	1 if state government worker; 0 otherwise.
Locgov	1 if local government worker; 0 otherwise.
THBsect	1 if defined as a "core" industrial sector by Tolbert, Horan, and Beck (1980); 0 if defined as a "periphery" sector.
Primseg 1	1 if defined as "control" workers by Gordon (1986); 0 otherwise.
Primseg 2	1 if defined as "technical and professional" workers by Gordon (1986); 0 otherwise.
Primseg 3	1 if defined as "craft" workers by Gordon (1986); 0 otherwise.
Primseg 4	1 if defined as "primary subordinated" workers by Gordon (1986); 0 otherwise.

dustries, or location in primary segments. (Reference groups are private, periphery, and secondary workers, respectively.)

The major findings are now summarized, in relative order of importance:

1. Labor market location explains a substantial proportion of Hispanic wage differences. The overall proportion of the observed wage difference explained by primary segment location is between 16 and 19% for Hispanic men and between 36 and 58% for Hispanic women. Most of the wage gap explained by the primary segment location is attributable to location in control or professional and technical subsegments. The proportion of the wage gap explained by industrial core sector location was lower than the proportion explained by primary segment location. The percentage of the wage difference explained by core industrial location for Hispanic men was 7 to 14%; for Hispanic women, 4 to 7%.

Table 5. Decomposition of Wage Differences: Industrial Sector Model

	Black	Mexican	Puerto Rican	Cuban	Other-Hispanic
		Men			
Wage difference	.245	.351	.328	.162	.365
Discrimination	.647	.295	.337	.332	.486
Explained effect	.353	.705	.663	.668	.514
Human capital[a]	.253	.491	.512	.300	.380
Education	.339	.562	.552	.674	.442
Socioeconomic[b]	.045	.023	.010	.078	−.049
Immigrant[c]	.026	.082	.075	.129	.128
Government[d]	−.011	.016	.001	.021	.013
THBsect	.039	.093	.065	.141	.072
		Women			
Wage difference	.068	.258	.217	.128	.294
Discrimination	.323	.282	.277	.447	.243
Explained effect	.677	.718	.723	.553	.757
Human capital[a]	.700	.565	.661	.345	.528
Education	1.051	.590	.647	.701	.593
Socioeconomic[b]	.369	.162	.152	.098	.120
Immigrant[c]	.040	.086	.048	.114	.145
Government[d]	−.205	.005	−.028	.012	.018
THBsect	.142	.062	.042	.073	.066

[a]Sum of Educa, Exp, Expsq effects.
[b]Sum of Married, Children, Veteran, Notable effects.
[c]Sum of Nativity, Fluency, Natflu, Natexp effects.
[d]Sum of Fedgov, Stagov, Locgov effects.

2. Differences in measurable characteristics explain most of the wage gap for Hispanic men and women, but the effect of discrimination is very important for Hispanics and explains most of the wage gap for black men. Discrimination accounts for two-thirds of black, one-half of other Hispanic, and one-third of Mexican, Puerto Rican, and Cuban men's wage gap. Considering that women have smaller observed wage differences, black women's earnings are not substantially affected by discrimination. However, discrimination represents between one-fifth and one-half of the wage gap for Hispanic women.

3. Education is the single most important factor explaining earning differentials for all groups of men and women except for black and other-Hispanic men. The proportion of the wage gap explained by differences in education, however, varies greatly among ethnic groups. Considering differences in both education and experience, human capital variables

Table 6. Decomposition of Wage Differences: Segmentation Model

	Black	Mexican	Puerto Rican	Cuban	Other-Hispanic
		Men			
Wage difference	.245	.351	.328	.162	.365
Discrimination	.549	.340	.316	.334	.490
Explained effect	.451	.660	.684	.666	.510
Human capital[a]	.255	.355	.376	.165	.270
Education	.257	.426	.419	.511	.335
Socioeconomic[b]	.050	.036	.015	.102	.064
Immigrant[c]	.033	.100	.106	.204	.157
Government[d]	.022	.011	−.002	.030	.017
Primary segments	.219	.159	.189	.164	.159
Primseg 1	.129	.057	.098	.039	.086
Primseg 2	.096	.082	.084	.106	.069
Primseg 3	.006	−.005	.000	.025	−.007
Primseg 4	.012	.025	.006	−.006	.011
		Women			
Wage difference	.068	.258	.217	.128	.294
Discrimination	−.062	.231	.252	.245	.184
Explained effect	1.062	.769	.748	.755	.816
Human capital[a]	.355	.337	.417	.209	.320
Education	.684	.388	.421	.456	.399
Socioeconomic[b]	.300	.138	.129	.086	.106
Immigrant[c]	.004	.047	−.009	−.039	.067
Government[d]	.113	.006	−.021	.008	.010
Primary segments	.817	.378	.361	.577	.419
Primseg 1	.319	.154	.155	.213	.123
Primseg 2	.519	.137	.154	.213	.170
Primseg 3	.018	.005	.003	.008	.002
Primseg 4	.040	.083	.048	.143	.125

[a]Sum of Educa, Exp, Expsq effects.
[b]Sum of Married, Children, Veteran, Notable effects.
[c]Sum of Nativity, Fluency, Natflu, Natexp effects.
[d]Sum of Fedgov, Stagov, Locgov effects.

explain between one-fourth and one-half of ethnic men's wage differences and eliminate or reduce by more than half ethnic women's differences.

4. Immigrant background variables explain 8 to 20% of the wage differences for Hispanic men and 5 to 15% for Hispanic women. The Hispanic groups for whom immigrant background variables accounted for the largest percentage of wage differences were Cubans and other-

Hispanics, both men and women. However, the relative effects of immigrant background variables was substantially reduced in the segmentation model suggesting a strong association between segmentation and immigration.

These findings indicate that there are substantial variations in the relative effect of the independent variables on the different Hispanic groups. Furthermore, there are no consistent patterns for the importance of observable characteristics and discrimination among men and women of similar ethnicity or race. Obviously, segmentation variables explained a larger proportion of wage differences than did industrial location. As suggested by DeFreitas (1988), the explanatory power of dual-economy models may be limited by the exclusion of industries with a large number of immigrants from the periphery. The greater explanatory power of occupational segmentation when compared to that for industrial sector could also reflect the greater stratification of earnings within industries than between industries. However, recent studies by Davidson and Reich (1988) and Reich (1984) offer evidence that since the early 1970s interindustry inequality has increased, not decreased as should be expected in order to find a lower effect of industrial location on wages.

In comparison to previous studies of earnings for Hispanics, the present study suggests that race, ethnicity, and sex are significant factors stratifying earnings after controlling for human capital, immigrant background, and labor market location. In particular, labor market location captured some of the effect of immigrant background and discrimination, but it seems unwarranted to reduce the effects of ethnic related traits to an exclusive consequence of labor market location. In other words, labor market location affects the demand for Hispanic labor but does not constitute the most significant source of income inequality. However, the combined effect of discrimination and labor market location upon earnings is a determinant as important as, or more important than, other measurable characteristics for many Hispanic groups.

The effects of demand-side factors—such as labor market structure and discrimination—vary depending on the model utilized to measure these effects.[7] According to the industrial location model, demand-side factors account for 70% of black men's wage differences, between 30 and 60% of Hispanic men's, 46% of black women's, and between 30 and 52% of Hispanic women's. According to the segmentation model, demand-side factors account for 77% of black men's wage differences, between 50 and 65% of black women's, and between 60 and

---

[7]For analytical convenience, labor market policies could be classified as supply-side or demand-side. Supply-side policies are those that affect the quality and quantity of labor that is offered in labor markets. In my study, supply-side polices are those pertaining to the acquisition of human capital, or adaptation factors that ameliorate the effects of socioeconomic and immigrant background. Demand-side factors are those that affect employers' hiring, compensation, and promotion practices.

75% of Hispanic women's. However measured, demand-side factors account for a substantial proportion of wage differences in New York City. The relative importance of demand-side factors, however, varies between Hispanic groups and between men and women of similar ethnicity and race. Specifically, occupational segmentation seems to be a more important factor explaining wage differences among Hispanic women than is the case for Hispanic men. Conversely, industrial sector location seems to be more important for Hispanic men than for Hispanic women.

These findings restate the need to implement policies aimed at correcting the problematic concentration of Hispanics in periphery industries and low-wage occupational segments and attacking discrimination. They also indicate the need for flexible policies that take into account gender differences and the particular problems of different national origin groups within the Hispanic category.

POLICY IMPLICATIONS

The above analysis of wage differences is consistent with emphasizing the need for a more active public and civic intervention in the demand side of labor markets in New York City. Previous research on Hispanic earnings has focused on supply-side factors (human capital, immigrant background) and therefore emphasized policies pertaining to the adaptation of Hispanic immigrants in labor markets. The "immigrant model" approach assumes a significantly competitive labor market in which wage inequality based on differences in workers' attributes will disappear with time. To the extent that public policy accelerates their adaptation in labor markets, Hispanics, like previous European immigrants have, will achieve income parity.

The optimistic outlook of the immigrant model is tempered by the evidence. The findings of this study suggest that demand-side factors play an important role in explaining wage inequality in New York City. Thus, there is a need to pursue both supply- and demand-side policies as complementary strategies to increase the earnings for blacks, Hispanics, and white women. Concurrent with policy recommendations in previous studies, promoting education and providing training opportunities to increase skills, language fluency, and country-specific labor market experience for Hispanics are important. But these conventional policy recommendations are bound to stop short of correcting employers' discriminatory hiring, compensation, and promotion practices.

Policies that remedy employers' discriminatory valuation of workers' productivity in labor markets include affirmative action and pay equity. Affirmative action promotes equal treatment of minority workers in hiring, promotion, and employment security. Hispanics and blacks are extremely underrepresented in private core industrial employment and in the upper tier of primary segments.

Affirmative action will promote the mobility of workers from secondary jobs to good jobs with higher earnings, employment stability, and more advancement opportunities. In contrast, pay equity promotes the equal valuation of jobs in which minority workers are concentrated. Rather than simply provide access to good jobs (as affirmative action proposes) pay equity aims at transforming a poor job into a good job. Pay equity is a necessary policy when the concentration of minorities in a particular job is the main factor inducing the undervaluation of workers' productivity.

In addition to race- and gender-specific policies, such as affirmative action and pay equity, Hispanic workers will benefit from industrial policies that target smaller firms, promote workers' protection and unionization, and support local economic development initiatives. These are broad class-based strategies that will benefit all workers in an industry. Government programs and community initiatives are crucial in the development of local economic projects and in assisting smaller firms that are more susceptible to recessionary times. Similarly, unions tend to promote worker solidarity and to minimize differences in job categories and earnings within firms and industries.

Conventional wisdom proposes that supply-side policies are more politically viable than demand-side policies, to the extent that the latter are perceived as promoting preferential treatment for minorities. The truth is that demand-side policies will benefit the majority of workers in New York City. To the extent that the monetary gains represent workers' invested interest in alternative policy scenarios, reasonable conditions for a multiracial and multiethnic alliance exist to support affirmative action, pay equity, and other demand-side strategies. Hispanic men and women are among those who will benefit most from these policies.

Acknowledgments

Research for this chapter was supported by a grant from the Committee for Public Policy Research on Contemporary Hispanic Issues and by the Ford Foundation. I have benefited from helpful comments and suggestions by Clara E. Rodriguez and Janis Barry Figueroa. Any remaining errors or omissions are my own responsibility.

REFERENCES

Averitt, R. T. (1968). *The dual economy: The dynamics of American industry structure.* New York: W. W. Norton.

Bean, F., & M. Tienda. (1987). *The Hispanic population in the United States.* New York: Russel Sage.

Borjas, G. (1982). The earnings of male Hispanic immigrants in the United States. *Industrial and Labor Relations Review, 35,* 343–353.

Cain, G. (1976). The challenge of segmented labor market theories to orthodox theory: A summary. *Journal of Economic Literature, 14,* 1215–1257.

Carliner, G. (1976). Returns to education for blacks, Anglos, and five Spanish groups. *Journal of Human Resources, 11* (Spring), 172–84.

Carlson, L., & C. Swartz. (1988). The earnings of women and ethnic minorities, 1959–1979. *Industrial and Labor Relations Review, 41*(4), 530–546.

Chiswick, B. (1978). The effect of Americanization on the earnings of foreign-born Men. *Journal of Political Economy, 86,* 897–921.

Cotton, J. (1985). A comparative analysis of black-white and Mexican-American-white male wage differentials. *Review of Black Political Economy* (Spring), 51–69.

Davidson, C., & M. Reich. (1988). Income inequality: An inter-industry analysis. *Industrial Relations, 27*(3), 263–286.

DeFreitas, G. (1988). Hispanic immigration and labor market segmentation. *Industrial Relations, 27*(2) 125–214.

Edwards, R. (1979). *Contested terrain.* New York: Basic Books.

Garcia, P. (1984). Dual-language characteristics and earnings: Male Mexican workers in the United States. *Social Science Research, 13,* 221–235.

Gordon, D. (1986). *Procedure for allocating jobs into labor segments.* Unpublished manuscript, New School for Social Research.

Gordon, D., R. Edwards, & M. Reich. (1982). *Segmented work, divided workers.* Cambridge, England: Cambridge University Press.

Grenier, G. (1984). The effects of language characteristics on the wages of Hispanic-American males. *Journal of Human Resources, 19*(1), 35–52.

Gwartney, J. P., & J. E. Long (1978). The relative earnings of blacks and other minorities. *Industrial and Labor Review, 31*(3) 336–346.

Hirschman, C., & M. G. Wong (1984). Socio-economic gains of Asian Americans, blacks, and Hispanics: 1960–1976. *American Journal of Sociology, 90*(3), 584–607.

Kalacheck, E., & F. Raines. (1976). The structure of wage differences among mature male workers. *Journal of Human Resources, 11*(4), 484–506.

Long, J. E. (1977). Productivity, employment, discrimination and the relative economic status of Spanish origin males. *Social Science Quarterly, 58* (December), 357–373.

McManus, W. (1985). Labor market cost of language disparity: An interpretation of Hispanic earning differences. *American Economic Review, 75*(4) 818–827.

McManus, W., W. Gould, & F. Welch. (1983). Earnings of Hispanic men: The role of proficiency in English Language. *Journal of Labor Economics, 1* (April), 110–130.

Osterman, P. (1975). An empirical study of labor market segmentation. *Industrial and Labor Relations Review, 28,* 508–523.

Poston, D. L., D. Alvirez, & M. Tienda. (1976). Earning differences between Anglo and Mexican American male workers in 1960 and 1970: Changes in the "cost" of being Mexican American. *Social Science Quarterly, 57* (December), 618–631.

Reich, M. (1984). Segmented labour: Time series hypothesis and evidence. *Cambridge Journal of Economics, 8,* 63–81.

Reich, M., D. M. Gordon, & R. Edwards. (1973). A theory of labor market segmentation. *American Economic Review, 63* (May), 359–365.

Reimers, C. W. (1983). Labor market discrimination against Hispanic and black men. *Review of Economics and Statistics, 65*(4), 570–579.

Reimers, C. W. (1984). The wage structure of Hispanic men: Implications for policy. *Social Science Quarterly 65*(2), 401–416.

Reimers, C. W. (1985). A comparative analysis of the wages of Hispanics, blacks, and non-Hispanic whites. In G. Borjas & M. Tienda, Eds., *Hispanics in the U. S. economy.* Orlando, FL: Academic Press.

Stolzenberg, R. M. (1975). Occupations, labor markets and the process of wage attainment. *American Sociological Review 40* (October), 645–665.

Tienda, M. (1983a). Nationality and income attainment among native and immigrant Hispanic men in the United States. *Sociological Quarterly, 24* (Spring), 253–272.

Tienda, M. (1983b). Market characteristics and Hispanic earnings: A comparison of Latinos and immigrants. *Social Problems, 31*(1), 59–72.

Tienda, M., & L. J. Neidert. (1980). Segmented markets and earnings inequality of native and immigrant Hispanics in the United States. *Proceedings of the American Statistical Association, Social Statistics Section.*

Tolbert, C., P. M. Horan, & E. M. Beck. (1980). The structure of economic segmentation: A dual economy approach. *American Journal of Sociology, 85*(5), 1095–1116.

Torres, A. (1988). *Human capital, labor segmentation, and inter-minority relative status: Black and Puerto Rican labor in New York City.* Unpublished Ph.D. Dissertation. New School for Social Research.

Verdugo, N. T., & R. R. Verdugo. (1984). Earnings differentials among Mexican American, black, and white male workers. *Social Science Quarterly, 65* (June), 417–425.

6

Latinos and Industrial Change in New York and Los Angeles

VILMA ORTIZ

INTRODUCTION

That the nature of American cities has changed over the last 30 years is well established. We have seen a dramatic decline in the production sector overall, referred to as the deindustrialization of America (Bluestone & Harrison, 1981), and an increase in service-oriented jobs, particularly in the finance and the information-processing areas.

Despite the fact that deindustrialization has occurred in all regions of the country, the time period in which these changes were initiated, or the pace at which they have occurred, differs by city. For instance, New York City and Los Angeles are typically presented as examples of cities at opposite ends of the continuum of urban change. In the 1950s, New York began experiencing its decline as the manufacturing capital. Deindustrialization and other economic changes continued to the point that New York almost experienced a financial collapse in the mid-1970s. Los Angeles, on the other hand, has never experienced the same decline in the production sector and, in fact, has actually showed an expansion of manufacturing jobs.

VILMA ORTIZ • Department of Sociology, University of California, Los Angeles, California 90024.

Hispanics in the Labor Force, edited by Edwin Melendez *et al.* Plenum Press, New York, 1991.

119

Nevertheless, the changes in New York and Los Angeles are not at opposite ends of this continuum in all respects. New York's recovery, on the heels of its crisis during the mid-1970s, occurred almost entirely in the service sector, particularly in the information-processing and high-finance areas. And Los Angeles is similar to New York in that the growth of its service sector has overshadowed the production sector. The growth of both these cities has essentially evolved them into global cities (Sassen, 1987).

The different pattern of change in these cities has implications for the effects on their minority communities although different claims have been made about what these effects might be. Some critics have argued that these changes have displaced minority workers because decline has been in areas where minorities have traditionally been found—manufacturing, while growth has been in areas for which minorities do not have qualifications—high tech jobs (Karsada, 1989; Wilson, 1987). This explanation, referred to as the "skills-mismatch" hypothesis, has been used to explain the increased joblessness among blacks in northeastern and midwestern cities (Wilson, 1987).[1]

On the other hand, others have argued that the expansion of the service sector has led to increased opportunities in low-skill and unskilled jobs for minorities and immigrants (Sassen, 1987). This development can be referred to as the *service-sector expansion* hypothesis. Employment in this sector is usually very low-paying with poor working conditions. Undocumented immigrants are especially likely to be employed in this sector because they are less likely to be in a legal position to object to such exploitative conditions (Morales, 1983). Under this scenario, we should see, not increased joblessness as cities evolve, but a changing concentration from production jobs to service-sector jobs.

A third explanation about the changing opportunities for minorities and immigrants in these world centers is the concept of job queues based on theories proposed by Lieberson (1980). For instance, Waldinger (1986) examined industrial change in New York City for blacks, foreign-born Hispanics, and foreign-born Asians between 1970 and 1980 as a means of testing the job-queue hypothesis. Basically, he argued that whites, historically the preferred group in the labor market, moved out of New York City in dramatic numbers during this period. Blacks, in turn, moved into many of the positions vacated by whites, particularly

---

[1]Another aspect of the skills-mismatch hypothesis is the *spatial dimension*. Accordingly, one way in which minorities are disadvantaged is that jobs are no longer in the inner city but are now in the surrounding areas and that minorities, particularly youth, have limited access to get to these jobs. The evidence regarding the spatial hypothesis is varied: although Karsada (1989) found that distance from jobs is a concern for youth, Ellwood (1986) concluded it was not. This finding may be a very important factor in explaining the experiences of minority populations in New York City and Los Angeles, but it is not possible to address this issue with the data used in this study because detailed geographic information is not available. For this reason, I do not discuss this hypothesis in any detail in this chapter.

in the public sector, and foreign-born Asians and Hispanics, being in the lowest positions in this stratification, moved into the bottom-most positions. Since the foreign-born groups moved into declining sectors (e.g., manufacturing) as well as expanding ones, he argued that the concept of ethnic queues is a better explanation for the changes that have occurred than the skills-mismatch hypothesis or the expanded service-sector explanation.

These explanations make different predictions about the effect of economic changes on minority populations. The skills-mismatch hypothesis predicts that joblessness has increased as result of the lack of jobs in the inner city. The service-expansion hypothesis predicts that disadvantaged groups, especially immigrants, have increased their representation in service sectors, particularly at the low-wage end. Finally, the job-queue hypothesis predicts that the minorities move into sectors vacated by groups higher than themselves in the job queue.

Most of the studies testing these explanations focus on one location or on one racial/ethnic group at a time. Thus, the explanations that may be supported in one study on a particular group or location may not generalize to other groups or areas. In this chapter, I compare several racial/ethnic groups—whites, blacks, Mexicans, and Puerto Ricans—focusing on two major urban centers—New York City and Los Angeles—and comparing immigrants and native-born Latinos.

What predictions can be made then concerning these groups in these cities? While it has been documented that the skills-mismatch hypothesis makes sense for blacks in midwestern cities, such as Detroit, where blacks have been displaced out of high-paying, unionized, heavy industry manufacturing jobs (Karsada, 1989), it is unclear whether this argument also applies to blacks in other areas or to Puerto Ricans or Mexicans. However, it makes sense to expect this explanation to be important for Puerto Ricans, since they are concentrated in northeastern cities and originally migrated to the United States to fill vacancies in New York's manufacturing industries.

On the other hand, we expect that the effects of industrial change will be quite different in Los Angeles. Evidence that the manufacturing sector has declined particularly in areas near or in the black community of Los Angeles (Soja, Morales, & Wolff, 1983), coupled with the extreme residential segregation of blacks, suggest that there are negative economic impacts for blacks. It is less clear, however, whether the skills-mismatch theory is relevant for Mexicans, although they, too, have been heavily involved in production industries in Los Angeles. Moreover, the dramatic increase of immigration from Mexico suggests that immigrant Mexicans may have moved into the low-skilled expanded opportunities—the unskilled service jobs and the downgraded manufacturing jobs (Sassen, 1987).

To examine these issues, 1970 and 1980 census data were used. Although these data are somewhat outdated at this point, they are the best sources for examining change at the metropolitan area level for specific racial/ethnic groups.

Other sources of data, such as the Current Population Survey (CPS), although more recent, do not have sufficiently large samples for focusing on these geographic areas and racial/ethnic groups. Moreover, the decade from 1970 to 1980 is a period during which key aspects of reindustrialization occurred in these cities and during which Latinos in these cities underwent dramatic changes.

METHODS AND DATA

The data for my analysis came from original tabulations of the 1970 and the 1980 Censuses. The analysis of the 1970 Census were from the Public Use Samples (PUS) 15% county sample file and the 1980 analysis from the Public Use Microdata Samples (PUMS) 5% data file. The racial/ethnic groups focused on in this analysis were whites and blacks in New York City and in Los Angeles, Puerto Ricans in New York, and Mexicans in Los Angeles.[2] In addition, Puerto Ricans and Mexicans were analyzed separately by place of birth—United States-born versus immigrant.[3]

In this analysis, I concentrated on changes in the industry distribution between 1970 and 1980 in New York City and in Los Angeles. Since the industry classification did not change between the two censuses, these comparisons were possible. The industry classification was regrouped into the following categories: *production* which included agriculture, forestry, mining, construction, and manufacturing (although manufacturing by far predominated in this category); *transport* which included transportation, communications, and utilities; *trade* which included wholesale and retail trade; *financial* which included finance, insurance, and real estate; *service* which included business and repair services, personal services, entertainment and recreation services, and professional and related services; and *public* which included all jobs in the public sector. The public category included all government employees and was based on the class of worker variable even if industry classification was something else (primarily professional service or transport industries). In some tables, the *transport* and *trade* industries were combined and so were the *financial* and *service* industries.

Industry distributions were also presented by education level—non-high

[2]For the 1980 data, the entire 5% sample of Puerto Ricans was used, whereas the other groups were subsamples since these groups had large populations in these locations. The Mexican sample is 1.67% of the population, the black sample is .25% of the population, and the white sample is .04% of the population. These subsamples were randomly selected from the PUMS sample.

[3]Among Puerto Ricans, those born in Puerto Rico are not technically considered immigrants because of the commonwealth status of Puerto Rico which grants U. S. citizenship to all Puerto Ricans. However, the distinct Latin American culture of Puerto Rico and the adjustment process experienced by Puerto Ricans when they migrate make their experiences comparable to other immigrants rather than to internal migrants.

school graduate versus high school graduate, since I expected different results for more skilled jobs versus less skilled ones.

In this analysis, I focused on SMSAs as defined by the Census Bureau, rather than the larger metropolitan area or the smaller urbanized area. Although both New York City and Los Angeles are part of larger metropolitan areas, the minority populations in these cities are concentrated within the SMSA rather than in the outlying areas. On the other hand, focusing on just the urbanized area or inner city as has been done by others (e.g., Karsada, 1989) is less reasonable, particularly in Los Angeles since large communities of Latinos and blacks reside in adjacent areas to the Los Angeles city limits (such as East Los Angeles and Compton). For purposes of comparability, the same geographic definition was used for the two locations.

RESULTS

Industry Change in New York and Los Angeles

Table 1 presents the changes in the number of jobs by industry and education level of workers in New York and in Los Angeles. First, we see dramatic declines in the number of jobs in New York City, particularly among the less educated. It is not surprising that among the less educated in New York, the industry category that lost the greatest number of jobs was production—over 270,000 jobs between 1970 and 1980 (although the percentage of decline for production jobs was not the largest decline of all industry categories because this category had a large base in 1970). Second, the next largest decline in number of jobs was in the trade category and, lastly, in transport and service categories.

Among the more educated, the declines were much smaller whether we compare the absolute numbers or the percentage of change. Again the declines in production were the largest—67,000 jobs were lost between 1970 and 1980. The second largest decline was in the public sector, which is not surprising given the fiscal crisis that occurred in New York during the mid-1970s.[4] The only industry category that grew was transport. The decline seen by industry reflects the overall decline in population in New York during this period—by more than 900,000 workers.

In Los Angeles, the pattern was different in that there was considerable growth overall. Yet the pattern was similar to that in New York with respect to educational differences: among less-educated workers, there were small de-

---

[4]These jobs were not lost by laying-off or firing employees but rather by not filling vacancies that resulted from retirement or resignations (Waldinger, 1986). The loss was relatively greater for more educated white employees, given the middle-class "white flight" from New York during this period.

Table 1. Change in the Number of Jobs by Industry

	Absolute number			
	1970	1980	Difference	Percentage of change
New York City				
Non-high school graduate				
Production	637,700	367.020	(270,680)	−42.4
Transportation	159,300	57,700	(101,600)	−63.8
Trade	501,400	295,280	(206,120)	−41.1
Financial	126,600	72,600	(54,000)	−42.7
Service	381,400	250,920	(130,480)	−34.2
Public	241,300	177,900	(63,400)	−26.3
Total	2,047,700	1,221,420	(826,280)	−40.4
High school graduate				
Production	697,400	630,300	(67,100)	−9.6
Transportation	264,600	292,440	27,480	10.5
Trade	629,700	625,200	(4,500)	−0.7
Financial	365,800	353,060	(12,740)	−3.5
Service	850,100	831,620	(18,480)	−2.2
Public	663,500	620,820	(42,680)	−6.4
Total	3,471,100	3,353,440	(117,660)	−3.4
Los Angeles				
Non-high school graduate				
Production	458,300	480,800	22,500	4.9
Transportation	47,300	44,920	(2,380)	−5.0
Trade	292,500	271,440	(21,060)	−7.2
Financial	28,900	22,500	(6,400)	−22.1
Service	224,500	194,760	(29,740)	−13.2
Public	78,800	76,180	(2,620)	−3.3
Total	1,130,300	1,090,600	(39,700)	−3.5
High school graduate				
Production	676,100	825,440	149,340	22.1
Transportation	152,700	200,800	48,100	31.5
Trade	501,200	595,660	94,460	18.8
Financial	186,500	231,000	44,500	23.9
Service	535,900	717,760	181,860	33.9
Public	419,700	459,160	39,460	9.4
Total	2,472,100	3,029,820	557,720	22.6

clines, while among more-educated workers, there was considerable growth. Production jobs actually increased in Los Angeles for both less- and more-educated workers. This increase has occurred primarily in the manufacturing of downgraded products (such as the garment industry, plastics, glass, etc.), jobs which are characterized by low wages and poor working conditions. The greatest deline in absolute numbers was in lower level services jobs—almost 30,000 jobs altogether. This was somewhat of a surprise given that service-sector expansion hypothesis.

Among the more educated in Los Angeles, the number of jobs increased dramatically, with the greatest growth in service-oriented jobs. The next largest growth, in absolute numbers, was in production and trade jobs. The growth as seen by industry category reflected the overall population expansion in the Los Angeles area during this period—by more than 500,000 workers in the SMSA.

Industry Change by Race/Ethnicity

Table 2 presents the change in the industrial distribution for racial/ethnic groups. In this table, the percentages of distribution by industry were presented instead of absolute numbers in order to control for differences in the size (and the changes in size between 1970 and 1980) of the racial/ethnic groups, which varied dramatically. For instance, the white population in New York declined by more than 1 million people (30% of the 1970 size) in this period, while the white population in Los Angeles declined to a much smaller extent (10% of its 1970 size). There was a small decline in the overall size of the black population in New York City, while there was an increase of blacks in Los Angeles. The Puerto Rican population in New York increased slightly during this period, due to slightly more migration from, than return migration to, Puerto Rico during this time. In contrast, the Mexican population in Los Angeles more than doubled during this period because of high immigration rates from Mexico.

In New York, less-educated whites experienced a decline in their concentration in production and slightly increased their representation in service/financial and public industries. More-educated whites increased their percentages in trade/transportation jobs and decreased in public-sector employment. However, we must keep in mind that given the dramatic decline in population size of whites, the absolute number of whites in each industry declined significantly. It is this phenomenon that Waldinger (1986) argued which allows for movement up the job queue.

Both the more- and the less-educated blacks in New York decreased their concentration in production jobs and increased their concentration in public-sector jobs, despite the fact that they were heavily concentrated in public-sector jobs to begin with. Less-educated blacks also declined in their representation in service/financial jobs during this time.

Table 2. Change in the Percentage of Distribution by Industry

	Whites			Blacks			US-born Puerto Ricans			Immigrant Puerto Ricans		
	1970	1980	Difference	1970	1980	Difference	1970	1980	Difference	1970	1980	Difference
New York City												
Non-high school graduate												
Production	27.7	24.2	-3.5	21.8	17.1	-4.6	25.1	24.7	-0.4	48.5	42.9	-5.6
Trade/transportation	37.1	37.4	0.3	24.9	23.8	-1.1	36.1	33.1	-3.0	25.5	22.0	-3.5
Service/finance	22.8	24.7	1.9	34.1	29.0	-5.1	22.4	25.0	2.5	18.4	21.8	3.4
Public	12.4	13.7	1.4	19.2	30.0	10.8	16.3	17.2	0.9	7.6	13.3	5.8
Total	1,050,200	436,800	(631,400)	334,600	208,000	(126,600)	26,300	43,120	16,820	178,300	129,740	(48,560)
High school graduate												
Production	20.2	19.3	-0.9	14.5	11.0	-3.5	19.2	16.1	-3.2	27.5	24.3	-3.2
Trade/transportation	25.9	29.9	4.0	22.6	21.1	-1.5	26.5	25.0	-1.5	23.8	20.4	-3.4
Service/finance	35.1	34.5	-5.0	31.2	32.3	1.1	33.8	36.6	2.8	30.6	30.8	0.2
Public	18.8	16.3	-2.5	31.7	35.6	3.9	20.5	22.4	1.9	18.0	24.5	6.5
Total	2,558,200	2,064,000	(494,200)	338,200	431,200	93,000	30,200	66,900	36,700	70,500	89,940	19,440

126

	Whites			Blacks			US-born Mexicans			Immigrant Mexicans		
Los Angeles												
Non-high school graduate												
Production	36.4	37.1	0.7	30.9	24.8	-6.1	52.5	43.2	-9.3	63.9	61.7	-2.2
Trade/transportation	34.7	37.7	3.0	22.2	23.1	0.9	24.2	28.1	3.9	18.5	19.4	0.8
Service/finance	22.5	20.5	-1.9	33.4	27.7	-5.7	15.0	17.3	2.3	14.6	15.3	0.6
Public	6.5	4.6	-1.8	13.4	24.4	10.9	8.2	11.4	3.2	3.0	3.7	0.7
Total	627,700	362,400	(265,300)	133,200	95,200	(38,000)	121,700	138,120	16,420	98,300	309,900	211,600
High school graduate												
Production	26.8	27.6	0.8	23.4	20.6	-2.7	32.5	28.3	-4.3	46.7	42.7	-4.0
Trade/transportation	26.8	27.2	0.4	21.5	21.2	-0.3	28.4	28.0	-0.4	23.9	23.9	0.0
Service/finance	29.9	32.3	2.4	23.8	28.3	4.5	23.1	25.1	2.0	22.5	21.8	-0.7
Public	16.4	12.9	-3.6	31.3	29.8	-1.5	15.9	18.6	2.7	6.9	11.6	4.6
Total	1,814,100	1,826,400	12,300	204,000	348,800	144,800	109,400	209,580	100,180	28,900	97,620	68,720

Puerto Ricans experienced the greatest losses in production, especially among island-born Puerto Ricans. They also experienced job losses in trade/transportation but increased their concentration in service/financial and public sector jobs, although not to the same extent as blacks.

In Los Angeles, less-educated whites increased their representation in trade/transportation and slightly decreased their concentration in service/financial and public sectors. Although the more-educated whites increased their representation in service/financial-sector jobs, they decreased their concentration in the public sector.

In Los Angeles, blacks lost jobs in production despite the overall growth in production jobs. To a large extent, this was due to the closing down and movement of factories in the south-central area of Los Angeles where blacks are concentrated (Soja *et al.*, 1983). Moreover, the decline of manufacturing jobs is greater for blacks in Los Angeles than in New York. It is possible that the decline of manufacturing jobs for blacks occurred in New York earlier than in Los Angeles, suggesting that comparisons between 1960 and 1970 might reveal a different picture.[5] Less-educated blacks in Los Angeles declined in their concentration in the service/financial sectors and increased their representation in the public sector, which is very similar to the changes among the less-educated blacks in New York. The more-educated blacks increased their representation in the service/financial sectors.

Mexicans, irrespective of place of birth and educational level, experienced great declines in production jobs. This decline was greatest among the less-educated United States-born Mexicans, coupled with an increase in their concentration in all other industries. Among the more-educated United States-born Mexicans, this decline was coupled with an increase in jobs in the service/financial and public sectors. Among less-educated immigrant Mexicans, the decline in production jobs was coupled with small increases in all other industries; but among the more-educated, there was an increase in public-sector jobs. We must keep in mind, however, that Mexican immigrants more than doubled in number during this period; consequently, the number of persons in each industry increased dramatically; for instance, the number in production among less-educated immigrants grew by more than 120,000 during this period.

The key findings from Table 2 include the following: (1) Production declined for all groups, but particularly in New York, among the less-educated group, and among Puerto Ricans and Mexicans.[6] (2) Public-sector employment

[5]Additionally, we might see even greater declines in the concentration of Puerto Ricans in manufacturing between 1960 and 1970.

[6]Racial/ethnic changes in manufacturing jobs vary for durable and nondurable industries. Among whites and blacks in New York, the decline is greater for jobs in the durable industries rather than in nondurable. Among Puerto Ricans, the decline is entirely in nondurable manufacturing, which is primarily in apparel, where Puerto Ricans were historically concentrated. In Los Angeles, the

Table 3. Change in the Percentage of Employment Rates

	Men			Women		
	1970	1980	Difference	1970	1980	Difference
New York City						
Non-high school graduate						
White	84.9	79.4	−5.5	40.0	39.3	−0.7
Black	75.6	58.3	−17.3	41.1	39.2	−1.9
US-born Puerto Rican	75.0	58.3	−16.7	26.2	26.4	0.2
Immigrant Puerto Rican	77.3	65.9	−11.4	22.0	23.4	1.4
High school graduate						
White	93.4	90.4	−3.0	49.8	62.9	13.1
Black	88.7	75.2	−13.5	60.1	65.8	5.7
US-born Puerto Rican	92.2	79.4	−12.8	43.5	59.5	16.0
Immigrant Puerto Rican	89.1	79.5	−9.6	44.1	48.3	4.2
Los Angeles						
Non-high school graduate						
White	81.3	78.0	−3.3	42.0	46.4	4.4
Black	69.1	57.8	−11.3	42.8	40.3	−2.5
US-born Mexican	81.5	75.5	−6.0	34.5	44.5	10.0
Immigrant Mexican	85.5	84.6	−0.9	36.2	43.1	6.9
High school graduate						
White	90.8	87.0	−3.8	51.1	65.0	13.9
Black	85.0	75.8	−9.2	60.8	72.0	11.2
US-born Mexican	91.0	86.5	−4.5	52.6	66.8	14.2
Immigrant Mexican	89.7	88.0	−1.7	48.8	54.9	6.1

expanded for minority groups, particularly for blacks in New York and in Los Angeles. (3) Employment in the service sector did not increase dramatically for any group.

Unemployment

The skills-mismatch hypothesis predicted that employment rates would decline as a result of being displaced from production jobs; employment rates by race/ethnicity and city are presented in Table 3. Among men, we see that employment has decreased the most among blacks in New York City and in Los

decline of manufacturing jobs for blacks are greater in the nondurable sector. Among Mexicans who were born in the United States, decline is greater in durable manufacturing whereas with immigrant Mexicans, decline is greater in the nondurable sector.

Angeles; among Puerto Ricans in New York; and among less-educated United States-born Mexicans in Los Angeles. In contrast, employment has decreased less among whites in New York City and in Los Angeles and among immigrant or more-educated Mexicans in Los Angeles.

Larger increases in employment can be seen among the more-educated women than among the less-educated. For the most part, employment among women in Los Angeles has increased to a greater extent than in New York. However, employment among women does not follow the same pattern of change as it does among men.

DISCUSSION AND CONCLUSIONS

How do the three explanations—skills mismatch, service expansion, and job queue—explain the finding for these racial/ethnic groups in these cities? The decline of production jobs among blacks in New York and in Los Angeles, among Puerto Ricans in New York, and among the less-educated United States-born Mexicans in Los Angeles supports the skills-mismatch hypothesis. This hypothesis is further supported by the increase in joblessness among black, Puerto Rican, and less-educated United States-born Mexican men. The exceptions are that less-educated United States-born Puerto Ricans experienced little decline in production jobs yet showed a decline in employment and that the more-educated Mexicans declined their representation in production jobs yet did not decline in employment.

The job-queue hypothesis is supported by the increased representation in the public sector among minorities, particularly since whites have declined their concentration in this sector. However, the decline in production jobs among these groups is not consistent with Waldinger's (1986) version of the job-queue hypothesis. Waldinger argued that as whites left sectors of the economy in New York City, other groups further down the job queue would take their place. However, blacks and Puerto Ricans did not move into vacancies in production-sector jobs, instead, they themselves moved out of these kinds of jobs. The groups to fill these jobs were newer immigrants from Asia and Latin America as Waldinger showed. Moreover, job queue makes less sense in Los Angeles where there has been only a small decline in the size of the white population.

The job-queue hypothesis might suggest a direct one-on-one replacement in the production sector (meaning that a new immigrant could fill a position previously held by a white or native minority). I would argue, however, that this is not case. Instead, vacated jobs were probably eliminated or redefined, while newly filled positions were created specifically to take advantage of the availability of workers who would take lower wages or poorer working conditions (e.g., downgraded manufacturing).

The service-expansion explanation is considerably less important for minorities since we see little growth in this category. Given the large numbers and character of Mexican immigration, we would expect to see an expansion in this category among immigrant Mexicans; yet this is not the case. The group that experienced the greatest change in this sector were blacks—declining among the less-educated, because of a decline in personal services, and increasing among the more-educated.

In sum, the skill-mismatch hypothesis is a much better explanation of the experiences of blacks, Puerto Ricans, and, to a limited extent, Mexicans than are the job-queue or the service-expansion hypotheses. These findings are relevant to the argument offered by Wilson (1987) regarding the urban underclass, since one of his key ideas is the link between industrial change and unemployment, which this study supports. Wilson went on to argue that the resulting male unemployment was related to increased family poverty. Although I do not address this issue in my present study, other data have shown that blacks and Puerto Ricans, the groups most affected by industrial change, have experienced increases in poverty. Thus, the process of reindustrialization is not only important to understand in and of itself but also in the manner in which it impacts on both individual and family lives.

Acknowledgments

I gratefully acknowledge comments by Melvin Oliver, James Johnson, Edwin Melendez, Ruth Milkman, Donald Treiman, and Antonio Serrata. This research was supported by the Faculty Senate, the Institute of American Culture, and the Chicano Studies Research Center at UCLA.

REFERENCES

Bluestone, B., & B. Harrison. (1981). *The deindustrialization of America: Plant closings, community abandonment, and the dismantling of basic industry*. New York: Basic Books.

Ellwood, D. (1986). The spatial mismatch hypothesis: Are there teenage jobs missing in the ghetto? In R. Freeman & H. Holzer, Eds., The black youth unemployment crisis. Chicago: University of Chicago Press.

Karsada, J. (1989). Urban industrial transition and the underclass. *ANNALS 501*, 26–47.

Lieberson, S. (1980). *A piece of the pie: Blacks and white immigrants since 1880*. Berkeley: University of California Press.

Morales, R. (1983). Transitional labor: Undocumented workers in the Los Angeles automobile industry. *International Migration Review 17*(4), 570–596.

Sassen, S. (1987). *The mobility of labor and capital: A study in international investment and labor flow*. Cambridge, England: Cambridge University Press.

Soja, E., R. Morales, & G. Wolff. (1983). Urban restructuring: An analysis of social and spatial change in Los Angeles. *Economic Geography* (April), 195–230.

Waldinger, R. (1986). Changing ladders and musical chairs: Ethnicity and opportunity in Post-industrial New York. *Politics and Society 15*, 369–402.

Wilson, W. (1987). *The truly disadvantaged: The inner city, the underclass and public policy*. Chicago: University of Chicago Press.

III

Government Employment

7

Hispanic Employment in the Public Sector

Why Is It Lower Than Blacks'?

CORDELIA REIMERS AND HOWARD CHERNICK

Government jobs have traditionally been viewed as "good" ones—more secure and with better fringe benefits, if not better paid, than jobs in the private sector that require similar levels of skill. Thus, they are potentially an important avenue for the economic advancement of minorities. Moreover, public-sector opportunities have been enhanced by the rapid expansion in the absolute and in the relative size of the public sector since World War II. Growth in total employment has been particularly rapid at the state and local levels. Although this growth has slowed somewhat in recent years, the shift of resources toward the public sector suggests that public employment would have been an important source of new jobs for all groups, even if hiring, promotion, and compensation patterns by race and gender were the same in the public and in the private sectors. Previous research indicates, however, that governments have been more "open" to blacks and women than have private firms. These groups have a higher percentage employed in the public sector, and a higher percentage in public-sector professional and managerial occupations, than do white men; moreover, blacks and

CORDELIA REIMERS and HOWARD CHERNICK • Department of Economics, Hunter College and the Graduate School of the City University of New York, New York, New York 10021.

Hispanics in the Labor Force, edited by Edwin Melendez *et al*. Plenum Press, New York, 1991.

women earn more for given human capital characteristics in the public sector than they do in the private sector (Reimers, 1985; Smith, 1977).

Some evidence suggests that the favored position of women and blacks has not extended to Hispanics. Using data from the 1970s, researchers found that Hispanics were less likely than both blacks and white non-Hispanics of the same gender to be employed by state and local governments, and less likely than blacks to be employed by the federal government (Abowd & Killingsworth, 1985; Reimers, 1985; Smith, 1977).

PUBLIC-SECTOR EMPLOYMENT AND EARNINGS BY ETHNIC/GENDER GROUP

Sectoral Distribution of Employment

Table 1 shows the percentages of employed civilians, classified according to gender, ethnic, and racial groups, who were in the local, state, and federal sectors, as well as the private sector, in 1980. Overall, 17.1% of the work force were government employees. For all ethnic groups, women are more likely than men to work in the public sector. Within the public sector they are much more likely than men to work for local and state governments, whereas men are slightly more likely than women to work for the federal government. Black and Other non-Hispanic (i.e., Native Americans and others who are neither white, black, nor Asian) participation in the public sector is about ten percentage points higher than that of whites of the same gender. These groups are more likely than whites to work in all levels of government.

Hispanics, on the other hand, are much less likely than blacks, and about as likely as whites, to work in the public sector. True, Puerto Rican men are more likely than white men to have a government job, but Cuban males and females and Other-Spanish females are less likely than whites of the same gender to do so. The other groups of Hispanics have rates of public-sector employment similar to those of whites of the same gender.

When we disaggregate the public sector by level of government, we find that for both men and women, Hispanics are less likely than whites to work for state governments; whereas, with the exception of Cubans, they are at least as likely as whites to work for the federal government. Puerto Ricans have higher rates of employment at the federal level than other Hispanic groups and whites, whereas Mexicans and whites have about the same rate.

At the local level, the Hispanic-white pattern differs by gender. Among women, Cubans and Other-Spanish are less likely than whites to work for a local government, while Mexicans and Puerto Ricans are only slightly more likely to do so than whites. Among men, Mexicans and Puerto Ricans are more likely than whites to be in the local public sector, with Puerto Ricans being the most

Table 1. Sectoral Distributions of All Employed Civilians,
by Gender, Race, and Ethnicity

| | Percentage employed in | | | |
Group	Local government	State government	Federal government	Private sector
All females	11.3	5.7	3.6	79.5
White non-Hispanic	10.9	5.3	2.9	80.9
Black non-Hispanic	15.3	8.5	7.7	68.5
Mexican	11.6	4.6	3.6	80.2
Puerto Rican	11.8	4.3	4.6	79.3
Cuban	7.2	2.8	1.8	88.1
Other-Spanish	8.3	4.9	3.8	83.0
Asian non-Hispanic	6.8	7.2	4.1	81.8
Other non-Hispanic	13.1	7.3	11.6	68.0
All males	6.7	3.8	4.1	85.5
White non-Hispanic	6.3	3.7	3.7	86.2
Black non-Hispanic	10.9	4.8	7.2	77.1
Mexican	6.5	2.4	3.6	87.5
Puerto Rican	8.1	2.8	4.5	84.6
Cuban	4.8	2.1	1.9	91.2
Other-Spanish	5.8	3.4	4.3	86.6
Asian non-Hispanic	4.7	5.8	5.5	84.0
Other non-Hispanic	9.5	5.1	9.1	76.3
Total population	8.7	4.6	3.9	82.9

SOURCE: U. S. Bureau of the Census, 1980 Census of Population, Vol. 1, *Characteristics of the Population,* Chapter C, General Social and Economic Characteristics, Part 1, U. S. Summary (Washington, DC: U. S. Government Printing Office, December 1983), Table 168, p. 165.

likely. Cubans are the most underrepresented Hispanic group at all levels of government; indeed, their rates of employment at the state and federal level are lower than any of the groups we analyzed, and at the local level, only Asians have a lower rate.

Sectoral Distribution of Earnings

Why is access to public-sector jobs important to Hispanics? One reason is that these jobs yield above-average incomes. For example, focusing just on the local level, if we divide jobs into three categories by level of pay for a full year of work, the middle third of jobs would pay between $13,000 and $26,000 in 1982 (i.e., $15,000–$30,000 in 1987 dollars). As shown in Table 2, for every gender/ethnic group, local government jobs were more likely than other jobs to carry a salary above $13,000 in 1982. The income discrepancy between sectors is especially large for Mexican and Other-Spanish men and for Cuban, Other-

Table 2. Income Bracket and Local Government Employment (Full-Time, Full-Year, Wage and Salary Workers)

	Mexicans	Puerto Ricans	Cubans	Other-Spanish	Non-Hispanic blacks	Asians, Other non-Hispanics	Non-Hispanic whites
Males							
% in local government sector							
Of total group	8.8	10.2	3.1	6.1	12.9	4.9	8.6
Of lower income[a]	6.8	8.9	2.6	4.0	12.1	4.3	7.2
Of middle income[b]	10.7	9.2	2.8	8.4	14.4	5.6	10.7
Of upper income[c]	9.0	19.3	5.5	4.4	9.5	4.4	6.5
% lower income[a]							
Of total group	41.5	37.4	44.2	32.8	37.9	18.8	16.2
Of local government workers	31.9	32.6	37.6	21.5	35.5	16.2	13.7
% middle income[b]							
Of total group	43.3	51.9	42.4	45.9	48.9	48.2	46.3
Of local government workers	52.5	47.0	38.8	63.1	54.8	54.5	57.7
% upper income[c]							
Of total group	15.2	10.7	13.4	21.3	13.2	33.0	37.4
Of local government workers	15.6	20.4	23.6	15.5	9.7	29.3	28.6

Females

% in local government sector							
Of total group	13.7	6.9	3.6	10.0	16.5	6.8	12.7
Of lower income[a]	13.3	6.7	2.0	5.7	13.9	4.7	8.5
Of middle income[b]	14.6	7.7	5.6	15.9	20.5	9.0	16.2
Of upper income[c]	13.7	0.0	22.9	15.4	11.0	6.1	17.1
% lower income[a]							
Of total group	66.4	55.4	71.0	57.2	54.9	45.2	46.0
Of local government workers	64.5	54.1	39.8	32.3	46.5	31.2	30.8
% middle income[b]							
Of total group	31.2	41.0	26.1	35.8	40.7	45.4	47.1
Of local government workers	33.1	45.9	41.2	56.9	50.6	60.3	59.9
% upper income[c]							
Of total group	2.4	3.6	3.0	7.0	4.4	9.4	6.9
Of local government workers	2.4	0.0	19.1	10.8	2.9	8.5	9.3

[a] Annual wage and salary income = $1–$12,999 in 1982.
[b] Annual wage and salary income = $13,000–$25,999 in 1982.
[c] Annual wage and salary income = $26,000+ in 1982.
SOURCE: March 1983 CPS Annual Demographic Microdata File, authors' tabulations (using population weights). *Full-time* = 35+ hours/week; *full-year* = 50+ weeks.

Spanish, Asian, and white women. For example, in 1982, only 29% of Cuban women who worked full time earned over $13,000, but 60% of those who worked for local governments did so.

Jobholders were more likely to earn over $26,000 in 1982 ($30,000 in 1987 dollars) in the local public sector than elsewhere if they were Puerto Rican or Cuban men, or Cuban, Other-Spanish, or white women. For instance, only 3% of Cuban women, and 10% of Puerto Rican men, who worked full time earned over $26,000 in 1982, but 20% of those who worked for a municipal government earned that much. For white and Other-Spanish men, and Asians and blacks of both sexes, these high-salaried jobs are more likely to be outside the local public sector.

With a couple of notable exceptions (Mexicans and Puerto Ricans), women have more to gain from access to local government jobs, in terms of higher rates of pay, than men of the same ethnic group. They are also more likely than men of the same group to work in local government. However, Cubans are much less likely than other groups to work in local government, even though their salaries tend to be higher in that sector than elsewhere.

In this chapter, we report on part of a larger project whose goal is to explain access to government employment by Hispanics. In the next section, we outline four hypotheses: the first emphasizing human capital considerations; the second, redistributive goals of public managers; the third, private-sector discrimination; and the fourth, individual preferences, that could account for variations in public employment across gender/ethnic groups. In the third section, we describe the cross-sectional data set that we constructed to analyze the reasons for the observed intergroup differences. As a preliminary investigation that focuses on the local level, we then present some simple adjustments of percentages that are employed in local government, controlling for education, occupation, nativity, citizenship, and English. Next, we extend the analysis to a multivariate model and to all levels of government. We present estimates of a multinomial logit model of employment sector that tests for the effect of human capital, citizenship, and location and that distinguishes among four sectors: local, state, and federal government and the private sector. We then summarize our conclusions in the final section.

HYPOTHESES TO EXPLAIN VARIATIONS IN PUBLIC-SECTOR EMPLOYMENT

Human Capital

Four hypotheses (not necessarily mutually exclusive) may be advanced to explain differential access to public-sector jobs. The first two emphasize the demand side of the public-sector labor market, while the last two emphasize differences in supply. On the demand side, the first hypothesis is in the human capital tradition. All employers, including those in the public sector, are assumed to value certain productivity-related characteristics, and make hiring and promotion decisions accordingly. Insofar as public-sector outputs differ from those of private-sector firms, they require a different skill mix of labor inputs. If the groups themselves differ on average with respect to these characteristics, we would expect differential hiring patterns to emerge. For example, both Blank (1985) and Smith (1977) found a more educated work force in the public sector. We would therefore expect groups with higher educational attainment to be more likely to be employed by government.

A natural way to test this "human capital" hypothesis is to control for personal characteristics of all employees. Since the average educational level of minorities is below that of whites, we would not expect human capital to explain the higher rate of public employment for blacks, though it could help explain the lower rate for Hispanics. Unless other characteristics outweigh the effect of education, we would expect the residual difference between minorities and whites to be larger (i.e., more positive), but that between blacks and Hispanics to be smaller, than the raw difference.

Redistributional Goals of Public Managers

In the second and third hypotheses, we assume that public- and private-sector managers pursue different objectives or face different constraints. In the second hypothesis, which is the more common view in the literature, we assume that public managers face an excess supply of labor because they set a common civil service wage for a given level of human capital, which is above the private market wage for all groups. Thus, observed differences in employment rates across groups reflect the demand of public employers. Among the goals of government are redistribution of resources, promotion of equality of opportunity, and conflict resolution. Redistribution may be implemented not only through taxation, transfer payments, and service provision, but also through choices of whom to hire and from whom to purchase nonlabor inputs. Moreover, government managers, being more bound by civil service rules and affirmative-action goals, may be less likely to practice discrimination than would private-sector employers.

If redistribution through input choices is one of the goals pursued by public-sector managers, then factors that affect the government's budget constraint and/or its political and administrative structure may also influence the hiring of minorities. This model would predict variations in public employment of minorities and women which depend primarily on the characteristics of governments rather than on individual differences; and if this model were correct, we would expect variations across governmental units to be at least as important as individual differences in explaining employment patterns.

Group Differences in Labor Supply to the Public Sector

The third hypothesis is an alternative to this demand-driven "government preferences" model. Different groups may have different degrees of access to the private sector, resulting in differences in their average supply price to the public sector. In contrast to private employers, who discriminate against certain groups, public employers are indifferent among groups. However, when they set a common wage (as they must under civil service rules), they passively attract a mix of groups that is weighted toward those who have least access to the private sector. In this "private-sector discrimination" model, differences in the degree of private-sector discrimination would show up as differential probabilities of public-sector employment across groups. Characteristics of the government itself would bear little or no relation to the sectoral distribution of minorities and women.

The fourth hypothesis also stresses differences across groups in the supply of labor to the public sector. However, in this model, supply differs, not because of private-sector discrimination, but because groups differ in their average preferences for particular job characteristics, which, in turn, differ by sector. Without observable data on individual preferences, we cannot investigate this possibility.

To summarize these four hypotheses, in the human capital model, discrimination—either in the private sector against minorities or in the public sector in their favor—has no role. In the government preferences model, there is a common supply price across all groups. Political and financial characteristics of the government, by affecting public managers' preferences, determine employment choices. In the private-sector discrimination model, the supply price differs across groups, and government characteristics do not matter. Rather, differences across labor markets in the degree of private-sector discrimination would be significant.

TESTING THE HUMAN CAPITAL HYPOTHESIS

Observable personal characteristics from the 1980 census permit a direct test of the first hypothesis, the human capital model. Although this approach has been used before in the study of government employment (Blank, 1985; Bloch & Smith, 1977), the innovative feature of our research is its focus on distinctions among Hispanic groups and its use of a data set that is larger and more recent, as well as more suitable for the analysis of Hispanics.

The Data Base

The data come from the 1980 U. S. Census of Population Public Use Microdata Sample A (PUMS A Sample). For each gender/ethnic group (male and female Mexicans, Puerto Ricans, Cubans, Other-Spanish, and white, black, Asian, and Other non-Hispanics), we drew random samples of the entire population of employed civilians in the United States aged 16 or over. For the preliminary standardizations, we used everyone aged 18 to 64 in these national random samples. The resulting sample sizes (listed at the bottom of Table 3) range from 4,259 for Puerto Rican women to 20,785 for Asian men.

We estimated the multinomial logit model on a pooled national sample of all gender and ethnic groups. For each of the eight ethnic groups listed above, we selected a random sample of approximately 250 male and 250 female employed civilians from the entire population, with the total sample size being 3,927 persons. We constructed variables (defined in Table 4) measuring sector of employment (local, state, or federal government, or private), age, education, veteran status, disability, nativity, citizenship, English fluency, occupation, location of residence, gender, and ethnicity.

Standardizations for Education, Occupation, Citizenship, and English

Method

First, we investigated the roles played by education, occupation, citizenship, and English in the observed intergroup differences in local-government employment. Groups like Hispanics that are less educated have a lower chance of holding public-sector jobs (Blank, 1985; Bloch & Smith, 1977). These jobs tend to be more highly skilled white-collar and professional positions that require more education than the average job. Citizenship has a direct effect in that some public employees are required to be citizens. Consumers of public services presumably prefer public employees who are fluent in English to those who are not, even though they may desire bilingual public servants in jurisdictions with many residents who speak another language.

To find out how much difference each of these factors made by itself, from the national random samples we calculated for each gender/ethnic group the minority/white ratio of percentages of employed civilians who were in local government. These percentages are standardized, in turn, for level of education, occupation, citizenship, and English. The standardized ratios are then compared with the unadjusted minority/white ratio of percentages employed in local government.

To standardize for education we distinguished four levels of schooling: high school dropout, high school graduate, some college, and college graduate. Another standardization was performed with 16 occupational categories: management, engineers and scientists, health professionals, teachers, librarians, social workers, lawyers, artists, technicians, sales, administrative support, protective service, other service, farm, crafts, and operatives and laborers combined. We subdivided professional and service workers to separate the occupations that are concentrated in the public sector from the others. We also compared the rates of local public-sector employment across gender/ethnic groups for noncitizens with English deficiencies, and for native-born citizens who spoke English only or very well.

When performing any standardization, one has to confront the question of which group's composition to use as weights. To deal with this "index number" problem, we calculated Fisher's ideal index (Kitagawa, 1964), which is the geometric mean of the two indexes, one using the weights of the minority and the other using the weights of the white non-Hispanics. Fisher's ideal index is attractive because it decomposes the unadjusted ratio into two component indexes, one reflecting group differences in sector of employment within a demographic category (i.e., education level or occupation), and one reflecting differences in educational attainment (or occupation) across groups.

Results

We see in Table 3 that the percentage in local government rises monotonically with education (except for Other non-Hispanic and white men), and is much higher for college graduates than for others. The local public sector accounts for over 20% of the jobs held by college-graduate Hispanic women, regardless of group, and by Mexican men. It accounts for fully 37% of the jobs held by college-graduate Mexican women, a figure nearly as high as the 40% for black women.

Not surprisingly, teaching and the protective services stand out as local public-sector occupations; and craft workers, operatives, and laborers are much less likely than average to work in the local public sector. For most gender/ethnic groups non-protective service workers, health professionals, and clerical workers have above-average percentages employed by local governments. (In the latter two occupations, this is true for women in more ethnic groups than for men.) Among males of most ethnic groups, managers also have an above-average chance of working in local government. The reverse is true for women, however; those in management are less likely than the average woman to work in local government.

We also see that nativity, citizenship, and English together have an enormous impact on access to municipal-government jobs within every gender/ethnic group. Since Hispanics have less education than blacks and are less likely to be fluent in English and (apart from Puerto Ricans) are also less likely to be citizens, these differences may help explain the difference in their access to job opportunities in local government.

The bottom panel of Table 3 shows the unadjusted minority/white ratio of

Table 3. Percentage Employed in Local Government, by Education, Occupation, Nativity, Citizenship, English, and Veteran Status: National Samples of Employed Civilians Aged 18–64

Males

	Mexicans	Puerto Ricans	Cubans	Other-Spanish	Non-Hispanic blacks	Non-Hispanic Asians	Other non-Hispanics	Non-Hispanic whites
Sample size	9,248	6,462	5,488	8,327	5,350	20,785	7,675	11,042
Percentage in local government of total	6.4	8.4	4.7	6.3	11.0	4.6	9.4	5.9
Of ED = 0–12	4.4	6.7	3.0	4.6	9.4	2.5	10.0	5.1
Of ED = 12	6.2	8.0	4.2	5.1	9.5	3.6	7.5	4.5
Of ED = 13–15	8.4	11.4	4.1	6.7	11.0	5.1	9.5	5.2
Of ED = 16+	21.3	17.8	9.4	12.1	23.1	5.7	12.7	9.7
Of managers	9.5	6.0	2.9	6.7	15.5	4.2	11.4	5.9
Of health professionals	9.1	12.5	7.9	6.7	4.2	4.4	7.3	2.3
Of teachers	58.9	54.9	49.5	49.0	56.6	21.9	36.5	46.9
Of clericals	7.0	8.0	4.9	5.0	9.4	6.1	8.8	3.4
Of protective service	46.5	46.4	40.3	49.2	37.3	40.1	41.6	53.3
Of nonprotective service	9.9	13.0	8.3	6.6	15.8	3.5	15.9	10.9
Of crafts	3.4	4.1	2.4	2.4	6.0	2.7	5.1	2.5
Of operators/laborers	4.0	4.7	2.7	4.1	7.6	2.2	6.6	3.2
Of foreign-born non-citizens with poor English	1.3	1.9	3.1	2.1	5.6	2.3	3.2	2.4
Of U. S.-born citizens with good English	8.5	9.3	8.4	9.5	11.1	7.1	9.3	6.0

(continued)

Table 3. (*Continued*)

	Mexicans	Puerto Ricans	Cubans	Other-Spanish	Non-Hispanic blacks	Non-Hispanic Asians	Other non-Hispanics	Non-Hispanic whites
Minority/white ratio								
Unadjusted	1.08	1.42	0.80	1.06	1.85	0.78	1.58	1
Standardized for education[a]	1.41	1.70	0.84	1.14	2.11	0.69	1.66	1
Standardized for occupation[a]	1.25	1.32	0.87	1.08	1.70	0.76	1.45	1
U. S.-born citizens with good English only	1.42	1.55	1.40	1.58	1.85	1.18	1.55	1
				Females				
Sample size	5,604	4,259	4,373	6,611	5,455	18,242	5,771	7,978
Percentage in local government of total	11.4	11.3	7.0	8.5	15.8	6.6	13.3	11.1
Of ED = 0–12	6.9	7.2	3.3	5.1	9.6	2.6	11.6	5.2
Of ED = 12	11.5	9.8	4.4	7.6	12.8	4.5	12.0	7.2
Of ED = 13–15	16.1	14.7	6.2	8.5	16.3	6.2	12.9	8.0
Of ED = 16+	37.3	29.1	20.7	21.9	40.5	11.3	25.0	30.4
Of managers	11.3	9.1	5.6	6.3	13.8	5.8	11.8	5.6
Of health professionals	19.6	10.8	6.7	10.9	21.1	9.5	14.4	13.2

Of teachers	64.3	60.3	58.5	55.1	65.2	39.9	45.9	57.7
Of clericals	15.5	12.8	5.7	9.4	16.7	7.0	13.8	7.9
Of protective service	35.3	61.9	45.5	37.9	48.5	16.7	34.1	47.5
Of nonprotective service	13.6	14.6	8.5	9.0	12.7	4.8	14.3	10.7
Of crafts	2.5	1.9	1.0	0.4	4.0	1.2	4.1	1.6
Of operators/laborers	1.7	1.6	0.8	2.0	3.0	0.7	5.0	1.9
Of foreign-born non-citizens with poor English	2.6	2.6	3.7	2.4	15.4	3.3	3.0	7.1
Of U.S.-born citizens with good English	13.7	12.7	8.1	12.5	15.9	9.2	13.6	11.3
Minority/white ratio								
Unadjusted	1.02	1.02	0.63	0.76	1.42	0.60	1.20	1
Standardized for education[a]	1.48	1.28	0.67	0.90	1.63	0.49	1.38	1
Standardized for occupation[a]	1.40	1.28	0.87	0.98	1.45	0.71	1.25	1
U.S.-born citizens with good English only	1.21	1.12	0.72	1.11	1.41	0.81	1.20	1

[a]Fisher's ideal index of local government employment: $[(\Sigma_i w_i p_i / \Sigma_i w_i p_i')(\Sigma_i w_i' p_i / \Sigma_i w_i' p_i')]^{1/2}$, where w_i (w_i') is the fraction of minority group members (white non-Hispanics) in category i, and p_i (p_i') is the minority's (white non-Hispanics') percentage in local government within category i.

SOURCE: 1980 Census, Public Use Microdata Sample A, authors' calculations.

percentages in the local public sector, the ratios (i.e., Fisher's ideal indexes) when we standardize for education and occupation, and the ratios when we consider only native-born citizens with fluent English. Controlling for education dramatically increases the local public-sector percentage for Mexicans and Puerto Ricans relative to whites. It does the same for blacks, however, so that less than one quarter of the gap between blacks and Mexican men, or Puerto Ricans of either sex, is closed. On the other hand, two thirds of the gap between Mexican and black women is due to education differences alone. To draw these conclusions, we divided the unadjusted Hispanic/white ratio in Table 3 (e.g., 1.08 for Mexican men) by the unadjusted black/white ratio (e.g., 1.85 for men). We then compared the result with the result of performing this division for the standardized ratios (e.g., 1.41 and 2.11).

The common perception is that certain occupations (namely, those in human services) are primarily in the public sector and that college-educated minorities are more likely to go into the human service professions. However, it should be kept in mind that minorities are less likely to go to college. Putting these ideas together would imply that minorities are less likely to be in the local public sector than whites because they are less likely to have the requisite education for the "public-sector" professions. If so, controlling for occupation would tend to increase the minority/white ratio of percentages in the local public sector.

We find that controlling for occupation does have this effect for Mexican and Cuban men. However, it reduces the percentage of Puerto Rican and black men in the local public sector relative to whites. The result is that over half of the gap between black and Mexican men is closed, and about 15% of the gap between black and Cuban or Other-Spanish men, but the gap between black and Puerto Rican men remains unchanged. As expected, for women of all Hispanic groups, the standardization for occupation increases the percentage in the local public sector relative to whites, bringing Other-Spanish women up to par with white women. Since the black/white ratio is scarcely affected, changing only from 1.42 to 1.45, the Hispanic/black ratio is increased for every group. In fact, Mexican women are almost as likely to work in local government as are black women, once occupational differences are factored out.

For Cuban and Other-Spanish men and for Other-Spanish women, eliminating the noncitizens and those without good English makes more difference than controlling for education. When we consider only United States-born citizens with good English, all groups of Hispanic men are at least 40% more likely than white men, and apart from Cubans, Hispanic women are 10 to 20% more likely than white women, to work in local government. None of the standardizations performed brought Cuban women up to par with white women. Nativity, citizenship, and English account for 65% of the gap between black and Other-Spanish men, 58% for Cuban men, 45% for Mexican men, and 30% for Puerto Rican men. These three factors account for 54% of the gap between black and

Other-Spanish women, 50% for Mexican women, 25% for Puerto Rican women, and 12.5% for Cuban women.

These standardizations, which control for one factor at a time, show that sectoral distributions for Hispanics begin to look more like that of blacks when we take into account citizenship or human capital. In the next section we will extend this analysis to a multivariate model.

A Multivariate Model to Test the Human Capital Hypothesis

Multinomial Logit Specification

The standardizations reported in the previous section can account for just one factor at a time. To test the hypothesis that intergroup differences in sector of employment are due to differences in human capital, citizenship, location, and occupation, we estimated a multinomial logit model. The dependent variable is the probability of being employed in each of four sectors: local, state, federal, or private (including self-employed). The independent variables include those already examined (education, occupation, citizenship, and English fluency), plus age, veteran status, and location. Other research (Blank, 1985) has found that government employees tend to be older than the average; if so, a group such as Hispanics that is younger than the average would have a lower chance of holding public-sector jobs. Moreover, Hispanics often lack the advantages that are conferred by veterans preference in the civil service because many of them immigrated as adults and so are less likely to have served in the armed forces.

We also included a number of dummy variables indicating location: center city, suburban, or rural (the omitted reference category), southern region of the country, and "large metropolitan area" for residents of New York, Chicago, Los Angeles, and Houston. Since the relative size of the public sector varies by location, and the groups show different regional concentrations and different degrees of urbanization, omitting these variables could bias the estimated coefficients on the group dummy variables. In this specification, we treated the occupation as predetermined, and included a single occupation variable for teachers, librarians, and social workers—the public-sector human service professions.

We allowed for differences among groups by including dummy variables for gender, race, and detailed Spanish origin, with white males being the reference group. This specification restricts the slope coefficients to be the same across groups. Any group differences among persons with otherwise similar personal characteristics will show up as shifts of the intercept (i.e., as differences in the group dummy variables). A significant coefficient on any of these group dummy variables indicates that the group is more (or less) likely to be employed in a branch of the public sector than whites with similar personal characteristics.

Thus, estimation of such a pooled sample has the advantage of summarizing group differences with a single, easy-to-interpret measure.

Results

The definitions of the variables in the model we have estimated are in Table 4 and the means are in Table 5. Coefficient estimates are reported in Table 6. The coefficients show the effects of the variables on the log odds of being in the given sector versus the private sector. The slopes have a more intuitive interpretation; they give the impact of a one-unit change in the variable on the probability of being in the given sector, evaluated at the means of the independent variables.

Of our human capital variables, we found that, as expected, education was highly significant and positive for all three public sectors. Veteran status mattered at the state level, but not elsewhere. However, contrary to Blank's (1985) findings, age was not significant (except for state government at the 10% significance level). The difference between the two results may reflect our smaller sample size, which reduced the precision of our coefficient estimates, or differences in the specific control variables included in our model and hers.

Table 4. Definitions of Variables

AGE	= age in years.
ED	= highest grade completed.
VET	= 1 if veteran; 0 otherwise.
DISABLED	= 1 if work or public transportation disability; 0 otherwise.
RCITIZEN	= 1 if citizen; 0 otherwise.
ENGHOME	= 1 if speaks only English at home; 0 otherwise.
RENGLISH	= 1 if speaks English only or very well; 0 otherwise.
CENTCITY	= 1 if resident of center city; 0 otherwise.
SUBURB	= 1 if resident of suburb; 0 otherwise.
SOUTH	= 1 if resident of South region; 0 otherwise.
LGSMSA	= 1 if resident of New York, Los Angeles, Chicago, or Houston SMSA; 0 otherwise.
HUMSRV	= 1 if teacher, librarian, or social worker occupation; 0 otherwise.
FEMALE	= 1 if female; 0 otherwise.
WHITENH	= 1 if white non-Hispanic; 0 otherwise (reference group).
BLACKNH	= 1 if black non-Hispanic; 0 otherwise.
ASIAN	= 1 if Asian non-Hispanic; 0 otherwise.
OTHERNH	= 1 if other non-Hispanic; 0 otherwise.
MEXICAN	= 1 if Mexican origin; 0 otherwise.
PRICAN	= 1 if Puerto Rican origin; 0 otherwise.
CUBAN	= 1 if Cuban origin; 0 otherwise.
OTHSPAN	= 1 if Other-Spanish origin; 0 otherwise.

Table 5. Means of Variables in Pooled
National Sample of Employed Civilians

Variable	Mean
Employed in local government	0.087
Employed in state government	0.047
Employed in federal government	0.050
Employed in private sector (reference category)	0.815
AGE	36.1
ED	11.8
VET	0.131
RCITIZEN	0.812
ENGHOME	0.455
CENTCITY	0.375
SUBURB	0.453
SOUTH	0.315
LGSMSA	0.248
HUMSRV	0.051
FEMALE	0.504
WHITENH	0.125
BLACKNH	0.125
ASIAN	0.131
OTHERNH	0.119
MEXICAN	0.125
PRICAN	0.131
CUBAN	0.127
OTHSPAN	0.117

In any case, our results suggest that the younger average age of Hispanics was not a major factor in explaining their underrepresentation in government employment.

Citizenship was positive and significant at the 5% level for local and state government, and at the 10% level for federal government. The language variable had no effect at the local and federal level, whereas those who spoke another language at home were actually more likely to work in state government. This variable was defined quite stringently—that only English could be spoken in the home. In effect, this became a measure of the ethnicity of the household as well as proof of the command of English; since even a second generation immigrant with perfectly fluent English, but living with parents from abroad, would be coded zero under our criteria (as would a native English-speaker with a foreign-born spouse). This definitional problem may help to explain the insignificance of the language variable at the local and federal level. At present, we have no explanation for its unexpected sign at the state level.

Table 6. Estimates of Multinomial Logit Model of
Sector of Employment in Pooled National Sample of
Employed Civilians, 1980 Census

Sample size: 3,927 (stratified by gender and ethnicity)

Variable	Coefficient	Standard error	Slope[a]
Sector: Local government			
INTERCEPT	−4.454	0.461	−0.2641**
AGE	0.006	0.005	0.0004
ED	0.056	0.020	0.0031**
VET	0.127	0.206	0.0064
RCITIZEN	0.706	0.237	0.0425**
ENGHOME	−0.084	0.179	−0.0038
CENTCITY	−0.061	0.188	−0.0015
SUBURB	−0.443	0.173	−0.0273**
SOUTH	0.159	0.143	0.0106
FEMALE	0.351	0.136	0.0215**
BLACKNH	1.049	0.243	0.0637**
ASIAN	0.012	0.310	−0.0011
OTHERNH	0.634	0.254	0.0361**
MEXICAN	0.628	0.291	0.0409**
PRICAN	0.443	0.305	0.0274
CUBAN	−0.041	0.330	−0.0010
OTHSPAN	0.489	0.293	0.0296*
LGSMSA	−0.014	0.169	0.0011
HUMSRV	2.706	0.202	0.1698**
Sector: State government			
INTERCEPT	−5.848	0.641	−0.1810**
AGE	0.011	0.006	0.0003*
ED	0.115	0.025	0.0036**
VET	0.874	0.211	0.0295**
RCITIZEN	1.089	0.358	0.0347**
ENGHOME	−0.725	0.211	−0.0246**
CENTCITY	−0.356	0.233	−0.0112
SUBURB	−0.317	0.204	−0.0092
SOUTH	−0.034	0.180	−0.0015
FEMALE	0.321	0.177	0.0097*
BLACKNH	1.607	0.329	0.0515**
ASIAN	0.130	0.406	0.0036
OTHERNH	1.480	0.320	0.0479**
MEXICAN	−0.253	0.460	−0.0107
PRICAN	0.772	0.391	0.0253**
CUBAN	−0.821	0.517	−0.0280
OTHSPAN	0.659	0.383	0.0208*
LGSMSA	−0.422	0.229	−0.0139*
HUMSRV	0.895	0.340	0.0208**

Table 6 (*Continued*)

Variable	Coefficient	Standard error	Slope[a]
	Sector: Federal government		
INTERCEPT	−5.185	0.570	−0.1726**
AGE	0.006	0.006	0.0002
ED	0.121	0.026	0.0042**
VET	−0.062	0.269	−0.0038
RCITIZEN	0.450	0.270	0.0133*
ENGHOME	0.045	0.217	0.0029
CENTCITY	−0.579	0.244	−0.0209**
SUBURB	−0.363	0.204	−0.0118*
SOUTH	−0.042	0.183	−0.0020
FEMALE	0.284	0.172	0.0092*
BLACKNH	0.451	0.317	0.0117
ASIAN	0.576	0.323	0.0212*
OTHERNH	0.673	0.287	0.0212**
MEXICAN	0.396	0.360	0.0133
PRICAN	−0.059	0.417	−0.0045
CUBAN	0.123	0.380	0.0058
OTHSPAN	0.320	0.353	0.0096
LGSMSA	−0.356	0.242	−0.0126
HUMSRV	2.136	0.249	0.0708**

[a]Impact of a one-unit change in the variable on the probability of being in the given sector, evaluated at the means of the independent variables.
**Significant at the .05 level; *significant at the .10 level.

The locational variables showed several interesting results. At the local level, we were surprised to find that center city residents were no more likely than non-metropolitan area residents to work for local government. By contrast, suburbanites were significantly less likely than center city or non-metropolitan residents to be in the local public sector. Evaluated at the mean, a suburbanite was almost three percentage points less likely than his or her center city counterpart to work for local government. This result may reflect the U-shaped cost curve for many local public services, with the minimum cost and therefore minimum employment at about 10,000 service recipients (Hirsch, 1984, pp. 271–274). It could also be that people with higher-paying private-sector jobs in the city are more likely to move to the suburbs and become commuters, thus increasing the private-sector percentage among those living in the suburbs.

By contrast, the likelihood of being employed by the federal government is lowest for center city dwellers and highest for non-metropolitan area residents. This may reflect the rural location of federal facilities that directly produce services: military installations, nuclear weapons plants, Department of Agriculture, Bureau of Reclamation, Indian Affairs, etc. Federal regional offices in big cities are grant-administering and regulatory rather than service providers and thus may have lower levels of employment relative to budget.

Examining the occupation variable, we find that members of the female-dominated human service professions (i.e., teachers, social workers, librarians) are, as expected, far more likely to work in the public than in the private sector. The female-male differential in local government is narrowed to 2.1 percentage points when we control for human capital, citizenship, location, and occupation. Even within occupation group (human services vs. all others), women are at least 25% more likely than males with similar characteristics to work in government. This differential access may reflect the fact that women are more likely than men to be in such occupations as teaching that are primarily employed in the public sector. It may also reflect less discrimination in the public sector, a preference by women for public-sector employment, or probably, a combination of all three.

We began with the observation that women and blacks were much more likely to be employed in government than were other groups, whereas Hispanics as a whole were about the same as whites (therefore less likely than blacks). These raw figures would suggest that the public sector was not playing its traditional role as a source of opportunity for the Hispanic minority. However, when we controlled for personal characteristics, location, and occupation, we found that the Hispanic groups' likelihoods of being employed by local government were raised relative to those of whites and blacks. Mexican Americans were 4 percentage points more likely than white non-Hispanics with similar characteristics to be employed by local government. The differential is 3 percentage points for Other-Spanish, 2.7 points for Puerto Ricans, and 0 for Cubans. Although the black-white differential was widened from 4.9 to 6.4 percentage points, most Hispanic-white differentials increased by even more than 1.5 points. Thus, with the exception of Puerto Ricans, the black-Hispanic differentials in local government employment, though still present, were narrower when we controlled for certain personal characteristics (education, age, veteran status, citizenship, English, location, and gender) than in the unadjusted rates. This finding suggests that local government was continuing to play its traditional role but, as of 1980, had not yet assumed the same importance for Hispanics as for blacks.

At the state-government level, Puerto Ricans and Other-Spanish were, respectively, 2.5 and 2.1 percentage points more likely than were white non-Hispanics to be employed by state governments, once demographic characteristics were controlled for. This was the reverse of the "raw" probabilities, where these groups were less likely than whites to be in state government. The negative Mexican-white differential remained unchanged, but the Cubans lagged even further behind whites in state-government employment when we controlled for personal characteristics than when we did not. The female-male differential in state-government employment for otherwise-similar individuals was only 1 percentage point, whereas the unadjusted differential was well over 2 points. On the other hand, the black-white differential increased to 5 percentage points.

There were no significant differences in the likelihood of federal employment between Hispanics and whites with similar characteristics; the higher rate for Puerto Ricans and the lower rate for Cubans in the unadjusted data both disappeared. The four-point higher rate of federal employment for blacks almost disappeared, too, becoming only 1 point above that of whites. Whereas men and women differed little in their unadjusted likelihoods of working for the federal government, a difference of 1 percentage point in favor of women appeared when we controlled for human capital, location, and occupation.

Here, as in the case of age, our findings differ somewhat from those of Blank (1985), who found in her research no significant gender difference in federal versus private employment; whereas we found that women were more likely than men to be employed in the federal sector. The divergence in results between the two studies may again reflect differences in model specification, particularly the inclusion by Blank of a greater number of occupational categories. However, our finding that being female or being black was strongly associated with employment in the state and local sectors is similar to hers.

CONCLUSIONS

In summary, the differences in individual characteristics, such as education, citizenship, veteran status, location, and occupation, though they contribute to variations in public employment across groups, are unable to explain these patterns fully. Only for Cubans at the local level, for Mexicans at the state level, and for all Hispanics at the federal level did the "human capital" hypothesis explain the differences between Hispanics and whites that are revealed in Table 1. Women, blacks, and Native Americans were significantly more likely than were white males to be employed in the state and local public sector, both before and after controlling for personal characteristics.

Moreover, differentials appeared for Hispanics at the local and state levels that were obscured by group differences in personal characteristics. Since education and citizenship improved access to local- and state-government jobs, and veteran status increased access at the state level, the lower educational attainment of Hispanics and their smaller numbers of citizens and of veterans proved to be a handicap for them relative to whites and blacks in getting government jobs at both local and state levels. When individuals with similar characteristics were compared, we found that Mexicans, Puerto Ricans, and Other-Spanish were more likely than were whites, but less likely than blacks, to work in local government. The same held true for Puerto Ricans and Other-Spanish in state government.

No.

156

CORDELIA REIMERS and HOWARD CHERNICK

Thus, the human capital model tells only part of the story. It seems to explain the differences in likelihood of employment in the federal sector, but not at the state and local level. The model reveals that, were it not for the lower educational levels and citizenship status of Hispanics, all except Cubans would be more likely than whites, but still less likely than blacks, to work in local government.

Once these differences in personal characteristics are controlled for, what then explains the greater access of Hispanics than whites to the local public sector? We began by delineating three other hypotheses: government managers' preferences, private-sector discrimination, and individual preferences for job characteristics, in addition to human capital, to explain differences in rates of public-sector employment. In research reported elsewhere, we have investigated the role of local-government managers' goals (Reimers & Chernick, 1990). In our preliminary results, the government variables that were presumed to influence those goals did not tell a consistent story. The most important variable affecting the rate of local public employment was still education.

The differential rates among Hispanic groups, blacks, and whites are not adequately accounted for by the combination of human capital and government variables. A full explanation no doubt involves a combination of both the demand factors—human capital and managerial preference—and the supply factors—private-sector "push" and individual tastes.

ACKNOWLEDGMENTS

This research was supported by grants from the Committee for Public Policy Research on Contemporary Hispanic Issues of the Social Science Research Council/Inter-University Program for Latino Research and from the PSC-CUNY Research Award Program of the City University of New York. We thank Demetris Papaiacovou, Diego Velez, and especially Franco Pignataro for invaluable assistance in data collection and preparation. We also thank Sharon Smith and Harriett Romo for helpful comments.

REFERENCES

Abowd, J. M., & M. R. Killingsworth. (1985). Employment, wages, and earnings of Hispanics in the federal and nonfederal sectors: Methodological issues and their empirical consequences. In G. J. Borjas & M. Tienda, Eds., *Hispanics in the U. S. economy* (pp. 77–125). New York: Academic Press.
Blank, R. M. (1985). An analysis of workers' choice between employment in the public and private sectors. *Industrial and Labor Relations Review, 38*, 211–224.
Bloch, F. E., & S. P. Smith. (1977). Human capital and labor market employment. *Journal of Human Resources, 12*, 550–560.
Hirsch, W. Z. (1984). *Urban economics*. New York: Macmillan.

Kitagawa, E. M. (1964). Standardized comparisons in population research. *Demography, 1,* 296–315.

Reimers, C. (1985). A comparative analysis of the wages of Hispanics, blacks, and non-Hispanic whites. In G. J. Borjas & M. Tienda, Eds., *Hispanics in the U. S. economy* (pp. 27–75). New York: Academic Press.

Reimers, C., & H. Chernick. (1990). *Hispanic employment in municipal government: Factors facilitating and hindering access to jobs.* Working Paper No. 8, IUP/SSRC Committee for Public Policy Research on Contemporary Hispanic Issues, The Center for Mexican American Studies, The University of Texas at Austin.

Smith, S. P. (1977). *Equal pay in the public sector: Fact or fantasy.* Princeton: Industrial Relations Section, Princeton University.

U. S. Bureau of the Census. (December, 1983). *1980 census of population, Vol. 1: Characteristics of the population,* Chapter C: General social and economic characteristics, Part 1, U. S. Summary. Washington, DC: U. S. Government Printing Office.

8

Racial, Ethnic, and Gender Employment Segmentation in New York City Agencies

WALTER STAFFORD

INTRODUCTION

Despite the media's growing concern about Hispanic influence on the political process, very little has been written about their involvement in urban government (Mladenka, 1989). This omission has been especially noticeable for Puerto Ricans, whose association with big city government is one of the longest among Latino groups in the nation. Indeed, the Puerto Rican economic and political experience in the United States has largely been shaped by resource allocations in New York City. Given the lack of a viable entrepreneurial base and a continuing history of discrimination among private employers, the progress of a large segment of the Puerto Rican population has been influenced by local governmental decisions about resources for education, welfare, and jobs (Falcon, 1984; Rodriguez, 1989).

Sections of this chapter were published in *Employment Segmentation in New York City Agencies* (Community Service Society: New York, 1989).

WALTER STAFFORD • Urban Research Center, Robert F. Wagner Graduate School of Public Service, New York University, New York, New York 10003.

Hispanics in the Labor Force, edited by Edwin Melendez *et al.* Plenum Press, New York, 1991.

Because of the close interrelation of local governmental decision-making and economic opportunities, Puerto Rican researchers and activists have in recent years given closer attention to their access to city agencies (Institute for Puerto Rican Policy, 1990; Torres, 1988). Their emphasis on government is in keeping with traditional routes of social and economic mobility among most racial and ethnic groups. Although the extent of ethnic mobility through government is often overemphasized (Erie, 1985), there is little doubt that governmental employment has assisted the Irish, Jews, Italians, and blacks in achieving a middle-class base. Racial and ethnic groups have also utilized local government to build and protect their niches within the market.

The problem facing Puerto Ricans in New York city has been competition with the widest assortment of racial and ethnic groups in the nation in seeking resources, contracts, and jobs from city government. Although both Mayor Robert Wagner in 1964 and Mayor John Lindsay in 1973 issued reports on the racial and ethnic composition of New York City government in which they stressed the need for increasing the employment of Puerto Ricans, the number of Puerto Ricans in government has remained insignificant, largely because Edward Koch, who was mayor throughout the 1980s, refused to develop programs to increase their participation. By the end of the 1980s, New York City was the only major city in the nation without a public-sector affirmative-action or set-aside program. Largely as a consequence of Mayor Koch's adamant stance against affirmative-action programs, Puerto Ricans were one of the few groups in the city whose share of jobs under the mayor remained smaller than their share of the labor force. The only other group with a below-average government participation rate was Asian-Americans, who have followed the "middle-man" approach to economic integration and have not actively sought a base of jobs in local government.

In this chapter I examine Hispanic employment in New York City's mayoral work force. I argue that the traditional focus of researchers on access to government jobs is too narrow. It is not merely the access to governmental jobs that benefits racial and ethnic groups, but the types of agencies where these groups gain access. Borrowing on segmentation theories and concepts that focus on primary and secondary industries and jobs, and protected and unprotected markets (Beck, Horan, & Tolbert, 1980), I argue that the influence of groups in government is largely determined by the types of agencies in which groups gain dominance. Although the concepts of primary and secondary in the private and public sectors are not parallel, I have structured the sectors around the salaries of employees. The highest salaried agencies are those where decisions about development, the environment, and social control are made. The lower-paying agencies are usually involved with welfare and social problems. A basic source of funding for the lower-paying agencies often consists of federal grants in aid, which influence the administrative structure of the agencies and salaries.

I also contend that one of the political trade-offs that white ethnic groups in New York City made with blacks, and to a lesser degree Hispanics, was to provide them access to jobs in lower-paying agencies while retaining the base of jobs and influence in those providing higher salaries. Erie (1985) makes a similar point. He noted that in cities controlled by political machines such as Chicago, as well as reform cities like New York, blacks were channeled into federally funded social welfare agencies to minimize racial and ethnic conflict with traditional police and fire departments. Although the 1972 Civil Rights act mandated an end to employment discrimination in local government, Puerto Ricans and blacks in New York remained largely concentrated in a narrow group of low-paying agencies.

A contrasting view of New York City is provided by Waldinger (1987). Borrowing on Lieberson (1980), he argues that as whites decline in the labor queue, a vacancy chain emerges allowing nonwhites to move up the job ladder as replacements. This argument is interesting, but limiting. Indeed, Waldinger provided evidence of industries where whites maintain dominance despite their decline, such as the construction industry. Other studies have revealed that blacks and Hispanics were narrowly confined to a small array of positions in banking, insurance, social services, retail, and manufacturing, despite the decline of whites in the labor force (Stafford, 1985; Torres, 1988). More specifically, with respect to government, Waldinger argued that it became a stronghold of blacks in large part because it was a declining industry and held little importance to Hispanics and Asians. Since Waldinger did not focus on the racial and ethnic composition of agencies, or on the economic and political benefits to whites, his position is limited. Blacks never gained a stronghold in the public sector; rather, they gained access to a narrow group of agencies where they were employed in low-wage jobs. The concentration of blacks in these agencies started well before the decline of whites in the public sector, and they would remain the base of black hiring once the white decline began. As blacks consolidated a base in low-wage jobs, Puerto Ricans were also seeking entry. However, they enjoyed little political power, and they were effectively blocked by white unions and civil service procedures (Stafford, 1989).

Several areas of the public service remain important to whites, whether their numbers are growing or declining. Whites, as was evident in the reverse discrimination cases filed by white firefighters in cities during the 1980s, have been reluctant to allow black and Hispanic entrants into these sectors even in cities with black mayors, such as Birmingham, Alabama, or large black populations. Basically, the protected services (fire, police) have provided high wages to generations of white males with minimum education. The other agencies where whites have maintained a majority control are agencies that control the development process where billions of dollars are at stake in contracts from city governments. The historical exclusion of blacks from city contracts is well documented (Bloch, 1969; Higginbotham, 1978). Any discussion of government employment that ignores this political reality is fraught with difficulty.

To show the importance of agencies in the composition of racial and ethnic employment, four areas are analyzed in this chapter: changes in the level of employment of groups between 1975 and 1986; the access of groups to high wages; the access of groups to occupations, and their access to high wage agencies.

Methods and Data

This chapter builds on a prior study of New York city government (Stafford, 1985). The principal sources of data on city employment consisted of summaries of the work forces of 66 city agencies compiled by the City Commission on Human Rights. Work force summaries of these agencies are submitted annually to the Equal Employment Opportunity Commission in Washington, DC, as required by the 1972 Civil Rights Act.

The city work force data are analyzed by occupation, race, ethnicity, and sex for the years of 1975 to 1986. Six groups were studied with regard to changes in employment, as well as occupational and agency segmentation: black males, black females, Hispanic males, Hispanic females, white males, and white females. The occupational categories include officials/administrators, professionals, clerical workers, technicians, protective service workers, paraprofessionals, skilled craft workers, and service/maintenance workers. Salary and occupational data for the population groups are analyzed by agencies for 1981 and 1986.

The following procedures were used to measure changes among groups:

1. To uncover changes in employment patterns between 1975 and 1986, the city work force data were computerized, and programs were run to show the annual percentage share of each group in the eight occupational categories listed above, as well as the net changes. Percentage share and net changes were also compared for 1975 and 1986. Each group's share of the city jobs was compared with its share of the total work force.
2. The representation and distribution of each group by occupation was calculated for 1981 and 1986. The group's share of an occupational category and salary interval were compared with its 1980 labor force share. In 1980, whites made up 65% of the labor force, blacks made up 23%, Latinos comprised 17%, and Asians were 4%.
3. Agencies were ranked for each group's representation in the seven occupational categories. The ten leading agencies in each occupational

category were used as the index for discussion of differences among groups.

The following procedures were used to assess agency segmentation. First, each of the 66 agencies was classified as a high-, middle,- or low-wage agency.[1] In 1986, 17% of the employees in the 66 agencies earned $43,000 or more. We shifted the interval to 20% and determined that all those agencies in which 20% or more of the workers earned $43,000 and above would be considered high-wage agencies. Fifty-six (56) percent of all city employees in 1986 earned between $25,000 and $42,999; agencies in which 56% of the employees earned salaries between these amounts were classified as middle-wage agencies. Twenty-nine (29) percent of the employees earned $25,000 or less in 1986. Agencies in which 29% or more of the work force earned less than $25,000 were considered low-wage agencies. Second, the racial, ethnic, and gender representation and distribution were calculated for each agency by salary classifications. Third, the representation and distribution of high- and low-wage employees in high- and low-wage agencies were calculated by race, ethnicity, and sex. Fourth, the racial and ethnic share of each of the agencies by high-, middle-, and low-wage status was compared with their share of the total New York City labor force.

Three measures of segmentation are used in the findings:

1. The proportion of the total employment of each group in an agency was calculated to determine its concentration. The higher the proportion of a group in an agency or occupation, the greater the segmentation. A group can be highly concentrated in a small number of agencies and yet be highly diversified occupationally within these categories. For example, the findings show that white males are narrowly employed as a group in a few agencies. However, they have access to the top official and administrative positions in all agencies.

2. A group's share and the proportion of the group employed in high-, middle-, and low-wage agencies is the second measure discussed in the findings. This measure is used to determine whether the concentration of a group is related to the proportion of employees in one of the three salary intervals. It is also used to determine if groups are over- or underrepresented in agencies that provide access to high, middle, or low salaries.

3. The third procedure is to compare a group's share within agencies with their share of the New York City labor force. This procedure shows under- and overrepresentation.

[1]This classification is not always exact, since some agencies contain large proportions of high- *and* low-wage workers. Notable among these are: the Law Department, Department of General Services, Office of the Mayor, and the Fire Department.

FINDINGS

The statistical analysis that follows supports the findings of earlier studies on the changes in racial and ethnic employment in local government following passage of the 1972 Civil Rights Act (Moss, 1988). The data show that despite numerical gains by African-Americans and Latinos in city government since 1975, these groups remained concentrated in a narrow array of agencies. These agencies typically employed a high proportion of the low-wage workers in city government. The lack of access among African-Americans and Latinos to agencies with a high proportion of high-wage jobs was a major reason for the inequality in salary structure of both groups in comparison to that of whites.

An analysis of employment trends in New York City government shows that between 1975 and 1986, the city work force increased by 0.5%, from 134,856 to 135,583. The increase was not an even progression, however; rather, there were three periods of growth (1978–1979, 1980–1982, and 1983–1986) and three periods of decline (1975–1977, 1979–1980, and 1982–1983).

The major shift in job structure occurred with the decline of clerical and service/maintenance employment and the rise of officials and administrators. In 1975, clerical workers accounted for 22% of the employment; service/ maintenance, 17%; and officials and administrators, 3%. By 1986, officials and administrators had increased to almost 9% of the total work force, while clerical and maintenance jobs declined to 17% and 13%, respectively. Other shifts in the share of the work force occurred among skilled craft workers, who increased from 2% to 4%; technicians, from 7% to 8%; and paraprofessionals, from 2% to about 4%. Like clerical and service/maintenance workers, the proportion of professional workers declined from 1975 to 1986.

Between 1975 and 1986, the representation of African-Americans and Hispanics in city government increased significantly. In 1975, African-Americans represented nearly one quarter (24.5%) of that work force. By 1980, they had increased their share to about 29%, and by 1986 to 32.5%. This was significantly higher than the proportion of African-Americans in the total city labor force, which was 23% in 1980 (Table 2).

Unlike African-Americans, the proportion of whites, Latinos, and Asian workers in the city government work force fell below their proportion of the total city labor force (Table 2). The share of Latinos in city government increased significantly from 5% to nearly 10%. Even with this increase, they remained below their proportion of the city's total civilian labor force, which was 16% in 1980.

The only group that declined in its share of city government jobs was whites. In 1986, white workers represented 56% of the work force, down from a high of nearly 70% (69.6%) in 1975.

Changes in the Employment of Latino Men

The share of government jobs held by Latino men increased from 3% to 6% between 1975 and 1986 (Table 1). Their share of government jobs in 1986 was about four points lower than their proportion of the total city labor force.

During the fiscal crisis of 1975–1976, Latino men lost jobs in every occupational category. Newly won jobs in the protective services were especially vulnerable. These job losses continued throughout the 1970s, despite small gains (72 jobs) during the 1976–1977 period.

In the 1980s, Latino men began to recapture the protective service jobs they lost in the 1970s. However, there were few significant gains in any other occupational category. This observation is illuminated in the calculations on net changes: from 1975 to 1986, 58% of the occupational gains by Latino men occurred in the protective services. This was the largest gain in a single occupation by any male group.

Changes in the Employment of Latino Women

The share of Latino females in the city government workforce remains below their share of the total city labor force. As shown in Table 1, in 1975 they

Table 1. Percentage of Distribution of Employment in
New York City Government

Race/ethnicity and sex[a]	1975	1980	1986
Total employment[b]	134,856	111,622	135,583
All males	73.7	72.2	68.5
All females	26.3	27.8	31.5
Hispanic workers	5.1	6.4	9.5
Males	3.4	4.3	6.1
Females	1.7	2.0	3.4
Black workers	24.5	28.8	32.5
Males	10.9	12.8	14.0
Females	13.7	16.0	18.5
White workers	69.6	63.9	56.4
Males	58.9	54.3	47.2
Females	10.7	9.6	9.1

[a]These are mutually exclusive categories.
[b]Total employment includes only full-time workers.
SOURCE: New York City Commission on Human Rights.

were about 2% of the city government workforce. By 1986 they accounted for 3.4%—less than half of their 7% share of the labor force. Even with a small number of employees, Latino women suffered major declines during the 1970s. In 1975–1976 they had a net loss of 474 jobs. Nearly 70% of that decline occurred in office/clerical and professional jobs. In the late 1970s, there were small increases in the number of women employed in government agencies, mostly in clerical positions. However, the gains in clerical jobs were not able to offset the losses suffered during the fiscal crisis.

In the early 1980s, Latino females regained some of their losses in office/clerical jobs. Between 1982 and 1983, of the 187 jobs gains, more than half (54%) were office/clerical jobs. During the growth period of 1983–1986, the majority of Latino women's employment gains were in protective services and office/clerical occupations.

Changes in the Employment of Black Men

In 1975, African-American men constituted 10.9% of city government workers. By 1986, they represented 14% (Table 1), about 3% higher than their labor force representation of 11%.

During the first period of decline in the city's workforce, African-American men suffered large losses in protective service jobs, as well as in service/maintenance jobs. During 1975 and 1976, 2,399 jobs were lost, one quarter of which were in protective services and 30% in service and maintenance.

By the end of the 1970s, there was an increase of black males in office, clerical, and paraprofessional jobs, largely due to the CETA program. Black males also recaptured some of their base in service and maintenance occupations, as well as in the protective services. This upward trend in employment continued throughout the 1980s, particularly in service/maintenance and protective services occupations. Overall, between 1975 and 1986, African-American men had a net gain of 4,343 jobs.

Changes in the Employment of Black Women

African-American women had the largest net gains in employment of any group: an increase of 6,623 jobs between 1975 and 1986. Their share of the city government workforce increased from 14% in 1975 to almost 19% in 1986 (Table 1). During the declining period, 1975–1977, African-American women lost more than 2,000 jobs, the majority during 1975 and 1976. Nearly 60% of the losses in this period were office and clerical jobs. Toward the end of the decade, African-American women began to gain in official/administrative and protective services occupations.

During the 1980s, official and administrative jobs represented the major growth area for black women. Much of this growth was the result of the "broad-banding" of clerical titles by the Department of Personnel. As discussed later, the effect of this practice was an increase in the number of African-American women ostensibly holding administrative jobs without receiving commensurate salary compensation. The job expansion was not confined to official and administrative jobs, however; African-American women also increased their representation in professional occupations and the protective services. Overall, however, it was the increase in jobs classified as official and administrative that characterized employment changes for black women. The gain of 2,784 in these jobs was the highest of any of the groups between 1975 and 1986; it also accounted for nearly 42% of their net job growth. Black women were also second to Latino males in the number of jobs gained in the protective services.

Changes in the Employment of White Men

In 1975, white males constituted 58.9% of the city government workforce; by 1986, their share had declined to 47% (Table 1). Despite this sharp decline, the proportion of white male workers in the government far exceeded their proportion of the total labor force, which was 37% in 1980 (Table 2).

The decline in white male employment during the 10-year period occurred largely between 1975 and 1977. However, it was during 1975 and 1976 that the sharpest decline occurred. At the time, white male employment declined by 10,457, more than 80% of the total loss for all city employees. Most of the occupational decline of white males in the 1970s occurred in protective service and service/maintenance jobs. One area where they gained employment was official and administrative positions.

In the early part of the 1980s, white male employment continued to decline, though at a much slower pace than in the 1970s. Most of the declines during this period occurred in protective service and service/maintenance jobs. The turn-around in white male employment began after the 1981–1982 economic downturn. From 1983 to 1986, white men gained a total of 5,203 jobs, the largest net gain of any group. Nearly half (46%) of the gains resulted from increases in skilled craft jobs. Slightly more than one quarter (27%) of the growth was attributed to gains in protective service jobs.

Changes in the Employment of White Women

Like their male counterparts, white women also suffered declines in their share of the workforce, though the declines were not as significant. In 1975, white women made up 10.7% of the city's employees; by 1986, the figure had dropped to 9.1% (Table 1).

The major changes in the structure of white female employment were the

Table 2. Representation of Ethnic Groups by Sex in New York
City Government Work Force and New York City
Civilian Labor Force

Race/ethnicity and sex	City government work force 1986	New York City civilian labor force 1980
Total number	135,583	3,161,321
Percentage male	69	55
Percentage female	32	45
Total percentage Hispanic[a]	10	16
Percentage male[b]	6	10
Percentage female	3	7
Total percentage black	33	23
Percentage male	14	11
Percentage female	19	12
Total percentage white	56	65
Percentage male[a]	47	37
Percentage female	9	29

[a]There is an overlapping of figures which stems from two questions posed in the 1980 Census. One question asked respondents whether or not they were of Hispanic origin (ethnicity), and the other asked about race.

[b]Within each of the ethnic groups the breakdown by sex represents the percentage of the total; white men are 47% of the total number of employees in city government.

Note: Figures may not add up to 100 due to rounding.

SOURCE: The New York City Civilian Labor Force Statistics, which includes government and nongovernment workers 16 years and over, are from the U. S. Department of Commerce, Bureau of the Census. 1980 Census of population, characteristics of people and housing for New York City. New York City government work force data were obtained from the New York City Commission on Human Rights.

large declines in office and clerical jobs and increases in official and administrative jobs. Major losses in employment occurred in 1975–1976, totaling more than 2,000 jobs. The loss of jobs, particularly clerical ones, continued throughout the second half of the 1970s. Clerical jobs accounted for virtually all the net job losses between 1975 and 1986.

In the 1980s, the number of white women in clerical jobs continued to decline. However, significant gains were made in official and administrative jobs. Between 1975 and 1986, the proportion of official and administrative positions held by white women doubled from 11.2% to 22.9%. The other source of employment gains was in the protective services.

Changes in the Access of Groups to High-Wage Jobs between 1975 and 1986

Even with a greater share of jobs, blacks and Hispanics failed to make significant gains in salary. The major reason is that they were denied access to high-paying jobs in agencies where they were historically concentrated and in those agencies where whites had a traditional base. The following analysis shows that the share of blacks and Latinos in higher-paying occupations remained below their proportion of the work force in 1986.

In 1986 the salaries of the mayoral work force had risen significantly. The top range of $25,000 and above in 1980 was comparable to $43,000 and above in 1986. White men constituted nearly three fourths (74%) of the employees earning $43,000 or more, and white women made up 8%. Blacks constituted 11% of those earning above $43,000 (8% black males and 3% black females). Hispanics, who made up about 10% of the workers, accounted for about 4% (3% male and 0.5% female) of those earning $43,000 and above.

At the bottom of the salary scale, African-American and Latinos were the dominant groups. In 1975, they constituted 62% of the employees earning $10,000 or less. In 1986, they accounted for 80% of all of the employees earning less than $20,000.

As shown in Table 3, in 1986 the distribution structure within and among groups retained its disparity and inequitability, especially for African-American and Latino women. Among white men, 27% earned $43,000 or more, and 84% earned above $33,000. Among white women, 45% earned $33,000 or more, and 15% earned $43,000 or more. Less than half (48%) of the black men earned above $33,000, and 37% earned less than $25,000. Nearly two thirds (64.6%) of all black women earned less than $25,000. Only 17% earned $33,000 and above.

Among Latinos, 54% of the men earned $33,000 or more and 32% earned under $25,000. Sixty-eight (68) percent of the Latino women earned less than $20,000. Only 18% earned $33,000 or more.

OCCUPATIONAL AND AGENCY STRATIFICATION

The agency and occupational stratification of African-Americans and Latinos is the principal reason for their lack of access to higher-paying jobs. There are four major findings regarding segmentation or stratification of blacks, Latinos, and whites by agencies.

1. Despite their decline in employment, whites have remained above their work force proportion of the labor force in 28 of the agencies that report

Table 3. Percentage Distribution of Full-Time
Government Employees in Selected Salary Ranges by
Race/Ethnicity and Sex, New York City, 1986

Salary range	NYC total	Hispanic	Black	White
Male				
$43,000+	21.3	9.1	9.3	26.5
$33–42,999	51.8	45.2	38.3	57.0
$25–32,999	11.5	13.9	15.0	10.1
$20–24,999	11.3	24.0	25.9	5.2
$16–19,999	4.0	7.8	11.4	1.2
$12–15,999	0.0	0.0	0.1	0.0
$8–11,000	0.0	0.0	0.0	0.0
$1–7,999	0.0	0.0	0.0	0.0
Column total	100.0	100.0	100.0	100.0
Female				
$43,000+	6.2	2.6	2.6	14.7
$33–42,999	19.1	15.2	14.4	29.8
$25–32,999	18.5	14.3	18.3	20.2
$20–24,999	40.6	49.4	46.0	26.7
$16–19,999	15.6	18.4	18.6	8.4
$12–15,999	0.0	0.0	0.0	0.1
$8–11,000	0.0	0.0	0.0	0.0
$1–7,999	0.0	0.0	0.0	0.1
Column total	100.0	100.0	100.0	100.0

SOURCE: New York City Commission on Human Rights.

to the Equal Employment Opportunity Office. Most of these agencies
offer high salaries.

In 1986, whites were above their labor force proportion of 65% in 28
agencies. Included in this total were the city's principal policymaking and development agencies, as well as the Police and Fire Departments.

Most of the agencies in which whites are above their proportion of the labor
force historically have had barriers to African-American and Latino employment.
A comparison of this report with the 1964 and 1973 reports issued by Mayors
Wagner and Lindsay, respectively, shows that there were 10 agencies in 1963,
1971, and 1986 in which whites made up 70% or more of the work force. The
predominantly white agencies included: Board of Standards and Appeals; Office
of Comptroller; President, Borough of the Bronx; Department of Sanitation;
Department of Ports and Terminals; Board of Ethics; District Attorney Queens
County; President, Borough of Queens; Public Administrator, Kings County;
City Sheriff; Public Administrator, New York County; and the Fire Department.

A comparison of 1971 and 1986 reveals twenty agencies in which whites constituted 65% or more of the employees. With the exception of the Board of Elections, the City Sheriff, and the Public Administrators of Richmond, Kings, and New York countries, each of the agencies in which whites were above their proportion of the labor force had a high proportion of employees earning high wages (i.e., agencies where 20% or more of the employees earned $43,000 or more).

2. Lack of access to skilled jobs and inequities in salaries within official/administrative and professional occupations continue despite numerical gains among African-Americans and Latinos.

African-Americans and Latinos remain excluded from the skilled crafts despite their employment gains. In 1975 and 1986, white males held 90% of all craft jobs. Forty-two (42) percent of these jobs paid $43,000 or more.

African-American females, who had the largest net gains in total employment and in official/administrative jobs, continued to comprise a high proportion of low-wage workers. Between 1975 and 1986, black females gained a total of 6,623 jobs, 42% of which were in official/administrator categories. Nevertheless, in 1986, 65% of all African-American women earned less than $25,000. Next to Latino females, who had significantly smaller gains, African-American women had the highest proportion of low-wage earners in the city work force.

This seeming disparity is because the "official/administrator" category used by the city includes clerical jobs. The number of African-Americans and Latinos in this classification, as well as in professional occupational categories, is a misleading measure of their progress. This "broadbanding" of occupational categories results in an inflation of the progress of African-Americans and Latinos.

Disparities in the salary distribution of groups in these categories document this inflation. In 1986, 91% of the 4,590 white men and 68% of the 2,714 white women in official/administrator jobs earned above $33,000. By comparison, only 36% of the 2,933 black women in these positions earned above $33,000. (Seventy-six [76] percent of the black men earned above $33,000. However, there were only 860 black men in these positions in 1986.) The number of Latinos in official/administrator occupations is very small. Forty-five (45) percent of the 365 females and 78% of the 242 males in this category earned $33,000 and above.

Similar disparities were found among professional jobs. In 1986, 89% of the 9,056 white males and 71% of the 2,774 white females in professional jobs earned $33,000 or more. By comparison, 56% of the 2,304 African-American males and 40% of the 3,792 African-American females earned $33,000 or more.

Among Latinos, 54% of the 730 males and 29% of the 671 females earned above $33,000.

3. Most employment increases by blacks and Latinos occurred in the narrow group of agencies in which they have traditionally found employment. The exception was the Police Department, which was mandated by the courts to increase African-American and Latino employment.

In 1986 there were 66 agencies listed in the EEO reports submitted to the federal government. Many of these were small, with less than 100 employees. However, there were 13 agencies/departments whose work forces exceeded 1,000, and four agencies with more than 10,000 employees. These included: Sanitation, 12,632; Fire Department, 13,752; Social Services, 24,639; and the Police Department, 32,703. Together these four agencies accounted for the employment of 62% of all workers.

An examination of Table 4 shows that blacks and Latinos, especially women, are the lowest paid. White females are the most diversified and white males the most concentrated.

Occupational and Agency Segmentation of Latino Men

In 1981 and 1986, the largest employers of Latino men were Police, Social Services, Correction, Sanitation, Parks and Recreation, Fire, Environmental Protection, General Services, Human Resources, Transportation, and Health. In Police, Correction, Sanitation, Fire, Parks and Recreation, and Environmental Protection, the majority of the men earned between $33,000 and $42,999 in 1986. In the Departments of Social Services, Parks and Recreation, Transportation, General Services, and Health, two thirds or more of the men earned less than $25,000 (Table 4).

A distinguishing feature of the occupational structure of Latino men is the small number working as officials/administrators. In 1986, there were only 242 officials/administrators and 730 professionals among the 8,209 Latino male employees. The officials/administrators were dispersed among agencies, with the largest proportion working in the Department of Social Services. However, the largest proportion was only 22%. Among the professionals, 46% were employed in the Department of Social Services, as were 67% of the clerical workers.

The Police Department was the leading employer of protective service workers. In 1986, 57% of the Latino male protective service employees worked in the Police Department.

Table 4. Concentration of Racial/Ethnic and Gender Groups in City Agencies by Salary Level, 1986

Salary level	Latino men $43,000 and above	Latino men $25,000 to $42,999	Latino men $24,999 and under	Latino women $43,000 and above	Latino women $25,000 to $42,999	Latino women $24,999 and under	Black men $43,000 and above	Black men $25,000 to $42,999	Black men $24,999 and under	Black women $43,000 and above	Black women $25,000 to $42,999	Black women $24,999 and under	White men $43,000 and above	White men $25,000 to $42,999	White men $24,999 and under	White women $43,000 and above	White women $25,000 to $42,999	White women $24,999 and under
All agencies[a]	9.1	59.0	31.8	2.6	29.5	67.8	9.3	53.3	37.4	2.6	32.7	64.6	26.5	67.0	6.4	14.7	50.0	35.3
Correction	5.6	90.0	4.5	1.2	80.2	18.6	8.9	83.3	7.8	3.7	78.4	18.0	17.4	80.3	2.3	12.6	48.1	39.3
Environment protection	7.4	78.2	14.4				5.6	72.6	21.8				24.0	68.6	7.3	13.6	45.6	40.8
Finance										2.6	27.3	70.1	29.7	55.0	15.3	11.3	57.0	31.7
Fire	11.2	80.3	8.4				15.8	75.7	8.6				22.6	77.0	0.3			
General services	7.4	26.0	66.5	0.8	15.1	84.1	5.7	27.7	66.5	2.2	18.9	78.8	31.3	53.1	15.6			
Health	2.7	20.6	76.7	2.2	21.9	75.8	4.1	25.6	70.1	1.5	40.9	57.6						
Housing preservation and development				0.5	32.9	66.7				2.2	31.7	66.0				21.1	48.5	30.4
Human Resource Administration				7.4	55.3	37.3												
Mayoralty	1.5	31.9	66.5	9.5	46.6	43.9	4.4	40.5	55.0				17.0	57.7	25.2	32.3	54.6	13.1
Parks and Recreation	15.9	76.2	7.8	2.8	48.5	48.6	20.0	62.4	17.5	1.9	25.9	72.1	28.3	69.8	1.9	7.6	61.8	30.6
Police				1.8	41.8	56.3				2.8	47.3	49.8				7.5	40.2	50.7
Probation	10.1	73.5	16.4				9.4	72.3	18.2	1.8	21.7	76.4	27.9	68.1	3.9			
Sanitation	3.9	23.5	72.1				5.8	31.5	62.6	2.4	29.6	67.9	21.9	58.2	19.9	5.6	37.9	56.4
Social services	3.6	28.5	68.0	1.6	16.9	81.5	3.0	23.1	73.9	0.6	21.4	77.8	22.5	56.9	20.5	12.8	49.0	38.2
Transportation				0.6	10.3	89.1										7.9	36.9	55.2

[a]All agencies, including those not listed in the table.

Note: Totals may not add up to 100 due to rounding.

SOURCE: New York City Commission on Human Rights.

Occupational and Agency Segmentation of Latino Women

In 1981 and 1986, the leading employers of Latino women were Social Services, Police, Health, Housing Preservation and Development, Transportation, Correction, General Services, Office of the Mayor, Probation, and Human Resources. In 1986, the Department of Social Services accounted for 40% of total female Latino employment.

In six of the above agencies (Social Services, Health, Housing Preservation and Development, Transportation, General Services and Probation) more than half of the women earned less than $25,000. The only agency in which the majority earned $33,000 or more was the Department of Correction (Table 4).

The majority (52.5%) of Latino women in 1986 were employed as office and clerical workers. Slightly more than half (51%) of the clerical employees worked in the Department of Social Services, as did 68% of the professionals. Fifty-nine (59) percent of the protective service employees worked in the Police Department.

There was only a small number of Latino women in official/administrative jobs, and those who were employed in these positions were diversified. The highest proportion (34%) was employed in the Department of Social Services.

Occupational and Agency Segmentation of Black Men

In 1981 and 1986, African-American men were limited to a narrow group of mayoral agencies. In 1986, 87% of them were employed in 10 agencies: Social Services, Police, Correction, Sanitation, Transportation, Parks and Recreation, Health, Fire, General Services, and Environmental Protection. In the Police, Fire, and Correction Departments, more than 70% of the black men earned $33,000 or more. The five in which the majority earned less than $25,000 were Social Services, Transportation, Parks and Recreation, Health, and General Services (Table 4).

The narrow agency concentration affects all occupational arrangements of black men. Thirty-two (32) percent of the officials/administrators were employed in the Department of Social Services, as were 47% of the professionals and 58% of the clerical workers. The Department of Correction provided most of the jobs in the protective services. Nearly four of every ten men in service/maintenance worked in the Sanitation Department. Those able to find jobs in the skilled crafts were fairly diversified.

Occupational and Agency Segmentation of Black Women

In 1981 and 1986, nearly nine of every ten black women worked in one of ten agencies. In rank order in 1986, these were the Departments of Social

Services, Police, Health, Correction, Transportation, Housing Preservation and Development, General Services, Finance, Probation, and Sanitation. The Department of Social Services accounted for 47% of their employment in 1981, and 44% in 1986. In 1986, the Correction Department was the only agency in which a majority (64%) of the women earned $33,000 or more. In the Department of Social Services, their leading agency of employment, 68% of the women earned less than $25,000 (Table 4).

Because of their narrow concentration in the Department of Social Services, a high proportion of black women on all occupational levels were found in that agency. In 1986, 60% of the officials/administrators, 63% of the professionals and 51% of the clerical employees worked in the Department of Social Services. The majority of the protective service employees worked in the Department of Correction.

Occupational and Agency Segmentation of White Men

In 1981, two thirds (66%) of all white males worked in three mayoral departments: Police, Fire, and Sanitation. In 1986, these three departments accounted for 65% of white male employment. Overall, white men are the most concentrated of all the major groups. In 1986, 90% of these men worked in 10 mayoral agencies: Police, Fire, Sanitation, Social Services, Environmental Protection, Transportation, Department of Correction, Parks and Recreation, General Services, and Finance. More than half of the men in each of the 10 agencies earned $33,000 or more, and at least 15% earned more than $43,000. In the three leading agencies—Police, Fire, and Sanitation—85% of the men earned $33,000 or more (Table 4).

Even though white males are concentrated in three agencies, their managerial and professional bases extend to all of the mayoral agencies. In contrast to blacks and Latinos, only 11% of the white male officials/administrators worked in the Department of Social Services. Their next highest concentration was in the Fire Department. Their professional jobs were also diverse. Twenty-three (23) percent worked in the Fire Department, followed by the Department of Social Services. An examination of the concentrations for white males reveals that only in the protective services and service and maintenance is there a high concentration by occupation. Fifty-eight (58) percent of the protective service workers were employed by the Police Department and 67% of the service and maintenance workers were employed by the Department of Sanitation.

Occupational and Agency Segmentation of White Women

White women are the most diversified of the major groups analyzed in this study. In 1981, their 10 leading agency employers accounted for 70% of their employment. By 1986 only 68% of the city's white women worked in their 10 leading agencies of employment.

The 10 leading agencies of employment for white women in 1986 were: Social Services, Police, Health, Transportation, Environment, Parks and Recreation, Finance, Housing Preservation and Development, Sanitation, and the Office of the Mayor. In Police, Housing Preservation and Development, and the Office of the Mayor, the majority of the women earned $33,000 or more. There were three agencies where the majority earned less than $25,000; these were the Sanitation, Parks and Recreation, and Transportation Departments. Like white males, a high percentage of white females in their principal employment bases earned $43,000 or more in 1986. In the Department of Social Services, 13% earned $43,000 or more and 42% earned above $33,000. In the Department of Health, 11% earned above $43,000, as did 32% in the office of the Mayor, and 21% in Housing Preservation and Development (Table 4). What is most striking about the data for white women is the shift upward in salaries between 1981 and 1986. While in 1981 a substantial percentage of the white female workers earned between $12,000 and $16,000 in their 10 leading employers, only a few of the women employed in their principal base earned less than $20,000 in 1986.

White women, as they moved out of clerical jobs, have diversified their base of employment. This expanded base of employment was reflected in their diversification among agencies in the higher-paying official/administrator jobs. In 1986, 21% of all white females worked as officials/administrators in the Department of Social Services, lower than any group with sizable number of officials and administrators, except white males. Their next highest concentration as officials and administrators was in legal offices (District Attorney, New York County and the Law Department). The occupational distribution of professionals was less diverse. Nearly 40% worked in the Department of Social Services, followed by 9% in the Department of Health.

4. Blacks and Hispanics are usually sparse in high-wage agencies concerned with policy and development, and overrepresented in agencies with a high proportion of lower-wage employees concerned with social problems.

In the prior discussion, salaries and agencies were examined according to the concentration of the group. Here we examine the relationship of the salary structure of agencies with their functions, as well as their racial, ethnic, and gender composition. This is important because salary structure only partially reflects opportunities for advancement. We have characterized the high-paying agencies by the percentage of employees earning above the highest salary interval. In 1986, 17% of all employees earned $43,000 or more; those agencies in which at least 20% of employees had earnings in this range are considered to have a concentration of high-wage employees. The second group of agencies were those where 56% or more of employees earned between $25,000 and $42,999. Agencies characterized by a concentration of low-wage employees were those in which 29% of the employees earned below $25,000. There are three main characteristics of the agencies with a high proportion of employees earning $43,000 or more. First, except for the City Council President's Office and Manhattan Borough President's Office, the staff earning over $43,000 are predominately white in these agencies. In fact, in the majority of the high-wage agencies, over 85% of the higher paid staff are white men and women. Second, with the exception of the uniformed services, few of these offices use extensive civil service requirements for employment. Third, most of these agencies are concerned with policy development, budget, and employee reviews. These are the critical policy positions for the city.

In 1986, these agencies employed 21% of all white men and 4% of white women. Less than 1% (0.8%) of African-American women and 5% of African-American men were employed in these agencies. Among Latinos, 7% of the men and 1% of the women worked in these agencies. In the second group of agencies—those in which 56% of the employees earned between $25,000 and $42,999—blacks and Latinos generally have greater access to the middle-range jobs, but not to those paying high salaries. These agencies employed 53% of white males, 46% of Latino men, 36% of African-American men, 20% of white women, 15% of Latino women, 12% of Asian-American women, and 10% of African-American women. Included in this group are the protective services, Environmental Protection, and agencies concerned with social control and secondary-level policy, such as the Commission on Human Rights.

The third group of agencies, those in which a high proportion of the employees (29% or more) earned less than $25,000, are characterized by their redistributive functions—that is, by their transfer of resources to clients. These agencies, 38 altogether, tend to be involved with the city's poor, the majority of whom are African-Americans and Latinos. They also included tax and public administration offices.

These agencies employed 50% of all African-American women in 1986 and 30% of African-American men. They accounted for 54% of the Latino women employed by the city and 27% of the Latino men. By contrast, only 4% of the white men and 22% of the white women worked in these agencies.

Despite the high share of African-Americans and Latinos in these agencies, more of the higher-paying jobs are held by whites. In 20 of the 37 agencies, at least 60% of the workers who earned less than $25,000 were African-Americans and Latinos.

CONCLUSION

The data in this study show that Hispanics remain underrepresented in local government relative to their share in the labor force. The major points of access for Hispanics in New York City government have been agencies dealing with the welfare state. Although these agencies are highly unionized, the salaries are significantly lower than agencies dealing with protective services and development, there are limited opportunities for mobility, and the supervisory and managerial staff are usually white. These are also the same agencies that have provided blacks their points of access to government, and tensions have increased with Hispanics, mainly Puerto Ricans, over the limited turf.

The narrow points of access of Hispanics and blacks to city government jobs supports the observation of Erie (1985), who found that in machine and reform cities the political elite conceded welfare state agencies while maintaining control of the higher-paying agencies responsible for development and policy. The exceptions to this pattern have been the increases of Puerto Ricans of both genders and black men in the Police Department. These increases are directly attributable to lawsuits by groups representing black and Latino policemen.

The data show less support for the labor queue theories. This argument, as articulated by Waldinger (1987), maintains that as whites decline in the labor force, blacks and Hispanics gain greater access to better jobs. This study shows that even with a decline in the labor force, whites have retained the majority share of high-wage agencies. Their control of Police, Fire, and Sanitation has permitted them to retain a base of high-wage jobs that require limited education. Their control of the development agencies means that the physical and environmental planning for the city remains outside of the access range of blacks and Hispanics.

What is not known about Hispanics in local government is whether their initial access points will lead to greater diversity, and which of the Hispanic groups are benefiting. Even though the 1972 Civil Rights Act mandated an end to discrimination in local government, neither blacks nor Puerto Ricans significantly diversified their base of jobs within agencies in New York City during the 1970s and 1980s. One of the basic reasons for the limited diversity was the refusal of Mayor Koch to develop an affirmative-action plan.

The 1990s represent a new era for Puerto Ricans. David Dinkins defeated Edward Koch in 1989, making him the city's first black mayor. In the general election between David Dinkins and the Republican candidate Rudolph Giuliani, Dinkins attracted 64% of the Puerto Rican and other Latino votes (Institute for Puerto Rican Policy, 1989). Dinkins' campaign was a local version of Jesse Jackson's "Rainbow" coalition, and the expectations were high among Puerto Ricans that the new administration would provide them wide access to new power and resources. Although Mayor Dinkins appointed a number of Puerto Ricans to head agencies, later assessments will determine whether and how Puerto Ricans benefit from the election of a black mayor.

In addition to the questions of changes in political leadership, researchers also need to develop clearer perspectives on employment and politics in local government. Changes in the access of Puerto Ricans and blacks to lower- and middle-level jobs in higher-paying or more traditional agencies in government is a slow process. These civil service jobs have been part of the bulwark of the white middle class in New York and other cities. The rules and procedures for entry and access to these jobs is a political as well as a management task that has to be studied carefully. We also need a better understanding of how the contracting process in local government is related to the dominance of agencies by certain groups. Until these questions are explored, the Puerto Rican political experience in local government will continue to be viewed in a narrow perspective.

REFERENCES

Beck, E. M., P. Horan, & C. Tolbert. (1980). The structure of economic segmentation: A dual economy approach. *American Journal of Sociology, 85*, 1095–1116.

Bloch, H. (1969). *The circle of discrimination. An economic and social study of the black man in New York*. New York: New York University Press.

City Commission on Human Rights. (1964). *The ethnic survey: A report on the number and distribution of negroes, Puerto Ricans, and others employed by the City of New York*. New York: Author.

Erie, S. (1985). Urban ethnicity in the United States. In L. Maldonado & J. Moore, Eds., *Urban ethnicity in the United States* (pp. 249–275). Beverly Hills, CA: Sage Publications.

Falcon, A. (1984). A history of Puerto Rican politics in New York City. In J. Jennings & M. Rivera, Eds., *Puerto Rican politics in urban America*. Westport, CT: Greenwood.

Falcon, A. (1988). Black and Latino politics in New York City: Race and ethnicity in a changing urban context. In F. Chris Garcia, Ed., *Latinos and the political system* (pp. 171–195). Notre Dame, IN: Notre Dame Press.

Higginbotham, A. (1978). *In the matter of color: Race and the American legal process*. New York: Oxford University Press.

Institute for Puerto Rican Policy. (1989). *Towards a Puerto Rican-Latino agenda for New York*. New York: Author.

Institute for Puerto Rican Policy. (1990). *The 1989 mayoral election and charter revision vote in New York City: The role of the Puerto Rican/Latino voter*. New York: Author.

Lieberson, S. (1980). *A piece of the pie*. Berkeley, CA: University of California Press.

Mladenka, K. (1989). Barriers to Hispanic employment success in 1,200 cities. *Social Services Quarterly, 70*, 391–405.

Moss, P. (1988). Employment gains by minorities, women in large city government, 1976–1983. *Monthly Labor Review, 1988*, 18–24.

New York City Commission on Human Rights. (1973). *The employment of minorities, women and the handicapped in city government: A report of a 1971 survey*. New York: Author.

Rodriguez, C. (1989). *Puerto Ricans*. Boston: Unwin Hyman.

Stafford, W. (1985). *Closed labor markets*. New York: Community Service Society.

Stafford, W. (1989). *Segmentation in municipal agencies*. New York: Community Service Society.

Torres, A. (1988). Human capital, labor segmentation and inter-minority relative status: Black and Puerto Rican labor in New York City, 1960–1980. Doctoral Dissertation, New School for Social Research.

Waldinger, R. (1986–1987). Changing ladders and musical chairs: Ethnicity and opportunity in post-industrial New York. *Politics and Society, 15*(4) 369–401.

IV

Women, Family, and Work

9

A Comparison of Labor Supply Behavior among Single and Married Puerto Rican Mothers

JANIS BARRY FIGUEROA

When the U. S. Census figures from 1960 to 1980 showed an increased number of female-headed households among all ethnic/racial groups, economists assumed that other things being equal, the lack of a second, male wage-earner would motivate many single mothers to enter the labor force, and supply more labor than would otherwise be the case. Among white women, female heads of households with minor children are more likely to be in the labor force than married women with children who live with their spouse (Kamerman & Kahn, 1988). Paradoxically, among black and Puerto Rican female householders with minor children, participation rates since 1960 appear to have stayed well below those of their spouse-present counterparts (Tienda & Glass, 1985). The literature has not specified why headship status *per se* should cause some women to work more and other women to work less.

LABOR SUPPLY DIFFERENCES BETWEEN SINGLE AND MARRIED MOTHERS

In a paper on poverty and the family, Smith (1988) noted that "women heading families are unlikely to be random draws from the population, but are

JANIS BARRY FIGUEROA • Division of the Social Sciences, Fordham University at Lincoln Center, New York, New York 10023.

Hispanics in the Labor Force, edited by Edwin Melendez *et al.* Plenum Press, New York, 1991.

more likely to come from impoverished backgrounds" (p. 161). His research on household composition changes showed that between 1960 and 1980, the characteristics of both black and white female householders had changed. In 1980, female heads were more likely to be young and never married than those women who headed families in the 1960s. He concluded that "more so than in the past, these families are now [headed by] young unwed mothers, women with low earning capacities" (p. 162). Smith does not provide any empirical evidence for this conclusion. However, both the younger age and never-married status of this group suggest the existence of time and money constraints that can only exacerbate labor market entry problems.

It is important to determine whether the variation in labor market behavior between married and single mothers is more a function of personal characteristics or of differing individual circumstances. Spouse-present women are assumed to be able to realize the benefits of joint-household production and consumption activities, as well as increases in the household's resource base resulting from their husband's earnings. For married mothers who live with their husbands, the decision to work for pay and to work full or part time is assumed to be an interdependent family decision that takes into account the cross-effects of the husband's labor supply choices.

Female heads, however, may live alone with their children and be solely dependent on their market earnings for their family's economic well-being. If these earnings are inadequate for family support, then they may seek eligibility for state-provided assistance. Undoubtedly, single mothers have greater access to public-income assistance when compared to married mothers with husbands. Rexroat's study (1990) on the effect of household structure on female family heads showed that women living in extended families were much less likely to be receiving assistance than were heads living alone with their children. Therefore, while household labor supply may fall because of an income maintenance program, female heads may actually increase their labor supply if they live in an extended family arrangement.

The wide variation evidenced in women's labor supply suggests that fixed costs are probably operating to constrain workers to work a minimum number of hours per week or weeks per year. Working mothers must earn enough to pay for child care expenses and many other services that they traditionally perform in the home. Yet many of the services provided by the mother (and this is especially the case for the single mother) cannot easily be substituted with goods and services bought in the marketplace. Therefore, family living arrangements in which there are other individuals who can substitute for the working mother or who, through their earnings, can increase the flexibility of the household in procuring needed goods and services are expected to play a large role in constructing the work decisions of single women with children at home.

This chapter will examine the significance of household composition characteristics that contribute to the variations in labor force participation and annual hours and weeks worked among a sample of Puerto Rican single and married mothers. Results from the empirical tests indicate that extended household forms are more important in explaining the probability of labor force entry and the variation in annual hours and weeks worked among Puerto Rican single mothers.

In the first section of this chapter, I will broadly look at the descriptive evidence on the labor market behavior of women who are distinguished by their headship status. In the second section, I will discuss the labor market behavior and individual characteristics of Puerto Rican women living in New York City. In the third section, I will describe the data used in the probit and regression estimates and present a theoretical model of labor supply choice in which the labor-force participation, annual hours-worked, and annual weeks-worked decisions are analyzed separately. Lastly, I will summarize the empirical results and suggest areas for future research.

IS HEADSHIP STATUS REALLY THE PROBLEM?

Investigations of the labor supply decisions of married women with children whose spouse is present have been the focus of the majority of labor supply studies written during the last twenty years. However, increased research on the employment problems of female householders in the 1980s paralleled the growing interest in welfare reform and workfare programs. The current literature on this group shows that the female headship category captures a number of diverse individuals, some of whom are lacking on-the-job training, education, assistance from the absent parent, and general support from both inside and outside the home (Kamerman & Kahn, 1988, p. 22).

The economic significance of the headship-status distinction in differentiating women's labor force participation and/or the number of hours worked has not been researched enough to allow any conclusions to be drawn. However, studies on the effect of government tax and transfer programs (Hausman, 1981; Levy, 1979; Masters & Garfinkel, 1977), household composition patterns (Rexroat, 1990; Stewart, 1981; Tienda & Glass, 1985), the significance of child-care costs for working mothers (Prescott, Swidinsky, & Wilton, 1986), and the employment opportunities that result from industrial restructuring (Cooney & Colon-Warren, 1979) have provided evidence suggesting that married mothers have different responses than do single mothers to identical economic incentives and constraints. Additionally, research by Blank (1988) and Ellwood (1988) support the contention that working female householders confront unique obstacles to choosing low levels of weeks or hours.

We know that recent studies on changing family structure and the "feminization of poverty" have highlighted important differences in the economic circumstances of single and married mothers, as well as variations among white, black, and Hispanic female heads of household. The dramatic increase in Puerto Rican family poverty is of particular concern. In 1988, 38% of all Puerto Rican families lived below the poverty level. A low rate of labor force participation among all Puerto Rican women and a large percentage of families that are female-headed are thought to be two major factors contributing to this high poverty rate (Smith, 1988). Therefore, it is important that policymakers gain more insight into the labor market behavior of Puerto Rican women in general and Puerto Rican female householders in particular.

Between the years 1960 and 1985, the rate of female headship among Puerto Rican families increased dramatically from 16 to 44%, with a correspondingly large increase for black families of from 21 to 44% and for non-Hispanic white families of from 8 to 12% (Sandefur & Tienda, 1988, p. 10). During this same period, the proportion of single-parent families (most headed by females) with the head not employed rose from 10 to 34% for Puerto Ricans, from 12 to 25% for non-Hispanic blacks, and from 5 to 6% for non-Hispanic whites (Tienda & Jensen, 1988, pp. 55–56).

Thus, it was not merely the rise in the number of female-headed families that hurt Puerto Rican family income so much more than that of other groups, but rather the greater probability that Puerto Rican female householders would be out of the labor force.

Female householders who receive means-tested transfers such as Aid to Families with Dependent Children (AFDC) are assumed to have a lower earnings capacity relative to those single mothers who do not receive aid. This is due to the fact that the program imposes high marginal tax rates on earnings, and thus reduces work incentives for those who could expect to earn only minimal wages (Ellwood & Summers, 1986). The percentage of female householders who received AFDC payments varies by racial and ethnic classification, but recently, Puerto Rican female-headed families are more likely than other groups to be receiving this form of income assistance (Bean & Tienda, 1987, p. 359).

Both Levy and Michel (1986) and Ellwood (1988) have argued that the present accounting structure of the welfare system forces low-income householders to choose between full-time work or no work at all. Further, according to Ellwood's figures (1988, p. 43), full-time work only makes sense for a single mother if she can earn a relatively high wage and has modest day-care costs. Low-waged householders may rationally calculate that the implicit value of their eligible benefits, which include health insurance, is greater than the total compensation they could earn if they worked at a full-time job. Assuming that those single mothers with higher earnings capacities are already in the labor force and generally working full time, then the problem of nonlabor force participation evidenced among Puerto Rican householders is in part due to their human capital deficiencies rather than to their headship status *per se*.

THE EMPLOYMENT SITUATION OF PUERTO RICAN
WOMEN IN NEW YORK CITY

In 1987, Puerto Ricans comprised 13% of New York City's population and they constituted its largest group of Hispanic residents. According to data from the 1987 *Current Population Survey,* they remain one of the city's most economically disadvantaged groups, with almost 50% of the population realizing an income that was below the census-defined poverty level in 1987. In 1987 New York City labor-force participation rate for Puerto Rican females was 31.0%, well below the comparable rates for non-Hispanic black and white women.

The relative constancy of the labor-force participation rate for Puerto Rican women living in New York City between the years 1970 (29.2%) and 1987 (31.0%) and the recorded declines in their participation between 1950 and 1970 are considered anomalous because their trends of increasing education, lowered fertility rates, increases in the percentage born in the United States, increases in the proportion heading a household, and decreases in the number of primary child-bearing age should have increased participation rates over time (Cooney & Colon, 1980).

By 1980, the relative occupational status of employed Puerto Rican women living in New York City had improved. The 1980 Census data showed a greater percentage working in lower and upper white-collar jobs than in the lower blue-collar jobs that this group had held traditionally. But the high rates of nonlabor force participation among Puerto Rican women limit the overall significance of this movement from blue- to white-collar jobs among the employed population.

Studies have found that differences in productive characteristics and hours worked provide a large part of the explanation for Puerto Rican women's lower participation rates and earnings when compared to their non-Hispanic white or Asian counterparts (Carliner, 1976, 1981; Carlson & Swartz, 1988). Working from within the human capital framework, ample research exists on the importance of English language skills, education, and job-specific experience for obtaining better employment opportunities and wages. Yet, for some analysts, the disadvantaged economic status of Puerto Rican women points out the need to consider important demand-side factors that also are shaping labor market outcomes. These factors include the decline in the number of light-manufacturing jobs in New York City, which had the effect of displacing large numbers of Puerto Rican women from their workplace (Bean & Tienda, 1987, p. 282; Cooney & Colon, 1980).

Mothers' Responsiveness to Economic Incentives and Constraints

An important question that I address in this chapter is whether female heads have greater or less responsiveness than married mothers to "economic" incentives and constraints, such as wages, exogenous income, young children at home, and other adults living in the household when making their labor supply decisions. To test this hypothesis, I created two samples by distinguishing all spouse-present, married Puerto Rican women aged 18–64 who had children under the age of 18 living at home from those women who had identical characteristics, but were female heads of households (single mothers).

The data used in this analysis are taken from the 1980 U. S. Census 5% Public Use Microdata Sample (PUMS) for New York City. The regional/urban focus of much of the recent work on the employment prospects of the disadvantaged, in combination with New York City's large Puerto Rican population, informed my decision to use New York City data.[1] Table 1 provides the mean characteristics of the working and the total populations.

The data show that Puerto Rican single mothers living in New York City had much lower employment levels (22%) than Puerto Rican wives (35%). According to the table, single mothers have lower levels of education, exogenous income, lower rates of English language proficiency and higher rates of work disabilities. They also report having larger numbers of children (aged 7–17) and other adults living in their households. And they are more likely to report unemployment. The raw differences in Table 1 for the working population show that annual hours and weeks worked are similar for both groups. Yet a breakdown of the pattern of hours and weeks worked over the year shows that 55% of all Puerto Rican single mothers worked full time/full year (35 hours or more a week and between 47 and 52 weeks a year) while only 49% of all married mothers did the same. Thus, the two samples differ with regards to their participation rates and their propensity to work full or part time, which refers to weekly hours, and full or part year, which refers to annual weeks. In the next section, I will discuss the factors that can account for these differences.

A MODEL FOR ESTIMATING WOMEN'S LABOR SUPPLY

A work-not-work function, based on a comparison between the wage and the reservation wage, and an hours and weeks-of-work function were estimated for the labor supply analysis. Both hours and weeks of work are conditional on the decision to be in the labor force. Blank's (1988) research on the labor supply of female household heads showed that the weeks and hours decisions are separate from the labor-market participation decision, but are also different from each

---

[1] The more recent 1987 *Current Population Survey* (CPS) was not chosen for my analysis because the Puerto Rican sample size was inadequate for my regional focus. Additionally, the Census Bureau has stipulated that the 1980 Census remains the best source for data on Puerto Ricans because of undercounting problems in the CPS sample.

Table 1. Variable Means for Puerto Rican Women[a]

	Working		Total population	
Variable	Married mother	Single mother	Married mother	Single mother
Wagert	5.01	5.06	2.12	1.31
	(1.70)[b]	(1.76)[b]	(4.37)[b]	(4.61)[b]
AnnHrs	1328	1359	491	299
	(681)	(728)	(777)	(667)
WeeksWrk	40.2	41.0	14.3	8.57
	(15.4)	(15.7)	(21.3)	(18.4)
LnWageRt	1.61	1.62	.565	.334
	(.532)	(.566)	(.831)	(.705)
ExogInc	1895*	1534	2315	1412
	(4069)	(3495)	(4903)	(4045)
LnExogInc	3.23	2.75	3.47	2.25
	(3.87)	(3.75)	(3.99)	(3.62)
Unemp	.192*	.247	.093	.094
	(.394)	(.431)	(.291)	(.292)
HusInc	11746	—	.05E-04	—
	(8063)	(—)	(8086)	(—)
HomeOwnr	.229*	.046	.168	.016
	(.420)	(.210)	(.374)	(.129)
ForBir	.700*	.755	.228	.198
	(.458)	(.430)	(.419)	(.398)
Exp	16.0*	17.3	17.9	18.1
	(9.14)	(9.24)	(10.1)	(10.2)
ExpSq	341*	387	424	432
	(368)	(389)	(447)	(465)
NoEnglish	.134	.144	.238	.321
	(.341)	(.352)	(.426)	(.466)
Education	11.2*	10.5	10.1	8.99
	(2.80)	(3.17)	(3.18)	(3.36)
Hus>65	.005	—	.006	—
	(.069)	(—)	(.081)	(—)
HusEmp	.038	—	.031	—
	(.190)	(—)	(.173)	(—)
Kids≤6	.690*	.485	.802	.764
	(.734)	(.676)	(.862)	(.871)
Kids7–11	.486	.501	.591	.633
	(.682)	(.678)	(.760)	(.801)
Kids12–17	.610*	.734	.705	.782
	(.845)	(.909)	(.938)	(1.02)
AdltR≥16	.280*	.342	.328	.303
	(.607)	(.675)	(.697)	(.670)
AdltR>65	.036*	.013	.023	.009
	(.207)	(.114)	(.163)	(.098)
AdltNonR	.014*	.090	.012	.056
	(.141)	(.296)	(.123)	(.243)

(continued)

Table 1. (*Continued*)

Variable	Working		Total population	
	Married mother	Single mother	Married mother	Single mother
FemAdltR	.033	.032	.041	.052
	(.226)	(.204)	(.356)	(.241)
EmpAdltR	.151	.179	.168	.123
	(.446)	(.462)	(.481)	(.394)
Notable	.028*	.063	.083	.180
	(.165)	(.244)	(.277)	(.384)
NevMarr	—	.256	—	.337
		(.437)	(—)	(.472)
Separate	—	.335	—	.371
	(—)	(.472)	(—)	(.483)
Widow	—	.056	—	.048
	(—)	(.231)	(—)	(.215)
Married	—	.039	.100	.041
	(—)	.195	(—)	(.200)
Divorced	—	31.1	—	.200
	(—)	(—)	(—)	(.400)
Labor force participation rate (%)	.35	.22	—	
$n=$	1,248	755	3,560	3,660

[a]Includes all women 18–64 years of age with children under age 18 living at home.
[b]Standard deviations are in parentheses.
*Difference in means significant at $\leq.05$ (2-tail prob.).

other. For that reason, annual hours and weeks worked are treated as separate variables in the labor supply model.

The procedure used in this model of the labor market accounts for the simultaneous nature of the participation and annual hours and weeks-worked decisions, and for the possibility of sample selection bias. In a single-period decision model, the decision to work and the number of hours or weeks that an individual works are the result of both supply and demand factors. On the demand-side specification, market wages (Equation 1) are assumed to be given independently of hours or weeks and are determined by a semi-log earnings function which includes years of completed schooling, English language proficiency, a proxy for labor market experience and its square, and a control for work disabilities. These variables are defined in Table 1.

The first equation shows

$$ln(W_i) = X_{1i}b + u_i \tag{1}$$

where $ln(W_i)$ is the natural log of the wage offer available to individual i, and X_{1i} is a row vector of observed individual characteristics with the associated parameter vector b. The mean-zero random disturbance term u_i represents the effects of unobserved factors (e.g., motivation) on market wages and is assumed to be a normal variate with classical properties for all i.

On the supply side we have

$$ln(W_{*i}) = X_{1i}c_* + X_{2i}d_* + u_{*i} \qquad (2)$$

where $ln(W_{*i})$ is the ith individual's reservation wage. Working women maximize their utility by combining household production time with market goods and services. The amount of labor supplied will depend on the value of the reservation wage, and this is a function of individual characteristics contained in X_{1i}, where c_* is the associated coefficient vector. The other observed variables measure property income, characteristics of other household members, and taste factors relating to household composition and leisure time. These variables are contained in the row vector X_{2i}, and d_* is the associated coefficient vector. The random disturbance term u_{*i} refers to unobservable factors and is assumed to be a normal variate with classical properties for all i.

The reservation wage (Equation 2) reflects the fixed costs of working in the market and the value given to nonmarket time. In this specification, the greater the amount of the husband's income (if the woman is married) or level of exogenous income, the greater the probability that the benefits of extra wage income diminish. Home ownership, an asset proxy, is usually assumed to increase the value of nonmarket time, although this variable may capture the association between past labor supply and ownership ability.

The number of children in the household under the age of 6, between the ages of 7–11, and between the ages of 12–17 is assumed to affect the reservation wage through increasing the fixed time and money costs associated with working. Household composition variables, including the number of adult relatives aged 16–64 and over age 65 who live in the household, as well as controls for the number of adult nonrelatives (fictive kin), female adult relatives, and employed adult relatives, are included to test for intrahousehold labor supply patterns and the possible substitution of other household members for the mother in domestic production tasks.

The distinction made concerning the gender and employment status of the adult relatives residing in the household, as well as the differentiation involving the number of adult nonrelatives in residence, acknowledges the recorded variation in the household extension mechanisms available to single and married mothers (Tienda & Glass, 1985; Rexroat, 1990). Nativity is included to control for the effect of birth on the island of Puerto Rico. Marital status is used in the sample of single mothers to control for reasons for female headship. Other control variables thought to affect the reservation wage, but not of primary interest for this estimation are defined in Table 1.[2]

The procedure used here allows for the possibility that the lowest number of hours a worker will work may be greater than zero. Thus, there is a discontinuity in the labor supply function at the point of equality between $ln(W_i)$ and $ln(W_{*i})$ that may result from fixed costs of labor market entry or labor market constraints (Blank, 1988; Killingsworth, 1983). Reported unemployment by those both in and out of the labor force who are looking for work or are on layoff from a job is included in both the annual hours and weeks regressions. As Blank argued (1988, p. 183) this variable could capture preferences of those who wish to work only part-year for reasons associated with children's school schedules, the nature of the job, or with eligibility constraints imposed by certain government transfer programs (e.g., unemployment compensation, welfare). However, Blank's study also suggests that slack labor demand may keep employees from working as many weeks as they want, thereby creating a discontinuity between desired and observed weeks of work.

Thus, the final equation shows that the number of hours supplied is a discontinuous function of the market wage,[3] where

$$H_i = a \, ln(W_i) + X_{1i}c + X_{2i}d + e_i \text{ for } ln(W_i) > ln(W_{*i})$$

and

$$H_i = 0 \text{ for } ln(W_i) < = ln(W_{*i}) \tag{3}$$

But if only those women with positive hours in the sample are observed, our dependent variable is limited (censored), and the use of ordinary least square (OLS) to estimate the parameters of both the wage and hours/weeks equations will cause biased estimates, as the conditional mean of the error term in the sample of workers is generally not zero. Additionally, the use of OLS to estimate the labor supply function can give inconsistent estimates of the parameters because of the possibility of a nonzero covariance between e_i (Equation 3) and u_i (Equation 1).

Thus, we first estimate a reduced-form probit equation for labor force

---

[2]In the samples of spouse-present women, controls for husband's age (over 65) and for his self-employment status are included in the regression analysis. A control for a work disability is also added.

[3]The relationship between Equations 2 and 3 arises from the fact that since reservation wage W_{*i} equals the greatest wage offer consistent with zero hours of labor supply, then $c_* = -c/a$, $d_* = -d/a$, and $u_{*i} = e_i/a$. See Prescott, Swidinsky, and Wilton (1986), p. 136; also see Killingsworth (1983), pp. 157–161.

participation, and then use the estimated coefficients to compute a selection bias correction variable (λ_i). The dependent variable in the probit model signifies employment for at least one week in 1979 and positive reported 1979 hours and earnings. The second stage of this procedure uses a selection bias-corrected regression to estimate the market wage, using only the data on workers, There are no right-hand-side endogenous variables in this reduced-form equation which includes the set of regressors contained in X_{1i} and lambda. The third stage of this procedure involves estimating the parameters of the both the annual hours and weeks equation, again using a selection bias-corrected regression on the sample of working women to acknowledge the nonrandom process by which subsamples of workers and nonworkers get constructed. Lastly, predicted wages for working women were used as an instrument for actual wages in the estimation of the annual-hours and weeks regression to correct for the simultaneous equation bias of the OLS estimator.

LABOR FORCE PARTICIPATION FINDINGS

Table 2 provides the probit estimates for Puerto Rican married and single mothers, respectively. Of particular interest is the finding that participation in the labor force is more likely for single mothers if there are adult nonrelatives and employed adult relatives living in the household. It is assumed that the presence of adult nonrelatives (fictive kin) in the home increases work probabilities because other household members substitute their domestic production skills for those of the mother. Having employed adult relatives living in the household could indicate the household's greater ability to purchase day-care services, or it could signify increased access to a job-information network via the employed family member. Both of these situations would increase the work probabilities of the single mother.

Married mothers with adult relatives over age 65 living in the household were also more likely to work. The positive impact of older family members on the participation probabilities of married mothers could reflect either the greater need to generate income to support elderly dependents or the substituting of these family members for the mother in household tasks. Although household structure affects participation probabilities of both married and single Puerto Rican mothers, extension mechanisms are more important in determining the work decision of single mothers.

As the greater difference between the two groups is found in their rates of participation, it is somewhat surprising that the probit results show a fair amount of similarity. However, labor market experience is not significant in explaining participation probabilities for married mothers, but is important for understanding the labor force entry of single mothers. The presence of children in the

Table 2. Coefficients of Probit Model
for Labor Force Participation for
Puerto Rican Women[a]

Variable	Married mother	Single mother
Constant	−.707**	−1.13**
	(.171)[b]	(.198)[b]
LnExogInc	−.005	.010
	(.006)	(.008)
HusInc	.00001**	—
	(.00003)	(—)
HomeOwnr	.285**	.805**
	(.063)	(.187)
Experience	.015	.033**
	(.010)	(.012)
ExpSq	−.0005**	−.0005**
	(.0002)	(.0002)
ForBir	−.109	−.081
	(.060)	(.071)
NoEnglish	−.238**	−.419**
	(.065)	(.069)
Education	.071**	.092**
	(.010)	(.010)
Hus>65	.333	—
	(.335)	(—)
HusEmp	−.028	—
	(.126)	(—)
Kids≤6	−.377**	−.515**
	(.037)	(.047)
Kids7–11	−.264**	−.287**
	(.035)	(.040)
Kids12–17	−.148**	−.182**
	(.032)	(.035)
AdltR≥16	−.103	−.078
	(.060)	(.065)
AdltR>65	.324**	−.132
	(.142)	(.248)
AdltNonR	.115	.335**
	(.183)	(.098)
FemAdltR	.028	−.049
	(.070)	(.128)
EmpAdltR	.063	.213**
	(.083)	(.095)
Unemp	.989**	1.07**
	(.080)	(.077)
NevMarr	—	−.321**
	(—)	(.077)

(*continued*)

Table 2. (*Continued*)

Variable	Married mother	Single mother
Separate	—	−.195**
	(—)	(.071)
Widow	—	−.090
	(—)	(.134)
Married	—	−.234
	(—)	(.146)
Notable	−.642**	−.813**
	(.107)	(.098)
Loglikelihood	−1949	−1424
n	3,560	3,660

*a*All women are aged 16–64 and have children under 18 living at home.
*b*Standard errors in parentheses. Dependent vari-
able-employed; estimation method: maximum
likelihood.
**$\leq$.01; *$\leq$.05.

household has a greater negative impact on the work probabilities of single
mothers which suggest the unique problems faced by the single parent. Home
ownership is a positive factor in determining participation probabilities, especially among single mothers. But the raw averages show that this form of
asset-holding is more prominent in the married mothers sample.

Reported unemployment which was, on average, comparatively higher for
working single mothers has a more significant impact on increasing their probabilities of being in the work force. English language skills, work disabilities,
and educational level are also particularly important in determining work
probabilities among single mothers. Overall, the results show similarity in
the variables that determine participation probabilities for both groups. However, the magnitude of the associated coefficients differs between the two samples.

The wage–rate regression results (not shown here) showed English language proficiency to be important in explaining wage variations among Puerto
Rican spouses, but not among female family heads. This may partly reflect the
occupational distribution of working female householders, who, according to the
Census data, tended to be more concentrated in lower blue-collar jobs where
proficiency skills are not as highly valued. Additionally, labor market experience
and its square explained a significant amount of the variation in wages only in the
single mother's regression, giving support to the idea that female family heads
may be working in different jobs from those of married mothers.

Table 3. Estimates of Annual Hours and Weeks, Conditional on
the Labor Force Participation of Puerto Rican Women[a]

	Annual hours		Annual weeks	
Variable	Married mother	Single mother	Married mother	Single mother
Constant	1583**	1176**	21.0	36.9**
	(760)[b]	(610)[b]	(16.6)[b]	(12.1)
LnExogInc	−14.3**	−1.16	−.352**	−.202
	(5.60)	(7.80)	(.122)	(.154)
HusInc	.003	—	−00006	—
	(.002)	(—)	(.00006)	(—)
HomeOwnr	19.8	−45.1	1.45	−.173
	(62.0)	(136)	(1.35)	(2.68)
ForBirth	−11.3	69.3	−.661	.704
	(47.5)	(57.4)	(1.04)	(1.13)
PredWage	115	355	14.75	8.62
	(368)	(318)	(8.06)	(6.30)
Hus>65	277	—	8.03	—
	(263)	(—)	(5.78)	(—)
HusEmp	71.9	—	.261	—
	(95.3)	(—)	(2.09)	(—)
Kids≤6	−21.8	−38.4	−2.66	−4.76**
	(66.0)	(75.4)	(1.44)	(1.49)
Kids7–11	−16.9	40.8	−1.73	.021
	(52.1)	(51.7)	(1.14)	(1.02)
Kids12–17	32.7	21.2	.046	.066
	(39.3)	(39.2)	(.863)	(.719)
AdltR≥16	36.4	140**	1.33	2.54**
	(54.9)	(60.1)	(1.20)	(1.19)
AdltR>65	25.8	169	2.60	3.27
	(10.3)	(205)	(2.25)	(4.08)
AdltNonR	−77.0	−80.1	−1.55	−2.26
	(129)	(86.8)	(2.82)	(1.72)
FemAdltR	103	95.4	2.78	1.90
	(84.1)	(117)	(1.84)	(2.33)
EmpAdltR	13.9	−183**	−1.02	−1.83
	(66.6)	(86.0)	(1.46)	(1.70)
Unemp	−723**	−800**	−14.2**	−18.8**
	(158)	(123)	(3.47)	(2.44)
NevMar	—	−60.9	—	1.32
	(—)	(72.7)	(—)	(1.52)
Separate	—	−129**	—	−2.71**
	(—)	(63.7)	(—)	(1.26)
Widow	—	−53.2	—	−.560
	(—)	(108)	(—)	(2.15)
Married	—	−42.5	—	.094
	(—)	(127)	(—)	(2.52)

(*continued*)

Table 3. (*Continued*)

Variable	Annual hours		Annual weeks	
	Married mother	Single mother	Married mother	Single mother
Notable	−253	−15.6	−9.26**	−1.43
	(174)	(130)	(3.83)	(2.59)
Lambda	−249	−198	−2.72	−1.91
	(254)	(159)	(5.57)	(3.16)
Adjusted $R^2=$	.13	.22	.19	.35
$n=$	1,248	755	1,248	755

*a*All women are aged 18–64 and have children under 18 living at home.
*b*Standard errors are in parentheses.
** $\leq$ .01; * $\leq$ .05.
SOURCE: 1980 United States Census, 5% PUMS for New York City.

HOURS AND WEEKS WORKED ESTIMATES

Table 3 provides information on the annual hours and weeks-worked estimates for both groups. The dependent variable is either the average number of hours worked per year during 1979 or the average number of weeks worked per year. Working Puerto Rican householders and married mothers appear to have different responses to economic incentives and constraints. After controlling for labor force participation, such factors as the number of children six years or younger living at home, the number of adult relatives living in the household, the level of asset (exogenous) income flowing into the household, and work disability status all have mixed impacts on the hours and weeks worked by each group.

The annual hours regressions show that household composition factors are significant in explaining hours variations for single mothers, but not married mothers. Controlling for all other factors, the presence of adult relatives increases work hours significantly. The presence of employed adult relatives, conversely, decreases work hours suggesting that single mothers and other family members are substitutes in household production. However, the adult relative variables (e.g., AdltR $\geq$ 16, FemAdltR, and EmpAdltR) all increment each other, so that the impact of a working grandmother under the age of 65 would be the sum of the above variable coefficients. In such a case, the negative cross-substitution effect of an employed adult relative would be outweighed by the positive impact of other household members on the hours worked by the householder.

The estimation of a separate annual weeks equation increases the explanatory power of the model. After accounting for the labor force participation decision, the impact of adult relatives on the weeks-worked decision of single mothers remains strong, but the presence of employed adult relatives no longer significantly affects this decision. The presence of young children at home significantly diminishes the number of weeks worked supporting the contention that single mothers with small children may face constraints in working full-year jobs.

Estimates from the weeks-worked regression for married mothers show that work disabilities affect weeks but not hours worked. This may reflect budget constraints imposed by disability insurance programs. In addition, the wage just barely escapes significance (at 0.06) in the married mother's sample this time, suggesting that wage rates play a more important role in determining weeks rather than hours worked other things being equal.

The unemployment variable in both the annual hours and weeks equations are associated with significantly lower hours and weeks worked for both groups, although the impact is more pronounced in the regressions for single mothers. This could be due to the fact that 22% of the single mothers who worked in this sample received public assistance. If a woman receives assistance, such as AFDC, she is likely to work less, and net wages will be lower because of the implicit earnings tax contained in the program. The attempt to integrate work, welfare, and parenting, as a significant number of part-year, part-time Puerto Rican mothers do, is a difficult combination.

Even after controlling for individual and household characteristics, the unemployment variable accounts for a large proportion of the negative residuals in the hours and weeks equations. However, the interpretation of this variable is not straightforward. It could be capturing preferences and household constraints that are omitted from the present model or it could reflect the existence of labor rationing at high levels of weeks. Census data does confirm that in 1980, Puerto Rican women living in New York City had significantly higher unemployment rates than non-Hispanic black and white women and that unlike the other groups, these rates were higher in 1980 than those observed in 1960.

Although the explanatory power of the estimated labor supply equations are comparable to other results provided in the literature, there is still a significant amount of information that is not captured with these models. We do know that after accounting for the labor force participation decision, employed female heads and married mothers are not deterred from longer work hours by the presence of young children at home, although young children do diminish the number of weeks worked by single mothers. The findings also indicate that single mothers benefit from an intrahousehold labor supply pattern and that other household members contribute to her ability to vary the number of hours or weeks worked over the year. Increases in the level of exogenous income diminish the hours and weeks worked by married mothers, and work disabilities cause this group to work part-year. Single mothers who are separated work fewer hours and weeks than do divorced single mothers, and both single and married mothers who report unemployment work less hours and fewer weeks.

SUMMARY

The participation regressions for single and married mothers reveal a large degree of similarity in the factors determining the work decision. Alternatively, the factors influencing the number of weeks and hours worked are rather different between the two groups. Of particular interest is the finding that single mothers who have other adults living in the household are more likely to participate in the labor force and to increase their working hours and weeks, although controlling for other factors the presence of employed household members acts to decrease the number of hours worked. Overall, these results support the contention (traditionally made most strongly in the research on black women) that household extension mechanisms can serve as an economic lifeline for female heads of household (MacPherson & Stewart, 1989; Tienda & Glass, 1985).

A comparative analysis of working Puerto Rican, non-Hispanic white, and non-Hispanic black female heads living in New York City showed that access to extended family networks had a consistently significant impact on the participation and hours/weeks decisions of black and Puerto Rican single mothers. However, extended households were not as important in determining the labor supply of married mothers or white householders, suggesting the need for further research into the economic importance of familial functioning and structure between household types and across racial and ethnic groups (Melendez & Barry Figueroa, 1990).

The present study of Puerto Rican female labor supply is regionally specific and the findings on the determinants of the participation and hours and weeks-worked decisions may be distinguishing particular patterns of economic survival that are unique to Puerto Rican women living in New York City. A recent study shows a tremendous diversity in family structure, employment status, income, and poverty rates among Puerto Ricans who live in areas outside of New York City (Bose, 1989). A few researchers have argued that economic strategies for Puerto Ricans seem to change on the basis of housing and transportation proximity, access to social service agencies, and employment opportunities in the local economy (Pelto, Roman, & Liriano, 1982; Rodriguez, 1989).

The public's increased expectation that single mothers not only work, but work enough hours and weeks to be able to support themselves and their children, implies that more information on the factors that affect this group's labor supply is needed. It is possible that housing constraints, social service agency rules on cohabitation, inadequate day-care services, low wage levels, and slack labor demand have acted to keep more Puerto Rican single mothers from participating in the New York City labor market, and from working full time, full year, than would otherwise be the case. The findings on the effect of reported unemployment imply the need for more studies into preferences for part-year work and the extent of labor-market rationing.

The findings do support the need for further inquiry into the factors encouraging extended household arrangements. Housing programs that provide the space for extended families to live together, if they so choose, could have a positive employment impact on single mothers. The empirical results indicate that working single mothers are depending on family and friends for their childcare needs. As MacPherson and Stewart (1989) noted, increasing the supply of low-income housing could encourage extended family arrangements that would allow participants to pool resources and capture the benefits of the scale economies.

ACKNOWLEDGMENTS

Funds for this research were provided by the Inter-University Program for Latino Research/Social Science Research Council Grants Program. The excellent programming assistance of Craig Plunkett is gratefully acknowledged. I also would like to thank Edwin Melendez, Cordelia Reimers, and Kacey Chuilli for their helpful suggestions.

REFERENCES

Bean, F., & M. Tienda. (1987). *The Hispanic population of the United States.* New York: Russel Sage.

Blank, R. (1988). Simultaneously modeling the supply of weeks and hours of work among female household heads. *Journal of Labor Economics, 6*(21), 177–204.

Bose, C. (1989). *Ethnicity, women and poverty.* Unpublished manuscript, State University of New York at Albany, Department of Sociology.

Carliner, G. (1976). Returns to education for blacks, Anglos, and five Spanish groups. *Journal of Human Resources 2,* 172–83.

Carliner, G. (1981). Female labor force participation rates for nine ethnic groups. *Journal of Human Resources 16,* 286–293.

Carlson, L., & C. Swartz. (1988). The earnings of women and ethnic minorities. *Industrial and Labor Relations Review, 41*(4), 530–552.

Cooney, R. S., & A. Colon Warren. (1979). Declining female participation among Puerto Rican New Yorkers: A comparison with native white non-Spanish New Yorkers. *Ethnicity, 6,* 281–297.

Cooney, R. S., & A. Colon. (1980). Work and family: The recent struggle of Puerto Rican females. In C. Rodriguez, V. Sanchez-Korrol, & J. O. Alers, Eds., *The Puerto Rican struggle: Essays on survival in the U. S.* Maplewood, NJ: Waterfront Press.

Ellwood, D. (1988). *Poor support: Poverty and the American Family.* New York: Basic Books.

Ellwood, D., & L. Summers. (1986). Poverty in America: Is welfare the answer or the problem? In S. H. Danziger & D. H. Weinberg, Eds., *Fighting poverty: What works and what doesn't.* Cambridge: Harvard University Press.

Hausman, J. (1981). Labor supply. In H. Aaron & J. Pechman, Eds., *How taxes affect economic behavior*. Washington, DC: Brookings Institution.

Kamerman, S., & A. Kahn. (1988). *Mothers alone: Strategies for a time of change*. Dover, MA: Auburn House.

Killingsworth, M. (1983). *Labor supply*. New York: Cambridge University Press.

Levy, F., & R. Michel. (1986). Work for welfare: How much good will it do? *American Economic Review, 76*, 339–404.

Levy, F. (1979). The labor supply of female household heads, or AFDC work incentives don't work too well. *Journal of Human Resources, 4*, 56–79.

MacPherson, D., & J. Stewart. (1989). The labor supply and school attendance of black women in extended and non-extended households. *American Economic Review, Papers and Proceedings*, (May), 71–74.

Masters, S., & I. Garfinkel. (1977). *Estimating labor supply effects of income maintenance alternatives*. New York: Academic Press.

Melendez, E., & J. Barry Figueroa. (1990). *An investigation of the labor participation and supply decisions of Puerto Rican, non-Hispanic black and white women: An inter-city examination of variations in employment*. Report for the Social Science Research Council/Inter-University Program for Latino Research Grants Program.

Pelto, P., M. Roman, & N. Liriano. (1982). Family structures in an urban Puerto Rican community. *Urban Anthropology, 11*(1), 39–58.

Prescott, D., R. Swidinsky, & D. Wilton. (1986). Labour supply estimates for low-income female heads of household using Mincome data. *Canadian Journal of Economics, 19*(1), 134–141.

Rexroat, C. (1990). Race and marital status differences in the labor force behavior of female family heads: The effect of household structure. *Journal of Marriage and the Family, 52*, 591–601.

Rodriguez, C. (1989). *Puerto Ricans: Born in the U. S.A.* Boston: Unwin Hyman.

Sandefur, G. D., & M. Tienda, Eds. (1988). *Divided opportunities: Minorities, poverty, and social policy*. New York: Plenum Press.

Smith, J. P. (1988). Poverty and the family. In G. D. Sandefur & M. Tienda, Eds., *Divided Opportunities: Minorities, Poverty, and Social Policy*. New York: Plenum Press.

Stewart, J. (1981). Some factors determining the work effort of single black women. *Review of Social Economy, 40*, 30–44.

Tienda, M., & J. Glass. (1985). Household structure and labor force participation of black, Hispanic and white mothers. *Demography, 22*(3), 381–394.

Tienda, M., & L. Jensen. (1988). Poverty and Minorities: A quarter-century profile of color and socioeconomic disadvantage. In G. D. Sandefur & M. Tienda, Eds., *Divided opportunities: Minorities, poverty, and social policy*. New York: Plenum Press.

APPENDIX

Variable Definitions for Table 1

Employed = 1 if respondent worked at least one week during 1979 and reported positive hours and earnings; 0 otherwise.

WageRt = real average hourly earnings in 1979, computed as annual earnings divided by weeks worked in 1979 $\times$ hours worked in 1979.

AnnHrs = weeks respondent worked in 1979 × hours worked in 1979.

WeeksWrk = weeks respondent worked in 1979.

LnWageRt = natural logarithm of real average hourly 1979 earnings.

ExogInc = other household income excluding all earning of respondent or husband (if applicable) or public assistance payments.

LnExogInc = natural logarithm or exogenous income.

Unemp = 1 if respondent reported looking for work or was on layoff from a job; 0 otherwise.

HusInc = husband's 1979 annual income (includes wages, salary, and self-employment income).

HomeOwnr = 1 if respondent owned the home in which she resided; 0 otherwise.

ForBir = 1 if born outside of U. S. mainland; 0 otherwise.

Exp = age of respondent in years minus completed education minus six.

ExpSq = experience squared.

NoEnglish = 1 if respondent's English proficiency was poor; 0 otherwise.

Education = number of years of education completed.

Hus >65 = 1 if respondent's husband was 65 years or older.

HusEmp = 1 if husband was self-employed; 0 otherwise.

Kids $\leq$ 6 = number of children 6 years or younger living in household.

Kids 7–11 = number of children 7–11 years old living in household.

Kids 12–17 = number of children 12–17 living in household.

AdltR$\geq$16 = number of nuclear adults aged 16–64 living in household (does not include respondent, husband, or children aged 16–17).

FemAdltR = number of female nuclear adults living in household.

EmpAdltR = number of employed nuclear adults living in household.

AdltR>65 = number of nuclear adults over age 65 living in household.

AdltNonR = number of nonnuclear adults (fictive kin) aged 16–64 living in household.

Notable = 1 if respondent reported work or transportation disability; 0 otherwise.

NevMarr = 1 if single mother was never married; 0 otherwise.

Separate = 1 if single mother was separated from spouse; 0 otherwise.

Widow = 1 if single mother was widowed; 0 otherwise.

Married = 1 if single mother was married, but not with spouse; 0 otherwise.

Divorced = 1 if single mother was divorced; 0 otherwise.

10

Work and Family Responsibilities of Women in New York City

Terry J. Rosenberg

INTRODUCTION

National studies of family income and poverty have shown that Puerto Rican families are concentrated in the lowest income levels, and that Puerto Rican families are among the poorest in the United States (Tienda & Jensen, 1987; U. S. Bureau of the Census, 1987). Likewise, in the New York Metropolitan Area and in New York City itself, Puerto Rican families—whether compared to all other families or to other Hispanic families—have very low incomes and extremely high rates of poverty (Cooney & Colon, 1980; Rosenberg, 1987, 1989).

These trends are of concern not only in terms of current living standards, but because they impact negatively on future generations. National and local birth statistics indicate that Puerto Rican children already start with significant problems related to the poverty status of their mothers. For instance, among all births nationally, Puerto Rican babies have the highest rate of low birthweight, 9.1% (Ventura, 1985; Ventura & Taffel, 1985). In New York City, where 64.7% of Puerto Rican births are financed by Medicaid, 27.8% of all Puerto Rican mothers have not had adequate prenatal care and 8.6% of all Puerto Rican babies are low

TERRY J. ROSENBERG • Community Service Society, 105 East 22nd Street, New York, New York 10010.

Hispanics in the Labor Force, edited by Edwin Melendez *et al*. Plenum Press, New York, 1991.

birthweight babies (special runs from the New York City Health Department 1985 Births Master File).

A number of phenomena are related to the income deficits found among Puerto Rican families across the United States: (1) There has been an increase in Puerto Rican female-headed families; (2) Puerto Rican women have a low rate of labor force participation; and (3) Puerto Rican families have, more than other families, depended on income-transfer programs such as Aid to Families with Dependent Children (AFDC). Within New York City, dramatic declines in the number of available manufacturing jobs have paralleled these other trends, and have had a further negative impact on the employment of Puerto Rican women (Cooney & Colon, 1980; Korrol, 1980; Tienda & Glass, 1985; Tienda & Jensen, 1987).

Since previous studies have only described the Puerto Rican population as a whole, or have studied Puerto Rican women in very broad categories, I thought that it would be worthwhile to consider in more detail the experiences of separate female age cohorts for one region. This effort, it was hoped, would clarify whether there are any differences among Puerto Rican women by age groups in terms of employment and family responsibilities that are also related to family income. Because New York City is still the major center for Puerto Rican settlement in the United States, it was chosen as the site for this analysis, even though the situation of Puerto Ricans in New York City may not be fully generalizable. We further chose to look at women in the childbearing years so as to better understand whatever conflicts there may be between work and childrearing for Puerto Rican women.

Additionally, the analysis sought to compare Puerto Rican women with other women in the city. By means of these comparisons, it was thought that some better understanding of differentials among Puerto Rican women in various life-cycle stages could be gained, at the same time as we measured the gap between Puerto Rican women and others within age groups.

DATA AND METHODS

Previous large-scale studies of the Puerto Rican population have most often depended upon census data, specifically on the Public Use Microdata samples (PUMS). These sources, of course, provide very detailed information on a large number of cases. As an alternative and much more recent source, the March Current Population Survey (CPS) has also been used for studies at the national level.

Since the March Current Population Survey contains much of the information that is found on the PUMS tapes, it is an appealing data source. The major disadvantage of the CPS, however, is that its small sample size limits local analysis. To compensate for this, we have merged three years of the survey, 1985, 1986, and 1987. The resulting CPS sample for New York City is still not as large as the 1980 Census PUMS sample, but it is a reasonable compromise given our interest in recent information.

Without weighting, the merged CPS sample of women 15–49 in New York City includes over 4,000 women. The weighted totals for these women, when divided into age groups, very closely approximate the age groups found in the 1980 Census. Furthermore, when they are subdivided into three racial/ethnic groups, non-Hispanic whites, non-Hispanic blacks, and Puerto Ricans, the proportional distribution by age again approximates that of the 1980 Census. In short, therefore, the merged sample appears to provide a reasonable basis for recent descriptive information about women in New York City.

It is worth noting, nonetheless, that the survey has undergone changes in the period considered which may affect the data on Hispanics in general, and on Puerto Ricans in particular. From 1985 through 1987, the CPS altered both the Hispanic sample and the weights used for Hispanic subgroups. On a national level, these changes are thought to be partly responsible for an unexpected decline in the number of Puerto Ricans from 1985 to 1986, and then again to 1987 (U. S. Bureau of the Census, 1987). Since there has been no official formula offered to correct for this problem, however, we have used the CPS data as originally distributed.

Four age groups are considered here: 15–19, 20–29, 30–39, and 40–49, which are assumed to represent age cohorts or life-cycle stages. In addition, three separate, mutually exclusive racial/ethnic groups are considered: non-Hispanic whites, non-Hispanic blacks, and Puerto Ricans (with the respective, unweighted, sample sizes in the final analysis being 1,524, 854, and 893). All three of the racial/ethnic groups include women born on the United States mainland as well as women born elsewhere, since the CPS does not include information on place of birth.

Of the variables found in the CPS, two basic indicators were chosen to measure a women's marketability and employment status: these were highest grade completed, and labor force status at the time of the interview. As indicators of family structure and child care responsibilities, we used martial status, relationship to householder, and the number of householder's own children under 18. For the youngest women in the sample, the last variable is an indicator of the number of siblings or other young children with whom a woman resides. For older women in the sample, this variable is an index of their own fertility. In either case, assuming that teenagers and older women in a household may share child care tasks, this variable is an indicator of the child care responsibilities shouldered by all women in the household.

The one measure of family economic status considered is the degree of family poverty calculated in each of the CPS samples by using the appropriate federal poverty threshold for each year. So, for instance, the incidence of poverty in the 1985 CPS is based on the poverty threshold for that year. Since the threshold is automatically adjusted for changes in the cost of living, this variable required no extra adjustment for inflation in the merged New York City sample.

FINDINGS

Labor Force Characteristics by Cohort

Table 1 and Figure 1 present the results of the analysis for all women 15 to 49 years of age. Tables 2 to 5 then present results for each of four cohorts separately. Taken together these tables allow for a full, detailed examination of differences across racial/ethnic groups and across age cohorts.

Among all women 15–49, Puerto Rican women clearly have the lowest educational levels. Although more than half of all Puerto Rican women have not completed high school, only 14.5% of all white women and 31.7% of all black women have less than a high school education. At the highest end of the scale, less than 5% of all Puerto Rican women have completed college, as compared to 34.5% of all white women and 13.1% of all black women.

Even in the youngest age cohort, women 15–19, there is an apparent lag in educational attainment for Puerto Rican women, though it is not as dramatic as it becomes in later years. It is really among women 20–29 that Puerto Ricans seem to fall far behind other women in completed years of education. At this stage in the life cycle, 45.6% of all Puerto Rican women have not completed high school, whereas only 5.8% of white women and 22.8% of black women are not high school graduates.

Among women 30–39, the highest level of educational attainment is found for all three racial/ethnic groups, with Puerto Rican women still being the least educated. Finally, for women 40–49, almost two thirds of Puerto Rican women have not finished high school, compared to 13.9% of white women and 28.2% of black women. The differences between Puerto Rican women and other women become most exaggerated in this last age group.

As has been shown in other studies (e.g., Rosenberg, 1987, 1989), Table 1 here reveals that Puerto Rican women are less likely to be employed than other women, whether full time or part time. Even though 68.1% of all Puerto Rican women reported that they were not in the labor force, only 36.1% of white women and 46.0% of black women were not. Overall, it appears that white and black women have similar patterns of labor force participation, and that the experiences of Puerto Rican women are unique.

For the youngest cohort of women 15–19, there are already proportionately more white and black women in the labor force than there are Puerto Rican

Table 1. Percent Distribution of Labor Force and Family Characteristics
for Women 15–49 by Race/Ethnicity

Characteristics	Total	Group[a]		
		White	Black	Puerto Rican
Highest grade completed				
Less than high school	29.7	14.5	31.7	55.9
High school	28.1	31.0	28.2	23.9
Some college	20.9	20.0	26.9	15.5
College or more	21.3	34.5	13.1	4.7
Labor force status				
Employed full time	42.0	49.3	41.4	23.6
Employed part time	8.7	11.6	6.8	4.0
Unemployed[b]	4.1	3.0	5.8	4.2
Not in labor force	45.2	36.1	46.0	68.1
Marital status				
Married	38.3	45.7	26.9	29.0
Widowed	2.1	1.9	2.8	2.3
Divorced	7.2	7.6	7.0	8.8
Separated	7.0	2.6	8.3	12.4
Never married	45.4	42.3	55.0	47.5
Relationship to householder				
Householder	37.1	31.9	44.6	44.9
Spouse of householder	29.6	37.6	17.7	22.8
Child of householder	24.2	22.4	28.8	25.2
Other relative	5.3	2.5	6.9	5.3
Nonrelative	3.9	5.6	2.1	1.8
Householder's own never-married children under 18				
None	44.0	58.0	36.8	28.6
1 child	23.8	21.0	26.6	24.6
2 children	19.5	14.5	21.4	26.4
3 or more children	12.6	6.5	15.2	20.5
Family poverty status[c]				
Below poverty level	23.8	8.2	30.4	49.9
100–149% poverty	10.8	6.6	13.6	13.5
150% and over	65.4	85.2	56.0	36.7

[a]These are mutually exclusive groups.

[b]This category includes unemployed persons with and without prior work experience.

[c]The poverty status considered here is the status of the main family, even in households with subfamilies.

SOURCE: Merged file with 1985, 1986, and 1987 March Current Population Survey data for New York City.

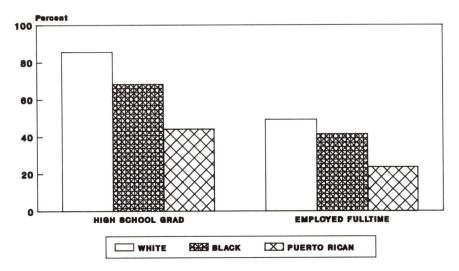

Figure 1. Labor force characteristics of women 15 to 49 by race/ethnicity.

women. Quite clearly, white women are more likely to be employed part time at this life-cycle stage than are either blacks or Puerto Ricans.

Through all the remaining age cohorts, the profile of work responsibilities remains relatively unchanged for Puerto Rican women. Approximately 40% of Puerto Rican women are in the labor force for all the older cohorts, and approximately 60% are not in the labor force. Among black women, there is an increase in labor force participation from ages 20–29 through ages 40–49, with the peak employment levels reached by the oldest women. Among white women, levels of employment are fairly steady across the life-cycle stages. Apparently, white women enter the labor force full time at the ages of 20–29 and stay in the labor force whether they are employed full time or part time in the older ages. Black women may enter the labor force later, but by the oldest ages they outpace white women with regard to levels of participation. Variations in the labor force participation of Puerto Rican women after the teen years are very slight. In every cohort, quite consistently, both white and black women are much more likely to be in the labor force and to be employed full time than are Puerto Rican women.

Family Characteristics by Cohort

Table 1 and Figure 2 indicate that, among all women, Puerto Ricans and blacks are less likely to be currently married than are white women. Compared to blacks, however, Puerto Ricans are more likely to have ever been married, and compared to all other women, Puerto Rican women are the most likely to be

Table 2. Percent Distribution of Labor Force and Family Characteristics
for Women 15–19 by Race/Ethnicity

		Group[a]		
Characteristics	Total	White	Black	Puerto Rican
Highest grade completed				
Less than high school	74.2	64.5	75.6	87.4
High school	8.8	11.5	9.3	4.8
Some college	16.9	24.1	15.1	7.3
College or more	.1	0.0	0.0	.5
Labor force status				
Employed full time	6.1	8.6	7.0	2.0
Employed part time	7.1	15.1	3.2	3.1
Unemployed[b]	3.7	4.2	5.5	2.1
Not in labor force	83.1	72.2	84.3	92.9
Marital status				
Married	2.1	1.2	0.0	5.6
Widowed	0.0	0.0	0.0	0.0
Divorced	.2	0.0	0.0	.6
Separated	.2	0.0	0.0	1.1
Never married	97.5	98.8	100.0	92.7
Relationship to householder				
Householder	1.0	.7	.6	1.4
Spouse of householder	1.5	0.0	0.0	4.5
Child of householder	87.5	94.4	84.2	87.1
Other relative	9.0	4.0	13.4	7.0
Nonrelative	.9	.9	1.8	0.0
Householder's own never-married children under 18				
None	20.0	25.6	17.2	19.5
1 child	34.1	40.8	31.1	27.9
2 children	24.0	21.9	26.7	20.3
3 or more children	22.0	11.6	25.1	32.3
Family poverty status[c]				
Below poverty level	32.7	7.1	40.0	59.3
100–149% poverty	12.9	9.4	14.0	13.8
150% and over	54.3	83.5	46.0	26.9

[a]These are mutually exclusive groups.

[b]This category includes unemployed persons with and without prior work experience.

[c]The poverty status considered here is the status of the main family, even in households with subfamilies.

SOURCE: Merged file with 1985, 1986, and 1987 March Current Population Survey data for New York City.

Table 3. Percent Distribution of Labor Force and Family Characteristics
for Women 20–29 by Race/Ethnicity

Characteristics	Total	Group[a]		
		White	Black	Puerto Rican
Highest grade completed				
Less than high school	19.1	5.8	22.8	45.6
High school	28.9	31.2	26.0	27.8
Some college	30.0	26.8	39.5	22.5
College or more	22.0	36.2	11.7	4.1
Labor force status				
Employed full time	44.1	58.2	31.8	26.3
Employed part time	6.8	10.1	5.5	3.0
Unemployed[b]	4.9	2.8	8.0	6.3
Not in labor force	44.2	28.9	54.7	64.6
Marital status				
Married	30.2	33.1	19.8	24.5
Widowed	.4	.2	.3	1.2
Divorced	2.5	1.6	1.8	6.1
Separated	4.8	.9	3.8	11.4
Never married	62.0	64.1	74.3	56.8
Relationship to householder				
Householder	32.7	26.0	37.2	47.7
Spouse of householder	22.3	27.3	10.9	19.2
Child of householder	31.1	32.0	41.1	24.5
Other relative	6.9	3.3	8.0	5.7
Nonrelative	7.0	11.4	2.8	3.0
Householder's own never-married children under 18				
None	54.7	74.8	40.1	34.5
1 child	22.0	15.5	27.3	25.6
2 children	16.2	7.9	22.5	24.1
3 or more children	7.2	1.8	10.1	15.8
Family poverty status[c]				
Below poverty level	24.6	8.3	32.8	50.7
100–149% poverty	12.0	9.1	11.8	15.8
150% and over	63.4	82.5	55.4	33.5

[a]These are mutually exclusive groups.

[b]This category includes unemployed persons with and without prior work experience.

[c]The poverty status considered here is the status of the main family, even in households with subfamilies.

SOURCE: Merged file with 1985, 1986, and 1987 March Current Population Survey data for New York City.

Table 4. Percent Distribution of Labor Force and Family Characteristics
for Women 30–39 by Race/Ethnicity

| Characteristics | Total | Group[a] | | |
		White	Black	Puerto Rican
Highest grade completed				
Less than high school	22.9	8.1	21.8	44.4
High school	29.2	31.0	32.2	28.6
Some college	18.3	17.3	25.1	17.5
College or more	29.5	43.6	20.9	9.4
Labor force status				
Employed full time	48.9	52.6	52.6	31.9
Employed part time	8.7	10.5	10.0	3.0
Unemployed[b]	3.4	2.7	5.4	4.0
Not in labor force	38.9	34.2	32.0	61.1
Marital status				
Married	52.5	58.8	43.7	37.9
Widowed	1.5	.9	2.1	1.8
Divorced	9.6	11.3	7.7	11.9
Separated	9.0	3.2	9.4	17.5
Never married	27.5	25.7	37.0	30.8
Relationship to householder				
Householder	48.0	41.9	58.2	58.4
Spouse of householder	39.6	47.6	28.7	28.8
Child of householder	5.6	5.1	6.9	5.6
Other relative	3.2	1.5	3.4	4.6
Nonrelative	3.7	3.9	2.8	2.6
Householder's own never-married children under 18				
None	37.2	51.5	27.7	18.7
1 child	20.5	18.3	22.8	22.0
2 children	24.3	20.1	25.9	33.5
3 or more children	18.0	10.1	23.7	25.8
Family poverty status[c]				
Below poverty level	22.7	8.3	29.4	50.4
100–149% poverty	9.5	4.6	15.8	9.2
150% and over	67.9	87.1	54.8	40.3

[a]These are mutually exclusive groups.
[b]This category includes unemployed persons with and without prior work experience.
[c]The poverty status considered here is the status of the main family, even in households with subfamilies.
SOURCE: Merged file with 1985, 1986, and 1987 March Current Population Survey data for New York City.

Table 5. Percent Distribution of Labor Force and Family Characteristics
for Women 40–49 by Race/Ethnicity

		Group[a]		
Characteristics	Total	White	Black	Puerto Rican
Highest grade completed				
Less than high school	28.9	13.9	28.2	64.9
High school	36.5	39.2	38.0	26.1
Some college	13.1	12.7	19.2	6.6
College or more	21.5	34.1	14.5	2.3
Labor force status				
Employed full time	50.4	50.0	62.6	24.9
Employed part time	10.5	13.8	7.2	8.5
Unemployed[b]	3.1	3.1	3.6	2.8
Not in labor force	36.0	33.1	26.6	63.8
Marital status				
Married	52.1	63.3	34.1	44.6
Widowed	6.7	6.4	8.5	7.2
Divorced	15.1	13.8	17.4	16.5
Separated	11.6	5.1	18.0	16.3
Never married	14.6	11.4	22.0	15.4
Relationship to householder				
Householder	49.7	39.2	66.0	57.4
Spouse of householder	43.0	53.7	25.3	36.8
Child of householder	2.5	2.8	3.0	1.7
Other relative	3.6	2.3	5.2	4.0
Nonrelative	1.2	2.0	.5	0.0
Householder's own never-married children under 18				
None	51.6	58.5	53.9	40.1
1 child	25.1	23.8	27.0	23.4
2 children	15.3	12.2	11.9	25.6
3 or more children	7.9	5.6	7.3	11.0
Family poverty status[c]				
Below poverty level	18.9	8.6	22.7	39.1
100–149% poverty	9.6	4.6	13.2	15.2
150% and over	71.5	86.8	64.1	45.7

[a]These are mutually exclusive groups.
[b]This category includes unemployed persons with and without prior work experience.
[c]The poverty status considered here is the status of the main family, even in households with subfamilies.
SOURCE: Merged file with 1985, 1986, and 1987 March Current Population Survey data for New York City.

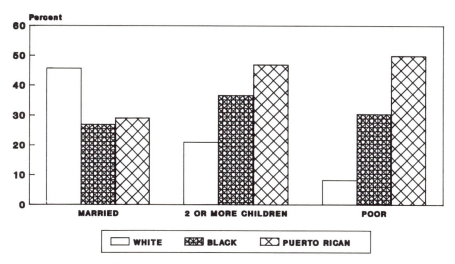

Figure 2. Family characteristics of women 15 to 49 by race/ethnicity.

currently separated or divorced. These marital status differentials are reflected in group differences in householder status. Approximately 45% of Puerto Rican women and black women are single householders, while 31.9% of all white women head their own households.

Very clearly, among Puerto Rican women, we find the lowest percentage living in households with no minor children—28.6% as compared to 36.8% of all black women and 58.0% of all white women in the same situation. From the opposite end of the scale, when compared to other women, Puerto Rican women are the most likely to reside in households with three or more minor children.

Puerto Rican poverty levels for all women 15–49 are much higher than they are for the other racial/ethnic groups. While 49.9% of the Puerto Rican families fall below the poverty level, 30.4% of all black families and 8.2% of all white families are poor. Among all Puerto Rican families in this sample, nearly two thirds are below 150% of poverty.

If we examine the youngest cohort, women 15–19, there are suggestions of early family formation among Puerto Rican women that are not found among either white or black women. (Because of the small sample size, evidence of this pattern in the CPS data cannot be conclusive.) At these ages, Puerto Rican women appear to be the most likely to have been married and the most likely to be either a householder or a spouse of the householder. Whatever their marital status and relationship to the householder, Puerto Ricans are also the most likely to live in a household with numerous minor children.

Although it is not possible to determine from the CPS data what the actual completed fertility of these young women may be, independent estimates show that the early fertility of both Puerto Rican and black adolescents are similar, and higher than that of whites. Using data from the 1985 New York City Health Department Births Master File and the age cohort estimates from the CPS, we calculated the 1985 birthrates for women 15–19. They are 68 per 1,000 for Puerto Ricans; 66 per 1,000 for blacks; and, 11 per 1,000 for whites. Thus, the data suggest that Puerto Rican and black women both begin bearing children earlier than do white women. However, the evidence from the merged CPS sample suggests that the family context in which they raise these children may not be the same at the earliest ages. Although young Puerto Rican women may start their own households when they give birth, blacks may remain within their family of orientation.

By ages 20–29, Puerto Rican women have an intermediate marital status distribution compared to black and white women, with 24.5% of Puerto Rican women currently married. Of all women in this age group, Puerto Ricans are the most likely to have ever been married, and by far the most likely to be separated or divorced. At this same point in the life cycle, fully 47.7% of Puerto Rican women head their own households, are the least likely to live in households without minor children (who are probably their own), and the most likely to be in households with more than three minor children.

Puerto Rican women and black women begin to share similar marital status and family relationship patterns in the age group 30–39, and both diverge sharply from the experience of white women at this stage. For women 30–39, 37.9% of all Puerto Rican women, 43.7% of all black women, and 58.8% of all white women are married. From another perspective, at this stage, 58.4% of all Puerto Rican women, 58.2% of all black women, and 41.9% of all white women are single householders. (The CPS data do not allow any analysis of differential remarriage patterns among divorced women, which obviously affect the current marital status of all women in the sample.)

Puerto Rican and black women 30–39 also appear to have similar child care responsibilities, as compared to whites. Although 18.7% of all Puerto Rican women and 27.7% of all black women live in households with no minor children, fully 51.5% of all white women live in childless households (including women who never had children and those whose children have grown and moved out of the household). Furthermore, Puerto Rican and black women reveal similar proportional distributions among those households with at least one minor child.

In the oldest age cohort, women 40–49, Puerto Rican and black women are still more similar to each other than they are to white women on the family structure variables. Puerto Rican and black women are less likely to be currently married and more likely to be single householders than are whites. If 57.4% of

Puerto Rican women and 66.0% of black women in this cohort are single house-holders, only 39.2% of white women head their own households.

Compared to both black and white women, Puerto Rican women 40–49 are the least likely to live in households with no minor children. Since almost 95% of these women are either the householder or the spouse of the householder, the minor children are their own, reflecting the continued childbearing of Puerto Rican women in older ages. Once more, data from the vital statistics complement our findings. Birth data for the 1980s show that older Puerto Rican women in New York City have the highest parity in comparison to all other women (Chavkin, Busner, & McLaughlin, 1987).

Poverty among Puerto Rican families is consistently higher than that of either blacks or whites through all the age cohorts. For Puerto Ricans and blacks, compared to whites, there is a decline in poverty rates from the youngest women to the oldest women. Among Puerto Rican women 15–19, 59.3% live in poor families; among Puerto Rican women 20–29, 50.7% are poor; among Puerto Rican women 30–39, 50.4% live in poor families; and among Puerto Rican women 40–49, 39.1% are poor. The comparable figures for blacks are 40.0%, 32.8%, 29.4%, and 22.7%. For whites the poverty rates are very low and there is little change evident from one age group to the next.

Puerto Rican women aged 40–49 are the most likely of all Puerto Rican women to be the householder's spouse, perhaps reflecting a stronger propensity to marry in their generation. Because they have a spouse present, they may also be the most likely to have an adult male wage earner in the household. If this is, in fact, the case, it explains why the oldest group of Puerto Rican women is the least likely to live in a poor family. It might also be true that older Puerto Rican women live in households with teenaged children who are working and contributing to the family income. Again, if this is the case, it explains the relative well-being of Puerto Rican women 40–49 as compared to other Puerto Rican women. Further analysis is needed to evaluate either of these possibilities.

A Focus on Married Women 30–39

In an effort to control for level of education and for marital status while considering other aspects of women's work and family responsibilities, I will next focus on married women who are 30–39 at three educational levels. These women were selected because they were thought to have relatively intact families, and to be at a stage where they had completed their education. Given these characteristics, I sought to uncover any differences by educational level and race/ethnicity in labor force status, the presence of children in the household, the total number of family members in the labor force, and the family's poverty status. The results of my analysis are shown in Tables 6 to 8 and in Figure 3.

Table 6. Percent Distribution of Labor Force and Family Characteristics
for Women 30–39, Who Completed High School, and Are Married
with Spouse Present, by Race/Ethnicity

Characteristics	Total	Group[a]		
		White	Black	Puerto Rican
Labor force status				
Employed full time	48.4	42.2	67.3	37.1
Employed part time	9.9	11.1	11.0	4.2
Unemployed[b]	1.3	1.6	0.0	1.5
Not in labor force	40.4	45.1	21.7	57.2
Householder's own never-married children under 18				
None	26.4	31.1	25.9	9.2
1 child	25.2	26.8	18.4	31.3
2 children	31.0	28.9	32.0	34.2
3 or more children	17.4	13.2	23.7	25.2
Householder's own children under 6				
None	58.2	57.7	61.8	54.7
1 child	32.0	32.1	29.4	33.6
2 or more children	9.8	10.2	8.8	11.8
Number of family members in the labor force				
None	2.1	1.9	2.3	7.1
1	40.6	44.8	24.4	51.5
2 or more	57.3	53.4	73.3	41.4
Family poverty status[c]				
Below poverty level	5.1	2.7	7.3	13.9
100–149% poverty	6.5	3.9	9.7	10.3
150% and over	88.5	93.5	82.9	75.9

[a]These are mutually exclusive groups.
[b]This category includes unemployed persons with and without prior work experience.
[c]The poverty status considered here is the status of the main family, even in households with subfamilies.
SOURCE: Merged file with 1985, 1986, and 1987 March Current Population Survey data for New York City.

In each of the tables, Puerto Ricans reveal different work and family responsibilities as compared to whites or blacks. (The relevant chi-square statistics for each set of figures are all highly significant.) Although the controls for age, marital status, and education are imperfect, these findings suggest that the simple socioeconomic variables examined here can only explain part of the work and

Table 7. Percent Distribution of Labor Force and Family Characteristics
for Women 30–39, Who Completed Some College, and Are Married
with Spouse Present, by Race/Ethnicity

| Characteristics | Total | Group[a] | | |
		White	Black	Puerto Rican
Labor force status				
Employed full time	59.1	55.6	71.1	45.7
Employed part time	7.6	6.5	13.2	8.7
Unemployed[b]	1.0	1.3	0.0	0.0
Not in labor force	32.4	36.7	15.6	45.6
Householder's own never-married children under 18				
None	33.7	41.4	24.9	15.8
1 child	25.4	26.9	21.0	28.4
2 children	26.8	22.7	29.6	40.2
3 or more children	14.1	9.0	24.5	15.6
Householder's own children under 6				
None	59.3	58.8	62.7	64.5
1 child	30.9	31.0	28.0	30.2
2 or more children	9.9	10.3	9.3	5.3
Number of family members in the labor force				
None	.8	.6	0.0	6.0
1	35.3	39.2	21.2	42.4
2 or more	63.8	60.2	78.8	51.5
Family poverty status[c]				
Below poverty level	3.1	2.6	5.5	7.2
100–149% poverty	4.2	3.1	4.5	0.0
150% and over	92.7	94.4	90.0	92.8

[a]These are mutually exclusive groups.

[b]This category includes unemployed persons with and without prior work experience.

[c]The poverty status considered here is the status of the main family, even in households with subfamilies.

SOURCE: Merged file with 1985, 1986, and 1987 March Current Population Survey data for New York City.

family differentials among women of separate racial/ethnic groups. Within any given subcategory of women, controlling for a number of characteristics, Puerto Rican women are always the least likely to work.

Whatever educational level is examined in these tables, Puerto Rican women have the lowest labor force participation rates. Black women have the highest

TERRY J. ROSENBERG

Table 8. Percent Distribution of Labor Force and Family Characteristics
for Women 30–39, Who Completed College, and Are Married
with Spouse Present, by Race/Ethnicity

| Characteristics | Total | Group[a] | | |
		White	Black	Puerto Rican
Labor force status				
Employed full time	67.6	66.3	81.4	58.9
Employed part time	7.2	5.8	15.9	7.0
Unemployed[b]	1.1	1.0	0.0	0.0
Not in labor force	24.1	26.9	2.7	34.1
Householder's own never-married children under 18				
None	39.5	45.9	39.1	25.9
1 child	28.8	27.1	34.5	39.8
2 children	22.7	19.6	15.7	34.3
3 or more children	9.0	7.4	10.7	0.0
Householder's own children under 6				
None	57.9	57.4	71.5	60.9
1 child	31.4	31.3	23.8	31.2
2 or more children	10.7	11.3	4.7	7.9
Number of family members in the labor force				
None	.4	0.0	0.0	8.7
1	28.4	31.4	7.8	33.5
2 or more	71.2	68.6	92.2	57.8
Family poverty status[c]				
Below poverty level	2.5	3.8	0.0	0.0
100–149% poverty	3.0	1.8	0.0	0.0
150% and over	94.4	94.5	100.0	100.0

[a]These are mutually exclusive groups.

[b]This category includes unemployed persons with and without prior work experience.

[c]The poverty status considered here is the status of the main family, even in households with subfamilies.

SOURCE: Merged file with 1985, 1986, and 1987 March Current Population Survey data for New York City.

labor force participation rates, with white women in an intermediate position. For the highest level of educational attainment, college or more, slightly less than 60% of Puerto Rican women are working full time, compared to 81.4% of black women and 66.3% of white women.

The family responsibilities of Puerto Rican women appear somewhat lighter

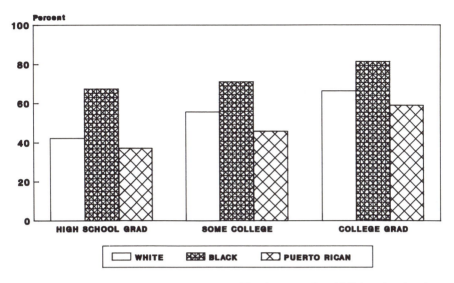

Figure 3. Percentage of married women, aged 30 to 39, who are employed full time, by education and race/ethnicity.

than those of black women, if the total number of minor children in the household is considered. However, if the measure used is the number of children who are under 6 years of age, Puerto Rican women appear to have a heavier burden of child care responsibilities as compared to blacks, but less responsibility as compared to whites.

For each educational level, Puerto Rican women are in families with fewer family members in the labor force—in part because of their own relatively low labor force participation rates. At the highest level of educational attainment, for instance, 57.8% of Puerto Rican women live in families with two or more members in the labor force. In contrast, 68.6% of white women and 92.2% of black women live in families with two or more members in the labor force.

Although the poverty rates shown in all three tables (Tables 6 to 8) are much lower than those seen earlier, the poverty rates for Puerto Rican families continue to be the highest. Among women with a high school education or better, 13.9% of all Puerto Rican women live in poverty; at the same educational level 7.3% of black women live in poverty and 2.7% of white women live in poverty. These differentials may be related to the lower level of labor force participation of Puerto Rican women and the lower likelihood of Puerto Rican families to have two or more working members.

There are important gradients for Puerto Rican women as well as for other women from the lowest level of educational attainment to the highest. Figure 3 graphically demonstrates the increase in full-time employment for each racial/ethnic group as level of education increases. For Puerto Ricans, as well as whites and blacks, women with the highest levels of education are the most likely to work full time.

In one further effort to explain the lower labor force participation of Puerto Rican women, I hypothesized that an earnings differential among women might discourage Puerto Rican women from joining the labor force, and from working full time. For women working full time in the selected group of married women 30–39, therefore, I calculated median annual earnings. In fact, the median for Puerto Rican women is the lowest of all three groups; for Puerto Ricans the figure is $15,500, for blacks it is $17,000, and for whites it is $20,000. Puerto Rican women who have not joined the labor force, therefore, may rationally calculate that their earnings capacity is low, even with a high school diploma, and may consequently decide not to seek employment.

Interestingly enough, however, when we evaluated the relative contribution of Puerto Rican women who work full time to their family's total income we discovered a more complex picture. The median earnings of Puerto Rican women constitute 51.7% of the entire median income for their families. By comparison, the respective figure for black women is 46.1% and for white women it is 34.2%. In other words, Puerto Rican women who work full time contribute relatively more to their families than do other women. Following this logic, one could say that the earnings of Puerto Rican women are even more crucial to their families' economic well-being than that of either black or white women. Still, the low level of wages they can expect with a limited education may keep many out of the labor force.

SUMMARY AND RECOMMENDATIONS

This analysis confirms and elaborates upon patterns found in previous research (Rosenberg, 1987, 1989; Tienda & Jensen, 1987). For women 15–49 in New York City, one sees consistent differences between Puerto Rican women and other women. Puerto Ricans in each of four age cohorts have lower educational levels and lower employment levels than blacks or whites. The gap between Puerto Rican women and others, however, varies by age group.

Within age cohorts, Puerto Rican women are more likely to be married than black women, and less likely to be married than white women. Early marriage, and early separation or divorce, appear to be distinctive experiences among Puerto Rican women. Thus, the high percentages of female-headed households found among Puerto Ricans and among blacks are probably not the result of the same family formation and dissolution processes.

Puerto Rican women live throughout their life spans in households that have more minor children, and throughout the life span they are also more likely to be found in poor families than are other women. These experiences vary somewhat among age cohorts.

Considering only a selected group of mature married women, there are still clear differences between Puerto Rican women and others. Puerto Rican women in this subsample, at every educational level, are less likely to be in the labor force, and less likely to work full time, than are other women. With lower percentages of families having two or more members in the labor force, these Puerto Rican women are more likely to live in poverty than either blacks or whites.

Although I have been able to further specify some general patterns, unfortunately I have not been able to provide complete explanations for these patterns. Numerous questions requiring more research attention in the future emerge from my findings. One of these has to do with the *timing* of education, employment, and childbearing in a women's life. It may be that teenage motherhood among Puerto Rican women is more likely to prevent high school completion and entry into the labor force than is the case for other women. It may also be that whatever their level of education, Puerto Rican women may stay out of the labor force longer and attend exclusively to child care responsibilities more than do other women. In both instances, during the time these women are in the home, they lose a competitive edge to other women in an already difficult labor market.

Given the presence of small children, another question relates to the influence of alternative income sources on the propensity of women to enter the labor force and work full time. In this study, I have not presented any data on program participation among Puerto Ricans versus others, but prior studies clearly illustrate the high percentages of Puerto Rican families receiving public assistance (Tienda & Jensen, 1987). Young mothers who are on welfare for a certain period of time, as compared to mothers who are temporarily supported by extended family members, may be less likely to seek outside employment. To the extent that Puerto Rican women may now be forced to receive welfare, in the absence of extended family members who can assist them, they may then be further discouraged from joining the labor force. And, in turn, their own dependence on welfare may subsequently increase the likelihood that their daughters will be on welfare and perpetuate their high poverty rates. (This forecast was found to hold true among whites and blacks in McLanahan, 1988.)

Since World War II, the two-earner strategy has become the most realistic choice for American families who desire a moderate level of living, or who even just want to stay above poverty. Whatever factors have hindered the labor market success of Puerto Rican women have also inhibited their families' economic progress. Without an increase in women's earnings, Puerto Rican families will continue to fall behind other families and will continue to decline into poverty.

In the current political climate with new welfare legislation, moreover, it is certain that more demands will be placed on women receiving transfer payments, and more stringent guidelines instituted with regard to their employment outside the home. Puerto Rican women, along with other women receiving AFDC, will soon be required to work in spite of their family responsibilities. A better understanding of why these women have thus far not joined the labor force, and why they have not found reasonably well-paying jobs, is crucial to any program that attempts to provide them with job skills and employment opportunities in a shrinking job market.

REFERENCES

Chavkin, W., C. Busner, & M. McLaughlin. (1987). Reproductive health: Caribbean women in New York City, 1980–1984. *International Migration Review, 21,* 609–625.

Cooney, R. S., & A. Colon. (1980). Work and family: The recent struggle of Puerto Rican females. In C. E. Rodriguez, V. S. Korrol, & J. O. Alers, Eds., *The Puerto Rican struggle: Essays on survival in the U. S.* (pp. 58–73). New York: Puerto Rican Migration Consortium.

Korrol, V. S. (1980). Survival of Puerto Rican women in New York before World War II. In C. E. Rodriguez, V. S. Korrol, & J. O. Alers, Eds., *The Puerto Rican struggle: Essays on survival in the U. S.* (pp. 47–57). New York: Puerto Rican Migration Consortium.

McLanahan, S. S. (1988). Family structure and dependency: Early transitions to female household headship. *Demography, 25,* 1–16.

Rosenberg, T. J. (1987). *Poverty in New York City: 1980–1985.* New York: Community Service Society.

Rosenberg, T. J. (1989). *Poverty in New York City, 1985–1988: The crisis continues.* New York: Community Service Society.

Tienda, M., & J. Glass. (1985). Household structure and labor force participation of black, Hispanic, and white mothers. *Demography, 22,* 381–394.

Tienda, M., & L. Jensen. (1987). *Poverty and minorities: A quarter-century profile of color and socioeconomic disadvantage.* Institute for Research on Poverty, Conference Paper. University of Wisconsin-Madison.

U. S. Bureau of the Census. (1987). *Current Population Reports: The Hispanic population in the United States: March 1986 and 1987 (advance report).* Washington, DC: U. S. Government Printing Office.

Ventura, S. J. (1985). Births of Hispanic parentage, 1982. *Monthly Vital Statistics Report, 34,* 1–16.

Ventura, S. J., & S. M. Taffel. (1985). Childbearing characteristics of U. S. and foreign-born Hispanic mothers. *Public Health Reports, 100,* 647–652.

V

Policy

11

Wage Policies, Employment, and Puerto Rican Migration

Carlos E. Santiago

INTRODUCTION

It is necessary to understand the forces influencing Puerto Rican migration to truly assess the economic status of Puerto Ricans in the United States. The migratory response reflects the aspirations of workers and their families and represents a relative dissatisfaction with economic conditions on the island. Moreover, the Puerto Rican migratory phenomenon is fundamentally different from the place-to-place European migrations of the twentieth century or the periodic movements of workers from Yugoslavia and Turkey to Western European countries. The Puerto Rican experience is characterized by both features. There is a good deal of cyclical mobility of workers between the island and the United States and longer-term secular movements from the island to the United States. My contention in this chapter is that we must examine both the cyclical

An earlier version of this chapter was presented at a seminar on *Employment Policy: Puerto Ricans and Jobs,* in Cambridge, Massachusetts, on April 8, 1988. This research has been partially funded by the Inter-University Program for Latino Research and the Social Science Research Council. The usual disclaimers apply.

CARLOS E. SANTIAGO • Department of Economics, State University of New York at Albany, Albany, New York 12222.

Hispanics in the Labor Force, edited by Edwin Melendez *et al.* Plenum Press, New York, 1991.

and secular nature of Puerto Rican migration to fully comprehend its effects on the economic status of the Puerto Rican population in the United States.

The objective of this chapter is two-fold. First, to highlight the role of migration in Puerto Rico's demographic transition. Second, to show that net migration was affected by increases in island minimum wages. Thus, the causal links to be identified are presented in reverse order—from migration to population growth first, and from wage policies to migration second. The results demonstrate the extensive influence of Puerto Rican migration on population growth. Its effects largely overshadow the influence of natural increases in the population. The finding that minimum wage hikes in Puerto Rico reduced net emigration is theoretically consistent, but quite unusual. Increases in island minimum wages in the mid-1970s, in conjunction with the extension of transfer benefits (such as the U. S. Department of Agriculture's Food Stamp Program) were seen as methods of reducing Puerto Rican migration to economically depressed urban centers in the northeast. Using monthly observations of wages and migratory movements between 1970 and 1987, the empirical analysis suggests that minimum wage shocks did reduce the net outflow of workers from the island.

The chapter is divided into five main sections. In the first section I examine the significance of Puerto Rican migration in the important process of growth of human resources on the island. In the second section, I discuss the Puerto Rican experience with minimum wage policies in the postwar period. Then in the third section, I present a simple behavioral model to help analyze the impact of wage hikes on labor mobility within island labor markets as well as between Puerto Rico and the United States. In the next section, I empirically test the sensitivity of net migration to wage shocks and the underlying employment effects on the island. In the final section, I provide concluding comments and notes for further research.

MIGRATION AND THE DEMOGRAPHIC
TRANSITION IN PUERTO RICO

Population growth plays a rather unique role in economic development. On the one hand, it can be related to an economy's potential output because it reflects changes in the stock of human resources. On the other hand, it also mirrors the claims on total product. This dual function implies that to assess the economic status of Puerto Ricans in the United States and on the island, it is necessary to understand the forces influencing population growth in Puerto Rico.

Between 1940 and 1985, the Puerto Rican population grew at an average annual rate of 1.2%; numbering roughly 1.9 million for the earlier year, and 3.3 million for the later one. This low rate of population growth masks important changes, foremost among which is the demographic transition experienced over this 45-year period. The demographic transition is represented by stages. The initial stage is one of high and stable birth and mortality rates. The second stage consists of high and stable birthrates and falling mortality rates. Historically, the reductions in birthrates prove to be the greatest challenge in the attempt to reduce population growth. Declines in mortality often occur quickly in response to improvements in health delivery systems, control of infectious diseases, and increased nutritional intake of the population. In the third stage, birthrates begin to decline, while in the final stage both birth and mortality rates converge at low levels. The theory of the demographic transition postulates that these temporal changes are largely influenced by the level of per capita income as well as the rate of economic growth.

In 1940, the Puerto Rican population experienced high birth and high mortality rates. Currently, the population is characterized by low birth and low mortality rates. Thus, dramatic structural changes in the size and composition of the population and labor force accompanied rapid industrialization.[1] Birthrates in Puerto Rico have remained consistently higher than birthrates in developed countries and somewhat lower than developing countries. In fact, prior to the industrialization push of the 1950s, the Puerto Rican birthrate was higher than the world average and only fell below that average after the industrialization process was well underway. The trend has been for birth rates in Puerto Rico to approach those of developed countries.

During the early stages of the demographic transition, population growth in Puerto Rico was considerably less than countries at similar levels of development. More recently, however, despite industrialization and economic maturity, population growth on the island is now much higher than experienced by countries at similar stages of development. The point is that although a demographic transition took place, population growth in Puerto Rico has not exhibited the patterns that are evident when countries move to higher stages of development. For example, population grew at an average annual rate of 1.67% from 1940 to 1950, slowed to 0.58% between 1950 and 1960, and then increased again by 1.54% between 1960 and 1980. Although trends in births and deaths have certainly altered the rate at which the Puerto Rican population has been growing, the primary determinant of population growth on the island has been migration.

[1]Using guidelines set forth by the World Bank, whereby birth rates of 30 or higher are classified as high and mortality rates of 15 or higher are considered high, Puerto Rico would be designated as a high birth–high mortality area in 1940, a high birth–low mortality are in both 1950 and 1960, and a low birth–low mortality area in 1970. Using this classification scheme to compare average annual population growth rates in Puerto Rico with other regions shows that population growth in Puerto Rico has remained below the world average for every period except the post-1960 period where it exceeds the world average for the low birth–low mortality rate group.

Population growth is generated by changes in births, deaths, and migration. In simple terms, total population in time period t, p_t, is expressed as

$$p_t = p_{t-1} + b_t - d_t + im_t - om_t \qquad (1)$$

where b_t is the number of births, d_t is the number of deaths, im_t is the number of immigrants, and om_t is the number of emigrants. Equation 1 can also be written as

$$p_t - p_{t-1} = \Delta p_t = nat_t + nm_t \qquad (2)$$

where nat_t is the natural increase in the population and nm_t is net migration.

For most countries, only the first element of the right-hand side of Equation 2 need be considered. But in Puerto Rico, it is the last term, more than anything else, that has influenced population growth in the postwar period. Figure 1 illustrates total population and its rate of growth in Puerto Rico from 1950 to 1984. Two observations are noteworthy. First, the population growth rate exhibits considerable cyclical variability. Second, it does not reflect a declining trend so characteristic of countries experiencing rapid economic growth. What makes the latter so unusual is that both crude birth and crude mortality rates have declined considerably over the postwar period. These changes are largely the

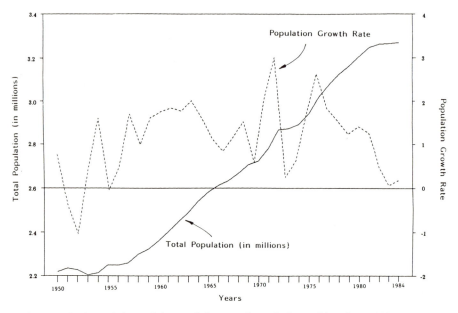

Figure 1. Total population and the population growth rate in Puerto Rico, from 1950 to 1984.

result of rising standards of living, improvements in educational attainment, and increases in female labor force participation.

Between 1940 and 1985, the birthrate (per 1,000 population) has been cut in half, falling from 40.1 to 19.2. The mortality rate declined from 18.4 to 6.6 over the same period. The infant mortality rate (per 1,000 live births) has dropped from 109.1 in 1940 to 17.3 in 1983. The sharp fall is partly due to improved medical facilities and ease of access to them. The forces responsible for declines in both infant and general mortality are also responsible for increasing life expectancy from 46 years in 1940, to 74 years in 1982. The latter increase is truly dramatic in such a short span of time (by 1960 life expectancy reached 69 years of age). These favorable demographic trends have been the result of rapid economic expansion and have led to continued growth of income per capita.

To better understand the dynamics of population growth, an autoregressive-moving average (ARMA) class model is specified for the Puerto Rican population growth rate. The univariate ARMA(p,q) model is represented by

$$\Phi_p(B)y_t = \delta + \Theta_q(B)\varepsilon_t \qquad (3)$$

where

$$\Phi_p(B)y_t = y_t - \phi_1 y_{t-1} - \ldots - \phi_p y_{t-p} \qquad (4)$$

and

$$\Theta_q(B)\varepsilon_t = \varepsilon_t - \theta_1 \varepsilon_{t-1} - \ldots - \theta_q \varepsilon_{t-q} \qquad (5)$$

Φ_p and Θ_q are autoregressive and moving average parameters in the lag operator B $(B^k y_t = y_{t-k})$, respectively. y_t is an endogenous variable and δ is a constant.

To determine which model best replicates the underlying time series process of the variable y_t, we minimize the Akaike Information Criterion (AIC).[2] This

---

[2] The Akaike Information Criterion provides an efficient method of choosing one of many competing models. Let us express the competing models $L(\alpha_1), L(\alpha_2), \ldots, L(\alpha_k)$ as $\bar{L}(\alpha)$. The AIC is defined by a loss function based on the difference between the true and estimated distribution of a fitted model. The error is expressed as a function of the likelihood ratio of two probability distributions and measured by Kullback and Leibler's mean information for discrimination. The loss function proposed by Akaike is

$$W(\Theta_o,\bar{\alpha}) = -2/T \int [log\bar{L}(\alpha)/L(\Theta_o)]L(\Theta_o)dx$$

where $\bar{\alpha}$ is treated as a constant in the integration, Θ_o is a vector of parameters, and T is the number of observations. The AIC is the predictor of W and can be expressed as assures a stationary time series process and a "white-noise" distribution of residuals.[3] The time series realization of the population growth rate, $\dot{p}_t$, is best captured by a first-order moving average process represented by the following equation:[4]

$$\dot{p}_t = 1.124 + 0.672\hat{\varepsilon}_{t-1} \tag{6}$$

Equation 6 captures the cyclical movement of the population growth rate in Puerto Rico over the postwar period.

The cyclical pattern of the population growth rate is attributable to variations in the rate of net migration. Since a behavioral model of demographic change has not been developed, the relationship between the population growth rate and the rate of net migration is simply based on the identity in Equation 2. Figure 2 shows the close correspondence between these two variables and suggests that both the long-term trend and the cyclical movement of the population growth rate are primarily influenced by movements of people between the United States and Puerto Rico. This should not be surprising given the openness of the Puerto Rican economy.

The relevant question, then, is to what extent is population growth, influenced as it is by changes in births, deaths, and migration, the result of economic transformation in Puerto Rico? It is plausible that the Puerto Rican demographic transition was accelerated by the very forces that brought about structural transformation. However, it is important to remember that a more fundamental determinant of these dramatic demographic changes was the existence of a migratory outlet, or "safety valve," which reduced population pressures on the island.[5]

A multiple time-series framework is well suited to reproduce the dynamics of birth rates, mortality rates, and migration rates in the course of Puerto Rican

---

$$AIC = (-2/T)log\tilde{L}(\alpha) + 2p/T$$

where p is the dimension of vector α. The objective is to find the specification which minimizes the AIC. See Amemiya (1985) for a discussion of the use of the AIC.

[3]In contrast to the classical multivariate regression approach, the error structure in the ARMA model, ε_t, is not assumed to be normally distributed with $E[\varepsilon_t] = 0$, $Var[\varepsilon_t] = \sigma^2$ for all t and $E[\varepsilon_t, \varepsilon_{t-j}] = 0$ for $j \neq 0$. Instead, these properties, which reflect a "white-noise" time-series process, are modeled. The implication is that model specification depends crucially upon the data. The rationale for this procedure is to eliminate effects of random drift, seasonality, and other "noise" from the series.

[4]Based on a chi-square test of the Box-Ljung Q-statistic, the residuals of this equation are white noise.

[5]The size of the Puerto Rican migration stream relative to the size of the population makes it a factor that cannot go unnoticed. Much has been written on the experience of the migrant population from a sociological perspective, whereas fewer works have appeared from a purely economic point of view. Notable exceptions are Friedlander (1965); Fleisher (1963); and Maldonado (1976).

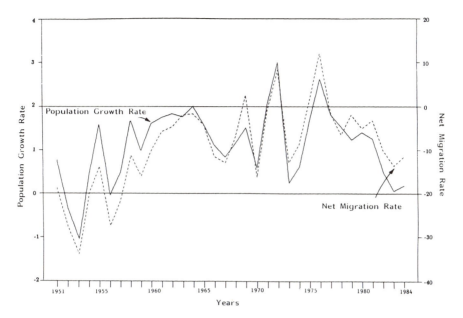

Figure 2. Population growth and the net migration rate in Puerto Rico, from 1951 to 1984.

industrialization. It is crucial, however, that endogenous and exogenous relations be specified *a priori*. The multiple time series model is as follows:

$$\begin{bmatrix} H_{11}(B) & H_{12}(B) \\ H_{21}(B) & H_{22}(B) \end{bmatrix} \begin{bmatrix} y_t \\ x_t \end{bmatrix} = \begin{bmatrix} F_{11}(B) & F_{12}(B) \\ F_{21}(B) & F_{22}(B) \end{bmatrix} \begin{bmatrix} \epsilon_{1t} \\ \epsilon_{2t} \end{bmatrix}$$

where y_t is a vector of endogenous variables, x_t is a vector of exogenous variables, and H_{ij} and F_{ij} are parameter matrices, elements of which are polynomials in the lag operator B. Each ε represents a white-noise disturbance with ε_{1t} referring to the variables in y_t and ε_{2t} referring to the variables in x_t. Since the elements of y_t are endogenous while the elements of x_t are exogenous, and assuming $E[\varepsilon_{1t}, \varepsilon_{2t}] = 0$, it is possible to simplify the expression above by maintaining that $H_{21}(B) \equiv 0$, $F_{12}(B) \equiv 0$, and $F_{21}(B) \equiv 0$.

The endogenous variables of vector y_t are the birthrate, b_t, the mortality rate, d_t, and the net migration rate, nm_t. The exogenous variables of vector x_t include real per capita income, g_t, and the rate of growth of per capita income, $\dot{g}_t$. Multivariate transfer functions were estimated for each of the endogenous variables. The results are as follows:

$$b_t = -1.915 - [0.9499(B) + 0.4828(B^2)]b_t + 0.00024g_t + 0.0056g_t$$
$$+ [0.6310(B) + 1.149(B^2)]\hat{\varepsilon}_{11t} \qquad (7)$$

$$d_t = -0.032 + [0.6091(B) - 0.0578(B^2)]d_t + 0.00005g_t + 0.0001\dot{g}_t$$
$$- 1.0890(B)\hat{\varepsilon}_{12t} \qquad\qquad (8)$$

$$nm_t = -18.06 + 0.4810(B)nm_t + 0.01307g_t - 0.8662\dot{g}_t \qquad (9)$$

In the equation for the birthrate, only the downward trend, $\delta = -1.915$ and the autoregressive and moving average parameters are found to be statistically significant. In the mortality rate equation, only the first-order autoregressive and moving average parameters are statistically significant. For the net migration equation, only the first-order autoregressive parameter is significant. Both the birthrate and the mortality rate required first differencing to attain stationarity. Puerto Rico certainly experienced a demographic transition in the postwar period, when per capita income and growth was rising. However, it is noteworthy that we cannot statistically link these major demographic movements with changes in either the level or growth of per capita income on the island.

The migration equation is particularly revealing. The level of per capita income in Puerto Rico is not temporally related to the net migration rate. However, the effect of changes in the growth rate is -0.8662, but its standard error is large, 0.6310. This result, though not strong, does suggest some countercyclical response of net migration. A rise in the Puerto Rican growth rate results in an increase in net emigration. One might consider this result contrary to *a priori* expectations. But, if migratory flows are viewed as responsive to relative economic conditions in the United States and Puerto Rico, and more responsive to the former than the latter, the result is not all that unusual. As an appendage of the United States economy, improvements in the Puerto Rican economy follow favorable movements in the United States. Thus, a positive growth rate in Puerto Rico simply signals that the United States economy has been strong, resulting in migratory movements from the island to the United States. This provides some evidence that it may be the pull of economic conditions in the United States rather than the push of economic conditions in Puerto Rico that most affects migratory flows.

We have shown that migration is a determining factor in the change in the stock of human resources in Puerto Rico. Its effects outweigh those of the natural increase in the population brought about by the demographic transition. The results also suggest that net migration is not very sensitive to the level of island per capital income or its growth leading one to conclude that human resource growth in Puerto Rico is, to a great extent, influenced by policies and economic conditions outside of Puerto Rico.

WAGE POLICIES AND PUERTO RICAN
ECONOMIC DEVELOPMENT

Wage policies have fundamentally changed the structure of wages in Puerto Rico over the last fifty years. They have affected the growth of employment, job search behavior, and labor mobility. They also influence the composition of island output and its input mix. Foremost among these policies is the application of the United States statutory minimum wage to the island labor market. What makes the effect of minimum wages so much greater in Puerto Rico than elsewhere, is not solely the pervasive coverage and effective enforcement of minimum wages. The more influential aspect is that the statutory minimum that applies to the island is the same that applies to the United States. A statutory minimum tied to the economy of the United States truly integrated the Puerto Rican labor market into the American economic sphere.

Even as initially intended, the application of minimum wages to Puerto Rico was fraught with contradictions. The Fair Labor Standards Act (FLSA) of 1938, as amended by the Congressional Act of June 26, 1940, stipulated that the level of wages in Puerto Rico should increase as rapidly as economically practical to achieve equality with that of the United States. Thus, minimum wage boards were authorized to establish the highest minimum wage rates which did not significantly reduce employment within a particular classification. Moreover, the rates were not to be set so low that island industries would have an advantageously competitive position vis-à-vis American industries.[6] The inherent contradiction here is the attempt to achieve minimum wage parity without sacrificing employment.

The administration of minimum wages in Puerto Rico has undergone significant changes. In the period from 1938 to 1940, the statutory minimum in the United States covered all activities involved in interstate commerce on an industry-wide basis. During the longer period from 1941 to 1973, minimum wage boards recommended exemptions to the statutory minimum on an individual industry basis. Since 1973, however, industry-specific minimum wage exemptions have been gradually eliminated. This continued until by 1977 across the board parity with the statutory minimum was achieved for most industries.

A fundamental change in the way the statutory minimum wage applied to Puerto Rico occurred in 1974. The Fair Labor Standards Act was amended in 1974 to provide for automatic annual increases in minimum wages in Puerto Rico until the statutory level of $2.30 per hour was reached (for all industries) by the end of the decade.[7] Approximately 75% of island employment was covered by

[6]See Reynolds and Gregory (1965), Reynolds (1965), and Rottenberg (1950) for a discussion of these issues.
[7]See U. S. Department of Commerce (1979).

the FLSA. The 1974 amendment called for automatic annual increases of 12 cents per hour for those industries with minimum wages below $1.40 per hour and annual increases of 15 cents per hour for those industries with minimum wages at or above $1.40 per hour. Industry boards recommended additional increases on an industry-by-industry basis. By 1977, of the 38 industries covered by wage orders, 17 provided for the payment of the $2.30 mainland statutory level. Many classifications within the 21 remaining industries also achieved the targeted level. By the end of 1977, 64% of all workers covered by the FLSA were subject to the $2.30 rate, while an additional 29% were in classifications calling for a $2.00 rate. Thus, only 7% of those workers covered by minimum wages were in classifications below $2.00 per hour.

Political pressure in both Washington and San Juan was such that the industry-specific exemptions to the statutory minimum granted by the minimum wage boards were gradually eliminated. It is quite possible that a political trade-off existed at the time in which further island participation in federal programs required the elimination of special exemptions granted to Puerto Rico. It is also conceivable that federal authorities felt it preferable to raise island standards of living through increased transfers and higher minimum wages rather than subsidizing Puerto Rican families in the already depressed urban centers of the United States. The intent was to eliminate differentials between the statutory minimum and the many industry-by-industry minima that existed in Puerto Rico. The result was twofold. First, industry differentials within Puerto Rico were eliminated. Second, differentials between the United States and Puerto Rico disappeared. It was necessary to promote rapid automatic annual increases of the minima to achieve this over a short period of time (1974–1979). This permitted employers to accurately gauge movements in wages and adjust their work force accordingly.

The new policy took effect just as the Puerto Rican economy slumped. The American economy was entering a severe recession influenced by dramatic oil price increases in 1973–1974. The slump led to a corresponding decline in economic activities on the island, led by the virtual disappearance of the petroleum refining industry. The island government, by then a primary employer of labor, found itself unable to pursue vigorous countercyclical policies. Likewise, growth of "formal" sector employment slowed somewhat, partially due to structural changes coinciding with the emergence of new industries with limited potential for absorbing the growing labor force. To further compound matters, there was evidence of net in-migration during the early 1970s.

The labor market adjusted very rapidly to the higher and more uniform minimum. The employment population ratio and labor force participation rates, already exhibiting slow downward trends, fell sharply. The unemployment rate increased to unprecedented levels, reaching 20% before 1979. These are not transitory changes, since they showed remarkable stability in the face of cyclical economic movements.

The structure of island wages was correspondingly affected. Average hourly earnings were rising less rapidly than the minimum for most industrial classifications, which resulted in a compression of the wage distribution with more workers concentrated at or slightly above the statutory minimum. Upon achieving the target rate of $2.30 per hour (which most industrial classifications did by 1977), future increases matched movements in the minimum wage. Thus, by 1981, these same industry groups (and most of the remaining ones) were paying the statutory minimum of $3.35 per hour. The little employment that remained at subminimum rates in 1981 was in agriculture, small leather goods, rubber and nonrubber footwear, hosiery, textiles, and tobacco.

Other notable changes were evident in island labor markets between 1970 and 1980. Formal sector employment growth slowed as public sector and manufacturing jobs became difficult to come by. Although there is little evidence of growth in informal sector employment during this period, wages do appear to have declined precipitously in these activities.[8] Santiago and Thorbecke argued (1988) that one reason for the apparent lack of growth of informal sector employment is that working at informal sector jobs and being unemployed are not mutually exclusive activities in Puerto Rico. Some of these changes can be attributed to the way minimum wages applied to Puerto Rico after 1974.

LABOR MIGRATION AND WAGE SHOCKS

Let us assume that initially we have two distinct labor markets, a and b. Although there is complete labor mobility between the two markets, they are geographically separate. Thus, it is not costless to migrate from one market to the other. The costs of migration are represented by c. If wages are equivalent in both markets there is no incentive for workers to migrate from one location to the other. Therefore, only with the incentive of a wage premium would labor migration occur. If w_a and w_b are the prevailing market wages in a and b, respectively, and τ is the premium required to induce migration from one market to the other ($-\infty \leq \tau \leq +\infty$), the two markets would equilibrate when

$$w_a(1 + \tau) = w_b - c \qquad (10)$$

This expression is designated the migration response function, μ.

If τ is zero, then the wage differential between locations equals the costs of

---

[8]See Santiago and Thorbecke (1984, 1988) for a discussion of some of these issues.

migration and workers have no incentive to move. But, if $\tau > 0$, and $|w_a(1 + \tau)$ $- w_b| - c > 0$, labor migrates from b to a, while if $\tau < 0$, and $|w_a(1 - \tau) - w_b|$ $- c > 0$, the migratory flow is in the opposite direction. Thus, migration depends upon the wage premium (τ), relative market wages (w_a and w_b), and the costs of migration, c. In equilibrium, labor migration between locations a and b alters the wage differential until the point where $\mu = 0$ or

$$\mu = |w_a(1 + \tau) - w_b| - c = 0 \tag{11}$$

There are two important points about the relation between labor markets a and b. The first is that they are geographically separate, necessitating the incursion of tangible costs of migration to move from one to the other. Second, a dynamic interaction exists between the two labor markets represented by τ. This term captures differential exogenously induced wage growth.

For the moment let us assume that $\tau > 0$, indicating that relative wages are higher in a than in b. Thus, absolute value signs in Equation 11 can be removed without loss of generality. Now let us turn to the labor market in b independently of that of a. In b, we have a single market for homogeneous labor. The market clears at a wage of w_b and all workers with reservation wages at or below that level are hired resulting in an employment level of e_o. The labor force is assumed to be variable and nonmarket activities are possible. Workers with reservation wages above w_b do not participate in labor market activities.

A fixed above equilibrium wage of w_m, call it the minimum wage, is applied to market b, but only with partial coverage k. The application of the minimum immediately results in a disemployment effect as workers with a value of marginal product below w_m are laid off. Defining $\dot{w}_m$ as the minimum wage hike ($\dot{w}_m = ln\ w_m - ln\ w_b$), $\dot{e}_m$ as the proportional change in employment ($\dot{e}_m = ln\ e_m - ln\ e_o$), and η as the absolute value of the wage elasticity of demand in the covered sector, the direction and magnitude of the covered sector disemployment effect is determined by the expression

$$\dot{e}_m = -\eta \dot{w}_m \tag{12}$$

Thus, the disemployment effect is proportional to the size of the minimum wage hike. Because of partial coverage, the minimum wage hike then results in an excess supply of workers in the covered sector and the emergence of an uncovered labor market (informal sector). In the uncovered sector, minimum wages are not binding and competitive conditions hold. With excess supply of workers in the covered sector and some degree of labor turnover (δ) in that sector, job rationing occurs.

Of major concern is the direction and extent of internal labor mobility that results from the minimum wage hike in b. It is possible for disemployed workers to (1) remain in the covered sector and continue searching for jobs there (job search option), (2) obtain employment in the uncovered sector (informal sector option), (3) withdraw from (or delay) labor force activities (nonparticipation option), or (4) migrate to market a (migration option). The analytical model suggests that, *a priori*, the direction of labor mobility within b is indeterminate and depends on the elasticities of labor demand in both covered and uncovered sectors (η and ε, respectively), the degree of minimum wage coverage (k), the separation or vacancy rate in the covered sector (δ), the elasticity of labor supply (s), and the size of the minimum wage hike ($\dot{w}_m$). It can be shown that the direction of labor mobility between covered and uncovered sectors within b is determined by ($\eta - \delta$). According to Mincer (1976), if $\eta > \delta$, $\dot{w}_n$ is positive (negative), indicating mobility from the covered (uncovered) to the uncovered (covered) sector.

Labor mobility between covered and uncovered labor markets within b will cease when expected wages in both are equal. Since jobs are rationed in the covered sector, but not in the uncovered sector, labor mobility ceases when

$$w_m \rho = w_n \tag{13}$$

where ρ represents the probability of obtaining covered sector employment and w_n is the wage in the uncovered sector. The simplest way of representing job rationing in the covered sector is to assume that all workers have equal opportunity to obtain these jobs.[9] That is,

$$\rho = \frac{\delta e_m}{U + \delta e_m} \tag{14}$$

where ρ is the probability of getting a job in the covered sector, δ is the rate of job turnover as mentioned above, e_m is total covered sector employment, and U is the number of unemployed job seekers. We can now express the maximum expected wage in b's covered sector as $w_m \rho = w_b$.

Returning to the issue of labor mobility between markets a and b, migration now equilibrates when

$$\mu = w_a(1 + \tau) - w_m \rho - c = 0 \tag{15}$$

or

$$\mu = w_a(1 + r) - w_m \left[\frac{\delta e_m}{U + \delta e_m} \right] - c = 0 \tag{16}$$

[9]This formulation is similar to that found in Harris and Todaro (1970). An extension of this approach, which introduces the intensity of job search, is found in Fields (1975).

The objective is to determine how migration between a and b responds to increases in the minimum wage in b, w_m. A minimum wage increase in b will have a dual effect on migration because of its impact on expected wages in b. First, it will increase the covered sector wage in b, and second, it will decrease the probability of obtaining covered sector employment in b. Since $e_m = F(w_m)$, Equation 16 can be written as

$$\mu = w_a(1 + r) - w_m\left[\frac{\delta f(w_m)}{U + \delta f(w_m)}\right] - c = 0 \tag{17}$$

Differentiating Equation 17 with respect to w_m gives

$$\frac{d\mu}{dw_m} = -w_m\frac{d\left[\dfrac{\delta f(w_m)}{U + \delta f(w_m)}\right]}{dw_m} - \left[\frac{\delta f(w_m)}{U + \delta f(w_m)}\right], \tag{18}$$

or

$$\frac{d\mu}{dw_m} = -w_m\frac{d\rho}{dw_m} - \rho, \tag{19}$$

which can be expressed as

$$\frac{d\mu}{dw_m} = -\rho(\epsilon_{\rho,w_m} + 1) \tag{20}$$

The change in the probability of obtaining covered sector employment given a change in the minimum wage is ϵ_{ρ,w_m}.[10] Since $(de_m)/(dw_m) = f'(w_m)$ is negative, ϵ_{ρ,w_m} will be negative.[11]

[10] It is very straightforward to show that

$$\frac{d\rho}{dw_m} = \frac{d\left[\dfrac{\delta f(w_m)}{U + \delta f(w_m)}\right]}{dw_m}$$

$$= \frac{[U + \delta f(w_m)]\delta f'(w_m) - \delta^2 f(w_m)f'(w_m)}{[U + \delta f(w_m)]^2}$$

$$= \frac{U\delta f'(w_m)}{[U + \delta f(w_m)]^2}$$

and since $f'(w_m)$ is negative,

$$\frac{d\rho}{dw_m} < 0$$

[11] It is interesting to compare ϵ_{ρ,w_m} with the wage elasticity of demand, η, of Equation 12. The former encompasses more than just job loss; it also captures changes in the pool of new job seekers, and hence the extent of competition for jobs within the covered sector.

The impact of the minimum wage hike on migration is now clear. It depends exclusively on the size of ε_{ρ,w_m}. To the extent that the minimum wage hike reduces the probability of finding employment in the covered sector by a considerable amount, net emigration will follow. More specifically, if $|\varepsilon_{\rho,w_m}| = 1$, there will be no migratory effect since any incentives to migrate from a to b because of the increase in the minimum wage in b will be exactly offset by a decline in the probability of obtaining employment in b's covered sector. On the other hand, if $|\varepsilon_{\rho,w_m}| > 1$, migration will result from b to a. Finally, if $|\varepsilon_{\rho,w_m}| < 1$, labor will migrate from a to b. These results are also affected by τ as shown below:

$$\text{If } |\epsilon_{\rho,w_m}| \begin{cases} >1, \text{ then, } \mu = 0 \text{ if } \tau < 0, \text{ and } b \Rightarrow a \text{ if } \tau \geq 0 \\ =1, \text{ then, } \mu = 0 \text{ for all values of } \tau \\ <1, \text{ then, } \mu = 0 \text{ if } \tau > 0, \text{ and } a \Rightarrow b \text{ if } \tau \leq 0 \end{cases}$$

The arrows represent the direction of migration between locations a and b.

This simple model suggests that wage hikes (or shocks) in b may or may not result in migration to a. Labor will migrate to a if a wage shock in b succeeds in lowering expected wages. This occurs only if the fall in the likelihood of finding a job in the covered sector outweighs the increase in the covered sector minimum wage. Moreover, the larger (smaller) the wage premium in a and the greater (smaller) the disemployment effects in b, the more (less) likely workers will migrate from b to a.

The analysis also provides some indication of the composition of potential migrants from b to a if an above equilibrium wage is imposed on b. Obviously, the workers most affected by this shock are those on the lower end of the wage scale and those with lower reservation wages. In effect, displaced workers in low-wage occupations (and presumably those with lower levels of educational attainment) would make up a disproportionate fraction of total migrant population.

The role of the uncovered or informal sector in b also becomes important in the process of migration. Recall that one possible result of increases in the minimum wage hike in b is to stimulate labor mobility from covered to uncovered sector activities. As more and more displaced workers move to the informal sector, wages will tend down. To the extent that these displaced workers accept informal sector employment and stop queuing up for scarce covered sector jobs, the probability of getting a covered sector job is less affected. But, if covered sector job search and informal sector employment are not mutually exclusive activities, the number of job seekers will not decline and the probability of finding covered sector employment will remain low. Thus, the likelihood of migration from b to a is reinforced by both continued declines in informal sector wages and longer spells of unemployment in b.

ESTIMATION OF THE MIGRATION RESPONSE FUNCTION

In this section, I will attempt to estimate the temporal relation between the net migration rate and minimum wages in Puerto Rico. One way to approach this conceptually is to view the migratory response function, μ, as a stationary state in equilibrium.[12] Although not a perfect representation, the multiple time-series framework of the first section provides an intuitively appealing approach to estimating this function.[13]

As indicated, migration is represented by the difference between the number of individuals arriving in Puerto Rico and the number of individuals leaving Puerto Rico in a given month. The difference in gross flows is divided by total civilian population (16 years of age and older) in Puerto Rico to obtain the net migration rate. Monthly observations from January 1970 to June 1987 are used to best capture the dynamics of the migration–minimum wage relation. These figures suggest that the net migration rate series contains considerable seasonality, largely capturing months of substantial tourist in-flow and out-flow in the course of the year. In addition, although there is some indication of nonstationarity in the variance of the series, it does not appear to trend from 1970 to 1987.

Four different minimum wage variables are used in the estimation of the migration response function. The first is the change in the nominal federal statutory minimum wage rate. The second is the change in the real minimum wage rate which consists of the federal statutory minimum wage divided by the consumer price index for Puerto Rico using 1967 as the base year. The real minimum wage rate increased dramatically in response to the post-1974 shocks, but since 1980 has declined steadily. The third is the change in the minimum wage ratio. The minimum wage ratio is represented by the economy-wide minimum wage divided by average manufacturing wages. This variable represents the impact of increases in the minimum wage on average wages in the economy, and hence, is a better indicator of the wage shock than the change in the nominal or real minimum wage rate. The unweighted minimum wage ratio remains high although the impact of the post-1974 shocks appear to have faded over time. An

---

[12]In the stationary state all relevant variables grow at a zero rate while in a steady state all relevant variables grow at a constant rate. Thus $d\mu/dt = 0$, where t is time.

[13]It should be noted that earlier studies, Fleisher (1963) and Maldonado (1976), used ordinary least squares to estimate an equation of the net migration rate of Puerto Rico. The advantage of this approach is that it allowed for the inclusion of many exogenous variables within their model. Unemployment rates and wages in the United States and in Puerto Rico were included. The disadvantage is that the assumptions regarding the underlying stochastic processes were not realistic. Our estimates avoid this through more careful attention to the structure of disturbances, but, at the same time, it reduces the feasibility of including additional variables because the cross-correlation patterns that result are too complex.

economy-wide minimum wage rate is most applicable after 1974, when industry-specific minimum wage boards were abolished. The fourth minimum wage variable is the change in the weighted minimum wage ratio. This variable captures the effects of the movement from a nonbinding economy-wide minimum wage prior to 1974, to one where coverage slowly increases. It is represented by the minimum wage ratio weighted by coverage, where coverage is estimated by a logistic function.[14] The weighted and unweighted ratios converge by 1977. The difference between the two ratios is that the latter measure assumes that coverage equals 1 throughout, while the former assumes that coverage increases gradually.

Table 1 presents parameter estimates of both the univariate model (column 1) as well as the transfer function (columns 3 to 5). The "best" univariate specification for the monthly net migration rate is one that contains a single seasonal moving average parameter. The seasonal moving average parameter remains stable under different specifications of the transfer function. Each of the four variables representing the exogenous impact of minimum wage hikes turn out to be positive and statistically significant. Likewise, the error structure portrays a white-noise process, providing further confidence that these results are not spurious. It is noteworthy that if ordinary least squares is used to estimate the parameters of a regression of the net migration rate on the change in the minimum wage ratio, a negative and statistically significant coefficient is obtained.[15] However, as indicated by the Q-statistic, the error structure is not well behaved. The autocorrelation function reflects considerable seasonality and noise, leading one to suspect that the model is not capturing the true relation between minimum wages and migration.

The parameter values in columns 2–5 of Table 1 are positive, indicating that minimum wage hikes in Puerto Rico after 1974 tend to increase labor migration from the United States to the island. According to the theoretical model, this implies that ε_{ρ, w_m} is less than 1. Some evidence to support this claim during the

---

[14]The procedure was to divide the time frame into equal periods and apply the logistic function to represent minimum wage coverage, k. In other words,

$$\kappa_t = \frac{e^x}{(1 + e^x)} \tag{21}$$

where e is the exponential function. Thus, k_t ranges between 0 and 1.

[15]The ordinary least squares estimate of the net migration rate equation is

$$mig_t = -0.0010 - 0.0974 \Delta MW_t \tag{22}$$

where mig_t is the net migration rate, and ΔMW_t is the change in the minimum wage ratio. The t-statistics for the constant and minimum wage parameter are -1.24 and -1.91, respectively. The Q-statistic is 622.25, which rejects the null hypothesis of a white-noise stochastic process.

Table 1. Parameter Estimates of the Migration Response Function
for Puerto Rico from January 1970 to June 1987

Independent variable	Dependent variable: Net migration rate				
	(1)	(2)	(3)	(4)	(5)
Seasonal moving average	-0.4430^a	-0.4827^a	-0.4944^a	-0.4608^a	-0.4554^a
	(-6.67)	(-7.410)	(-7.64)	(-6.97)	(-6.88)
Change in nominal mini- mum wage	0.0096^a (2.81)				
Change in real minimum wage		1.9194^a (3.15)			
Change in minimum wage ratio			0.0298^a (2.23)		
Change in minimum wage ratio $\times$ coverage				0.0172^a (1.72)	
R^2	0.9046	0.9083	0.9091	0.9071	0.9061
Q-statistic	52.62	49.22	50.70	52.74	53.67
Standard error	0.0036	0.0036	0.0036	0.0036	0.0036
Number of observations	186	186	186	186	186

Note: T-statistics are in parentheses.
[a]Indicates that parameters are statistically significant at the 10% level of significance.

1970s can be found in Santiago (1986, 1989).[16] Using quarterly data from 1974 to 1982, estimates of minimum wage elasticities of employment and unemployment (evaluated at the means) are found to be -0.1221 and 0.3987, respectively. Although not identical to ε_{ρ,w_m}, these results do suggest that the impact of the minimum wage on the probability of finding covered sector employment is probably inelastic.

The results also imply that $\tau \leq 0$. What this suggests is that the United States did not have a nonwage advantage over Puerto Rico during the 1970s. Recall that during the mid to late 1970s, New York City, the prime recipient of the Puerto Rican migrant population, was in severe financial distress. It certainly is conceivable that the New York City labor market was perceived as not as attractive to residents in Puerto Rico at that time. Federal transfer payments to island residents were increasing, among which the Department of Agriculture's Food Stamp Program became most important.[17] That most of these benefits were

[16]These articles focus on the post-1973 period and find that minimum wage hikes in Puerto Rico can be associated with declines in the employment–population ratio and increases in island unemployment.
[17]See Weisskoff (1985) for a discussion of the impact of federal transfers to the island economy during the 1970s.

available either in the United States or Puerto Rico reinforces the notion that, all things equal, more familiar surroundings are preferred to unfamiliar ones.

CONCLUSIONS

My study has reached three main conclusions. First, migration is the prime determinant of human resource growth and change in Puerto Rico. Migratory movements swamp changes in the natural increase of the population. Although this underscores the uniqueness of Puerto Rican economic development, it also suggests that the worldwide movement toward liberalization of factor mobility is best captured by an examination of Puerto Rican economic relations.

Second, the static model of expected wage differentials has held up quite well to empirical testing in the Puerto Rican context. This is not to say that all, or even most, of Puerto Rican migration can be explained by variations in wages and job opportunities, but these forces certainly influence the direction of net migratory flows.[18] Further research should determine whether economic factors are more relevant in explaining international migration than internal migration. The role of the nonwage premium, τ, is also crucial here, although it represents a measure of our ignorance more than anything else.

Third, minimum wage policies do impact the labor market sufficiently to influence the direction of labor migration. Supporting evidence for this claim can be found in analyses of the composition of Puerto Rican migration. Both Rivera-Batiz (1987) and Ortiz (1987) have found that the post-1974 migration stream consists, in large measure, of movements of relatively low-wage labor. This is in sharp contrast with research on minimum wages in the United States, where the potential migratory impact is ignored. It is conceivable, however, that minimum wage policies have influenced the regional migration of low-wage labor in the United States. To my knowledge, this issue has not received attention in the literature.

Disemployment and unemployment effects of minimum wages are the most studied aspect of this policy. The effects on the distribution of income and other welfare considerations are generally ignored. The same can be said of its potential impact on labor migration of low-wage workers. The Puerto Rican experience with minimum wages suggests that the migratory effects of minimum wage hikes needs careful and continued study.

[18]Contrast this with the recent work of Stark (1984) and Rosenzweig and Stark (1989) concerning the role of relative deprivation and risk-sharing in migration. Also see Fields (1982) and Schultz (1982), pp. 559–594.

ACKNOWLEDGMENTS

The comments of Edwin Melendez and Vilma Ortiz are especially appreciated.

REFERENCES

Amemiya, T. (1985). *Advanced econometrics*. Cambridge: Harvard University Press.

Fields, G. S. (1975). Rural-urban migration, urban unemployment and underemployment. *Journal of Development Economics, 2,* 165–187.

Fields, G. S. (1982). Place-to-place migration in Colombia. *Economic Development and Cultural Change, 30,* 539–558.

Fleisher, B. (1963). Some economic aspects of Puerto Rican migration to the United States. *Review of Economics and Statistics, 45,* 245–253.

Friedlander, S. (1965). *Labor migration and economic growth*. Cambridge: M.I.T. Press.

Harris, J. R., & M. P. Todaro. (1970). Migration, unemployment and development: A two-sector analysis. *American Economic Review, 60,* 126–142.

Maldonado, R. (1976). Why Puerto Ricans migrated to the United States in 1947–1973? *Monthly Labor Review, 99,* 7–18.

Mincer, J. (1976). Unemployment effects of minimum wages. *Journal of Political Economy, 84,* 87–104.

Ortiz, V. (1987). Changes in the characteristics of Puerto Rican migrants from 1955 to 1980. *International Migration Review, 20,* 612–628.

Reynolds, L. (1965). Wages and employment in the labor-surplus economy. *American Economic Review, 55,* 19–39.

Reynolds, L., & P. Gregory. (1965). *Wages, productivity, and industrialization in Puerto Rico*. Homewood, IL: Richard D. Irwin.

Rivera-Batiz, F. (1987). Is there a brain drain of Puerto Ricans to the United States? *Puerto Rico Business Review, 12,* 1–5.

Rosenzweig, M. R., & O. Stark. (1989). Consumption smoothing, migration, and marriage: Evidence from rural India. *Journal of Political Economy, 97,* 905–926.

Rottenberg, S. (1950). *Labor cost in the Puerto Rican economy*. Puerto Rico: Labor Relations Institute.

Santiago, C. E. (1986). Closing the gap: The employment and unemployment effects of minimum wage policy in Puerto Rico. *Journal of Development Economics, 23,* 293–311.

Santiago, C. E. (1989). The dynamics of minimum wage policy in economic development: A multiple time series approach. *Economic Development and Cultural Change, 38,* 1–30.

Santiago, C. E., & E. Thorbecke. (1984). Regional and technological dualism: A dual-dual development framework applied to Puerto Rico. *Journal of Development Studies, 20,* 271–289.

Santiago, C. E., & E. Thorbecke. (1988). A multisectoral framework for the analysis of labor mobility and development in LDCs: An application to postwar Puerto Rico. *Economic Development and Cultural Change, 37,* 127–148.

Schultz, T. (1982). Lifetime migration within educational strata in Venezuela: Estimates of a logistic model. *Economic Development and Cultural Change, 30,* 559–594.

Stark, O. (1984). Rural-to-urban migration in LDCs: A relative deprivation approach. *Economic Development and Cultural Change, 32,* 475–486.

U. S. Department of Commerce. (1979). *Economic study of Puerto Rico.* Washington, DC: U. S. Government Printing Office.

Weisskoff, R. (1985). *Factories and food stamps: The Puerto Rican model of development.* Baltimore: Johns Hopkins University Press.

12

Latino Research and Policy

The Puerto Rican Case

ANDRES TORRES AND CLARA E. RODRIGUEZ

INTRODUCTION

For quite some time students of the Latino experience have been aware that Latinos in the United States are in a difficult and vulnerable economic situation. Government policy addressing the economically disadvantaged position of Latinos has been limited and proven less than successful. This analysis will therefore focus on one Latino group to examine the reasons for this policy failure. As an extreme case of Latino disadvantage, the plight of Puerto Ricans provides a litmus test of the efficacy of policy as it affects all Latinos, as well as the commitment of the federal government to the eradication of inequality in all its forms.

We begin with a definition of poverty and its relationship to the labor force. We follow this with a description of the historical and current documentation of the disadvantaged situation of Puerto Ricans in the United States. We then comment on the labor market research on this population, calling attention to

ANDRES TORRES • Center for Puerto Rican Studies, Hunter College of the City University of New York, New York, New York 10021.   CLARA E. RODRIGUEZ • Division of the Social Sciences, Fordham University at Lincoln Center, New York, New York 10023.

Hispanics in the Labor Force, edited by Edwin Melendez *et al.* Plenum Press, New York, 1991.

problems in the research production process and the role of political considerations in the development of public policy agendas. We then review the current policy debates that pertain to the entire Latino population, indicating their lack of relevance to the unique situation of Latinos and conclude with two examples of policy recommendations that have been tailored to meet the needs of the Latino population.

DEFINITION OF POVERTY

Poverty is measured as a level of income falling short of a minimally acceptable standard of living. In 1987, the estimate of this minimum standard stood at $11,611 for a family of four (U. S. Bureau of the Census, 1989). Low incomes arise from any or all of four relationships to the labor force: (1) *low wages,* (2) *underemployment* (insufficient number of hours worked in the year, as with part-time or seasonal employment), (3) *unemployment,* or (4) *nonlabor force participation.* Roughly one half of the poverty in the United States is related to the first three components—in the sense that it consists of persons who are actively connected to the labor force (Sawhill, 1989). Here the problem is low or temporarily zero labor market earnings. These working poor are also those who receive the least amount of government assistance. The remaining cause of poverty has to do with lack of sustained access to employment (nonlabor force participation). Poverty that is due to nonlabor force participation is higher among Puerto Ricans than for most any other group.

PERSISTENT DISADVANTAGE

As mentioned, Puerto Ricans in the United States find themselves facing a difficult and vulnerable economic situation. Soon after the "great migration" of Puerto Ricans in the 1950s, government reports and the pronouncements of scholars investigating this area began to highlight the economic adversities that Puerto Ricans were experiencing in the United States (see, e.g., Bonilla & Campos, 1981; Hernandez, 1976, 1983; History Task Force, 1979; Lopez, 1973; Lopez & Petras, 1974; New York City Board of Education Study, 1958; Puerto Rican Community Development Project (PRCDP), 1964; Rodriguez, 1974, 1979; A. Torres, 1973; U. S. Bureau of the Census (1963); U. S. Commission on Civil Rights, 1972, 1976; U. S. Department of Labor, 1968; and Wagenheim, 1975). Despite these many reports, little was done.

There has also been, for some time, a distinct sense that the causes of this distress went well beyond the control of Puerto Ricans and were to be found in the structural changes of the economy and the position of Puerto Ricans within it.

Some observers anticipated that even with a booming economy, Puerto Ricans would not necessarily benefit. Indeed, the U. S. Commission on Civil Rights (1976) confirmed this perception in the mid-seventies when it said that

> the employment problems of Puerto Ricans have persisted for 25 years. . . . the mere growth of the economic pie would not assure a larger piece for Puerto Ricans and others suffering chronic poverty. (p. 64)

Despite these early warnings, the situation of Puerto Ricans was given scant attention until recently. Although some writings appeared in journals and periodicals that are not considered mainstream, the primary research market had little interest in these works. But more recently, Puerto Ricans

> have moved from being simply ignored in most research, to inclusion on the margin, and now emerge as prime suspects in the personification of the most menacing social ills of our time. (Bonilla, 1989, p. 2)

Much of the current interest in Puerto Ricans derives from the results of new studies that have found them to be uniquely disadvantaged relative to other groups in American society. During the 1980s, government data and research reports continued to provide growing evidence of the uniquely disadvantaged position of Puerto Ricans within postwar society, thus, reinforcing the earlier assessments (Bean & Tienda, 1988; Center on Budget and Policy Priorities, 1988; Community Service Society, 1989; Sandefur & Tienda, 1988). While other minorities experienced a period of socioeconomic advancement during the 1960s—which was followed by a phase of limited gains during the 1970s—the Puerto Rican experience is one of continuously growing disadvantage since 1960 (Sandefur & Pahari, 1988).

This deteriorating relative position is reflected in a variety of indicators. In 1960, the median family income was lower than that of blacks, other Latinos, and Native Americans. By 1980, the difference had widened. In 1987, median family income for Puerto Ricans was less than half that of whites (Center on Budget and Policy Priorities, 1988, pp. 18, 22). In relation to whites, Puerto Ricans were the only Hispanic group not to have narrowed the family income gap during the 1970s (Bean & Tienda, 1988, pp. 342, 344). During the late 1980s, the incidence of poverty among Puerto Ricans continued to be higher than for any other group, remaining similar to the poverty rate of a decade earlier (Center on Budget and Policy Priorities, 1988). In New York City, the extent of Puerto Rican poverty was higher than for any other measurable group (Community Service Society, 1989).

Data on labor force participation present a similar story of disadvantage. In 1980, Puerto Ricans exhibited participation rates lower than other groups, and those employed worked fewer hours on the average (Borjas, 1985, p. 153). Analysis of trends by gender indicates that participation rates for Puerto Rican males steadily declined between 1960 to 1980, while that of women improved modestly between 1960 to 1980 (Bean & Tienda, 1988, Table 9.1, p. 290). The disadvantaged situation of Puerto Ricans, relative to other groups, has been so severe that it has led some to speculate on whether Puerto Ricans are becoming a Hispanic "underclass" (Tienda, 1989).

ISSUES AND PROBLEMS IN PUERTO RICAN LABOR FORCE RESEARCH

Because the situation of Puerto Ricans has recently attracted a growing corpus of research, it is important to examine its direction in order to develop more effective labor force policies. In the following discussion, we will focus on some important issues and problems in the ongoing research on Puerto Ricans, with many issues also relevant to other Latinos. Some of the issues reflect current research conditions; for example, such intrinsic problems as methodological and data limitations. Other issues involve the explanatory power of models, the accessibility of research, the often tenuous connection between assumption and conclusion, and the consequences of these concerns for policy.

Inadequate Data

When doing research on Puerto Ricans, there are some inherent problems since much of the research performed is derivative of labor market studies concerning African Americans and Mexican Americans. Also, data limitations are severe because of the relatively small size of the Puerto Rican population. There is no reliable annual series on employment and income indicators. Furthermore, because of their status as United States citizens, Puerto Rican migratory patterns cannot be traced as they can for foreigners.

Some of these problems also apply to Latinos as a whole; for example, many national samples and regional surveys have tended to exclude Latinos. Thus, comparative analyses are often impossible. Nor do other Latinos have reliable regional annual series on employment and income indicators, making analyses of change over time difficult. Consequently, the literature on Latino inequality is characterized by a significant gap between theoretical conjecture and empirical testing. Not surprisingly, these realities severely hamper research and policy analysis.

Inadequate Models

Another recurring and significant problem is that the statistical models used in labor market research tend not to fit Puerto Ricans. For example, if we examine the regression results of a number of studies, we find the explanatory power (R^2) for the "Puerto Rican equations" to be consistently lower than for all other groups.[1] Key differentiating factors may be at work, which have not been effectively incorporated into the models thus far developed. These include (1) the multiracial character of the Puerto Rican population and the difficulties this presents vis à vis the racial dichotomy in American society; (2) the status of Puerto Ricans as colonial immigrants; (3) the influence of long-term structural-regional change on Puerto Rican communities; (4) the excessively high levels of urbanization; and (5) the impact of housing abandonment in areas of high Puerto Rican concentration. In addition, these models fail to capture the positive effect of a functional dual migration (FDM) experience. This last issue, which if quantified, might be termed the *FDM quotient,* is not to be confused with the *circulating migration* thesis that is commonly discussed in the research and journalistic literature.[2] Rather, it refers to the everyday need and ability of Puerto Ricans to function within family networks or communities that are both bilingual and bicultural—in the United States and in Puerto Rico. Although the circulating migration thesis implies a commitment to neither place, the FDM implies a commitment to both cultures.

Again, several of these difficulties also apply to Latinos as a whole. To one degree or another, all Latino populations are multiracial in character. Similarly, many Latino groups have a parallel historical relationship to the United States; for example, seventh or eighth generation Latinos living in Texas, California, or the Southwest, who call themselves Tejanos, Californios, or Hispanos. The effect of an FDM experience is also applicable to Latinos who return often to their countries, for example, Dominicans and Hispanics who return to Mexico frequently. Velez (1988) discussed this in his study of "exchange networks" on both sides of the United States–Mexico border. The influence of long-term structural-regional changes on Latino communities is also often neglected in analyses of their labor market experience. In short, the reductionism and simplistic causality underlying many models makes them woefully inadequate for analyzing much of the Latino labor force experience and population.

Accessibility and the Indigenous Factor

The trends toward increasing quantification and methodological abstraction result in research that is less accessible to those not trained to evaluate the methodological and theoretical premises underlying most research projects. Many people who advocate, design, or implement policy are not trained in these

---

[1]This observation appears to hold even after taking into account the smaller size of the Puerto Rican sample in these studies. For evidence of this, see Niemi (1974); Reimers (1983); Melendez (1988); A. Torres (1988).

[2]See Rodriguez (1989) for a discussion of this thesis.

areas. The research, therefore, is less accessible to such individuals and it is also less open to comment, evaluation, and review by people who have hands-on policy experience. In some cases, the distance between research and practice is so great that the research is often viewed by those within the Puerto Rican policy community as not reflective or representative of the Puerto Rican community, and as lacking in understanding and insight.

Some of the research is inaccessible not so much because it is methodologically abstract, but because it makes opaque what should be obvious. To apply *New York Times* columnist Leonard Silk's critique of many modern economic theories, they range from "cloaking the obvious in a little wild incomprehensibility" to "stupefaction of the exhaustingly clear" (Silk, 1990). Similarly, some of this research might be summarized as penetrating insights into the all too obvious.

However, highly quantitative work has come to be recognized as the most credible and as having the highest likelihood of funding and policy attention. Although quantitative methods can be very valuable, insistence on quantitative methods can often serve as an inadvertent screening device; thus limiting, from funding or publication, more qualitative or historical research. Much research in the quantitative area begins by testing abstract models or new methodological techniques on a convenient or appropriate sample. In some cases, the results demonstrate statistical significance about insignificant issues. Such research should only be used as a complement of, not a substitute for, research that begins with and builds on the historically unique and multifaceted reality of the group in question.

There has been a long-standing concern that the requirements of social science be reconciled with the notions and practical concerns that Puerto Ricans consider to be important. A decade ago, Hernandez (1980) argued that a relevant Puerto Rican research agenda should generate (1) appropriate concepts and explanatory models, (2) research methods producing valid and reliable information, and (3) activities that enhance professional capability and communication of knowledge. Thus, for quite some time, there has been an expressed need to reconcile indigenous concerns with those of social science research. The problems of accessibility noted in the Puerto Rican case are also reflected, to greater and lesser degrees, in other Latino communities.

In earlier periods, some credence was given to the need to incorporate the "indigenous factor" into analyses of groups that were culturally and/or racially different. There may have been some resistance to what some deemed a subjective view, but the view was, nonetheless, acknowledged as necessary. At present, we find little awareness of the need or desirability to incorporate this indigenous factor into the research process.[3]

---

[3]Other factors have intervened in the involvement of indigenous researchers. Many actual and potential Puerto Rican researchers have been siphoned off into administrative tracks; others have

Taking a retrospective view, we see a curious alteration in the extent to which studies were viewed as accurately reflecting the Puerto Rican community. Past studies, such as the New York City Board of Education (1958), PRCDP (1965), and the U. S. Commission on Civil Rights (1976), were not challenged with regard to how accurately they reflected the policy needs of the Puerto Rican community. Problems with these studies had to do with how seriously their recommendations were taken; that is, whether the policy prescriptions they advanced were pursued. Objections raised dealt with the official neglect demonstrated in response to these studies and their recommendations (see, for example, Jorge, 1984). In these studies, Puerto Rican researchers were intimately involved; the work of other Puerto Rican researchers was accurately incorporated; and the studies were subject to some community review.

Today, many of these conditions do not apply. Computerization and methodological abstraction restrict the number of participants in the research process to those attached to the principal universities and research institutes. Increasingly, the social science community regards as legitimate that work which is produced by these centers. Furthermore, highly quantitative work, often requiring extensive technical resources, is the sort of work that has come to be recognized by governmental and established funding institutions as the most credible. This is the work that receives funding and becomes the most widely distributed, referenced, and discussed at the policy level. Thus, access to technical resources, training, and knowledge have defined the research population involved in today's Puerto Rican labor force research.

Few current studies review any of the earlier literature on Puerto Ricans—indigenous or otherwise, which has led to the critique that much of the work done on Puerto Rican disadvantage is *ahistorical*. The shortage of indigenous input is not an abstract concern; it lowers the quality of the research in several ways. One type of input that is missing is the rich, insightful, and vital indigenous literature. Since much of the current work does not build on earlier research, the preceding writings become marginalized, undervalued, or totally forgotten.

A by-product of ignoring the prior research is that the wheel is constantly being reinvented, or, as an old expression put it, the Mediterranean is always being discovered. If we examine closely the earlier research, we find that many of the same issues noted then are surfacing again today, but with a new cast of characters. Puerto Rican poverty, for example, has been rediscovered, but it has

---

been overburdened by demands of a crisis intervention nature; while others have concluded that the type of research currently being produced seems unworthy of their efforts. Some of the early exits from the research path have been the result of discouragement. Much of the social science community will acknowledge the capacity of Puerto Ricans to be community organizers and advocates long before accepting them as researchers.

a new wrinkle; it is now seen as a *new poverty*. In point of fact, this is the same poverty that originated in the 1950s; it is a continuation of the same trend; now reaches into second and third generation families. Today, however, it has been given a new appearance and a new name (i.e., "the underclass").

Although there is no guarantee that including "indigenous factors" will result in research that is representative of the community, there is a greater likelihood that issues of community concern and alternative perspectives will be captured. There is also a greater likelihood that the research will be more accurate and the policy more useful. Moreover, there are serious consequences to omitting the indigenous factor. For example, the research produced may be seen as alien to the self-defined needs of the community. In essence, the terms within which policy and programs come to be discussed are the terms provided by policy researchers. Thus, the discourse on welfare reform turns on what is the most effective way of getting female heads of household to accept low-wage jobs, instead of addressing the question of whether such women should be given the option of enhancing their role as full-time môthers or becoming trained skilled employees.

Not surprisingly, many of the Puerto Rican community-based organizations do not realize the extent to which their own agendas have been driven by policy research that ignores the indigenous factor. Consequently, many community-based organizations seek funding for programs that are conceptualized externally and may not necessarily respond to their priorities, for example, constructing new housing when the needs for rehabilitation of existing housing and tenant organizing may be seen as more important. To be sure, ours is not a claim that only Latinos are entitled to perform research on Latinos. Rather we emphasize that the prevailing framework of research and policy formation relating to Latinos needs to be challenged by taking into account Latino perspectives in all their variety. Recent efforts in this direction include the notion that Latinos have developed, over the centuries, an intellectual tradition that can help define policy issues and construct responses to them. Latinos need to be appreciated as active agents, not merely passive inhabitants of a world controlled by others (Hayes-Bautista, 1990). Also, the new concern for respecting diversity in the social sciences is accompanied by an insistence that the experiences of subordinate groups are valuable sources for generating new insights on social reality (Rosaldo, 1989). In all of this, the intervention of the indigenous factor is crucial for producing research that might not otherwise materialize.

The Case of "the Underclass"

A prime example of the accessibility and indigenous factor problem is found in the underclass concept. Although this perspective has recently been quite influential in policy circles, the empirical and theoretical work in this area on

Puerto Ricans is only beginning to emerge (Aponte, 1988; Tienda, 1989). Plaguing this research are methodological disputes over measurement issues and causality (Sawhill, 1988). As Danziger (1989, p. 2) said "there is little consensus on the appropriate definition or measurement of the underclass."

The *underclass* means different things to different people. As defined within the social ecology literature, it involves individuals who are not working or looking for work, who are socially and spatially isolated from mainstream institutions and activities, and who are in a situation of persisting disadvantage. This latter characteristic is often understood to mean that there is an intergenerational transmission of poverty; that is, if a family is detached from the labor market and socially isolated, the probability is great that the children will repeat this pattern.

To some researchers and academics, the term *underclass* may be defined by how it is measured. Measures often used to approximate the characteristics might include (1) the percentage of individuals within an area who are out of the labor force, (2) persons dependent on welfare, (3) pregnant teenagers, (4) female heads of households, (5) high school dropouts, and (6) individuals involved in criminal activity. Areas that were found to contain high rates of these variables would be termed *underclass areas*.

Finally, and perhaps most importantly, the term *underclass* conveys—even to those who are quite distant from such discussions—an immediate, pejorative sense of class, that is, a position outside of or beneath the regular class structure. More journalistic, less precise, or pedestrian understandings of the term include a dimension of criminality, and attitudinal and/behavioral predispositions to not working. The problem, of course, is that since the word means so many things to so many people, it is not a very efficient term. Moreover, it is disparaging and stigmatizing. It is one matter to use imprecise terminology; it is another to employ offensive vocabulary.[4]

There are also more pragmatic problems that arise from the use of the term. It is difficult to determine who is and who is not a member of the underclass. Although many geographic areas could be defined as underclass areas according to these measures, these neighborhoods contain many individuals who do not conform to the underclass criteria. That is to say, they may live in underclass areas but they have jobs, spouses, high school degrees, and the like. In addition, there are others who may be representative of the data but who are still law-abiding, hardworking, and upstanding citizens of the community. For example, take a female head of household who received aid for her dependent children, and, in the informal economy, who takes care of another child. Such a woman

---

[4]In his presidential address to the American Sociological Association, August, 1990, William Julius Wilson alluded to the difficulties of the term *underclass* and suggested that the term *ghetto poor* be used instead.

may have been severed from the formal labor market for some time, and may not be a high school graduate; she may also have become pregnant at the age of 17. But she may be a good mother and babysitter, a good citizen, and be active in improving her community. Consequently, the term *underclass* has been widely criticized by Puerto Rican researchers (Bonilla, 1989; Hernandez, 1990) and others (McGahey, 1982; Morris, 1989).

The behavioral implications suggested by the term have not been supported; see, for example, Corcoran, Duncan, Gurin, and Gurin (1985), who find that the majority of the persistent poor do not fit underclass stereotypes. Moreover, Corcoran *et al.* (1985) also found that it is changes in economic circumstances that lead to changes in psychological attitudes and not vice versa. The term is perplexing to define (Ricketts & Sawhill, 1988). It is unclear what proportion of those in designated underclass areas have recently moved there and what proportion have been there for some time. Since we lack longitudinal data showing chronic and concentrated economic deprivation (Tienda, 1989), we cannot answer this question. Given the lack of data to prove the existence of an underclass, one wonders why speculations abound—why this has reached the level of a debate.

Yet, the underclass concept has been so often used in reference to Puerto Rican poverty that it recently warranted an article in the *Annals of the American Academy* on "Puerto Ricans and the Underclass Debate" (Tienda, 1989, p. 107). It is of interest to note that the article refers to what is a prevailing conception in many circles: that is, *not* that there is a growing sector within the Puerto Rican community which evidences a persisting disadvantage, but rather that the *whole* group is becoming an underclass. The article notes "the growing speculation that Puerto Ricans are becoming part of the urban underclass" and again it notes the "considerable speculation that Puerto Ricans have become part of the urban underclass" (Tienda, 1989, p. 107). Earlier the statement had been made that "Puerto Ricans have become the Hispanic underclass during the past two decades" (Tienda & Jensen, 1986, p. 41). Thus, we find that, in the case of Puerto Ricans, the term is not used to refer to a "residual" population, as is argued by Wilson (1987), but it is used to refer to the whole group. In effect, we have a most remarkable social science phenomenon, the assumption that an entire ethnic-racial group has become an underclass, that is, that the group does not display any variance.

From Conjecture to Conclusion

Discussion regarding the possible existence of a Puerto Rican underclass produced a modest channeling of resources to the question but few answers. A recent study concluded that until questions "are satisfactorily answered, discussions about the development of a Puerto Rican urban underclass will be largely speculative" (Tienda, 1989, p. 119). In the same way, other issues have similarly followed the path from ambiguous research results to premature assumptions or weakly established conclusions.

An example of this is the association that is often made directly or indirectly between work and welfare. Bean and Tienda (1988, p. 302) suggested that the lower labor force participation of Puerto Rican female heads of household may be because Puerto Rican women rely more on public assistance. The fact that this group has the highest poverty rate and the highest welfare rate suggests a linkage. They go on to say that this inference is "suggestive" rather than conclusive; however, they fail to examine or demonstrate the possible existence of a causal relationship. A relationship between Puerto Ricans and welfare has often been "suggested" in the literature. However, the empirical work substantiating the suggestion has been lacking. For example, it was often inferred that getting on welfare was an important motivation for Puerto Rican migration to New York. Yet, the one study that examined this notion refutes the idea (Maldonado, 1976).

POLICY

Many of the policy prescriptions advanced in studies on Puerto Rican disadvantage ignore the uniqueness of the Puerto Rican situation. Hence the recommendations that emerge are strikingly similar to those counseled for other groups who are mired in poverty. They also tend to be standard repetitions of earlier recommendations. The real question is to what extent do the policies proposed resolve the fundamental issue of Puerto Rican or Latino disadvantage and to what extent does the research enlighten our understanding.

It would seem that with the accessibility problems noted above and with the creation of models and concepts that inadequately explain Puerto Rican disadvantage, it is important for Puerto Rican community-based organizations to insist on greater access and review, as well as better accountability and input into the research process. Having policy research conducted in conjunction with those agencies most in touch with the Puerto Rican community may be the most productive route to useful research. This is assuming, of course, that the respective parties, that is, the community-based organizations and the researchers, undertake their responsibilities seriously and with mutual respect.

Debates on Policy Approaches

Three major areas of debate concerning policy for the disadvantaged may be discerned. These are whether to provide universal or targeted programs; pursue policies that improve incentive structures or alter individual behavior; and whether to pursue people-specific or place-specific policies. The logic underlying these debates makes manifest the political considerations that are intertwined in policy formulation. The impact on Latinos of these various perspectives is seldom addressed. Nonetheless, Latino disadvantage is often unconsciously subsumed under one or more of these perspectives—thus, ignoring the uniqueness of the various Latino situations and thereby reducing the efficacy of policy. We will review each of these debates.

Universal versus Targeted Programs

Broad-based policies designed to improve the standard of living of all working and poor people are viewed as the most appropriate for two reasons: they are effective in getting at the structural roots of inequality and poverty and they are politically more acceptable to a broad political spectrum (Wilson, 1987). In recent years, however, such universalistic approaches have come into less favor because they are perceived as more costly. Examples are full-employment strategies and income policies that set a minimum floor for an acceptable standard of living.

Targeted policies focus on specific demographic groups and are designed either to remove institutional barriers to upward mobility (i.e., affirmative-action programs) or to enhance productivity potential (i.e., educational and job-training programs for unemployed and poverty populations).

Policies That Improve Incentive Structures versus Those That Alter Individual Behavior

The debate over "welfare reform" illustrates this second area of controversy. The issue is whether to develop policies that improve incentive structures or those that alter individual behavior. Generally, policies that improve incentive structures are concerned with seeking and retaining employment by using incentives. Those who argue for providing incentives prefer programs that gradually phase out—as opposed to eliminating or greatly reducing—benefits upon employment. They maintain that this approach provides an orderly transition to the labor market. Furthermore child care and health insurance provisions must be maintained if job search is going to be effectively supported. On the other hand, policies geared toward changing the behavior patterns of the poor seek to raise the cost of nonmarket activity, such as unemployment, participation in transfer programs, and so forth. Workfare, "learnfare," and reduction of benefit levels in transfer programs are designed to meet this end.

People-Specific versus Place-Specific Policies

People-specific policies refer to programs that seek to enhance individual choice. Examples of this are voucher systems that subsidize the poor's expenditures on housing and education services. Providing transportation so that the inner city unemployed can find jobs in suburban areas with labor shortages is another example. Place-specific approaches, such as neighborhood revitalization strategies, local economic development programs, or urban enterprise zones address the spatial and environmental context of poverty. These programs may be initiated by governmental agencies or carried out through corporate–community partnerships (National Puerto Rican Coalition, 1988).

Employment-Oriented Policies

The following are examples of some general policy recommendations that are discussed with specific reference to Latinos. These specific recommendations should not be seen as sufficient by themselves but as illustrating how policies can be more tailored to the Latino situation. For a broader range of similar recommendations, the reader is referred to recent policy statements issued by other sources: Association of Puerto Rican Executive Directors (APRED) (1990); Hispanic Policy Development Project (1988); IUP/SSRC Committee for Public Policy Research (1990); Institute for Puerto Rican Policy (1989); National Puerto Rican Coalition (1988); and R. D. Torres (1989).

Policies Addressing Productivity Characteristics

Here the primary concern is with raising the human capital levels of the poor. An essential strategy is to support school programs that prepare students for the rising skill requirements of the labor market and that improve the transition from schooling to the work world. Other approaches involve the private sector in training entry-level workers for promotion to higher-paid jobs. Further on up the educational scale, it is argued that government needs to expand access to college education for the poor and the disadvantaged. Human capital enhancement approaches also encompass such programs as Head Start, the Job Training Partnership Act, and the Job Corps (Burtless, 1986).

Experts disagree, however, on which is the most crucial intervention point within the educational system. Glazer (1986) suggested that increased spending at the elementary level may be more cost-effective than investing in work-training programs for dropouts since only a few dropouts manage to benefit from these programs. On the other hand, Jencks (1986) suggested that providing

> resources in secondary schools is of prime importance because students there, unlike those in elementary schools, will not have another chance to improve skills. (p. 8)

In the case of Puerto Ricans, interventions at both levels would decrease grade-delay, one of the primary explanations of their high dropout rate (Fligstein & Fernandez, 1985; Cafferty & Rivera-Martinez, 1981). Measures that improve school environments (e.g., class size, physical plant) and promote the employment of multicultural teachers have also been advanced (Fligstein & Fernandez, 1985).

Policies Encouraging Minority Entrepreneurship

There is some indirect evidence that the degree of self-employment and entrepreneurship within the Puerto Rican and Mexican communities has declined over the years. The spread of giant chain stores and department stores during the 1950s and 1960s reduced many of the advantages which local *bodegas* and retail stores offered within these urban communities. In particular, many small businesses were eliminated, or more successful operations closed in urban areas in California and New York City when their owners retired. Still others suffered from the negative effects of urban decline, arson, urban renewal, and redlining of minority communities. The decline of many communities meant that market conditions were not propitious for long-term survival of these establishments.

Measures designed to overcome these obstacles and to facilitate the development of community-based enterprises include: subsidized small business loans and management consultancy, first-source contracting, set-asides for minority businesses and contractors. In the current political environment, many of these programs have met with opposition because of the perception that such initiatives promote "reverse discrimination." However, in local jurisdictions where Latinos and African-Americans constitute significant sectors of the electorate, such proposals have been fairly successful in obtaining approval. Although less supported in the contemporary period, strategies that promote worker-owned cooperatives and enterprises continue to draw attention as viable programs for job creation and economic development. Although not usually conceived of as ethnically oriented strategies for social mobility, these initiatives offer a clear alternative to marginal jobs and dependency for depressed communities. However, they require encouragement and support from government (Hirschman, 1984; Schorr & Schorr, 1988).

CONCLUSION

Few progressive-minded individuals would dispute the sensibility of instituting these social reform policies. For example, many would favor policies that aim for full employment, target unemployment in specific metropolitan areas, generate new employment in areas that have slack labor markets, or reform school programs and make greater job-training investments to address mismatch problems. The reality, however, is that, at bottom, policy debates and decisions involve the larger issues of resource allocation and priorities. These issues are, in turn, subject to political will.

We would be remiss if we did not acknowledge the role that politics plays in transforming policy research into public policy. Policy agendas and recommendations may be driven as much, or more, by political conditions as by research findings. Although some researchers may not necessarily conduct their work with reference to specific policy frameworks, their findings may be compatible with *various* policy approaches. Thus, the relationship between research agendas and policy prescriptions is often tenuous. Therefore, we should not mystify the role of the researchers in the development of policy. Nor should we underestimate the power of political action in bringing about change.

ACKNOWLEDGMENTS

The authors would like to thank Frank Bonilla, Antonio Lauria, Pedro Pedraza, Carlos Sanabria, and Zulema Suarez for helpful comments. All remaining errors are our responsibility. For institutional report, we are also thankful to the Center for Puerto Rican Studies, Hunter College of the City University of New York.

REFERENCES

Aponte, R. (1988). *Employment and poverty among blacks and Puerto Ricans in the urban north.* Paper presented at the Massachusetts Institute of Technology Seminar Series, "Puerto Ricans and the Changing Northeast Economy," Cambridge, MA.

Association of Puerto Rican Executive Directors (APRED). (1990). *A call to action.* Presented to the black and Puerto Rican caucus of the New York State Legislature, Albany, February 17, 1990.

Bean, F., & M. Tienda. (1988). *Hispanic population in the U. S.* New York: Russell Sage.

Bonilla, F. (1989). *Breaking out of the cycle of poverty.* Washington, DC: National Puerto Rican Coalition.

Binilla, F., & R. Campos. (1981). A wealth of poor: Puerto Ricans in the new economic order. *Daedulus, 110*(2), 133–176.

Borjas, G. (1985). Jobs and employment for Hispanics. In P. San-Juan Cafferty & W. C. McCready, Eds., *Hispanics in the United States.* New Brunswick, NJ: Transaction Books.

Burtless, G. (1986). Public spending for the poor: Trends, prospects, and economic limits. In S. H. Danziger & D. H. Weinberg, Eds., *Fighting poverty: What works and what doesn't.* Cambridge: Harvard University Press.

Cafferty, P., & C. Rivera-Martinez. (1981). *The politics of language.* Boulder, CO: Westview Press.

Center on Budget and Policy Priorities. (1988). *Shortchanged: Recent developments in Hispanic poverty, income and employment.* Washington, DC: Author.

Community Service Society. (1989). *Poverty in New York City, 1985–88: The crisis continues.* New York: Author.

Corcoran, M., G. Duncan, G. Gurin, & P. Gurin. (1985). Myth and reality: The causes and persistence of poverty. *Journal of Policy Analysis and Management, 4*(4), 516–536.

Danziger, S. (1989). Overview. *Focus, 12,* 1.

Fligstein, N., & R. Fernandez. (1985). Hispanics in education. In P. San Juan-Cafferty & W. C. McCready, Eds., *Hispanics in the United States.* New Brunswick, NJ: Transaction Books.

Glazer, N. (1986). Education and training programs and poverty. In S. H. Danziger & D. H. Weinberg, Eds., *Fighting poverty: What works and what doesn't.* Cambridge: Harvard University Press.

Hayes-Bautista, D. (1990). Intellectual framework for a multicultural society: Demographic change and intellectual traditions. Paper presented at the National Conference on Latino Research Perspectives in the 1990s, Pomona, California.

Hernandez, J. (1976). *Social factors in educational attainment among Puerto Ricans in U. S. metropolitan areas.* New York: Aspira of America.

Hernandez, J. (1980). Social science and the Puerto Rican community. In C. E. Rodriguez, V. Sanchez Korrol, & J. A. Alers, Eds., *The Puerto Rican struggle: Essays on survival in the U. S.* Maplewood, NJ: Waterfront Press.

Hernandez, J. (1983). *Puerto Rican youth employment.* Maplewood, NJ: Waterfront Press.

Hernandez, J. (1990). Latino alternatives to the underclass concept. *Latino Studies Journal, 1,*(1), 95–105.

Hirschman, A. O. (1984). *Getting ahead collectively: Grassroots experiences in Latin America.* New York: Pergamon Press.

Hispanic Policy Development Project. (1988). *Closing the gap for U. S. Hispanic youth: Public/private strategies.* Washington, DC: Author.

History Task Force, Centro de Estudios Puertorriquenos. (1979). *Labor migration under capitalism: The Puerto Rican experience.* New York: Monthly Review.

Institute for Puerto Rican Policy. (1989). *Toward a Puerto Rican/Latino agenda for New York City.* New York: Author.

IUP/SSRC Committee for Public Policy Research. (1990). *New directions for Latino public policy research.* Austin: The Center for Mexican American Studies, University of Texas.

Jencks, C. (1986). Comment. In S. H. Danziger & D. H. Weinberg, Eds., *Fighting poverty: What works and what doesn't.* Cambridge: Harvard University Press.

Jorge, A. (1984). *The Puerto Rican study 1953–57: Its character and impact on Puerto Ricans in New York City.* Unpublished doctoral dissertation, New York University.

Lopez, A. (1973). *The Puerto Rican papers.* New York: Bobbs-Merrill.

Lopez, A., & J. Petras. (1974) *Puerto Rico and Puerto Ricans.* Cambridge, MA: Schenkman.

Maldonado, R. (1976). Why Puerto Ricans migrated to the United States in 1947–73. *Monthly Labor Review, 99*(9), 7–18.

McGahey, R. (1982). Poverty's voguish stigma. *New York Times,* March 12, A29.

Melendez, E. (1988). *Labor market structure and wage inequality in New York City: A comparative analysis of Hispanics, non-Hispanic blacks and whites.* Cambridge, MA: MIT Department of Urban Studies and Planning.

Morris, M. (1989). From the culture of poverty to the underclass: An analysis of a shift in public language. *American Sociologist, 20*(2), 123–133.

National Puerto Rican Coalition. (1988). *Public policy agenda, 1988–1990.* Washington, DC: Author.

New York City Board of Education. (1958). *The Puerto Rican study, 1953–57.* (J. Cayce Morrison, Chair).

Niemi, A. M. (1974). Wage discrimination against Negroes and Puerto Ricans in the New York SHSA: An assessment of educational and occupational differences. *Social Sciences Quarterly, 55* (June).

Puerto Rican community development project (PRCDP). (1965). New York: Puerto Rican Forum.

Reimers, C. (1983). Labor market discrimination against Hispanic and black men. *Review of Economics and Statistics, 45* (November).

Ricketts, E., & I. Sawhill. (1988). Defining and measuring the underclass. *Journal of Policy Analysis and Management, 7*(2), 316–325.

Rodriguez, C. (1974). *The ethnic queue: The case of Puerto Ricans in the U. S.* San Francisco, CA: R & E Research Associates.

Rodriguez, C. (1979). *Economic factors affecting Puerto Ricans in the U. S.* In History Task Force, Centro de Estudios Puertorriquenos, *Labor migration under capitalism: The Puerto Rican experience.* New York: Monthly review.

Rodriguez, C. (1989). *Race, class and gender among Puerto Ricans in New York.* Report submitted to the Inter-University Program for Latino Research. Austin, TX: University of Texas.

Rosaldo, R. (1989). *Culture and truth: The remaking of social analysis.* Boston: Beacon Press.

Sandefur, G. D., & A. Pahari. (1988). *Racial and ethnic inequality in earnings and educational attainment.* University of Wisconsin-Madison, Institute for Research on Poverty, DP #863–88.

Sandefur, G. D., & M. Tienda. (1988). *Divided opportunities: Minorities, poverty, and social policy.* New York: Plenum Press.

Sawhill, I. (1988). Poverty in the U. S.: Why is it so persistent? *Journal of Economic Literature, 26*(3), 1073–1119.

Schorr, L., & D. Schorr. (1988). *Within our reach: Breaking the cycle of disadvantage.* Garden City, NY: Doubleday.

Silk, L. (1990). The denial of the obvious. *New York Times,* March 9, 1990, D2.

Tienda, M. (1989). Puerto Ricans and the underclass debate. *Annals, 501,* 105–119.

Tienda, M., & L. Jensen. (1988). Poverty and minorities: A quarter century profile of color and socioeconomic disadvantage. In G. D. Sandefur & M. Tienda, Eds., *Divided Opportunities: Minorities, poverty, and social policy.* New York: Plenum Press.

Torres, A. (1973). Puerto Rican employment in New York. *New Generation, 53*(4), 12–17.

Torres, A. (1988). Human capital, labor segmentation and inter-minority relative status. Doctoral dissertation, New School for Social Research, New York.

Torres, R. D. (1989). Latinos, economy and politics of inequality: Policy alternatives in the post-Reagan era. *La Red, 2*(4), 24–32.

U. S. Bureau of the Census. (1963). U. S. Census of Population: 1960, Subject Reports. *Puerto Ricans in the United States.* Final Report PC(2)-1D. Washington, DC: U. S. Government Printing Office.

U. S. Bureau of the Census. (1989). The Hispanic population in the U. S.: March 1988. Washington, DC: U. S. Government Printing Office.

U. S. Commission on Civil Rights. (1972). *Hearings on civil rights of Puerto Ricans. Demographic, social and economic characteristics of New York City and the New York metropolitan area.* Staff Report, February, 1972.

U. S. Commission on Civil Rights. (1976). *Puerto Ricans in the continental United States: An uncertain future.* Report submitted to the President and Congress, Washington, DC.

U. S. Department of Labor. (1968). Bureau of Labor Statistics. *Labor force experience of the Puerto Rican worker.* Regional Report No. 9 of Poverty Area Profiles, June, 1968, Washington, DC.

Velez, C. (1988). Networks of exchange among Mexicans in the U. S. and Mexico. *Urban Anthropology and Studies of Cultural Systems and World Economic Development, 17*(1), 27–52.

Wagenheim, K. (1975). *A survey of Puerto Ricans on the U. S. mainland in the 1970s.* New York: Praeger.

Wilson, W. (1987). *The truly disadvantaged: The inner city, the underclass and public policy.* Chicago: University of Chicago Press.

13

Latinos, Class, and the U. S. Political Economy

Income Inequality and Policy Alternatives

RODOLFO D. TORRES AND ADELA DE LA TORRE

INTRODUCTION

Few studies analyze the mechanisms that cause inequality in earnings, employment, and occupational achievement between Latino and non-Latino populations. Compared to analyses of income for blacks, relatively little attention has been devoted to the study of income determination among Latino populations. Previous studies consider income inequalities from the perspective of human capital theory. In this chapter, we will consider two dominant theoretical perspectives for explaining income inequality: the human capital model and the class/structural model. Then we will review related empirical studies of Latino

RODOLFO D. TORRES • Graduate Center for Public Policy and Administration, California State University Long Beach, Long Beach, California 90840.   ADELA DE LA TORRE • Health Care Administration Program, California State University Long Beach, Long Beach, California 90840.

Hispanics in the Labor Force, edited by Edwin Melendez *et al.* Plenum Press, New York, 1991.

populations. After critiquing the human capital and class/structural perspectives, we will discuss policy initiatives emerging from these two competing models on income inequality. Lastly, we will consider future research directions for the analysis of income determination and employment among Latinos in the United States and conclude with some thoughts on the challenges we face in the post-Reagan era in constructing policy alternatives and initiating a movement that secures economic and political justice.

Dramatic changes are expected in the racial and ethnic composition of new entrants into the labor force in southern California. Between 1980 and 1990, non-Latino whites are projected to compose only one out of five new workers; blacks will make up one out of six, and other non-Latino groups one in nine. About one-half of the expected expansion of the labor force will come from Latino residents, and most of these will be of Mexican origin (Muller & Espenshade, 1985, p. 166). Ethnic changes in southern California's labor force in the 1990s will be even greater. The number of non-Latino whites (female and male) will decline, and new workers of Mexican origin will account for three out of four new workers in the region. According to a recent study sponsored by the Urban Institute (Muller & Espenshade, 1985), even without further immigration or internal migration, the majority of workers added to the labor force in southern California over the next twenty years would be Latino, primarily of Mexican origin.

So, there is little doubt that Latinos compose one of the fastest growing groups in the labor market and will soon become the largest minority in the United States. However, little is known about the process by which Latinos enter and participate in the labor market, which is particularly troubling because of the continuing serious inequalities in income, wages, and occupational achievement compared to white non-Latino workers. Little research of a longitudinal nature has been completed, partly because of the difficulty, until recently, of identifying Latino national-origin groups in census information. Changes in census categories identifying Latinos have created problems of compatibility between 1950 and 1970. With the inclusion of Latino identifiers in the Census Bureau's annual Current Population survey since the 1970s, and with the release of the 1976 Survey of Income and Education (SIE) microdata file, empirical work has become more feasible. Now it is possible to distinguish considerable socioeconomic variation within national-origin groups, allowing for separate analysis of populations with origins in Mexico, Cuba, Puerto Rico, Central and South America, and a residual "other-Hispanic" grouping.

Theory determines to a considerable extent what we observe. Theory also determines what we do not observe. Theoretical perspectives facilitate our asking certain questions. Consequently, it is important to consider the theoretical perspectives shaping the empirical investigations discussed in this chapter.

INCOME INEQUALITY AND DISCRIMINATION: THE ROLE OF
HUMAN CAPITAL MODELS

There have been several major attempts to understand the persistence of discrimination in the market place. Clearly, this interest has stemmed from the empirical observations that show not only significant income differentials between black and white workers, at any given point in time, but continuing through many decades, and also the low occupational employment status for these workers (Bergmann, 1971; Brown, 1977; Reich, 1981). In addition to this concern for the plight of the black worker, recent empirical evidence on the Hispanic worker shows similar labor market trends and experiences (Rochin 1988).

Although several demand-side models have been developed to explain theoretically labor market discrimination, such as the Becker (1957) model, the Bergmann (1971) crowding model, and the Spence (1973) signaling model, the supply-side human capital models have been the major focus of several studies in economics and in sociology.

Supply-side models, such as the human capital model, shift the focus from employer tastes and informational problems within the labor market that result in discriminatory hiring/training policies, to those factors that affect workers' productivity before they enter the market place. Here, human capital theory is used in order to understand the investment decisions in general training by non-white workers and white workers. The implicit assumption in this model is that non-white workers and women are treated fairly in the labor market even though their opportunity sets may have been constrained prior to entering the market place; that is, from such institutional barriers as unequal access to quality school, limited access to social services, and the like.

Given that market forces are independent of institutional constraints, the low wages received by non-white workers and/or their occupational segregation is a result of their choice not to invest in training or education that would improve their social and economic status. Thus, the responsibility of low wages and low occupational status is a result of choices made by these workers not to obtain the work credentials necessary for employment in high-wage sectors. What appears as labor market discrimination, therefore, merely reflects non-optimal decision-making practices by non-white workers.

These non-optimal decisions that are made by non-white workers benefit some sectors of the economy, even though there is an overall misallocation of resources. In this model, those who gain from this misallocation are those who employ unskilled workers, which occurs because there is an artificially high supply of unskilled, potentially high productivity workers.

The human capital model, unlike the demand-side models, suggests that

there are no distortions in the labor market, and that both employer and workers
operate rationally in the labor market. The employer pays the workers the value
of their marginal product and the workers rationally weigh the returns they will
receive from investments in human capital. Thus,

> racism is embedded in political and social institutions . . . markets are affected only
> to the extent that they register the effects of racism while performing their technical
> task of guiding resources to their most efficient use. (Weaver, 1978, p. 306)

Other critics of the human capital model are concerned with the exclusion of
class and class conflict as important factors in explaining labor market phenomena. Bowles and Gintis (1975) argued that an adequate theory of human
resource utilization must include theories of production and of social reproduction. They claimed that human capital theory offered no theories of production
and of social reproduction. Class issues influence the demand for labor.
Ownership of capital and control structures in capitalist enterprises significantly
influence the incentive of workers. Although the human capital perspective
focuses on workers' individual characteristics and attributes, this perspective
seems to limit itself to consideration of their technical skills as related to productive capacity. The human capital perspective ignores labor history, wherein management has used race, sex, age, ethnicity, and formal educational degrees to
fragment the labor force. Issues of power and class are fundamentally involved in
accounting for labor demand in allocating workers to positions, structuring jobs,
and defining the productivity of workers. The complexity of the labor market is
not expressed by a human capital perspective that considers as free market
matching of technically defined skills with technically defined production requirements.

For the past twenty years, human capital explanations have provided explanations of income differences for black and white populations. Historically,
throughout the twentieth century, measured skill disparities between blacks and
whites have narrowed. However, income inequality between the two populations
did not begin to narrow until the 1960s. Using 1940 census data, Zeman focused
on years of schooling and on-the-job training, two of the most important determinants of income according to the human capital model. Incomes of both races
increased with schooling and age, but the rate of increase in income was much
higher for white men. Zeman's study suggested that giving blacks the same
amount of education as whites would accomplish little to reduce income inequality. Further research in the 1950s tended to confirm Zeman's findings
(Smith, 1984, p. 685). Even the early work of Thurow (1969), based on the
microlevel 1960 census tapes, continued to show low returns in schooling for
blacks in addition to dramatic declines in their relative earning potential throughout their careers. Economists focused on market discrimination against black
skilled labor and government discrimination, which contributed to lower quality

education in black schools, to explain declining black-white income ratios with schooling. Theories of discrimination accounted for differences in job investment: either blacks were seen as being denied jobs with human capital growth, or they were confined to secondary labor markets.

In the late 1960s and early 1970s, two factors contributed greater credibility to human capital analysis (Smith, 1984, p. 686). First, there was a continued substantial rise in black-white income ratios. Second, analysis based on microdata tapes from the 1967 Survey of economic Opportunity and the 1970 census suggested that rates of return to education appeared as high for blacks as for whites, the latter being especially true for higher education. Nevertheless, the historical validity of the human capital perspective continued to be questioned (Ashenfelter, 1977; Darity, 1982; Levin, 1978). The significant rise in relative black income that began during the mid-1960s coincided with the enactment of the 1965 Civil Rights Act. Some critics of the human capital model attribute considerable importance to antidiscrimination legislation as the explanation for this rise in black income (Freeman, 1973). The long historical record continued to show that although there had been a steady convergence in human capital characteristics between blacks and whites, income inequality for blacks had not changed much until the late 1960s.

A more recent, careful analysis of the historical trends in schooling, income, and labor market participation for blacks and whites indicates a stronger case for human capital explanations of these trends. Smith (1984, p. 695) found that generations of blacks who were born between 1886 and 1905 had an impact on the interpretations of time-series changes in their relative income that lasted for forty years. As long as they remained a large part of the total labor force, there was no reason to expect much convergence in income ratios based on human capital elements alone. Once these cohorts left the labor market in the 1960s and 1970s, improvements in economic conditions of black men became evident. Smith and others now argue that black men of recent cohorts do not encounter career prospects that differ from those of white men. They see the fundamental problems as the wide inequalities that exist when labor market competition begins. Smith (1984) concluded that the large income gap between white and black men that exists when careers begin may be due substantially to racial discrimination. However, this perspective now places more confidence in the human capital model, asserting that as the human capital of blacks increases relative to whites, black wages will also increase accordingly.

Empirical studies based on the extended human capital model vary considerably owing to differences in the variables that are included, definitions and ways of operationalizing the same variables, data sets applied, and measurement. However, these models do conform in certain general ways. Most studies find that, in contrast to studies of blacks, educational attainment is the most important income differential between the Latino and non-Latino white population. The low wages of Latinos in the labor market are not strongly accounted for by wage discrimination as occurs with black-white wage comparisons. Instead, wage differences between Latino and white workers are caused by the lower levels of human capital characteristics (i.e., education and job skills) found among the Latino population.

The research of Reimers (1985, p. 55) showed, for comparative purposes, a 23% wage-offer gap between black and white men. Less than one half of this gap can be explained by different individual characteristics. Educational differences account for only 10% of the inequality. As much as 14% of the wage-offer difference may be due to discrimination. The Reimers study identified a significant wage difference between Latinos and non-Latino white men. Educational differences accounted for about one half of the wage difference. Statistically controlling for differences in socioeconomic characteristics of the two groups, the wage gap was substantially reduced, to 6%. This residual, unexplained gap in income was attributed to discrimination.

In analyzing the differences in unemployment rates between Latino and non-Latino white populations, DeFreitas (1985) found that individual characteristics accounted for most of the gap. However, the residual or unexplained difference suggested that discrimination also played a role in creating the higher unemployment rates for Latinos compared to the white population.

The effects of education on income vary significantly across Hispanic-American groups. Generally, these studies indicate that income returns to education for Latinos are lower than they are for whites, but it varies by nationality. Using 1975 data, Reimers (1985) found that Hispanic-Anglo wage ratios for men ranged from low of seventy-two cents for Mexicans to a high of eighty-nine cents for Cubans.

Since a substantial number of Latinos are foreign-born, other variables enter the human capital equation, including nativity, English-language proficiency, length of time in the United States, and nationality. In particular, the impact of English-language proficiency has been the focus of several empirical studies. A study by Grenier (1984) concluded that language attributes play a significant role in wage levels of Hispanic male workers. In addition, he found that Hispanic workers whose mother tongue was Spanish had lower returns to education relative to those whose mother tongue was English. In a later study, McManus (1985) estimated the costs of language disparity for Hispanics and the impact of English language proficiency on wages of Hispanics. He estimated the aggregate cost of language disparity for three Hispanic male groups who had varying levels of English proficiency (i.e., those designated as "very well," "well," and "not well"). For his sample, he estimated an aggregate cost of language disparity of $45 million, which he suggested reflected an underestimate of the true cost of language disparity as Spanish-speakers account for approximately one half of the

English deficient speakers. A final study focusing on the impact of English language ability on labor market opportunities of Hispanics and East Asian immigrant men is by Kossoudji (1988) who also concluded that it was costly to lack English proficiency; however, this cost is not shared equally by all ethnic groups. Instead, at every skill level, Hispanics appear to bear a higher cost for their language deficiency relative to Asians owing to reduced observed earnings and fewer occupational opportunities. A critical assumption of many of these empirical studies is that the marginal value product of the individual worker is adversely affected by lack of English proficiency. If this assumption is valid and if the lower observed wages of Hispanics is explained primarily by the lack of English proficiency, then the obvious policy implication would be to increase the level of English proficiency for this group to enhance their wage level and occupational choice. At the same time, underlying this policy recommendation is the subtle suggestion that affirmative-action programs are not the best policy alternatives for increasing the income levels of Hispanics.

Similar policy implications can be gleaned from the Reimers (1985) study. She concluded that race had no significant impact on the wages of Latino men, and that discrimination in the labor market may be responsible for wage differences of 18% for Puerto Ricans, but only 6% for Mexican men compared to non-Latino white men (p. 55).

All Latino groups (except Mexican-Americans born in the United States) had lower returns to education than Anglo men (Reimers, 1985, p. 41). Compared to the earning increases of 6.1% per grade of additional schooling that was completed by Anglo men, other-Hispanics earned 3.4% and Mexicans 5.4%. Except for Cubans and other-Hispanics, foreign-born Latinos had lower returns from their education in the United States than native-born men of their ethnic group (Reimers, 1985, p. 44).

Studies show that returns to foreign work experience are much smaller than returns to work experience in the United States (Reimers, 1985, p. 45). Immigrants from Mexico, Puerto Rico, and Central and South America gain little in earnings based on their prior work experience outside of the United States. In terms of earnings, these immigrants are viewed the same as new entrants into the labor market. There are also differences in returns between immigrants to the United States and Americans with regard to their work experience. Mexican, other-Hispanic, and black male immigrants have higher initial returns to work experience in this country than their native-born counterparts. However, their experience also peaks more quickly. Puerto Rican, Cuban, and Central or South American immigrant men have lower initial returns to work experience than do the native-born (Reimers, 1985, p. 45). Reimers also found that in states where Latinos constituted a larger proportion of the population, white and Cuban men earned at least as much as they earned elsewhere (p. 49). However, Mexican,

Puerto Rican, and other-Hispanic men received lower wages than elsewhere, which may be evidence of discrimination affecting Latinos when they represent a larger proportion of the population. These conditions could also result from Mexicans and other-Hispanics choosing to work where there are many other Latinos, regardless of the lower wage rates in these regions.

Studies of the determinants of Latinas' wages show some differences from men. Reimers (1985) reported that Mexican women's average wage offers are 20% lower than white non-Hispanic women (p. 70). After compensating for regional cost-of-living differences, the gap narrowed to 16%. Years of schooling was found to account for 93% of the real wage offer gap. Puerto Rican and Cuban women's wages are about the same as that of white non-Hispanic women. The most likely explanation offered is that white non-Latin American women tend to be employed in white-collar jobs, whereas minority women with comparable education are more often employed in blue-collar jobs that provide higher wages. Again, just as for Latinos, Reimers (1985) argued that race is not an important factor in explaining the lower wages of Latin American women (p. 72). Immigrant status accounts for small differences in the wage gap for women, from 0.2% for Mexican women to 8% for Central and South American women. English language problems cause wage differences ranging from none for Puerto Rican women to 8% for Cuban women. The larger families of Mexican women are considered a factor in explaining the 3% wage gap when compared to their Anglo counterparts, but represent minimal differences for other groups of Latinas.

A study by Carlson and Swartz (1988), which examined wage disparities across racial and ethnic groups, found that women's earnings for all groups were less sensitive to human capital characteristics than that of white men. If Mexican and Puerto Rican women were paid, using the same white male earnings function, given their productive characteristics, less than one half of the observed earning gap between the two groups would have remained. From their empirical study, it was suggested that all groups of women experience a greater influence from discrimination than do men; however, much of the disparity in women's earnings can be attributed to productive characteristics and hours worked.

Generally, the human capital studies suggest that ethnic discrimination is not a major determinant in the earnings of Mexican, Puerto Rican, and Cuban women, although it is more of a barrier to Central and South American and other-Hispanic women. On the whole, all Latin American women receive lower returns for their work than do white non-Hispanic women (Reimers, 1985, p. 74). The reason for this is because Latin American women have less access to jobs with training and promotion opportunities, and often have more children than do white non-Hispanic women, which is another factor that lowers their wages.

THE CLASS/STRUCTURAL MODEL

Prior to the development of an articulated class/structural model of income determination by such labor economists as Reich, Gordon, and Edwards (1973), alternative explanations of wage and occupational determination were developed by institutional economists such as Fisher (1953), Kerr (1954), and Doeringer and Piore (1971) that challenged the accuracy of the human capital approach. In particular, the Doeringer and Piore (1971) dual labor market model provided critical contributions in understanding the role of nonmarket forces in labor market allocations.

The concept of the dual labor market was developed in response to the observation that no single labor market exists (Kerr, 1954). In fact, in certain sectors of the economy, the allocations of labor and the determination of wages appears to be insulated from market forces. Doeringer and Piore (1971) attempted to explain the mechanism and institutions that allocated labor under these conditions. In order to deal with the problem theoretically, their suggestion was to develop the concept to the internal labor market and the theory of the dual labor market. An internal labor market is defined as an "administrative unit within which pricing and allocation of labor is governed by a set of administrative rules and procedures" (Doeringer & Piore, 1971, p. 1). They attributed the emergence of this market to the rise of skill specificity, increased on-the-job training, and custom. According to them, it also evolved to give the worker and the employer more security in the work place. However, at the same time that the internal labor market stabilized the relationship between the worker and the employer, it also institutionalized discriminatory labor market practices.

The three major categories of instruments that can result in these discriminatory practices are: (1) entry, (2) job allocation, and (3) wage. Non-market entry requirements, such as union membership, by definition are discriminatory because they segregate a group of workers from the labor market as qualified only for certain jobs. Both job allocation and wages that are non-market determined (e.g., based on a seniority system), also promote differentiation within the work force that may have no relationship to productivity. Thus, with this system a more productive non-white or white worker may not receive a fair return on his or her skill level.

The persistence of low wages and low job status, however, must be analyzed within the broader framework of the dual labor market. The dual labor market consists of a primary and a secondary labor market. Generally, the primary labor market has the following features:

> high wages, good working conditions, employment stability, chances of advancement, equity, and due process in the administration of work rules. (Doeringer & Piore, 1971)

Given these characteristics, the development of an internal labor market follows within this sector as nonwage aspects of employment increase in importance. In contrast, jobs in the secondary labor market generally do not have internal labor markets and possess many of the following features:

> low wages and fringe benefits, poor working conditions, high labor turnover, little chance of advancement, and often arbitrary and capricious supervision. (Doeringer & Piore, 1971, p. 165)

The dual labor market analysis specifically arose as an attempt to understand the labor force problems of the disadvantaged, particularly non-white workers in urban areas, whose problems had previously been attributed to unemployment. A major conclusion drawn from the model was that non-white workers were confined to jobs in the secondary labor market, and that high unemployment rates were a characteristic of jobs in that sector. Thus, policy should be aimed at minimizing the entry barriers (e.g., via manpower training programs) into the primary labor market, or creating conditions so that jobs in the secondary sector can acquire some of the characteristics of the primary labor market in order to develop more stable work relationships.

The major problems that Doeringer and Piore attempted to approach with the dual labor market analysis is how to explain the persistence of non-white workers in jobs that were characterized as secondary labor market occupations. They attempted to explain this persistence by examining lower income life-styles and the characteristics of secondary jobs, such as lack of stability and low skill requirements. Thus, these workers have neither the incentive nor the model to acquire the necessary skills to enter the primary labor market. Furthermore, employers have no incentive to invest in training their workers, given their behavioral characteristics, nor do they have the incentive to stabilize the work relationship. The net effect is that non-white workers are caught in dead-end, low-paying jobs with slim chances of entering the primary labor market.

Although discrimination against non-white workers does and can occur in the primary labor market, this problem is of lesser importance than the problem of concentration of non-white workers in the secondary labor market—a problem deeply rooted in the subculture of non-white workers and the structure and nature of the secondary labor market. Discrimination against non-white workers, therefore, is a product of these two factors and can only be eliminated by breaking the links that attach the non-white workers to the secondary labor market.

The major weakness in the institutional models is that discrimination appears to be exogenously determined; that is, we are left with the question: How did discriminatory treatment of non-white workers arise in their model? Not attempting to explain the origins of discrimination results in a circular argument. For example: Why are non-whites overrepresented in the secondary labor market? Is this because they are discriminated against and less productive? But why are they less productive and discriminated against? Is this because they are in the secondary labor market where the proper skills and behavioral traits needed for the primary labor market are unattainable? And so the vicious circle continues.

Unlike the dual labor market analysis, which limits its discussion to the narrow confines of the labor market, a class/structural perspective considers three basic units of analysis: macrosocial structures, classes, and individuals, This perspective argues that social structures and classes are equally significant in determining individual income. In addition, the structuralist perspective considers these three units as interdependent. A fully developed theory of income inequality must recognize the characteristics of the social structures within which income is determined.

With an analysis of the social basis of the income determination process, specific analysis of income determination at the class level can take place. Income determination at the class level can be considered by two factors: the analysis of income determination within classes, and the analysis of the ways in which the entire income determination process is shaped by class conflict. Class relations are believed to influence income determination of individuals. Classes are organized social forces that enter into conflict and change social structures. According to Wright (1979), class conflict influences the income determination process in two basic ways: first, through union struggles over wages, unemployment insurance, and other social welfare benefits, and second, by transforming the social structures within which income determination occurs.

From the structural perspective, the analysis of individual-level income determination involves two dimensions: first, the way in which individual choices and actions can change a person's position within class relations through inter- or intraclass mobility, and second, the various processes which affect those specific individual choices influencing the individual's income within a certain class location. Certainly, the individual's education, for example, has a bigger impact on the income of a manager than for a worker. This perspective considers class and social structural relationships which influence individual consciousness.

Human capital research does not focus on wage discrimination as the most important form of discrimination occurring within the labor market. A class/structural perspective regards wage differences as the result of the location of workers within the labor market, in terms of industrial sector and occupation. Here we consider three major noncompetitive labor market structures: dual labor markets, occupational segmentation, and ethnic enclaves.

Industrial dualism argues that the organization of the product markets (as monopolistic or competitive) determines the relative bargaining of firms and workers (Gordon, 1972). Firms belong either in the core sector or the periphery. Higher earnings are realized in the core sector while lower wages are earned in the peripheral sector.

Occupational segmentation considers the degree of control an individual has in the work environment. Edwards (1979) identified three occupational segments. Secondary jobs are those requiring little formal training and are characterized by low pay, no career mobility, and high turnover. A subordinate primary segment are those jobs attached to the top segment requiring some formal training, and are characterized by limited career mobility, moderate pay and benefits, and some career mobility. The independent primary jobs, those requiring considerable training, are characterized by real career mobility opportunities, high pay, good benefits, and low turnover. About two thirds of the Latino labor force is located in the peripheral industries and more than 60% is concentrated in the low-wage occupational segment (Melendez, 1988, p. 1).

Empirical studies have found significant differences in earnings in core and peripheral industrial sectors after taking into account workers' characteristics. Workers in core industries earn 30 to 40% higher wages and experience lower turnover (Bibb & Form, 1977; Kallenberg & Althauser, 1981). Studies of occupational segmentation indicate that workers in secondary jobs do, in fact, experience less upward mobility and have lower wages, whereas those in primary sector jobs experience higher salaries and more job mobility (Gordon, 1972). The labor market segmentation models view the evolution of the labor market as a function of the level of the development of the productive forces. By examining the historical development of capitalism in the United States, it is possible to trace the corresponding changes in the labor market, that is, at each stage (competitive, monopoly, and advanced monopoly) the labor market must adapt in order to reproduce the social relations of production. However, in the latter two stages of capital accumulation, capital becomes concentrated at an uneven rate; thus, the production process itself becomes segmented into competitive and monopolistic sectors and the dual labor market that develops reflects this uneven sectoral growth.

In the segmentation model, racist labor practices are viewed as tools to aid in further dividing and conquering the working class. Any divisions within the working class are played upon in order to break down worker solidarity. Divisions that are due to both race and sex are a given in this model, resulting in a glossing over of the origins and processes by which a certain group is selected for discriminatory practice. Most empirical studies have focused on the black experience, with little research considering the Latino labor market experience.

A recent study by Melendez (1988) has examined the effects of labor market structure on Latino labor markets in New York City. Melendez considered several categories of Latinos: Mexicans, Puerto Ricans, Cubans, and other-Hispanics using the 1980 census data. The findings from his study indicate that labor market structures (in this case, industrial sectors and occupational segmentation) are important determinants of Hispanic, non-Hispanic, black, and white hourly wages in New York City. In fact, labor market structure explains a substantial proportion of Latino wage differences from non-Latino white populations. About 16 to 19% of the difference is explained by primary-segment location for Hispanic men and 36 to 58% for Hispanic women. Working within core industries can explain about 7 to 14% of the Latino wage gap for men and about 4 to 7% for women. Melendez found that discrimination is still important an factor in accounting for the wage gap for Latin Americans. Discrimination was responsible for about one third of the wage gap for Mexican, Puerto Rican, and Cuban men. Although the wage gap was much smaller for women than men, discrimination accounted for one fifth to one half of the gap. This study of the New York City labor force determined that whites have higher returns to education and job experience than do blacks and Latinos. Finally, Melendez found that education was the single most important factor for all Latino groups in explaining the earnings gap between them and the white population. However, the proportion of the wage gap explained by differences in education varies greatly among the different Latino groups. Human capital characteristics account for 25 to 50% of the ethnic wage differences and reduces by more than 50% women's wage differences.

Previous studies of structural theories of labor market segmentation have barely touched upon the interaction of class and ethnicity not much attention has been paid to ethnically organized economic activities. Recently, Portes and Bach (1985) integrated the concept of ethnic enclaves with analysis of segmented labor market theory. Their analysis involved a six-year period. Contrary to the human capital model, immigrants do not arrive as isolated individuals but rather have access to the resources of the larger groups to which they belong. Portes and Bach argued that an immigrants' ability to utilize individual human capital is influenced by class position, social networks, and state policies. State policies may work to direct immigrant groups into secondary markets. Ethnicity, rather than individual skills, may combine with an immigrant's working-class background to link secondary labor employers to new workers. For some immigrant groups, however, another structure operates within the labor market: the ethnic enclave.

Ethnic enclaves are distinct economic formations characterized by spatial concentrations of immigrants who organize a variety of enterprises to serve their own market and the general population (Portes & Bach, 1985, p. 203). Ethnic enterprises possess two essential traits: the presence of immigrants with sufficient capital to create new opportunities for economic growth and an extensive division of labor within the enclave. The enclaves develop as the first wave of immigrants send over an entrepreneurial class. The growth and diversification of this class offer subsequent immigrants from the same ethnic group employment opportunities unavailable to immigrants entering regular labor market sectors. Studies show that these entrepreneurial activities can expand because they are able to reproduce (on a local scale) some of the characteristics of monopolistic control that account for the success of firms in the larger economy. Ethnic entrepreneurs use new immigrant workers to suppress unionization and to capitalize through pooled savings and rotating credit systems (Cheng & Bonacich, 1984; Light, 1972). The labor organization of immigrant enclave economies requires recent arrivals to take the worst jobs first. Immigrants are willing to stay in these secondary-type jobs because they open paths of upward mobility that are unavailable outside the immigrant enclave. Expanding enclave firms are expected to create managerial-level openings or self-employment for members of the same minority.

Ethnic enclaves differ from the secondary sector: ethnic ties permeate the class relationship with a sense of collective purpose and solidarity forces discipline on the part of the workers; however, it also demands obligations from the managers to provide training and skill upgrading for the workers.

Portes and Bach (1985) showed how Cuban entrepreneurs in Miami merged into the local economy through the growth of a small-scale entrepreneurial class, which was assisted by the established social network within the Cuban community. However, it is also important to recognize that the majority of the sample had entered the outside economy, moving into the segmented primary and secondary sectors. They found that ethnicity in the secondary sector was associated with lower rewards and subordinate social and economic positions generally found among the immigrant minorities. Their study concluded that individual skills operated differently depending on where immigrants worked. In the enclave, Cuban education contributed to occupational gain early in the resettlement experience and over time. Also, workers benefited from work experience in Cuba and from the additional experience they gained in the United States. Outside the enclave in the secondary sector, there were few benefits or rewards for individual skills. Previous education in Cuba penalized occupational workers. Workers in the secondary sector moved upward by accumulating economic resources transferred from Cuba or acquired over time in the United States.

In all, Portes and Bach (1980, 1985) found that the process of occupational and income attainment among Cuban immigrants was significantly influenced by the availability of ethnically organized enclaves. Self-employment and economic returns on human capital, made possible through the operation of enclaves, had little to do with the individual abilities of immigrants. Instead, their upward economic achievements depended on the enclave social structures that received and supported them. In contrast, although many Mexicans had greater education and occupational training than did Cuban immigrants, few Mexican immigrants in the Portes study became small businessmen within six years of their arrival in the United States. Portes and Bach claimed that Mexican immigrants do not have an enclave option but, instead, are entrenched in a long historical working-class migrant flow.

Beginning with the works of Simmel, sociologists have been interested in how group size influences social behavior and social structure. Recently, labor market analysts have investigated how the relative size of minority populations in the labor market influences minority wages relative to the white majority. Studies have reached different conclusions, in part, because they use different dependent variables (income and occupational status) to demonstrate increasing or decreasing inequality. Also, most studies treat minority populations as homogeneous, with no attempt to account for the increasing heterogeneity found within minority groups today.

There are two general explanations for the widening disparity of income between the white majority and the minority populations. One argument is that discrimination increases as minority workers compete for scarce resources, thereby threatening the majority economically and politically. This results in discrimination against minorities both in access to educational institutions and to good jobs in the work place. A second explanation is that when threatened by growth of the minority population, the majority will use its control of capital to subordinate minority workers, using them as sources of cheap labor and for driving down wages (Bonacich & Modell, 1980). Consistent with other studies, Borjas (1985) and Tienda and Lii (1987) found that Latinos working in labor markets with larger shares of minorities earned less than Latinos working in areas with smaller minority concentrations. The losses of earnings of black, Latino, and Asian men associated with residence in areas with high minority concentrations were greatest among the college educated and lowest among those who had not completed high school. College educated whites gained most from these minority concentrations. Whites with less education did not gain from increased minority density. Tienda and Lii suggested that Asians and Latinos appear to compete more with each other than with whites in the markets where they are disproportionately represented (1987, p. 160). Significant disparities in earnings between highly educated men from minority groups and whites suggest that schooling, by itself, is not sufficient to narrow the earnings gap (p. 162). These findings coincide with other studies showing that socioeconomic inequalities between majority and minority income increase as the proportion of minorities in the labor market grows. Reich (1971) argued that racial/ethnic inequality increased owing to the suppression of labor union growth or labor militancy as well as the reduction in minority access to educations that are needed to make gains in the labor market.

Another perspective suggests a more positive relationship between increases in minority populations and minority income. Frisbie and Neidart (1977) found that in terms of occupational status, both majority and minority workers benefited from labor market concentration of minority workers, but that only white workers gained financially. They argued that discrimination might be lessened in areas of minority concentration if racial and ethnic minorities are successful in creating and developing economic enclaves that insulate minority workers from competition with the white majority. Once a minority population reaches a certain size, it develops internally high-status jobs and income generation through minority enterprises. Another explanation supporting this positive relationship is that as the minority population grows, so will its political power and its strength in economic bargaining (Reich, 1981). Increased political power will then lead to the enactment of legislation supporting equal opportunities or equal pay for equal work in the labor force for minority workers (Bonacich & Modell, 1980).

INDUSTRIAL POLICY

Conventional policy recommendations for reducing income inequality focuses on conclusions drawn from the human capital model. Proposals typically suggest increasing formal schooling, providing job training for minorities, and improving English-language fluency for immigrant groups. To the extent that differences in individual characteristics like education and job training explain differences in income, policies should emphasize education and job training. However, the human capital approach translates into a myopic view of policy changes that might contribute to a change in income disparities for the Latino population. It provides a narrow view of production and an even more limited understanding of social reproduction in the economy.

The human capital model, interpreted at face value, can be used to support a victim-blaming explanation of inequalities in income. The intense focus on individual characteristics suggests that the individuals are responsible for inadequate schooling, weak job skills, and a poor command of the English language.

Policy recommendations based on the class/structuralist model offer different solutions for rectifying the disparity of income for minorities. From this perspective, income inequalities result from the normal operation of the labor market. That is to say, income inequality is a structural aspect of the capitalist economy and does not derive entirely from individual differences in skills and competencies. More importantly, this model posits that class, which is defined as positions within the social relations of production, plays a central role in mediating income inequality in a capitalist society.

Since the middle 1970s, restructuring has radically influenced American corporations. Increasingly, foreign economic and political conditions are influencing domestic labor and welfare policies. During the 1970s, the economy in the United States moved rapidly from a goods-producing to a service-producing economy. Since the 1982 recession, most new jobs have been created in the service sector, and service-sector workers are worse off economically than their counterparts in the manufacturing sector.

These international economic and political changes have contributed to sharp declines in profits for corporations, which have responded by restructuring in ways that significantly affect labor and minority incomes. Some of the changes in corporate structure have had a clear impact on depressing labor conditions. Interregional corporate structures have had a clear impact on depressing labor conditions. Interregional and international shifts of capital have contributed to the highly visible cycles of plant closures in the United States. The plant closures that have received the widest attention occurred in such areas of the economy as the automobile, tire, and steel industries.

With introduction of new technologies, jobs in electronics and telecommunications face deskilling. Wage cuts accompany the process of deskilling occupations. Highly centralized companies with well-defined internal career paths are being replaced by smaller operations with fewer long-term career opportunities—even occupations are being "downsized." Management practices in the 1980s regularly demanded wage freezes, staff reductions, and two-tiered pay systems.

The impact of the tremendous growth in part-time employment or contingency work by Latinos in the labor force must be considered. In order to increase flexibility in organizations, a new emphasis has been placed on converting full-time jobs into part-time jobs, contracting jobs to non-union firms, and increasing numbers of new homeworkers, as a special labor version of "outsourcing." Informal estimates of part-time or contingent labor suggest an increase from eight million part-time workers in 1980 to 18 million today. Increasing the size of the contingent work force allows management to reduce the firm's benefit expenses. The Employee Benefits Research Institute in Washington, D.C., reported that, in 1986, 70% of all part-time employees had no company-provided retirement plan and 42% had no company-provided health insurance. Contingency workers also received a lower hourly wage compared to full-time employees. A recent study of 44 different service and manufacturing industries found that part-time workers were paid lower hourly wages than were full-time workers, and they were less likely to be covered by health insurance and pension plans, even after statistically controlling for differences in workers' characteristics (Ehrenberg, Rosenberg, & Li, 1991). These changes will heavily impact Latinos in the part-time labor force.

Current debates center on whether low-wage jobs are growing at the expense of high-wage jobs and whether the middle class is disappearing. In a recent study completed for the U. S. Congressional Joint Economic Commission, two economists, Bluestone and Harrison, were asked to address these issues (Harrison, 1987; Bluestone & Harrison, 1988). They found that average hourly, weekly, and annual wages and salary incomes of individual workers peaked in the early-to-mid 1970s. Since that time, incomes have either stagnated or fallen. Median weekly earnings have yet to reach their 1973 peak. Presently, real working-class incomes stand at about the same level as in 1960. Bluestone and Harrison also found that between 1973 and 1979, about one fifth of all net new employment created in the United States paid annual wages and salaries lower than the 1973 median wages (about $7,400 in 1986 prices). The trend subsequently worsened. Between 1979 and 1985, over 40% of all net new employment paid these low wages. Indeed, these changes strongly suggest a proliferation of low wages in our newly restructured economy.

All sectors of the economy have experienced increases in part-time labor, wage freezes, and union bashing. However, Bluestone and Harrison concluded that the growth of the service sector is particularly responsible for these dismal trends. They found that, between 1979 and 1985, only 6% of net new jobs in manufacturing paid yearly wages below $7,400. Forty percent of the jobs being created in the service sector were paying $7,400 or less. In their study, they determined that service sector workers are seven times more likely to earn wages below the poverty line than are manufacturing workers (Harrison, 1987, p. 10). Policy-makers need to consider reorganizing the performance and remuneration of service-sector jobs instead of denying their growth.

FUTURE RESEARCH

Certainly, the 1990 census should provide major new data for the exploration of income determination among minority populations. A methodological problem with human capital studies is that cross-sectional data are used to impute causal forces. Better longitudinal studies or time-series analyses are needed to explain more accurately gender differences in the determination of income. Far more research is needed on the ethnic enclave economies that are developing in Los Angeles, San Diego, and San Francisco–San Jose silicon valley, Houston, San Antonio and other urban areas in the Southwest. Los Angeles will provide the opportunity for researchers to explore relationships among several ethnic enclaves within the city including Korean, Chinese, Vietnamese, Mexican, and perhaps Central American entrepreneurs who establish themselves along with their labor forces. To what extent are these minority groups competing among themselves?

More research is needed on the impact of corporate restructuring of Latinos in the labor market. How are Latinos doing as contingent or part-time workers? How are they doing in the middle-class professions? In general, more research is needed on Latinos within specific labor markets.

Now that it is possible to differentiate among Latino groups in the measurement of factors determining their income, policy analysts should begin to consider the differential impact their policy recommendations will have on these groups. The human resource analysts have shown that Latinos are a heterogeneous group, and that their different locations within the work force must be taken into consideration when formulating labor and educational policies. Research that does not differentiate the Hispanic populations according to class and national origins will indubitably lead to misguided policy.

What effects will the new immigration law have on native-born Latino employment and income? Research is needed to better understand the impact of urban undocumented workers on the incomes of other minority groups. Further research is also needed to examine the relationship between local economic development and the growth of the marginal sectors of the labor market. Are we seeing the exacerbation of the problems of their sector and a formation of Chicano/Latino underclass in the urban political economy and social structure? How to create a substantial number of quality jobs for this group is of crucial importance to a comprehensive research agenda.

Last and most important, future empirical research on the Chicano/Latino economic condition must be recast in a more rigorous analytical and theoretical framework. A critical analysis of the capitalist state and class structure is conspicuously absent in studies of the Latino population. In particular, what is missing, in the growing body of quantitative approaches to the study of Chicano/Latino inequality, is a conceptualization of the centrality of class, both background and position, and the relationship of such positions in determining earnings, employment, and unemployment. The absence of an analysis of the capitalist wage–labor system and class relations with its structural inequalities of income and power is a serious shortcoming. Future investigation of income inequality must include class position within the social relations of production as an independent variable. For example, a landmark work—*Race and Class in the Southwest* by Mario Barrera (1979)—can serve as a guide for future research on Latinos in a changing political economy. His theoretical contribution that lay in defining, locating, and connecting the subordinate class position of Chicanos with the institutionalized patterns of discrimination and the interests of capital remains critical. However, his focus on structural relations needs to be integrated into a broader theoretical framework that allows for ideological, political, and cultural forms of resistance to capitalist hegemony. Recent work in state theory posits that the state rather than production is the site of conflict and counterhegemonic struggles. To what extent are racial/ethnic relations a sphere of action autonomous from economic relations? In what ways do race, gender, and class structure each other? What is the role of the state in this process? Research on the accumulation and legitimation needs of the state can provide needed theoretical clarify to an understanding of Chicano inequality, and what public policies are needed to address it, in a liberal capitalist democracy. Thus, the theoretical imperative of doing research should become the moral imperative of policy and social reconstruction.

Full employment and increased affirmative action should be two inseparable demands of a progressive program for economic democracy and Chicano/Latino equality in the post-Reagan era. A third demand should address both overall economic inequality and racial inequality in a programmatic manner (e.g., a national policy that would raise the wages of low-wage workers more rapidly than those of high-wage workers)—a solidarity wage. For a fuller discussion of a solidarity wage, see Bowles, Gordon, and Weisskopf (1983, pp. 283–284). This demand, in conjunction with the demands for full employment and affirmative action, represent what French sociologist Andre Gorz (1968, pp. 7–8) termed "non-reformist reforms"—that is, policy changes which bestow greater power and democratic rights to the "average" citizens in their daily lives as workers and consumers.

As indicated in this chapter, conventional policy recommendations for addressing income disparities among groups have indeed been based on human capital models. At the same time, there *are* a set of initiatives that have attempted to deal with a different category of problems. That is, we have seen special unemployment payments given to steel workers in the early 1980s to protect them from the effects of "unfair foreign competition," a lengthening of workers' compensation periods to handle the same problem, and the bailout of several large industrial and financial firms (such as Lockheed, Chrysler, First Republic Bank of Texas, and the Continental Bank of Illinois). The rationale for these government ventures into the marketplace was not based on a human capital model. Instead, they were "structural" in the sense that a situation was defined as being abnormal or outside the acceptable limits of the "structure of economic relations." Once trade, banking, and bankruptcy crises of these corporate giants were defined in this way, exceptions were made, and they could be administered to without disturbing the underlying corporate ideology.

Industrial policy is fundamentally structural, too. Its difference is that the above interventions have been crisis-oriented exceptions, whereas industrial policy implies the adoption of an ongoing explicit commitment to channel developments for the industrial structure as a whole. The question, then, is how should this be done? A democratic approach to industrial policy might insist on (1) equal representation of workers on supra-organizational boards; (2) initiatives that not only protect the established position of privileged workers, but also raise the access of unprivileged Chicano/Latinos workers to better and more stable jobs; and (3) geographic preference that channels quality jobs into Chicano communities, which are supported by local control and democratic participation.

In effect, what we are positing is that policy makers have already quietly recognized the need to correct economic outcomes when they are the result of warped or unacceptable structural disturbances. Perhaps, a point of departure relevant to Latino workers and communities would be to say, Why not define instances of structural inequality and resource deprivation as unacceptable, too? This could serve as the rationale for government interventions, just as the government has resolved to help big corporations who are in need.

Future policy research on contemporary Latino issues should be conducted within a framework of politics of social change. Advanced intellectual groundwork, though essential, cannot substitute for political practice. In these post-Reagan years, the struggle for economic and social justice will require the development or organizations and the marshaling of new social forces and movements that are committed to structural economic reforms. Also necessary is the advancement of a compelling vision of equity and grassroots participation upon which forms of economic democracy could be articulated and practiced in the electoral arena. The policy and political initiatives that are outlined in this chapter will only come at considerable cost, but the benefits could be enormous—a more democratic economy.

REFERENCES

Ashenfelter, O. (1977). Comments on Smith-Welsh's black-white male earnings and employment: 1960–1970. In T. Juster, Ed., *The distribution of economic well-being*. National Bureau of Economic Research Studies in Income and Wealth, No. 41. Cambridge, England: Bollinger.

Barrera, M. (1979). *Race and class in the southwest*. Notre Dame: University of Notre Dame Press.

Becker, G. S. (1957). *The economics of discrimination*. Chicago: University of Chicago Press.

Bergmann, B. (1971). The effects of white incomes of discrimination in employment. *Journal of Political Economy, 79*(2), 294–313.

Bibb, R., & W. Form. (1977). The effects of industrial occupational and sex stratification on wages in blue-collar markets. *Social Forces* (June), 974–996.

Bluestone, B., & B. Harrison. (1988). *The great U-turn: Corporate restructuring and the polarizing of America*. New York: Basic Books.

Bonacich, E., & J. Modell. (1980). *The economic basis of ethnic solidarity: A study of Japanese Americans*. Berkeley: University of California Press.

Borjas, G. (1985). Jobs and employment for Hispanics. In P. San Juan Cafferty & W. C. McCready, Eds., *Hispanics in the United States: A new social agenda*. New Brunswick, NJ: Transaction Books.

Bowles, S., & H. Gintis. (1975). The problem with human capital theory—A Marxian critique. *American Economic Review, 65*(2), 74–82.

Bowles, S., D. Gordon, & T. Weisskopf. (1983). *Beyond the waste land*. Garden City: Doubleday–Anchor Press.

Brown, P. (1977). *The inequality of pay*. Berkeley: University of California Press.

Carlson, L. A., & C. Swartz. (1988). The earnings of women and ethnic minorities, 1959–1979. *Industrial and Labor Relations Review, 41*(4), 530–545.

Cheng, L., & E. Bonacich. (1984). *Labor immigration under capitalism*. Berkeley: University of California Press.

Darity, W. A. (1982). The human capital approach to black-white earnings inequality: Some unsettled questions. *Journal of Human Resources, 18*, 72–93.

DeFreitas, G. (1985). Ethnic differentials in unemployment among Hispanic-Americans. In G. Borjas & M. Tienda, Eds., *Hispanics in the U. S. Economy*. New York: Academic Press.

Doeringer, P., & M. Piore. (1971). *Internal labor markets and manpower analysis*. Lexington, MA: Heath-Lexington Books.

Edwards, R. (1979). *Contested terrain*. New York: Basic Books.

Ehrenberg, R., P. Rosenberg, & J. Li. (1991). Part-time employment in the United States. In R. Hart, Ed., *Employment, unemployment and hours of work*. London, England: Allen & Unwin.

Fisher, L. (1953). *The harvest labor market in California*. Cambridge: Harvard University Press.

Freeman, R. (1973). Changes in the labor market for black Americans, 1948–1972. *Brookings Papers on Economic Activity, 1*, 67–120.

Frisbie, W. P., & L. Neidart. (1977). Inequality and the relative size of minority populations: A comparative analysis. *American Journal of Sociology, 82*, 1007–1030.

Gordon, D. M. (1972). *Theories of poverty and underemployment: Orthodox, radical and dual labor market perspectives*. Lexington, MA: D. C. Heath.

Gordon, D. M., R. Edwards, & M. Reich. (1982). *Segmented work, divided workers*. Cambridge, England: Cambridge University Press.

Gorz, A. (1968). *Strategy for labor*. Boston: Beacon Press.

Grenier, G. (1984). The effects of language characteristics on the wages of Hispanic-American males. *Journal of Human Resources, 19*(1), 35–52.

Harrison, B. (1987). The impact of corporate restructuring on labor income. *Social Policy, 18*(2), 6–11.

Kalleberg, A., W. Michael, & R. P. Althauser. (1981). Economic segmentation, worker power and income inequality. *American Journal of Sociology, 87*(3), 651–683.

Kerr, C. (1954). *Balkanization of the labor markets*. Berkeley, CA: Institute of Industrial Relations, Reprint No. 59.

Kossoudji, S. A. (1988). English language ability and the labor market opportunities of Hispanic and East Asian immigrant men. *Journal of Labor Economics, 6*(2), 205–228.

Levin, H. M. (1978). *Education and earnings of blacks and the "Brown" decision*. Unpublished manuscript.

Light, I. (1972). *Ethnic enterprises in America: Business and welfare among Chinese, Japanese, and blacks*. Berkeley: University of California Press.

McManus, W. S. (1985). Labor market cost of language disparity: An interpretation of Hispanic earnings differences. *American Economic Review, 75*(4), 818–827.

Melendez, E. (1988). *Labor market structure and wage inequality in New York City: A comparative analysis of Hispanic and non-Hispanic blacks and whites*. Unpublished manuscript, MIT, Department of Urban Studies and Planning, Cambridge.

Muller, T., & T. Espenshade. (1985). *The fourth wave: California's newest immigrants*. Washington, DC: Urban Institute.

Portes, A., & R. L. Bach. (1980). Immigrant earnings: Cuban and Mexican immigration in the United States. *International Migration Review, 14*, 315–341.

Portes, A., & R. L. Bach. (1985). *Latin journey: Cuban and Mexican immigrants in the United States*. Berkeley: University of California Press.

Reich, M. (1971). The economics of racism. In D. M. Gordon, Ed., *Problems in political economy: An urban perspective*. Lexington, MA: D. C. Heath.

Reich, M. (1981). *Racial inequality*. Princeton: Princeton University Press.

Reich, M., D. Gordon, & R. Edwards. (1973). A theory of labor market segmentation. *American Economic Review, 63*, 359–365.

Reimers, C. (1985). A comparative analysis of the wages of Hispanics, blacks and non-Hispanic whites. In G. Borjas & M. Tienda, Eds., *Hispanics in the U. S. Economy*. New York: Academic Press.

Rochin, R. I. (1988). *Economic perspective of the Hispanic community*. Unpublished manuscript, The Tomas Rivera Center, San Antonio, Texas.

Smith, J. (1984). Race and human capital. *American Economic Review, 74*(3), 685–698.

Spence, M. (1973). Job market signaling. *Quarterly Journal of Economics, 87*(3), 355–374.

Thurow, L. C. (1969). *Poverty and discrimination.* Washington, DC: Brookings Institution.

Thurow, L. C. (1975). *Generating inequality.* New York: Basic Books.

Tienda, M., & D. Lii. (1987). Minority concentration and earnings inequality: Blacks, Hispanics and Asians compared. *American Journal of Sociology, 93*(2), 141–166.

Weaver, F. S. (1978). Cui Bono and the economic function of racism. *Review of Black Political Economy, 8*(3), 302–313.

Wright, E. O. (1979). *Class structure and income determination.* New York: Academic Press.

Epilogue

Edwin Melendez, Clara E. Rodriguez, and Janis Barry Figueroa

In the Introduction of this volume, we noted that the economic and political landscape confronting the majority of Hispanic residents in this country was significantly different from that encountered by earlier European immigrants. Although over time the incorporation of Hispanics into the labor force appeared to replicate the traditional experience of immigrant's "crowding" into low-skilled, entry-level jobs, the upward occupational mobility that had characterized the assimilation process of earlier European immigrant groups was not evidenced in the socioeconomic profile of Hispanics.

A number of analysts have stated that the entry of new Hispanic immigrants, who are unskilled, have less formal education, and speak English less fluently than their native-born counterparts, has distorted the statistics used to chart Hispanic progress (Borjas, 1990; Chavez, 1989). Chavez stated that if only native-born Hispanics who had resided in the United States for at least 10 years were considered, their socioeconomic profile would be decidedly more like that of the middle class. According to some researchers, then, second-generation Hispanics are indeed making the kind of economic progress that earlier European arrivals achieved, and the real problem lies in "well-intentioned" government

EDWIN MELENDEZ • Department of Urban Studies and Planning, Massachusetts Institute of Technology, Cambridge, Massachusetts 02139.   CLARA E. RODRIGUEZ and JANIS BARRY FIGUEROA • Division of the Social Sciences, Fordham University at Lincoln Center, New York, New York 10023.

Hispanics in the Labor Force, edited by Edwin Melendez *et al.* Plenum Press, New York, 1991.

efforts, such as transfer payments and affirmative action, that act to hinder many Hispanics from making it on their own (Sowell, 1990).

Contrary to this line of thinking, other reports show that the presence of immigrants does not distort aggregate Hispanic poverty statistics. Recent Hispanic immigrants are just as likely to seek employment as their native-born counterparts, and their higher poverty rates reflect, in part, changes in the larger economy that have transformed work force demands, thus affecting the employment opportunities of native- and foreign-born populations alike (Ong, 1989; U. S. Department of Labor, 1989).

It is evident that the immigrant experience continues to be an important theme in the literature on the economic integration and social adjustment of today's Hispanics. Latino diversity is the other key element contributing to our knowledge about this population. Information on the vastly different immigration experiences of Cubans, Puerto Ricans, Mexicans, and other Hispanics has been greatly improved by research that provides a sociohistoric and economic context for examining the structure of Hispanic ethnicity (Bean & Tienda, 1987, pp. 7–35). Thus, the economic success of the Miami-based Cuban community can be understood in light of the entrepreneurial and social backgrounds of many of the early arrivals, as a function of the massive aid that was received from the federal government, and as a result of the community's ability to use the location of the enclave economy to promote international trade, especially with Latin America and the Caribbean (Wilson & Martin, 1982).

Similarly, the impact and legacy of the incorporation process of Mexican Americans and Puerto Ricans into distinct regional labor markets, where they were relegated to the most undesirable jobs and paid the lowest wages, had negative economic repercussions on these communities. Today many Puerto Ricans and Mexicans live in bilingual and bicultural urban communities in the Northeast and Southwest that are disintegrating under the weight of poverty and unemployment. For some individuals living in these communities, economic survival has mandated that workers maintain a familiarity with both the native and U. S. labor markets (see Chapter 12, this volume).

Therefore, when looking at the labor market status of Hispanics today, it becomes obvious that there are no simple answers to the many questions and controversies that have been derived from the data or raised in the literature. However, the recent trends in the data exhibited in the tables of Chapter 1 in this volume suggest that Mexicans and Puerto Ricans, for example, are not moving along the assimilation path predicted by the "immigrant model" in a linear fashion. Thus, the empirical evidence on Hispanic economic convergence with the majority population is mixed.

Although the immigrant paradigm remains important, and nativity or period of arrival are included in the empirical tests conducted by many of the authors represented in this volume, other concerns have gained prominence in the literature. In particular, Hispanics have increasingly identified themselves as a disadvantaged minority group, shifting both research and public policy toward accepting a set of postulates more associated with the civil rights movement of racial minorities and women.

Hispanic diversity, industrial and occupational change, region of residence, federal immigration policies, racial and gender discrimination, and visibility and strength of Hispanic political organizations are some of the key concerns in current Hispanic labor market studies. In many ways, the shift in emphasis away from the basic immigrant model represents a recognition of Hispanics as a distinct national minority, a diverse ethnic group that shares characteristics with past European immigrants and Native and African-Americans. Despite this change in research emphasis, the policy community is far from in agreement on which of the many concerns should be given priority and how the research community's information can be incorporated into the formulation of public and private programs affecting the Hispanic population.

LABOR FORCE ISSUES AND APPROACHES

In this section, we will summarize some of the basic themes related to Hispanic employment, earnings, and economic well-being which are found in the research on Hispanics in the labor force. In this volume we cannot attempt to offer a unified theoretical presentation of the main issues, but rather a diversity of approaches. Both conventional demand- and supply-side explanations have faced serious challenges from researchers, and there are competing perspectives on Hispanic labor market problems. At this point, analysts and practitioners are determining what information is most useful in describing, predicting, or influencing the individual behavior and institutional circumscription found in the labor market. Our intent then is to indicate how the scope of Hispanic studies is being expanded and, perhaps, some of the key controversies within the field resolved.

ISSUES

Data Problems

Presently, no clear consensus exists in the literature on what are the major factors contributing to the employment problems of Hispanics, nor what remedies are appropriate to improving their disadvantaged situation in the labor market. Apparently, the human capital perspective—as evidenced in the work of Rivera-Batiz (Chapter 3, this volume), and Reimers and Chernick (Chapter 7, this volume), for example—has been emphasized in both this volume and in earlier treatments of Hispanic economic well-being (e.g., Bean & Tienda, 1988; Borjas & Tienda, 1985; Sandefur & Tienda, 1988). This emphasis may be due as much to the data deficiencies that impinged on researchers' abilities to accurately test the human capital approach, as it was a function of the theory's capacity to resolve any enigmas regarding the disadvantaged status of Hispanics in the labor force.

Two important sets of data, the 1976 Survey of Income and Education and the 1980 United States Census, have allowed analysts to investigate the Hispanic population in depth and to look at differences between national-origin groups along many parameters. Yet the variables available from these data are often error prone, are difficult to translate into policy-relevant estimates of labor market outcomes, and are indirect in their measurement of demand and supply constraints.

Longitudinal data are also problematic. Even though the Survey on Income Program Participation (SIPP) has included Hispanics in the sampling, sample size has remained a problem for performing certain statistical tests. Further, data that include Hispanics (e.g., the National Longitudinal Survey of Labor Market Experiences of Youth and High School and Beyond) have limited use for certain tests of difference between national-origin groups.

Questions concerning Hispanic membership in the underclass clearly exemplify the data problem issue. In the Tienda (1989) study on Puerto Ricans and the underclass debate, the author admitted that she was limited by an inability to track individual employment patterns over time. Lacking the proper data to perform the required tests, the statistical evidence provided inconclusive interpretations. In his analysis of immigrant cohorts across censuses, Borjas (1990) noted that serious biases have been introduced into the estimates of immigrant labor market assimilation because of the incapacity to measure annual changes among the same group of individuals. Inevitably, controversy and distorted perceptions result when life-cycle judgments on Hispanic employment, poverty, welfare dependency, and so on are made from cross-sectional findings.

Labor Market Discrimination

Evidence presented in this book and elsewhere has shown that Hispanics remain concentrated in low-wage, blue-collar, and service jobs because of low educational levels and weaknesses in other productivity-related traits. Traditional economic theory claims that increased human capital investments should act to bring the lifetime earnings of Hispanic workers in line with other, similarly endowed workers. Consequently, much of the public- and private-sector efforts aimed at Hispanic employment advancement has been education and skill oriented. However, without more equal access to capital markets, for example,

Hispanics will be unable to make the required human capital investments. Thus, inequalities in earnings that have their basis in capital market imperfections will continue to be a chronic problem, even when labor market competition acts to level human capital returns among diverse ethnic and racial groups.

Yet competitive forces are not working uniformly, market failures are pervasive, and employer discrimination appears to be profitable. Hispanics and non-Hispanics do not face similar career job prospects, even after controlling for human capital assets. A recent Urban Institute Report (prepared by Cross, Kenney, Mell, & Zimmerman, 1990) on the hiring practices of employers in Chicago and San Diego found that there were noticeable differences in the treatment of Hispanic and Anglo job-seekers for low-skilled, entry-level jobs. Given the controls for education, work experience, and other factors that were made in the study, the authors concluded that discrimination against Hispanics accounted for a significant portion of the disparate hiring practices encountered by male Hispanic applicants.

The relative importance of discriminatory factors in explaining earnings and occupational achievements of Hispanic men and women continues to be debated. For example, Stolzenberg (1982) argued that occupational discrimination against Hispanics is felt only by first-generation, non-English-speaking immigrants. Yet Kossoudji (1988) found that Hispanics have a higher cost for English language deficiency than Asians at every skill level. Reimers (1985) found that the discrimination factor varied in its importance in explaining the wage gap between male, Hispanic national-origin groups and non-Hispanic white men. She also reported that discrimination was not a major factor in understanding the wage gap between non-Hispanic and Hispanic women. Melendez (Chapter 5, this volume) found that discrimination explained a large proportion of the wage gap between non-Hispanic and Hispanic New Yorkers. Yet Skerry (1990) has argued that Hispanics are not a race and therefore cannot be subject to racial discrimination in employment.

Inconsistent findings on the discrimination issue are as much a function of differing theoretical perspectives as they are variations in methodologies or samples employed. Neoclassical approaches have highlighted the role of human capital acquisition in employment and salary differences and have assumed that competitive forces will eliminate costly, discriminatory behavior. Institutionalists now contend that regional labor market characteristics (e.g., industrial structure, percentage of Hispanic representation in the community) influence the returns to productivity-related traits by determining the degree of competition among workers for jobs. Lastly, radical economists argue that earnings and employment differentials between Hispanic and non-Hispanics reflect not only economic outcomes, but also political forces that work to make ethnic and racial discrimination profitable for employers and useful for dividing worker unity.

In the previously cited Urban Institute study, white and Hispanic applicants of the same age applied for jobs with résumés that were similar, except for national origin. Employers regularly chose the white applicants despite similar human capital characteristics. Thus, it appears that fixed characteristics such as "foreign looking or sounding" (as were applied to the Urban Institute's Hispanic testers) receive unique "economic rents" that are not eliminated by the market. Certainly, the size of these returns can be affected by policies that affect the market and cause labor demand shifts (such as the 1986 Immigration Reform and Control Act), or alter individual choices about investments in general or specific training (such as the Civil Rights Act of 1990). But differential returns accruing to factors that are more or less given—such as race, ethnicity, sex, region of residence, family background, and first language—help to maintain the current structure of economic inequality by rationing people into jobs.

Potential employers may respond negatively to applicants' "Hispanicity," as reflected in their color, surname, and accent. Rodriguez (Chapter 4, this volume), while focusing on racial self-perception, confirmed the importance of Hispanicity. She found that Puerto Rican men who identified as other-Spanish were at a disadvantage in relative wages when compared to Puerto Rican men who identified as white. Focusing on interviewer identification of race, Telles and Murguia (1990) found racial difference imposed a cost on Mexican-Americans. Those workers with darker phenotypes received significantly lower earnings. Therefore, both subjective race (i.e., racial self-identification) and objective race (i.e., phenotype) are important labor market variables for Hispanics.

Labor Market Conditions

Demand-side analyses constitute a small proportion of the available studies on Hispanics in the labor force. Such structural factors as regional labor market conditions (e.g., unemployment and wage rates), general patterns of sectoral decline and growth, ethnic residential concentration, availability of labor substitutes, rates of unionization, and government regulation are some of the major determinants previously examined in studies of demand-side forces affecting Hispanic employment (Borjas, 1983; Cooney, 1979; Lii & Tienda, 1987; Sassen-Koob, 1985; Waldinger, 1985).

In Chapter 1 in this volume, we indicate in the accompanying tables that the distribution of jobs and wages over the past two decades diminished the probabilities of job advancement and improvements in salary for some Hispanic national-origin groups. The restructuring of labor demand that occurred in the Northeast is now recognized as a factor that contributed to the disadvantaged status of Puerto Ricans, although empirical testing on the specifics of how this process worked between 1960 and 1980 remains incomplete. Similarly, the economic progress of Mexicans during this period improved, but the recent data from the 1980s suggest a reversal in this trend. Economic declines in the Southwest region of the United States during the 1980s may have contributed to the slowdown in economic progress among Mexicans; but without case studies of changing employment structures, we can only speculate on the connections between uneven economic growth and income losses. Therefore, existing gaps in measures of economic well-being between Hispanics and non-Hispanics, that are not explicable by ethnic differences in personal and family variables, may result from job-access factors that were determined by the less than full-employment regional economies of the 1970s and 1980s (Chapter 6, this volume).

During the last 20 years and especially since 1979, the unemployment rate for the less-skilled male worker has increased and his wage rate declined in comparison to his skilled counterpart. Wage inequality among women over this same period has either fallen or remained stable. Industrial shifts, deunionization, technological progress, declines in the minimum wage, and changes in education contribute about equally to explaining the wage gap between college educated men and those who have a high school diploma or less (Blackburn, Bloom, & Freeman, 1990).

Because Hispanic males tend, on average, to be younger, to have lower rates of college attendance, and to be represented in declining sectors of the economy, they are more likely to be unskilled and to be subject to employment losses. The increased demand for skilled workers, and the relative undersupply of this type of worker among the Hispanic population, can only exacerbate the trend in earnings inequality between Hispanics and non-Hispanics (Chapter 2, this volume).

The Puerto Rican Worker

The disadvantaged labor market status of Puerto Ricans since 1970 has led some researchers to question whether Puerto Ricans present a special exception to the Hispanic population. Recent investigations of whether a Puerto Rican underclass exists (Tienda, 1989), and suggestions that the community is bifurcated between those who work and those who receive welfare (Chavez, 1989), are representative of this research tendency in the literature.

Recent attempts to disassociate and distinguish the underpinning of the socioeconomic profile of Puerto Ricans from those of other Hispanic groups are said to have their basis in the higher incidence of poverty found among Puerto Ricans, the relatively low, female labor-force participation rate, the high percentage of female-headed families who rely on government income-assistance, the steadily declining rate of male labor force participation, and the residential concentration of this population in the Northeast. Puerto Rican divergence from traditional benchmarks of economic progress is encouraging new studies of this group. The fact that Puerto Rican women had the highest labor force participation rate in the 1950s, but by 1970 the lowest rate among working women, should supply the motivation that is needed to help clarify the effect of industrial restructuring in the Northeast on the labor market behavior of this group.

Whether Puerto Ricans represent a "special case of the disadvantaged" based on the items described above is subject to multiple interpretations. Indications that Puerto Rican family structure has changed over time has broad implications for the community as a whole. As both Rosenberg (Chapter 10, this volume) and Barry Figueroa (Chapter 9, this volume) make clear, Puerto Rican families will continue to lag behind other families unless more Puerto Rican women join the labor force and earn enough money to support themselves and their families. Yet, in attempting to answer one set of questions, both chapters raise a variety of new ones. Torres and Rodriguez argue in their chapter that statistical models that ignore factors—such as the status of Puerto Ricans as colonial immigrants, the impact of urban decline on Puerto Rican neighborhoods, and the early positioning of Puerto Ricans in the labor hierarchy—fail to explain much about the difficulties confronted by this population. Specialists in minority education note that the traditional exclusion of Puerto Ricans from the more desirable occupations and the historic lack of correlation between educational advancement and social mobility may help explain the poor school performance of Puerto Rican youth (Ogbu, 1978).

Government's Role

In a complex and dynamic market economy like that in the United States, the forces shaping the demand and supply of labor are usually not coordinated. Public employment policies may be usefully developed in order to mediate mismatch problems, but their development will depend largely on the movement of the political pendulum that informs and supports these programs.

The dramatic social retrenchment of the 1980s, and the reluctance of the federal government to take the lead in constructing and funding effective employment programs, only contributed to the diminished employment prospects of the unskilled and discouraged worker, and thereby exacerbated the trend toward growing income inequality and poverty. Although evaluative studies are few and far between, it appears that existing employment and training programs that service Hispanics may be reaching only those applicants who come into the program with marketable skills, thus leaving many of those in the applicant pool underserviced and discouraged (Romero, 1989).

The importance of acquiring more and better quality education and skills for improving the employment situation of Latinos is unequivocally evidenced in much of the research in this volume. But primary and secondary educational institutions, especially those located in urban areas, seem unable to prepare Latino youth for job opportunities in the "postindustrial" economy of the 1990s. The federal government does not operate schools; state and local authorities do.

Therefore, while the federal sector can increase educational appropriations and encourage fundamental changes in the public school systems that service low-income students, states and localities make the real policy decisions.

Current attempts to make disastrously bad schools accountable to students and parents involve some degree of administrative reform of politically controlled systems, and/or systems of control modeled after choice-based economic markets. Educational reform is especially important for Hispanic populations. Improving the rate of qualified high school graduates would greatly diminish the need for work-training programs whose success in the Hispanic community still remains seriously in doubt (Romero, 1989).

One aspect of the political backlash of the 1980s and the ascendancy of laissez-faire economics is the American people's rejection of further redistribution of wealth and equality of access in the face of a sluggish economy. Harrison and Bluestone (1988) noted that stagnant economic growth, slowdowns in earnings and family income, and the preponderance of low-wage employment that characterized the 1970s caused many voters to reject further assistance for the poor. On the one hand, local government employment for Hispanics helped to support whatever economic progress was made between 1970 and 1980 (Chapters 7 and 8, this volume). On the other hand, the gutting of the social safety net took its toll on those communities operating at the margin.

Poverty among Hispanics has been increasing, and there is ample research on exactly who is poor, how poverty may be transmitted through an intergenerational process, the role of new immigrants in increasing Hispanic poverty, the inability of the labor market to reduce poverty through rising wages, and the role of past and present governmental policies in alleviating or encouraging continued economic deprivation (Sandefur & Tienda, 1988, pp. 265–270).

Yet the persistence of poverty among Hispanics and all the attendant ills associated with it—homelessness, broken families, crime, drugs, ravaged urban areas, inadequate clothing, housing, health care, and education—has many poverty researchers perplexed. In a discussion of the difference between the poverty problems of 1989 and those he investigated in 1964 as a member of the Kennedy–Johnson Council of Economic Advisors, Tobin (1990) stated: "I'm afraid that we don't know how to arrest and reverse the disintegration of these urban neighborhoods, with or without new infusions of public money" (pp. 6–7).

Clearly government has a role in assisting the discouraged worker and in providing for those who cannot work. But demographic changes, the slowdown in economic growth, and reshaped institutions of every sort have changed the context of public policy formulation in such a way that questions of equity as well as of efficiency should be given greater weight. According to Torres and Rodriguez (Chapter 12, this volume), the inclusion of "indigenous factors" in devising and implementing public policies that affect Latinos helps to ensure that earlier, useful research is not forgotten and that the community's needs are

298 EDWIN MELENDEZ *et al.*

effectively represented. Such an evaluation should help to diminish the number of unintentional negative policy outcomes and deepen our understanding of the complex problems that Hispanics face in the United States today.

REFERENCES

Bean, F. D., & M. Tienda. (1988). *The Hispanic population of the United States.* New York: Russel Sage.

Blackburn, McK., D. Bloom, & R. Freeman. (1990). The declining economic position of less skilled American men. In G. Burtless, Ed., *A future of lousy jobs: The changing structure of U. S. wages.* Washington, DC: Brookings Institution.

Borjas, G. (1983). The substitutability of black, Hispanic and white labor. *Economic Inquiry, 21,* 93–106.

Borjas, G. (1990). *Friends or strangers: The impact of immigrants on the U. S. Economy.* New York: Basic Books.

Borjas, G., & M. Tienda. Eds. (1985) *Hispanics in the U. S. Economy.* Orlando, FL: Academic Press.

Chavez, L. (1989). Tequila sunrise: The slow but steady progress of Hispanic immigrants. *Policy Review, 53,* 64–67.

Cooney, R. S. (1979). Intercity variations in Puerto Rican female participation. *Journal of Human Resources, 15*(2), 222–235.

Cross, H., G. Kenney, J. Mell, & W. Zimmerman. (1990). *Employer hiring policies: Differential treatment of Hispanic and Anglo job seekers.* Washington, DC: Urban Institute Press.

Harrison, B., & B. Bluestone. (1988). *The great U-turn: Corporate restructuring and the polarizing of America.* New York: Basic Books.

Kossoudji, S. (1988). English language ability and labor market opportunities of Hispanic and East Asian immigrant men. *Journal of Labor Economics, 6*(2), 205–228.

Lii, D.-T., & M. Tienda. (1987). Minority concentration and earnings inequality: Blacks, Hispanics and Asians compared. *American Journal of Sociology, 93,* 141–165.

Ogbu, J. (1978). *Minority education and caste: The American system in crosscultural perspective.* New York: Academic Press.

Ong, P. (1989). *The widening divide: Income inequality and poverty in Los Angeles.* Report from the Graduate School of Architecture and Urban Planning, University of California Los Angeles.

Reimers, C. (1985). A comparative analysis of the wages for Hispanics, blacks, and non-Hispanic whites. In G. Borjas & M. Tienda, Eds., *Hispanics in the U. S. Economy.* Orlando, FL: Academic Press.

Romero, C. J. (1989). *Services to Hispanics in JTPA: Implications for the system.* Report to the National Commission for Employment Policy.

Sandefur, G. D., & M. Tienda. (1988). *Divided Opportunities: Minorities, Poverty, and Social Policy.* New York: Plenum Press.

Sassen-Koob, S. (1985). Changing composition and labor market location of Hispanic immigrants in New York City, 1960–1980. In G. Borjas & M. Tienda, Eds., *Hispanics in the U. S. Economy.* Orlando, FL: Academic Press.

Sowell, T. (1990). *Preferential policies: An international perspective.* New York: William Morrow.

Stoltzenberg, R. (1982). *Occupational differences between Hispanics and non-Hispanics.* Report to the National Commission for Employment Policy.

Skerry, P. (1990). Hispanic job discrimination exaggerated. *Wall Street Journal,* April 27, p. A12.

Telles, E., & E. Murguia. (1990). Phenotypic discrimination and income differences among Mexican Americans. *Social Science Quarterly, 71*(4).

Tienda, M. (1989). Puerto Ricans and the underclass debate. *Annals, 501,* 105–119.

Tobin, J. (1990). The poverty problem: 1964 and 1989. *Focus, 12*(3), 6–7.

U. S. Department of Labor. (1989). *The effects of immigration on the U. S. economy and labor market.* Immigration and Policy Research Report 1.

Waldinger, R. (1985). Immigration and industrial changes in the New York City apparel industry. In G. Borjas & M. Tienda, Eds., *Hispanics in the labor force.* Orlando, FL: Academic Press.

Wilson, K., & W. A. Martin. (1982). Ethnic enclaves: A comparison of the Cuban and black economies in Miami. *American Journal of Sociology, 88*(1), 135–160.

Index